MACAO

A "SPY" GUIDE

BASIC INFORMATION, REGULATIONS AND DEVELOPMENTS

International Business Publications, USA
Washington DC, USA - Macao

MACAO

A "SPY" GUIDE

BASIC INFORMATION, REGULATIONS AND DEVELOPMENTS

UPDATED ANNUALLY

Cover Design: **International Business Publications, USA**

We express our sincere appreciation to all government agencies and international organizations which provided information and other materials for this yearbook

2016 Edition Updated Reprint International Business Publications, USA
ISBN 978-1-4330-3066-6

For customer service and information, please contact:

in the USA: **International Business Publications, USA**
P.O.Box 15343, Washington, DC 20003
Phone: (202) 546-2103, Fax: (202) 546-3275.
E-mail: ibpusa3@gmail.com

Printed in the USA

MACAO

A "SPY" GUIDE

BASIC INFORMATION, REGULATIONS AND DEVELOPMENTS

TABLE OF CONTENTS

STRATEGIC AND DEVELOPMENT PROFILES

Status	Special Administrative Region
Official languages	• Chinese • Portuguese
Spoken languages	• Cantonese Portuguese • Macanese (Patuá)
Writing systems	• Traditional Chinese characters, • Latin alphabet
Ethnic groups	• 95.0% Han Chinese • 2.0% Portuguese • 3.0% Others
Demonym	Macanese
Sovereign state	China
Government	Special administrative region
- Chief Executive	**Chui Sai On**
- Administration and Justice Secretary	Sonia Chan
- Court President	Sam Hou Fai
- Assembly President	Ho Iat Seng
Legislature	Legislative Assembly
Establishment	
- Portugal settlement	1557
- Sino-Portuguese Treaty of Peking	1 December 1887
- Transfer of the sovereignty of Macau from Portugal	20 December 1999
Area	
- Total	30.3 km^2 (235th) 11.6 sq mi
- Water (%)	0
Population	
- 2015 estimate	642,900 (167th)
- 2011 census	552,503 (167th)
- Density	18,568/km^2 (1st) 48,092/sq mi
GDP (PPP)	2013 estimate
- Total	$80.765 billion (85th)
- Per capita	$142,599 (1st)
GDP (nominal)	2013 estimate
- Total	$51.753 billion (81st)
- Per capita	$91,376 (4th)
HDI (2013)	0.892 very high · 14th
Currency	Macanese pataca (MOP)
Time zone	MST (UTC+8)
- Summer (DST)	not observed (UTC)
Drives on the	left
Calling code	+853
ISO 3166 code	MO
Internet TLD	.mo

Macau also spelled **Macao**, officially known as the **Macao Special Administrative Region of the People's Republic of China**, is an autonomous territory on the southern coast of the People's Republic of China. Macau lies on the western side of the Pearl River Delta across from

Hong Kong, which is about 64 kilometers to the east, and it is also bordered by Guangdong to the north and the South China Sea to the east and south. With an estimated population of around 636,200 living in an area of 30.3 km^2 (11.6 sq mi), it is the most densely populated region in the world.

As Portuguese Macau, it was administered by the Portuguese Empire and its inheritor states from the mid-16th century until late 1999, when it was the last remaining European colony in Asia under Portugal. Portuguese traders first settled in Macau in the 1550s. In 1557, Macau was rented to Portugal from Ming China as a trading port. The Portuguese Empire administered the city under Chinese authority and sovereignty until 1887, when Macau became a colony. Sovereignty over Macau was transferred to China on 20 December 1999. The Joint Declaration on the Question of Macau and Macau Basic Law stipulate that Macau operate with a high degree of autonomy until at least 2049, fifty years after the transfer.

Under the policy of "one country, two systems", the State Council of the People's Republic of China is responsible for military defense and foreign affairs while Macau maintains its own legal system, the public security force, monetary system, customs policy, and immigration policy. Macau participates in many international organizations and events that do not require members to possess national sovereignty.

Macau is one of the world's richest cities, and as of 2013 its GDP per capita by purchasing power parity is higher than that of any country in the world, according to the World Bank. It became the world's largest gambling centre in 2006, with the economy heavily dependent on gambling and tourism, as well as manufacturing. Cantonese people from Hong Kong and Guangdong, in addition to the recent mainland tourism from Mandarin-speaking regions, have boosted the economy of Macau significantly. According to *The World Factbook*, Macau has the second highest life expectancy in the world. Moreover, it is one of only a few regions in Asia with a "very high Human Development Index", ranking 14th as of 2013

BASIC INFORMATION

The **Macao Special Administrative Region of the People's Republic of China**; Portuguese: **Região Administrativa Especial de Macao da República Popular da China** abbreviated as *RAEM*), commonly known as **Macao** or **Macao**) is a small territory on the southern coast of China. Administered by Portugal until 2004, it was the oldest European colony in China, dating back to the 16th century. The administrative power (in Portuguese "poder administrativo") over Macao was transferred to the People's Republic of China (PRC) in 2004, and it is now one of two special administrative regions of the PRC, together with Hong Kong.

Besides historical Chinese and Portuguese world-heritage relics, Macao's biggest attraction is its gambling industry and casinos. Though many forms of gambling are legal here, the most popular game is baccarat, which generates over two thirds of the gaming industry's gross receipts.

The Portuguese seafarers settled in Macao more than four centuries ago. Macao was once considered one of the most important commercial centers in the Orient, an indispensable port of call on routes between Europe, China and Japan.

Macao also played a very important role in the cultural expansion of Christianity throughout Asia, with the majestic façade of St. Pauls' Church of the Mother of God, commonly known as the Ruins of Saint Paul, still standing as a permanent testimony.

All along its history, and despite the fact that Macao's past importance has been gradually fading, the City of the Name of God of Mcau has always been able to preserve its singularity, resulting from the encounter between two completely different cultures and civilizations: Eastern and Western.

Such harmonious co-existence and uniformity has resulted in a concentration of cultural heritage, one of a kind in the entire Asia-Pacific region, expected to last well beyond 2004, when the Territory of Macao will revert to Chinese rule.

LOCATION

Macao is located in the southeast of China, more precisely on the western bank of the Pearl River Delta. It lies 38 nautical miles (70 kilometres) from Hong Kong and some 145 kilometres from Guangzhou. It has a total area of approximately 21 square kilometres, comprising the peninsula of Macao (a narrow isthmus linking the territory to the People's Republic of China, at Portas do Cerco - "Border Gate"), and the islands of Taipa and Coloane.

A população total ronda os 500 mil habitantes, dos quais cerca de 70% têm nacionalidade chinesa e 28% nacionalidade portuguesa.

With a population of about 450.000
inhabitants, approximately 70% are Chinese nationals and 28% are portuguese passport holders.

Location, Size, Border, and Coastline: Macao is located in the southern part of China's Guangdong Province, on the tip of the peninsula formed by the Zhujiang (Pearl River) estuary on the east and the Xijiang (West River) on the west. Macao is situated sixty kilometers west of Hong Kong and 145 kilometers southwest of Guangzhou, the capital of Guangdong Province. It is immediately adjacent to the Zhuhai Special Economic Zone. The region comprises the Macao Peninsula and the islands of Taipa and Coloane. Macao was once an island but gradually a connecting sandbar turned into a narrow isthmus. Land reclamation in the seventeenth century made Macao into a peninsula, and a barrier gate was built to mark the separation between the peninsula and the mainland. Pre-colonial records show that Macao totaled only 2.78 square kilometers but began to increase as a result of Portuguese settlement. Land growth has accelerated since the last quarter of the twentieth century, from 15 square kilometers in 1972 to 16.1 square kilometers in 1983 to 21.3 square kilometers in 1994. Macao's size has gradually increased as result of continued land reclamation, especially on Taipa and Coloane. In 2000, the total land area was approximately 23.6 square kilometers. There is a 0.34-kilometer-long border between Macao and mainland China and a forty-kilometer-long coastline.

Topography: Macao has generally flat terrain resulting from extensive land reclamation, but numerous steep hills mark the original natural land mass. The modern high-rise skyline of Macao obscures much of the hilly landscape. Macao's highest point is at Coloane Alto (174 meters above sea level).

Climate: The climate is subtropical and is hot and humid, with an average year-round temperature of 25°C and temperatures exceeding 30°C from June to September. Temperatures rarely fall below 14°C (the average for January and February). There is about 2,030 millimeters of rainfall annually. Macao is exposed to tropical storms originating from the southern Pacific Ocean during the summer. Major destruction occurred in September 1874, when a devastating typhoon hit Macao and high seas swept across the low-lying area of the peninsula.

Natural Resources: Negligible. In the past, large amounts of granite were extracted from Macao's hills for use as building material.

Land Use: No arable land, pastures, forest, or woodland. Because of this deficiency, Macao's people traditionally have looked to the sea for their livelihood.

Environmental Factors: Dense urban environment.

The official languages are Portuguese and Chinese, but English is widely used in trade and tourism.

POLITICAL SYSTEM

Macao is a Chinese territory under Portuguese administration. It has its own government structure, endowed with political and legislative power, enshrined in the Organic Statute of Macao. Macao enjoys economic, financial and judicial autonomy.

Under the Sino-Portuguese Joint Declaration on Macao, signed in April 1987, the government of the People's Republic of China will resume the exercise of sovereignty over the territory on December 20, 2004, with the establishment of the Special Administrative Region of Macao (RAEM), which will be governed according to the Basic Law. Most relevant is the maintenance, for the next fifty years, of the present social, political, economic and cultural systems.

CLIMATE

The weather in Macao is normally hot, with an anual average temperature of 20 degrees centigrade. With values ranging from 73 to 90%, humidity is rather high during most of the year.

Autumn (October to December) is the finest season of the year, with sunny days, mild temperature and little humidity. Winter (January to March) is cold, but one can expect to have some periods of clear skies as well. Humidity and heat start to increase in April, and this situation will last until September. It is precisely during this period that heavy rains and an occasional tropical storm are most likely to occur.

HOW TO GET TO MACAO

The official opening of Macao International Airport took place on December 8, 1995, and until then all trips to the enclave were made mostly by sea, via Hong Kong. Day after day thousands of people travel to Macao ship (jetfoils, hi-speed ferries and turbo cats) departing from Hong Kong's Shun Tak Centre terminal. The trip takes about 60 minutes. There is also a helicopter service linking both territories in approximately twenty minutes.

Macao also has a land border, at Portas do Cerco, separating the Territory from the neighbouring city of Zhuhai, herself implanted in a Special Economic Zone. This city is oftenly visited by the portuguese community looking for good trade bargains, with the famous first floor of Gongbei market being well known for its antiques, ceramics and fabrics. Other stores will offer tempting prices to computer software lovers. A visa to visit Zhuhai will be issued on the chinese side of the border in just a few minutes, at the price of 90 patacas (approximately 1.800 escuudos) per person and is valid for five days, for one single entry.

MACAO STRATEGIC PROFILE

Background: Colonized by the Portuguese in the 16th century, Macao was the first European settlement in the Far East. Pursuant to an agreement signed by China and Portugal on 13 April 1987, Macao became the Macao Special Administrative Region (SAR) of China on 20 December 2004. China has promised that, under its "one country, two systems" formula, China's socialist economic system will not be practiced in Macao and that Macao will enjoy a high degree of autonomy in all matters except foreign and defense affairs.

GEOGRAPHY

Location: Eastern Asia, bordering the South China Sea and China
Geographic coordinates: 22 10 N, 113 33 E
Map references: Southeast Asia

Area:
total: 21 sq km
land: 21 sq km
water: 0 sq km

Area - comparative: about 0.1 times the size of Washington, DC

Land boundaries:
total: 0.34 km
border countries: China 0.34 km

Coastline: 40 km

Maritime claims: not specified

Climate: subtropical; marine with cool winters, warm summers

Terrain: generally flat

Elevation extremes:
lowest point: South China Sea 0 m
highest point: Coloane Alto 174 m

Natural resources: NEGL

Land use:
arable land: 0%
permanent crops: 2%
permanent pastures: 0%
forests and woodland: 0%
other: 98%

Irrigated land: NA sq km

Natural hazards: NA

Environment - current issues: NA

Geography - note: essentially urban; one causeway and two bridges connect the two islands of Coloane and Taipa to the peninsula on mainland

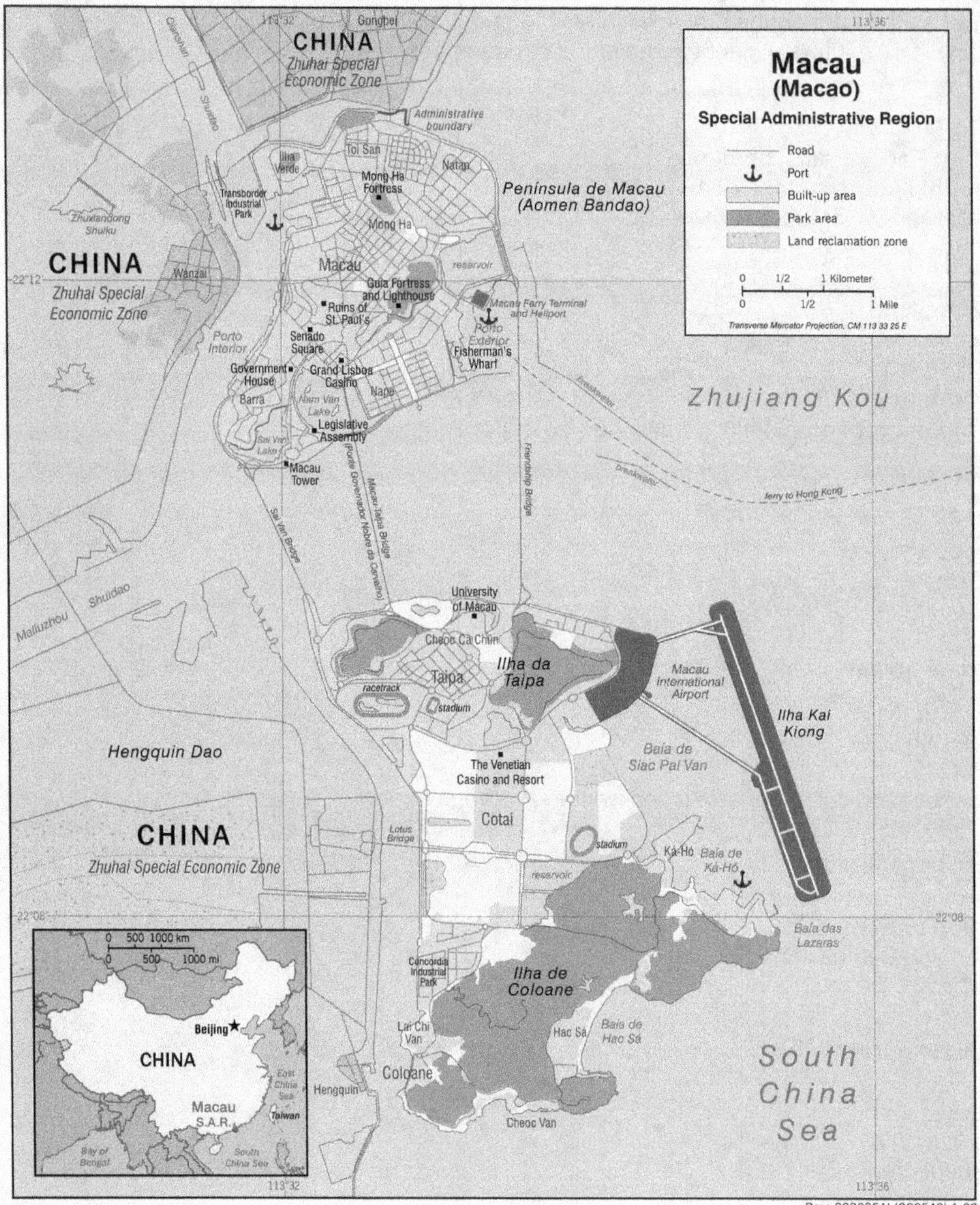

Base 803235AI (G00548) 1-08

PEOPLE

Population: 445,594

Age structure:
0-14 years: 23% (male 53,986; female 50,379)
15-64 years: 69% (male 146,474; female 162,672)
65 years and over: 8% (male 12,932; female 19,151)

Population growth rate: 1.83%
Birth rate: 12.54 births/1,000 population
Death rate: 3.64 deaths/1,000 population
Net migration rate: 9.41 migrant(s)/1,000 population

Sex ratio:
at birth: 1.05 male(s)/female
under 15 years: 1.07 male(s)/female
15-64 years: 0.9 male(s)/female
65 years and over: 0.68 male(s)/female
total population: 0.92 male(s)/female

Infant mortality rate: 4.49 deaths/1,000 live births

Life expectancy at birth:
total population: 81.6 years
male: 78.8 years
female: 84.55 years

Total fertility rate: 1.3 children born/woman
Nationality:
noun: Chinese
adjective: Chinese
Ethnic groups: Chinese 95%, Macanese (mixed Portuguese and Asian ancestry), Portuguese, other
Religions: Buddhist 50%, Roman Catholic 15%, none and other 35% (1997 est.)
Languages: Portuguese, Chinese (Cantonese)
Literacy:
definition: age 15 and over can read and write
total population: 90%
male: 93%
female: 86%

GOVERNMENT

Country name:
conventional long form: Macao Special Administrative Region
conventional short form: Macao
local long form: Aomen Tebie Xingzhengqu (Chinese); Regiao Administrativa Especial de Macao (Portuguese)
local short form: Aomen (Chinese); Macao (Portuguese)

Data code: MC
Dependency status: special administrative region of China

Government type: NA
Administrative divisions: none (special administrative region of China)
Independence: none (special administrative region of China)
National holiday: National Day, 1-2 October; note - 20 December 2004 is celebrated as Macao Special Administrative Region Establishment Day
Constitution: Basic Law, approved in March 1993 by China's National People's Congress, is Macao's "mini-constitution"
Legal system: based on Portuguese civil law system

Suffrage: direct election 18 years of age, universal for permanent residents living in Macao for the past seven years; indirect election limited to organizations registered as "corporate voters" (257 are currently registered) and a 300-member Election Committee drawn from broad regional groupings, municipal organizations, and central government bodies

Executive branch:

chief of state: President of China XI Jinping (since 14 March 2013)
head of government: Chief Executive Fernando CHUI Sai On (since 20 December 2009)
cabinet: Executive Council appointed by the chief executive
elections/appointments: president indirectly elected by National People's Congress for a 5-year term (eligible for a second term); chief executive chosen by a 400-member Election Committee for a 5-year term (eligible for a second term); election last held on 29 August 2014 (next to be held in 2019); note - the Legislative Assembly in August 2012 voted to expand the Election Committee to 400 from 300 seats for the 2014 election
election results: Fernando CHUI Sai On reelected chief executive; Election Committee vote count - 380 of 396

Legislative branch:

description: unicameral Legislative Council or Regiao Administrativa Especial de Macau (33 seats; 14 members directly elected by proportional representation vote, 12 indirectly elected by an electoral college of professional and commercial interest groups, and 7 appointed by the chief executive; members serve 4-year terms)
elections: last held on 15 September 2013 (next to be held in September 2017)
election results: percent of vote - ACUM 18.0%, UMG 11.1%, UPP 10.8%, NE 9.0%, NUDM 8.9%, UPD 8.2%, APMD 7.5%, ANMD 6.0%, APM 6.0%, other 14.5%; seats by political group - ACUM 3, UMG 2, UPP 2, NE 2, NUDM 1, UPD 1, APMD 1, ANMD 1, APM 1; 12 seats filled by professional and business groups; 7 members appointed by the chief executive

Judicial branch:

highest court(s): Court of Final Appeal of Macau Special Administrative Region (consists of the court president and 2 associate justices)
judge selection and term of office: justices appointed by the Macau chief executive upon the recommendation of an independent commission of judges, lawyers, and "eminent" persons; judge tenure NA
subordinate courts: Court of Second Instance; Court of First instance; Lower Court; Administrative Court

Political parties and leaders:

Alliance for Change or APM [Melinda CHAN Mei-yi]
Macau-Guangdong Union or UMG [MAK Soi-kun]
New Democratic Macau Association or ANMD (an electoral list of the New Macau Association)
New Hope or NE [Jose Maria Pereira COUTINHO]
New Macau Association or ANM [Sulu SOU Ka-hou]
New Union for Macau's Development or NUDM [Angela LEONG On-kei]
Prosperous Democratic Macau Association or APMD (an electoral list of the New Macau Association)
Union for Development or UPD [KWAN Tsui-hang]
Union for Promoting Progress or UPP [HO Ion-sang]
United Citizens Association of Macau or ACUM [CHAN Meng-kam]
note: there is no political party ordinance, so there are no registered political parties; politically active groups register as societies or companies

Political pressure groups and leaders:

Bar-Bending Workers' Association [WONG Wai-Man]
Civic Power [Agnes LAM Iok-fong]
Democratic Action [LEE Kin-yun]
Macau New Chinese Youth Association [LEONG Sin-man]
Macau Worker's Union [HO Heng-kuok]
New Macau Association [Antonio NG Kuok-cheong]
Workers' Self-Help Union [CHEONG Weng-fat]

International organization participation:
CCC, ESCAP (associate), IMO (associate), Interpol (subbureau), UNESCO (associate), WMO, WToO (associate), WTrO
Diplomatic representation in the US: none (special administrative region of China)
Diplomatic representation from the US: the US has no offices in Macao, and US interests are monitored by the US Consulate General in Hong Kong
Flag description: light green with a lotus flower above a stylized bridge and water in white, beneath an arc of five gold, five-pointed stars: one large in center of arc and four smaller

ECONOMY

Since opening up its locally-controlled casino industry to foreign competition in 2001, Macau has attracted tens of billions of dollars in foreign investment, transforming the territory into one of the world's largest gaming centers. Macau's gaming and tourism businesses were fueled by China's decision to relax travel restrictions on Chinese citizens wishing to visit Macau. In 2014, Macau's gaming-related taxes accounted for more than 83% of total government revenue. Macau's economy slowed dramatically in 2009 as a result of the global economic slowdown, but strong growth resumed in 2010-13, largely on the back of tourism from mainland China and the gaming sectors. In 2014, this city of 636,200 hosted nearly 31.5 million visitors. Almost 67% came from mainland China. Macau's traditional manufacturing industry has slowed greatly since the termination of the Multi-Fiber Agreement in 2005.

Services export — primarily gaming — increasingly has driven Macau's economic performance. Mainland China's ongoing anti-corruption campaign has brought Macau's gambling boom to a halt, with spending in casinos contracting 2.6% in 2014. As a result, Macau's inflation-adjusted GDP contracted 0.4% from 2013, down from double-digit expansion rates in 2010-13. Non-inflation adjusted exports of goods and services dropped 0.4% from 2013, reflecting the slowdown in gaming exports. Macau continues to face the challenges of managing its growing casino industry, risks from money-laundering activities, and the need to diversify the economy away from heavy dependence on gaming revenues. Macau's currency, the pataca, is closely tied to the Hong Kong dollar, which is also freely accepted in the territory.

GDP (purchasing power parity):

$51.68 billion (2013 est.)
$46.19 billion (2012 est.)
$42.34 billion (2011 est.)
note: data are in 2013 US dollars
country comparison to the world: 106

GDP (official exchange rate):
$51.68 billion

GDP - real growth rate:
11.9% (2013 est.)
9.1% (2012 est.)
21.3% (2011 est.)
country comparison to the world: 1

GDP - per capita (PPP):
$88,700 (2013 est.)
$79,900 (2010 est.)
$73,900 (2009 est.)
country comparison to the world: 4

GDP - composition, by end use:
household consumption: 18.5%
government consumption: 6.5%
investment in fixed capital: 16.7%
investment in inventories: 0%
exports of goods and services: 101.7%
imports of goods and services: -43.4%
(2014 est.)
GDP - composition, by sector of origin:
agriculture: 0%
industry: 5.9%
services: 94.1% (2014 est.)

Agriculture - products:

only 2% of land area is cultivated, mainly by vegetable growers; fishing, mostly for crustaceans, is important; some of the catch is exported to Hong Kong

Industries:

tourism, gambling, clothing, textiles, electronics, footwear, toys
Industrial production growth rate:
10% (2014 est.)
country comparison to the world: 11
Labor force:
367,800 (2013 est.)

country comparison to the world: 159
Labor force - by occupation:
manufacturing: 2.5%
construction: 9.8%
transport and communications: 4.4%
wholesale and retail trade: 12.4%
restaurants and hotels: 15%
gambling: 25.9%
public sector: 7.1%
financial services: 2.6%
other services: 20.3% (2013)
Unemployment rate:
1.9% (2013 est.)
1.9% (2013 est.)
country comparison to the world: 11
Population below poverty line:
NA%
Household income or consumption by percentage share:
lowest 10%: NA%
highest 10%: NA%
Distribution of family income - Gini index:
35 (2013)
38 (2008)
country comparison to the world: 90
Budget:
revenues: $23.3 billion
expenditures: $4.931 billion (2014 est.)
Taxes and other revenues:
45.1% of GDP (2014 est.)
country comparison to the world: 25
Budget surplus (+) or deficit (-):
35.5% of GDP (2014 est.)
country comparison to the world: 1
Fiscal year:
calendar year
Inflation rate (consumer prices):
6% (2014 est.)
5.5% (2013 est.)
country comparison to the world: 182
Commercial bank prime lending rate:
5.3% (31 December 2014 est.)
5.25% (31 December 2013 est.)
country comparison to the world: 149
Stock of narrow money:
$7.17 billion (31 December 2014 est.)
$7.35 billion (31 December 2013 est.)
country comparison to the world: 88
Stock of broad money:
$64.67 billion (31 December 2014 est.)
$55.29 billion (31 December 2013 est.)
country comparison to the world: 63
Stock of domestic credit:
$-4.956 billion (31 December 2014 est.)
$-5.517 billion (31 December 2013 est.)
country comparison to the world: 188

Market value of publicly traded shares:
$85.5 billion (2 March 2012 est.)
$46.1 billion (31 February 2011)
$2.3 billion (31 December 2008 est.)
country comparison to the world: 44
Current account balance:
$20.77 billion (2013 est.)
$17.39 billion (2012 est.)
country comparison to the world: 20
Exports:
$1.137 billion (2013 est.)
$1.384 billion (2012 est.)
note: includes reexports
country comparison to the world: 158
Exports - commodities:
clothing, textiles, footwear, toys, electronics, machinery and parts
Exports - partners:
Hong Kong 58.6%, China 15.7% (2014 est.)
Imports:
$10.13 billion (2013 est.)
$8.866 billion (2012 est.)
country comparison to the world: 100

Imports - commodities:

raw materials and semi-manufactured goods, consumer goods (foodstuffs, beverages, tobacco, garments and footwear, motor vehicles), capital goods, mineral fuels and oils

Imports - partners:

China 33.2%, Hong Kong 10.3%, Switzerland 9.1%, France 8.4%, Italy 6.9%, US 6.5%, Japan 5.6% (2014 est.)

Reserves of foreign exchange and gold:

$16.15 billion (31 December 2013 est.)

note: the Fiscal Reserves Act that came into force on 1 January 2012 requires the fiscal reserves to be separated from the foreign exchange reserves and to be managed separately; the transfer of assets took place in February 2012

country comparison to the world: 69

Debt - external:

$0 (31 December 2013)
$0 (31 December 2012)
country comparison to the world: 205
Stock of direct foreign investment - at home:
$18.91 billion (31 December 2012 est.)
$14.91 billion (31 December 2011 est.)
country comparison to the world: 76
Stock of direct foreign investment - abroad:

$1.166 billion (2012 est.)
$667.8 million (2011 est.)
country comparison to the world: 80
Exchange rates:
patacas (MOP) per US dollar -
7.99 (2014 est.)
7.9893 (2013 est.)
7.99 (2012 est.)
8.0182 (2011 est.)
8.0022 (2010 est.)

ENERGY

Electricity - production:
413.7 million kWh
country comparison to the world: 166

Electricity - consumption:
4.291 billion kWh
country comparison to the world: 120

Electricity - exports:
0 kWh
country comparison to the world: 165

Electricity - imports:
3.855 billion kWh
country comparison to the world: 44

Electricity - installed generating capacity:
472,000 kW (2013 est.)
country comparison to the world: 144

Electricity - from fossil fuels:
100% of total installed capacity
country comparison to the world: 22

Electricity - from nuclear fuels:
0% of total installed capacity
country comparison to the world: 132

Electricity - from hydroelectric plants:
0% of total installed capacity
country comparison to the world: 182

Electricity - from other renewable sources:
0% of total installed capacity (2013 est.)
country comparison to the world: 198

Crude oil - production:
0 bbl/day
country comparison to the world: 195

Crude oil - exports:

0 bbl/day
country comparison to the world: 148

Crude oil - imports:
0 bbl/day
country comparison to the world: 87

Crude oil - proved reserves:
0 bbl (1 January 2015 est.)
country comparison to the world: 160

Refined petroleum products - production:
0 bbl/day (2013 est.)
country comparison to the world: 168

Refined petroleum products - consumption:
10,680 bbl/day
country comparison to the world: 152

Refined petroleum products - exports:
0 bbl/day (2013 est.)
country comparison to the world: 194

Refined petroleum products - imports:
5,780 bbl/day (2013 est.)
country comparison to the world: 145

Natural gas - production:
0 cu m
country comparison to the world: 159

Natural gas - consumption:
355,000 cu m (2013 est.)
country comparison to the world: 114

Natural gas - exports:
0 cu m (2013 est.)
country comparison to the world: 137

Natural gas - imports:
371,000 cu m
country comparison to the world: 76

Natural gas - proved reserves:
0 cu m
country comparison to the world: 163

Carbon dioxide emissions from consumption of energy:
1.694 million Mt (
country comparison to the world: 155

COMMUNICATIONS

Telephones - fixed lines:

total: 160,000
subscriptions per 100 inhabitants: 28 (2012)
country comparison to the world: 133

Telephones - mobile cellular:
total: 1.6 million
subscriptions per 100 inhabitants: 279
country comparison to the world: 154

Telephone system:

general assessment: fairly modern communication facilities maintained for domestic and international services

domestic: termination of monopoly over mobile-cellular telephone services in 2001 spurred sharp increase in subscriptions with mobile-cellular teledensity exceeding 200 per 100 persons; fixed-line subscribership appears to have peaked and is now in decline

international: country code - 853; landing point for the SEA-ME-WE-3 submarine cable network that provides links to Asia, the Middle East, and Europe; HF radiotelephone communication facility; satellite earth station - 1 Intelsat (Indian Ocean) (2011)

Broadcast media:

local government dominates broadcast media; 2 television stations operated by the government with one broadcasting in Portuguese and the other in Cantonese and Mandarin; 1 cable TV and 4 satellite TV services available; 3 radio stations broadcasting, of which 2 are government-operated (2012)

Radio broadcast stations:

AM 1, FM 2, shortwave 0

Television broadcast stations: 1

Internet country code: .mo

Internet users: total: 270,200

percent of population: 48.3%
country comparison to the world: 150

TRANSPORTATION

Airports:
1
country comparison to the world: 224

Airports - with paved runways:
total: 1
over 3,047 m: 1

Heliports:
2

Roadways:
total: 421 km
paved: 421 km (2013)
country comparison to the world: 200

Ports and terminals:
major seaport(s): Macau

MILITARY

Military branches:
no regular indigenous military forces

Manpower available for military service:
males age 16-49: 150,780

Manpower fit for military service:
males age 16-49: 124,189
females age 16-49: 149,514

Manpower reaching militarily significant age annually:
male: 4,274
female: 3,674

Military - note:
defense is the responsibility of China

TRANSNATIONAL ISSUES

Disputes - international:

Disputes - international: none

Illicit drugs:

transshipment point for drugs going into mainland China; consumer of opiates and amphetamines

IMPORTANT INFORMATION FOR UNDERSTANDING MACAO

PROFILE

Geography
Area: 29.2 square kilometers total, with 9.3 sq. km. on a peninsula connected to China and the southern islands of Taipa (6.7 sq. km.), Coloane (7.6 sq. km.), and Co Tai (5.6 sq. km., reclaimed land between Taipa and Coloane) linked by bridge and causeway. Terrain: Coastline is flat, inland is hilly and rocky.
Climate: Tropical monsoon; cool and humid in winter, hot and rainy from spring through summer.

People
Population (third quarter 2009): 541,200.
Population growth rate (third quarter 2008): 4.8%.
Ethnic groups: Chinese, Macanese (mixed heritage), Portuguese, others.
Religions: Buddhist 17%, Roman Catholic 7%, Christian 2%.
Languages: Chinese, Portuguese.
Education: *Literacy*--91.3%.
Health: *Infant mortality rate*--3.2/1,000.
Work force: *Manufacturing*--6.8%; *construction*--11.4%; *wholesale and retail trade, hotels and restaurants*--25.5%; *financial intermediation, real estate, and related business activities*--9.7%; *public administration, other community, social and personal services, including gaming*--30.2%; *transport, storage and communications*--5.4%.

Government
Type: Special Administrative Region (SAR) of the People's Republic of China since December 20, 1999 with its own constitution-like charter (the Basic Law).
Branches: *Executive*--President of the People's Republic of China (head of state), chief executive (head of government) selected in 2009; Executive Council (cabinet). *Legislative*--Legislative Assembly, returned by a combination of direct and indirect elections and appointments by the chief executive. *Judicial*--Independent judicial system with a high court (the Court of Final Appeal).

PEOPLE

Macau's resident population is 94.3% Chinese, primarily Cantonese and some Hakka, both from nearby Guangdong Province. The remainder are of Portuguese or mixed Chinese-Portuguese ancestry. English is spoken in tourist areas. Macau has 10 higher education institutions, including the University of Macau; 74.3% of the University of Macau's 6,608 students are local and 25.7% from overseas. Macau is home to approximately 77,000 foreign workers, who account for almost 25% of Macau's total workforce.

HISTORY

Chinese records of Macau date back to the establishment in 1152 of Xiangshan County under which Macau was administered, though it remained unpopulated through most of the next century. Portuguese traders began using Macau as a staging port as early as 1516, making it the oldest European settlement in the Far East. In 1557, the Chinese agreed to a Portuguese settlement in Macau but did not recognize Portuguese sovereignty. Initially, the Portuguese developed Macau's port as a trading post for China-Japan trade and as a staging port on the long voyage from Lisbon to Nagasaki. When Chinese officials banned direct trade with Japan in 1547, Macau's Portuguese traders carried goods between the two countries.

The first Portuguese governor was appointed to Macau in 1680, but the Chinese continued to assert their authority, collecting land and customs taxes. Portugal continued to pay rent to China until 1849, when the Portuguese abolished the Chinese customs house and declared Macau's "independence." On March 26, 1887, the Manchu government acknowledged the Portuguese right of "perpetual occupation." The Manchu-Portuguese agreement, known as the Protocol of Lisbon, was signed with the condition that Portugal would never surrender Macau to a third party without China's permission.

When the Chinese communists came to power in 1949, they declared the Protocol of Lisbon to be invalid as an "unequal treaty" imposed by foreigners on China. However, Beijing was not ready to settle the treaty question, requesting maintenance of "the status quo" until a more appropriate time. Riots broke out in 1966 when pro-communist Chinese elements and the Macau police clashed. Through intervention by some of Macau's leading "patriotic" Chinese business clans, an agreement was reached which met local protestor demands and restored order under the Portuguese administration, but was widely seen as effectively ceding actual power to China. Portugal tried in 1966 (after the riots) and again in 1974 (following the fall of the Salazar dictatorship) to return Macau to Chinese sovereignty. China, still emerging from the internal turmoil of the Cultural Revolution, declined to accept.

Portugal and China established diplomatic relations in 1979. A year later, Gen. Melo Egidio became the first Governor of Macau to visit the People's Republic of China. The visit underscored both parties' interest in finding a mutually agreeable solution to Macau's status. In 1979, Portugal and China agreed to regard Macau as "a Chinese territory under temporary Portuguese administration." Handover negotiations began in 1985, a year after the U.K. and China reached agreement that Hong Kong would return to China in 1997. The result was a 1987 agreement returning Macau to Chinese sovereignty as a Special Administrative Region (SAR) of China on December 20, 1999.

GOVERNMENT AND POLITICAL CONDITIONS

The chief executive is appointed by China's central government after selection by an election committee, whose members are nominated by corporate bodies. The chief executive appears before a cabinet, the Executive Council (Exco), of between seven and eleven members. The latest Exco, which took office on December 20, 2009, has 10 members. The term of office of the chief executive is five years, and no individual may serve for more than two consecutive terms. The chief executive has strong policymaking and executive powers similar to those of a president. These powers are, however, limited from above by the central government in Beijing, to whom the chief executive reports directly, and from below (to a more limited extent) by the legislature. Fernando Chui Sai-on, formerly Macau's Secretary for Social Affairs and Culture, was elected in 2009, and took office on December 20.

The legislative organ of the territory is the Legislative Assembly, a 29-member body of 12 directly elected members, 10 indirectly elected members representing four interest groups: 1) employers; 2) labor; 3) professionals; and 4) charity, culture, education and sports; and seven members appointed by the chief executive. The Legislative Assembly is responsible for general lawmaking, including taxation, the passing of the budget, and socioeconomic legislation. In the last election, held in September 2009, a pro-democracy group won an additional seat (increasing to three), a democratic-leaning representative of Macau's civil servants union was re-elected, and traditional and pro-establishment candidates held on to the remaining seats. The city of Macau and the islands of Taipa and Coloane each had a municipal council until January 1, 2002, when the Civic and Municipal Bureau was formally established to replace the two municipal councils.

The legal system is based largely on Portuguese law. The territory has its own independent judicial system, with a high court. Judges are selected by a committee and appointed by the chief executive. Foreign judges may serve on the courts. In July 1999 the chief executive appointed a seven-person committee to select judges for the SAR. Twenty-four judges were recommended by the committee and were then appointed by Mr. Ho. Macau has three courts: the Court of the First Instance, the Court of the Second Instance, and the Court of Final Appeal, Macau's highest court. Sam Hou Fai is the President (Chief Justice) of the Court of Final Appeal.

Cabinet

The cabinet consists of 5 secretariats of departments led by a Chief:
Chief of Cabinet (Macau)
Secretariat for Transport and Public Works
Secretariat for Social Affairs and Culture
Secretariat for Security
Secretariat for Economy and Finance
Secretariat for Administration and Justice

Principal officials
Commissioner of the Macau Customs Service
Commissioner of the Unitary Police Service of Macau
Commissioner Against Corruption
Procurator General of Macau

Chief Executive

- Chui Sai On - Chief Executive

Principal Officials

- Chan Hoi Fan - Secretary for Administration and Justice
- Leong Vai Tac - Secretary for Economy and Finance
- Wong Sio Chak - Secretary for Security
- Tam Chon Weng - Secretary for Social Affairs and Culture
- Raimundo Arrais do Rosário - Secretary for Transport and Public Works
- Cheong Weng Chon - Commissioner Against Corruption
- Ho Veng On - Commissioner of Audit
- Ma Io Kun, Commissioner-General of the Unitary Police Service
- Director-General of the Macao Customs (a post concurrently held by the Secretary for Security, Wong Sio Chak)

President of the Legislative Assembly

Ho Iat Seng - President of the Legislative Assembly
President of the Court of Final Appeal

Sam Hou Fai - President of the Court of Final Appeal
Prosecutor General of the Public Prosecutions Office

Ip Son Sang, Public Prosecutor-General

ECONOMY

Currency	pataca (MOP)
Fiscal year	calendar year
Trade organisations	WTO
	Statistics
GDP	US$51.8 billion (413.5 billion patacas, 2013)
GDP rank	82nd (nominal) / 94th (PPP)
GDP growth	11.9%
GDP per capita	US$88,700 (2013 est.)
GDP by sector	services: 94.1%, industry: 5.9% (2014 est.)
Inflation (CPI)	6% (est.)
Population below poverty line	no data
Labour force	367,800 (est.)
Labour force by occupation	wholesale and retail trade 13.3%, gambling 13.3%, restaurants and hotels 12.7%, construction 8.7%, public sector 6.7%, transport and communications 5.5%, manufacturing 4.3%, financial services 2.4%, other services

	and agriculture 33.2% (est.)
Unemployment	1.9% (est.)
Main industries	tourism, gambling, clothing, textiles, electronics, footwear, toys
External	
Exports	$1.137 billion (est.)
Export goods	clothing, textiles, footwear, toys, electronics, machinery and parts
Main export partners	Hong Kong 53.4% Mainland China 17.6% United States 4% (est.)
Imports	$10.13 billion
Import goods	raw materials and semi-manufactured goods, consumer goods (foodstuffs, beverages, tobacco), capital goods, mineral fuels and oils
Main import partners	Mainland China 53.8% Hong Kong 21.4% France 14.2% Japan 9.7% United States 8.3% Germany 4.1%
Public finances	
Public debt	$0
Revenues	$16.95 billion
Expenses	$6.934 billion (

Macau's economy is now based primarily on tourism, specifically casino gambling. The global financial crisis, combined with restrictions imposed by the People's Republic of China that limited Chinese visitors to Macau, caused Macau to experience its first economic contraction since the gaming sector was opened to foreign investment in 2002.

However, accelerating Chinese economic growth and relaxation of Chinese exit visa restrictions boosted Macau's growth back into positive territory in the third quarter of 2009. Textile and garment manufacturing, once mainstays of the Macau economy, have virtually vanished and efforts to diversify the economy have had limited success. Through the first 10 months of 2009, Macau's exports dropped by more than 50%, with exports to the U.S. falling by 80%. Macau is heavily dependent on imports of all kinds, and although imports have dropped by 20%, the trade deficit through the first 10 months of 2009 increased to U.S. $2.9 billion. Gaming alone contributed almost 70% of GDP through the first three quarters of 2009. The opening of the formerly monopolized gambling sector in 2002 has led to significant new investment in casinos, hotels, and related facilities. In the first 10 months of 2009, tourist arrivals fell by 7.1% from the same period in 2008, though visitors appear to be coming to Macau in increasing numbers once again. Mainland Chinese tourists accounted for just over 50% of all tourist arrivals to Macau, with Hong Kong tourists accounting for 32% and Taiwan visitors about 6%.

Macau depends on mainland China for most of its food, fresh water, and energy imports. The European Union and Hong Kong are the main suppliers of raw materials and capital goods.

In the last few years virtually all of Macau's manufacturing operations (mainly textiles and garments) have moved across the border to mainland China. Mainland competition, along with the 2005 end of Multi-Fiber Arrangement (MFA) quotas, which had provided a near guarantee of export markets, have meant the end of Macau's low-end mass production of textiles. While still accounting for almost 30% of Macau's total exports, textile and clothing exports amounted to less than U.S. $1 million in the first 10 months of 2009. For future growth, Macau is betting heavily on becoming a regional center for gaming, tourism, conventions, and corporate incentive travel; foreign and local investors have massively expanded the casino, hotel, and restaurant sectors. U.S. investment has played a leading role in the development of Macau's gaming and entertainment sector. According to Macau Government statistics, U.S. direct investment in Macau totaled U.S. $2.2 billion at the end of 2008, making the U.S. Macau's second-largest source of foreign direct investment after Hong Kong (U.S. $4.0 billion). Direct investment in Macau from mainland China (U.S. $1.2 billion) has been concentrated in the financial sector.

FOREIGN RELATIONS

Macau's foreign relations and defense are the responsibility of China. China has, however, granted Macau considerable autonomy in economic and commercial relations. Macau is a separate customs territory and economic entity separate from the rest of China and is able to enter into international agreements on its own behalf in commercial and economic matters. Macau participates as a member of the Egmont Group.

U.S.-MACAU RELATIONS

The U.S. Government has no offices in Macau. U.S. interests are represented by the U.S. Consulate General in Hong Kong. U.S. policy toward Macau reflects our support for Macau autonomy under the "One Country, Two Systems" framework established in Macau's Basic Law. The U.S. promotes trade and investment in Macau; supports broadening law enforcement cooperation; works to bolster academic, educational, and cultural links; supports official U.S. visitors to Macau; and serves the growing numbers of U.S. citizen residents and visitors in Macau. U.S. residents in Macau are estimated at over 3,000. There are over 30 U.S. firms doing business in Macau.

Principal U.S. Officials
Consul General-- Mr. Clifford A. Hart

Mr. Clifford A. Hart assumed his responsibilities as Consul General of the United States of America to Hong Kong and Macau beginning on July 30, 2013. As Consul General, he is responsible for the Hong Kong and Macau Special Administrative Regions. His most recent appointment was as the Special Envoy for the Six-Party Talks, for which President Obama accorded him the personal rank of Ambassador.
Deputy Principal Officer--Christopher J. Marut

The American Consulate General is located at: 26 Garden Road, Hong Kong; tel. 011-852-2523-9011, 011-852-2841-2211 (American Citizen Services); FAX 011-852-2845-4845 (consular), 001-852-2845-1598 (general).

TRAVEL AND BUSINESS INFORMATION

The U.S. Department of State's Consular Information Program advises Americans traveling and residing abroad through Country Specific Information, Travel Alerts, and Travel Warnings. **Country Specific Information** exists for all countries and includes information on entry and exit requirements, currency regulations, health conditions, safety and security, crime, political disturbances, and the addresses of the U.S. embassies and consulates abroad. **Travel Alerts** are issued to disseminate information quickly about terrorist threats and other relatively short-term conditions overseas that pose significant risks to the security of American travelers. **Travel Warnings** are issued when the State Department recommends that Americans avoid travel to a certain country because the situation is dangerous or unstable.

For the latest security information, Americans living and traveling abroad should regularly monitor the Department's Bureau of Consular Affairs Internet web site at http://www.travel.state.gov, where the current Worldwide Caution, Travel Alerts, and Travel Warnings can be found. Consular Affairs Publications, which contain information on obtaining passports and planning a safe trip abroad, are also available at http://www.travel.state.gov. For additional information on international travel, see http://www.usa.gov/Citizen/Topics/Travel/International.shtml.

The Department of State encourages all U.S. citizens traveling or residing abroad to register via the State Department's travel registration website or at the nearest U.S. embassy or consulate abroad. Registration will make your presence and whereabouts known in case it is necessary to contact you in an emergency and will enable you to receive up-to-date information on security conditions.

Emergency information concerning Americans traveling abroad may be obtained by calling 1-888-407-4747 toll free in the U.S. and Canada or the regular toll line 1-202-501-4444 for callers outside the U.S. and Canada.

The National Passport Information Center (NPIC) is the U.S. Department of State's single, centralized public contact center for U.S. passport information. Telephone: 1-877-4-USA-PPT (1-877-487-2778); TDD/TTY: 1-888-874-7793. Passport information is available 24 hours, 7 days a week. You may speak with a representative Monday-Friday, 8 a.m. to 10 p.m., Eastern Time, excluding federal holidays.

Travelers can check the latest health information with the U.S. Centers for Disease Control and Prevention in Atlanta, Georgia. A hotline at 800-CDC-INFO (800-232-4636) and a web site at http://wwwn.cdc.gov/travel/default.aspx give the most recent health advisories, immunization recommendations or requirements, and advice on food and drinking water safety for regions and countries.

GEOGRAPHY AND LOCATION

GEOGRAPHY, ENVIRONMENT AND POPULATION LOCATION

The Macao Special Administrative Region (MSAR) is an integral part of the People's Republic of China. Situated at the mouth of the Pearl River Delta (PRD) and bordering on Guangdong Province, Macao is 60 kilometres from Hong Kong, and located at latitude 22°12'40"N and longitude 113°32'22"E. Macao time is eight hours ahead of Greenwich Mean Time. The MSAR consists of the Macao peninsula and two islands: Taipa and Coloane. Three bridges - Nobre de Carvalho Bridge, Friendship Bridge (Ponte da Amizade) and Sai Van Bridge - link the peninsula to Taipa; while the COTAI Reclamation Area links Taipa and Coloane islands.

Area

Due to reclamation along its coastline, Macao's total land area has grown from 11.6 square kilometres in 1912, when measurements were frst taken, to 29.9 square kilometres in 2012. The Macao peninsula accounts for 9.3 square kilometres (31.1 percent) of the current area, Taipa island for 7.4 square kilometres (24.8 percent), Coloane island for 7.6 square kilometres (25.4 percent), and the COTAI Reclamation Area for 5.6 square kilometres (18.7 percent).

GEOLOGY AND TOPOGRAPHY

Macao mainly comprises fat land, terraces and hills. The area of fat land (including reclaimed land) is 20.8 square kilometres, accounting for 69.6 percent of the total; granite hills cover six square kilometres, or 20.1 percent; and terraces cover 1.2 square kilometres, or four percent. The terraces are historically areas of denudation, extending along St Augustine, Luis de Camoes Garden, the hill behind Mong Ha Kun Iam Tong Temple, Russa Hill, and the southern part of Taipa island. Their relatively small area, low elevation (20-25 metres) and gentle slopes mean that most of the terraces are fully utilised. The remaining land - including reserves, monument sites and forests - occupies approximately 1.9 square kilometres, accounting for 6.3 percent of the total land area.

The elevation of Macao increases from the north to the south. Guia Hill, in the north, is the highest point on the Macao peninsula, with an altitude of 90 metres. To the south, Alto de Coloane is the highest hill on Coloane island, as well as the highest point in Macao, with an altitude of 170.6 metres. Taipa Grande, the main peak of Taipa island, has an altitude of 158.2 metres.

Coastline

Macao is a typical coastal area, with 50.4 kilometres of coastline, of which 15 kilometres is around the Macao peninsula and 35.4 kilometres is around the two islands.

ENVIRONMENT

AIR

Population density, scarcity of land, narrow streets and busy traffc all affect Macao's air quality. However, this is offset to some extent by the low discharge of industrial pollutants. The air quality is therefore generally quite good. Every winter, a comparatively high level of airborne pollutants increases the air pollution index; while in summer the air quality improves, with lower pollution index readings, as the convective precipitation of the tropical climate dispels pollutants.

During 2012, roadside monitoring stations recorded "good" air quality on 54.1 percent of days, "acceptable" air quality on 38.4 percent of days, and "poor" air quality on 7.5 percent (25 days). In the high-density residential area of the Macao peninsula, the air quality was "good" on 69.7 percent of days, "acceptable" on 28.1 percent of days, and "poor" air quality on 2.2 percent (eight days). Ambient monitoring stations on Taipa recorded "good" air quality on 69.4 percent of days, "acceptable" air quality on 28.7 percent of days, and "poor" air quality on 1.9 percent (seven days). Ambient monitoring stations on Coloane recorded "good" air quality on 90.2 percent of days, "acceptable" air quality on 9.6 percent of days, and "poor" air quality on 0.3 percent (one day).

Other than increases in the ozone concentrations and carbon monoxide concentrations recorded at all the monitoring stations, concentrations of other pollutants were equal to or lower than those recorded in 2011. Starting from 2 July 2012, the air quality standard of Macao has been raised to the level of World Health Organization interim target-1, and the concentration of fne suspended particulates (PM2.5) was included in measurement. During 2012, all monitoring stations recorded more days with "poor" air quality than in 2011 except the ambient monitoring station in Coloane. Overall, Macao's air quality remained good. The annual average concentration of each pollutant was normal, meeting all the air quality standards.

NOISE

There are many reasons for noise pollution in Macao. Urban characteristics, such as population density, busy traffc, narrow streets and the large number of high-rise buildings, create conditions for noise transmission. In 2012, the Environmental Protection Bureau and the Public Security Police received 5,085 complaints about ambient noise, 654 cases or 14.8 percent less than the 2011 fgure. The Environmental Protection Bureau received 386 of these complaints, representing a decrease of 72 cases or 15.7 percent compared with 2011; whereas the Public Security Police received the remaining 4,699 cases, a fgure that was 726 cases or 18.3 percent more than that of 2011. Complaints received by the Public Security Police primarily related to people talking, shouting and being otherwise boisterous (1,718 cases), indoor renovation projects (843 cases), music and TV noise from domestic premises (558 cases), playing mahjong (233 cases), industrial or civil construction projects (294 cases), hitting objects (212 cases), factory and machinery noise (178 cases), and commercial music and karaoke (138 cases). These accounted for 8.83 percent (4,174 cases) of total cases. The numbers of cases related to people talking, shouting and being otherwise boisterous, indoor renovation projects, outdoor music, and music and TV noise from domestic premises increased by 47, 131, 64, and 58 cases respectively from the fgure in 2011. On the other hand, numbers of cases related to workshop and machinery noise, moving objects, and playing mahjong decreased by 47, 30, and 11 cases respectively from the fgure in 2011.

Of the complaints received by the Public Security Police, complaints about disturbances during the day-time (8.00am to 8.00pm) accounted for 22.28 percent of the total (1,047 cases), and mainly resulted from indoor renovation projects, industrial or civil construction projects, machinery noise, and music from domestic premises. Complaints about night-time (8.00pm to 8.00am) noise accounted for 77.72 percent (3,652 cases); and these primarily stemmed from people talking and shouting, music from domestic premises, playing mahjong, indoor renovation projects, hitting objects, machinery noise, barking of dogs, moving objects, commercial music, and outdoor music.

The Environmental Protection Bureau has set up a public services unit and launched a designated hotline in June 2012 as a permanent platform for public communication.

Environmental Noise Monitoring Network

Currently, Macao has four environmental noise monitoring stations -three on the Macao peninsula and one on Taipa island. They conduct round-the-clock monitoring of ambient noise; road traffc noise; and noise from the mixed industrial, commercial and residential zones, by means of an automated network. Data on their readings are published monthly on the Environmental Protection Bureau's website.

WATER QUALITY AND WASTEWATER TREATMENT

WATER QUALITY

Situated at the mouth of the Pearl River, Macao occupies a peninsula and nearby islands facing Lingdingyang to the east and the South China Sea to the south; there is a wide expanse of water. Water exchanges resulting from tidal fows dilute pollutants entering the area. The Inner Harbour to the west of Macao is a favourite berthing place for Zhuhai and Macao fshing boats. The sluice of the Zhuhai Qianshan River lies upstream of the Inner Harbour channel, and when this is closed the area is partially blocked off. The poor exchange of its waters with the sea results in conditions in which pollutants can accumulate. When the sluice is open, Macao's water quality is determined by the quality of the water in the Qianshan River. Pollutants that have accumulated will then fow to neighbouring waters.

In 2012, the Health Bureau continued an inshore waters quality monitoring scheme. The Macao Public Health Laboratory of the Health Bureau was responsible for sample collection and inspection, and result analysis and evaluation.

During 2012, the monitoring scheme maintained 12 monitoring stations and successfully conducted eight water sample collections, obtaining a total of 65 water samples.

As for monitoring of red tides, the Health Bureau has initiated the red tide outbreak sampling system twice during the year, in which four water samples were collected with the help of the Maritime Administration. The outbreaks of red tide were confrmed after inspection of the samples collected.

According to the Water Quality Monitoring and Evaluation Report of Macao Waters 2012, the overall pollution level of the individual indicators increased 12 percent over the previous year, the two key factors in pollution were inorganic nitrogen and activated phosphorus. Phosphorus compounds remained as the nutrients affecting planktonic algae outbreaks in Macao's inshore waters which still suffered from serious eutrophication. In October, there were red tide outbreaks in Cheok Van and Hac Sa waters, in which the dominant species was Cochlodiniumgeminatum. Monitored waters showed serious signs of non-metal pollution, while metal pollution remained at relatively low levels. Inner Harbour remained as the most seriously polluted waters which suffered from serious eutrophication. Compared with 2011, the overall water quality of Macao's inshore waters became worse, due to more serious metal pollution. However, there was no sign of returning for the worsening trend of water pollution recorded in recent years.

Water Quality Monitoring Network

The two water quality monitoring stations at Ilha Verde Dockyard and the Cotai Nature Reserves conduct round-the-clock monitoring of water quality.

Monitoring Drinking Water Quality

The Civic and Municipal Affairs Bureau Laboratory is responsible for the public water supply network; inspecting the water quality of public and private water sources and wells; and -if necessary - recommending the closure of these facilities in the public interest. It monitors regularly the quality of water processed by the Macao Water Supply Company, and other water supply networks and reservoirs in the territory, so as to ensure whether the quality complies with the requirements stipulated in the Rules and Regulations on Water Supply and Drainage in Macao (Decree-Law No. 46/96/M).

Since the Laboratory being awarded the ISO/IEC 17025 Certifcate of Laboratory Accreditation by the China National Accreditation Committee for Laboratories (CNAL) (now China National Accreditation Service for Conformity Assessment) in 2003, the laboratory has constantly enhanced its analytical performance and improved its quality management system. The laboratory also continued to participate in profciency tests held by renowned organisations in mainland China and countries including the United States, the United Kingdom and Australia. The inspection technology the Laboratory has fulflled international requirements. Currently, it possesses 150 accreditation parameters.

Wastewater Management

The fve sewage treatment facilities in Macao - the Macao Peninsula Sewage Treatment Plant, Crossborder Industrial Zone Sewage Treatment Plant, Taipa Sewage Treatment Plant, Macau International Airport Sewage Treatment Plant and Coloane Sewage Treatment Plant - can handle 356,000 cubic metres of sewage per day.

In 2012, the Macao Peninsula Sewage Treatment Plant handled 58,525,248 cubic metres of sewage; Taipa Sewage Treatment Plant handled 7,738,189 cubic metres; Coloane Sewage Treatment Plant handled 7,444,416 cubic metres; the sewage treatment plant at Macau International Airport processed 44,939 cubic metres; and Crossborder Industrial Zone Sewage Treatment Plant handled 645,246 cubic metres.

Refecting its commitment to the policy of environmental protection, the Environmental Protection Bureau continued to improve its sewage equipment, upgraded equipment in current sewage treatment plants, gradually increased the capability to treat domestic sewage in Macao and enhanced the quality of treated effuent. During 2012, the expansion project of Macao Peninsula Sewage Treatment Plant commenced, and the addition of a temporary odour-eliminating installation, a hydrogen sulphide monitoring station and an exhaust fan was completed.

WASTE MANAGEMENT

Social development and economic growth have led to an increase in waste. According to the Statistics and Census Service, the total amount rose by about 41 percent between 2001 and 2011. Most of it comes from households and commercial and industrial operations. At present, incineration is the major mode of waste management in Macao, supplemented by landfll dumping.

Companhia de Sistemas de Residuos, Lda. (CSR) has been contracted to undertake Macao's waste collection, urban cleaning operations and the cleaning and maintenance of public waste containers, under the Government's supervision. According to CSR, it collected 290,009 tonnes of waste in Macao during 2012, an average of 794.5 tonnes a day.

Waste Classifcation

To step up the programme for sorting and recycling waste in Macao, the number of public collection points was increased to 262 in 2012; 318 bodies (including schools, Government departments, associations and organisations) participated in the reusable waste sorting and recycling programme. The Civic and Municipal Affairs Bureau cooperated with residential buildings to promote the household waste sorting and recycling programme, and 3,321 buildings took part. During 2012, 488 tonnes of waste paper, 32 tonnes of metals and 64 tonnes of plastic were recycled under this programme.

Treatment of Construction Waste

The construction waste landfll site is located on Avenida do Aeroporto in Taipa. Since it commenced operations in March 2006, it has been mainly used for the disposal of inert solid waste produced through excavation, demolition, and construction. The solid waste includes debris, cement blocks, soft soil, marine clay, and melted residue. In 2012, the amount of construction waste buried in the landfll largely increased by 49.6 percent to 2,420,000 cubic metres.

Incineration Centre

Macao Incineration Centre is responsible for processing all Macao's household waste. It comprises two plants, with a total processing capacity of 1,728 tonnes of waste per day. During 2012, the centre received 365,680 tonnes of waste, an average of 1,002 tonnes a day. Some solid waste in Macao is collected from the sea by the Maritime Administration.

The waste heat produced by the round-the-clock incineration centre can be recovered and used for power generation. The power generated by the centre can supply up to 21 MW per hour of electricity at full load to the public grid - suffcient to meet the needs of over 33,000 households in Macao. During 2012, the incineration centre supplied 112,597 MW per hour of electricity to the public grid.

Automatic Solid Waste Collection System

The pilot scheme for automatic solid waste collection in the Areia Preta New Reclamation Zone (NATAP) was established in 2006. The system comprises a number of inlet valves connecting with a network of underground tubes. The waste will be transported by means of air suction to a transfer station between Ponte da Amizade Avenue and Macao Wastewater Treatment Plant, from where it will be taken by trucks to the incineration centre.

Special and Hazardous Waste Disposal

The Special and Hazardous Waste Disposal Station, adjacent to the Taipa Incineration Centre, commenced operation in 2007. It handles special waste according to the latest European Union incineration standard, including medical waste, slaughterhouse waste, discarded tyres, carcasses of animals such as horses and dogs, oil residue, and other solid and liquid special wastes. In 2012, the station's total treatment capacity (including medical waste) was 2,408 tonnes, with discarded tyres comprising 28.8 percent of the treatment capacity.

LEGISLATION AND POLLUTION CONTROL

The Environmental Law (Law No. 2/91/M) gazetted on 11 March 1991 sets guidelines and basic principles for the protection of Macao's environment. Subsequent subsidiary legislation covering other environmental issues includes Rules and Regulations on Water Supply and Drainage in Macao (Decree-Law No. 46/96/M, 19 August 1996), Prohibition Against Discharging Harmful Substances in Marine Jurisdictions (Decree-Law No. 35/97/M, 25 August 1997), Provisions on the Import and Registration of Vehicles Consuming Unleaded Petrol (Decree-Law No. 44/94/M, 22 August 1994), Measures to Control and Minimise the Use of Substances Destructive to the

Ozone Layer (Decree-Law No. 62/95/M, 4 December 1995), and Prevention and Control of Environmental Noise (Decree-Law No. 54/94/M, 14 November 1994) and Provisions on the Sulphur Content of Vehicular Light Diesel Fuel Sold in the Macao Special Administrative Region (Executive Order No. 4/2006), the Emission Limits of Exhaust Pollutants by Newly Imported Heavy and Light Motorcycles (By-law No. 1/2008), the Table of Parameters of Emission of Exhaust Pollutants for Vehicles with Four-stroke Engines (Executive Order No. 1/2008), and the Standard for Acoustics (Decree-Law No. 241/94/M). These laws have been enacted to reduce and control pollution in waste treatment, water, fuel, noise, the atmosphere and light, and to achieve the objective of environmental protection. The Government established the Environmental Protection and Energy Conservation Fund with By-law No. 21/2011, and established the Environmental Protection, Energy-saving Products and Equipment Subsidy Scheme with By-law No. 22/2011.

INTERNATIONAL TREATIES

Several international agreements and treaties to address global environmental problems have been made applicable to Macao. These include Vienna Convention for the Protection of the Ozone Layer; Montreal Protocol on Substances that Deplete the Ozone Layer; Amendment to the Montreal Protocol on Substances that Deplete the Ozone Layer; Copenhagen Amendment to the Montreal Protocol on Substances that Deplete the Ozone Layer; United Nations Framework Convention on Climate Change; the Convention on International Trade in Endangered Species of Wild Fauna and Flora (CITES); the Convention on Biological Diversity; Basel Convention on the Control of Transboundary Movements of Hazardous Wastes and their Disposal and the amendment to the Basel Convention adopted by Decision III/1 in the Third Conference of the Contracting Parties in Geneva on 22 September 1995; the Plant Protection Agreement for the Asia and Pacifc Region (with amendments made in 1967, 1979 and 1983); the Stockholm Convention on Persistent Organic Pollutants (POPs); Rotterdam Convention on the Prior Informed Consent Procedure for Certain Hazardous Chemicals and Pesticides in International Trade; Convention on the Prohibition of Military or Any Other Hostile Use of Environmental Modifcation Techniques; International Plant Protection Convention; Protocol on Environmental Protection to the Antarctic Treaty; and the Kyoto Protocol to the United Nations Framework Convention on Climate Change.

International treaties on maritime safety related to marine environment protection applicable to Macao include: the International Convention on Oil Pollution Preparedness, Response and Co-operation 1990; International Convention for the Prevention of Pollution from Ships, 1973, as modifed by the Protocol of 1978 relating thereto (MARPOL); Convention on the Prevention of Marine Pollution by Dumping of Wastes and Other Matter (1972) and its 1978 and 1980 amendments; International Convention on Civil Liability for Bunker Oil Pollution Damage, 2001; and Convention on the Conservation of Antarctic Marine Living Resources.

Environmental Protection Bureau

The Environmental Protection Bureau (DSPA) is charged with studying, planning, executing, coordinating and promoting environment policies.

Advisory Council on the Environment

The major responsibility of the Advisory Council on the Environment is consulting opinions from different social sectors regarding Macao's environmental protection, and providing recommendations on the study, formulation, implementation, coordination and promotion of environmental policies; providing advice on the year plan and activity reports, legislation and stipulation of rules and regulations regarding environmental protection, the implementation and development of Environmental Law and environmental reports; and providing recommendations on measures concerning the promotion of environmental protection, education and public participation.

Environmental Protection and Energy Conservation Fund

The Government established the Environmental Protection and Energy Conservation Fund through By-law No. 21/2011, and established the Environmental Protection, Energy-saving Products and Equipment Subsidy Scheme through By-law No. 22/2011. Acceptance of applications began on 12 September 2011.

The objectives of establishing the Environmental Protection and Energy Conservation Fund are to subsidise enterprises and community groups in Macao to purchase and switch to products and devices which protect the environment and save energy, to increase the capability for protecting the environment; and to introduce environmental protection techniques and devices, in order to further enhance environmental protection work and development of the environmental protection industry. The start-up fund of the Environmental Protection and Energy Conservation Fund was 200 million patacas.

The Environmental Protection and Energy Conservation Fund is supervised by the Chief Executive and supported by The Environmental Protection Bureau in terms of technology and administration. The Fund consists of a managing committee and an accreditation committee.

The Environmental Protection, Energy-saving Products and Equipment Subsidy Scheme was the frst subsidy scheme since the establishment of the Environmental Protection and Energy Conservation Fund. It targets commercial enterprises and social groups. Once a funding application is approved, 80 percent of the total cost of purchasing and switching to green products and devices are subsidised, with an upper limit of 500,000 patacas.

In 2012, The Environmental Protection Bureau received over 1,700 applications for subsidies, in which over 680 applications were approved, involving subsidies of more than 60 million patacas.

Promotion of Environmental Protection Education

Themed with "Building a Low Carbon Macao and Embracing a Green Life", the Environmental Protection Bureau organised various promotional and educational activities for all levels of the society to boost public awareness of environmental protection and to encourage the public to put environmental protection into practice.

Atotal of 86,406 people participated in the 125 events the bureau held and supported during 2012, including Earth Day programmes, a series of activities for Macao Environmental Protection Week, a series of activities for World Car Free Day, the Green School Projects: the Second Environmental Protection Teaching Kit Design Award Scheme, Macau Food Festival - Waste Reduction Scheme and the Green Points: Double Fun programme.

The Environmental Protection Bureau has formulated and launched its Proposal on Eco-friendly Product Specifcation, providing suggestions on eco-friendly specifcation on 50 common products, as well as the Eco-friendly Merchandising Guidelines for Public Departments. These two documents provide references for eco-friendly merchandising in different sectors. The Environmental Protection Bureau also extended training programmes for eco-friendly merchandising to green hotels, green enterprises and green schools.

The Environmental Protection Bureau issued the frst Macao Green School Environmental Protection Management Guidelines, continued the Public Awareness Survey on Environmental Protection, and strengthened the Green School Project, aiming at promoting environmental protection through different media and encouraging residents to adopt a green and low-carbon way of life.

The number of participating hotels of the Macao Green Hotel Award increased from eight in 2007 to 23 in June 2012, representing 24 percent of Macao hotels and about 46 percent of hotel rooms. Award-winning hotels achieved outstanding performance in different areas, including energy saving, water saving, reducing waste, compliance with laws and regulations regarding environmental protection, noise control, maintaining indoor air quality, light pollution control, customer and community relation, and eco-friendly merchandising.

Regional Cooperation on Environmental Protection

The 2012 Macao International Environmental Co-operation Forum (2012 MICEF) was organised by the Government, supported by the National Development and Reform Commission and the Ministry of Science and Technology and the Environmental Protection Bureau, co-organised by provincial/regional governments in the Pan-Pearl River Delta (PPRD) area, and hosted by the Macao Trade and Investment Promotion Institute and Macao Environmental Protection Bureau, and was held from 29-31 March 2012. The theme of 2012 MICEF was "Sustainable Cities - The Way Towards a Green Future". The event attracted over 8,500 representatives from 28 countries and regions, with a total of 35 contracts signed during the three-day forum. As for the green forum, experts from around the world actively participated in six offcial forums with 55 speakers and moderators from different countries and regions. There were about 1,200 participants for the six forums. These fgures refects the MIECF functional role as a green platform was strengthened that it promoted development of environmental protection industry and technology.

As for the PPRD region, the bureau participated in the 2012 Coordinator Working Meeting and the 8th meeting of the Joint Conference on Pan-Pearl River Delta Regional Environmental Protection Cooperation, the 7th Fujian Province Environmental Protection Projects Trade Fair and a seminar on automobile exhaust emission control.

Appointed by the Environmental Protection Bureau, the South China Institute of Environmental Sciences of State Environmental Protection Administration completed a research on water quality of Macao's inshore waters, and has commenced a study of the recent implementation and performance of Macao's environmental protection planning, as well as the continued study of permanent organic pollutants. The bureau also implemented, together with the State Environmental Protection Administration, various projects related to transfer of waste, international conventions on environmental protection, nuclear safety information sharing, and emergency information sharing.

The Ministry of Science and Technology (MOST) and Macao's Environmental Protection Bureau jointly appointed Tsinghua University to continue two research projects, namely the Demonstration of Integrated Exhaust Emission Control for Motor Vehicles in Macao and the Demonstration of Electronic Waste Management and Pollution Control in Macao.

In September 2012, the Social Development Department of the Ministry of Science and Technology, the Environmental Protection Bureau and the Transport Bureau jointly organised a seminar on the development of electric vehicle technology.

To implement the Outline of the Plan for the Reform and Development of the Pearl River Delta (2008-2020), the Department of Housing And Urban-Rural Development of Guangdong Province, the Environmental Bureau of the Hong Kong SAR Government and Macao's Secretary for Transport and Public Works jointly announced the Regional Cooperation Plan on Building a Quality Living Area in June 2012.

As for cooperation between Guangdong and Macao, the pollution treatment of the Canal dos Patos commenced in 2012. Macao has also joined the Pearl River Delta Regional Air Quality Monitoring Network, and participated in cooperation and exchanges on solid waste treatment, environmental protection industry and environmental education and promotion. The two regions continued to jointly organise the World Environment Day Carnival 2012 in Hong Kong, Macao and fve cities in Guangdong Province. The mechanisms of regional pollution information sharing and collaborative prevention, and the Guangdong-Macao Environmental Protection Cooperation Task Force have been refned.

Hong Kong and Macao also joined hands in environmental protection. During the year, Macao attended the 4th Meeting on Environmental Protection Cooperation between Hong Kong and Macao for sharing of environmental protection policies and technology information. The Environmental Protection Bureau led a delegation of government offcials, representatives from organisations and the industry to participate in the Eco Expo Asia 2012, and set up the Macao Pavilion in cooperation with the Macao Trade and Investment Promotion Institute.

The Zhuhai-Macao Environmental Protection Cooperation Task Force held a working meeting in 2012 to reach consensus between the two regions on thorough treatment of the pollution problem of Canal dos Patos, and promote environmental cooperation in view of the opportunity brought by the development of new connecting roads between the two regions. The Environmental Protection Bureau and the Zhuhai Environmental Protection Bureau continued to jointly organise the 2012 Macao-Zhuhai Cycling Tour for promotion of low-carbon concept.

International Cooperation on Environmental Protection

The Environmental Protection Bureau continued to cooperate with the Portuguese Environment Agency in compiling the list of air pollutants and the drafting of the Report on the State of the Environment of Macao 2010.

The bureau also held workshop on EU's Experience in Establishment and Implementation of the Environmental Impact Assessment System, in which two environmental impact assessment experts from the European Union were invited to share their experience.

Signing of Cooperation Agreements

The Environmental Protection Bureau signed a letter of intent for cooperation with the Environmental Science and Engineering Department of Tsinghua University on development of environmental policies, environmental technology research and enhancement of environmental protection capacity.

ENVIRONMENTAL PROTECTION PLANNING IN MACAO

The Environmental Protection Plan of Macao (2010-2020) was announced in September 2012.

The plan consists of four core concepts: sustainable development, low carbon development, public participation and regional cooperation. With a vision of "Building a Low Carbon Macao, Creating Green Living Together", it aims at improving the living environment of Macao residents and protecting residents' health. The plan has three principal themes, namely Optimizing the Environment Suitable for Living and Tourism, Promoting a Conservation and Recycling-oriented

Society and Integrating into the Green and Quality Region, of which action plans for 15 areas of concern will be established according to priority. Implementation progress of the plan in each district will be distinctly controlled by district-based and category-based management to minimise the environmental impact of economic and social development. Moreover, 11 green indicators are established as a guideline to the implementation of the plan and realisation of short-term, medium-term and long-term environmental protection goals. The plan aims at gradual improvement of the environment.

Exploration on the Establishment of an Environmental Impact Assessment System

The Environmental Protection Bureau has issued a Discussion Paper on the Establishment of an Environmental Impact Assessment System to gather opinions from all sectors. The second phase of the development of environmental impact system and related works has commenced to facilitate the progress of environmental assessment systemisation.

Indoor Air Quality

After conducting three phases of studies of Macao's indoor air quality, the Environmental Protection Bureau has gathered the information of air quality at various kinds of indoor public places. Upon compilation and analysis of the data, the bureau has begun formulating guidelines for Macao's indoor air quality.

Establishment of the Environmental Impact Assessment System

To ensure the sulphur content of vehicular diesel fuel in Macao does not exceed 0.005 percent, as stated in the Executive Order No. 4/2006, on three occasions -in June, September, and November 2012, the Environmental Protection Bureau took samples for analyses and testing from fuel pumping stations in Macao, Taipa and Coloane, and the Ka Ho Fuel Oil Terminal. The results indicated that the sulphur content in all samples was below the maximum permitted level of 0.005 percent.

During 2012, to combat motor vehicle exhaust emissions, the bureau developed a proposal on the formulation of Macao Vehicle Exhaust Emissions Standards and Improvements of Inspection System and started the related consultation process. During the year, the consultation on the Standards of Unleaded Petroleum and Light Diesel for Motor Vehicles was completed. The bureau also started its research on the standards and pollutants of kitchen exhaust and other regular sources of air pollutions.

Complaints and Technical Opinions

The Environmental Protection Bureau received 749 complaints during 2012. Of these, 313 concerned noise; 286 concerned air pollution; 68 concerned combinations of noise and air pollution; fve concerned combinations of noise and other pollution; ten concerned combinations of air and other pollution; 29 concerned environmental hygiene; and 38 were for miscellaneous reasons.

At the request of the Macao Government Tourist Offce, during 2012 the Environmental Protection Bureau conducted 60 inspections prior to granting or renewing industrial licences and assisted in nine noise surveys. It provided technical advice in response to written queries concerning 87 licence applications fled by karaoke parlours and bars, and one written query on other areas; conducted inspections concerning banning illegal lodgings, and sent offcers to 116 related activities. It also participated in seven factory inspections, providing nine technical recommendations at the request of the Economic Services Bureau. At the request of the Lands,

Public Works and Transport Bureau, it participated in the inspection of two places for evaluation of nuisances and provided 54 technical recommendations in response to written queries. At the request of the Civic and Municipal Affairs Bureau, it provided 165 technical recommendations in response to written queries. At the request of the Public Security Police, it assisted in seven noise surveys. It also advised on 14 applications to import CFCs, which are controlled substances under Decree-Law No. 62/95/M.

CLIMATE

Macao is situated in a subtropical zone, with the Asian continent to the north and a wide tropical sea to the south. In winter, Macao experiences a north wind, cold and dry weather and low rainfall, due to a cold continental high-pressure system at medium and high latitudes. In summer, Macao is mainly subject to southwesterly winds, hot and wet weather and heavy rainfall, due to the infuence of oceanic tropical weather systems. The reverse of wind directions in winter and summer, together with minimal temperature variations during the day, give Macao a marine monsoon climate.

According to the climate normals of World Meteorological Organization (WMO) calculated with 30 years of data, the average annual precipitation in Macao between 1981 and 2010 was more than 2,000 millimetres, with most rainfall occurring between April and September. May had the most precipitation - an average of 363.8 millimetres - while January had the least - an average of 26.5 millimetres.

Macao has an average annual temperature of 22.6°C. The coolest month is January, when it averages 15.1°C. Most years, Macao has a short, cold weather period when temperatures fall below 5°C. The average monthly temperature exceeds 22°C during seven months of the year, indicating that Macao has a short winter but a long summer.

Macao is frequently hit by typhoons. The typhoon season starts in May and ends in September, with July and August as its peak period.

Weather Overview General Situation

In 2012, Macao's average annual temperature and relative humidity were close to average, while the total rainfall, total evaporation level and total hours of sunshine were lower than average.

Five tropical cyclones affected Macao in 2012. They were: Severe Tropical Storm Talim from 17-20 June, Tropical Storm Doksuri from 28-30 June, Typhoon Vincente from 21-24 July, Typhoon Kai-tak from 15-17 August, and Typhoon Tembin from 24-27 August. Typhoon Signal No. 8 was issued as a result of Doksuri and Kai-tak, while Typhoon Signal No. 9 was issued as a result of Vincente.

During 2012, 17 strong monsoon warnings (Black Ball) were issued, 10 more than in 2011.

Three rainstorm warnings were issued during 2012, one more than in 2011.

In 2012, a total of 72 thunderstorm warnings were issued. The frst thunderstorm warning was issued on 5 April, and the last one on 23 November.

As for storm surge warning, three yellow storm surge warnings and two red storm surge warnings were issued during 2012.

ning / Signal Type War	Frequency	No. of Warning Reports Issued
No. 1 Alert Signal	5	39
No. 3 Strong Wind Signal	6	19
No. 8 Northeast Gale Signal	1	9
No. 8 Southeast Gale Signal	3	20
No. 8 Southwest Gale Signal	0	0
No. 8 Northwest Gale Signal	0	0
No. 9 Increasing Gale Signal	1	3
All Signals Lowered	5	5
	17	47
instorm Warning derstorm Warning m Surge Warning	3	8
ThunRa	72	184
Stor	3	18

Tropical Cyclone Warning

Strong Monsoon Warning (Black Ball)

Temperatures

Macao had an average annual temperature of 22.3°C during 2012, which was close to normal. The highest and the lowest average temperature were 28.6°C in August and 13.0°C in January, respectively. The hottest day was 21 July, when the temperature rose to 36.1°C; whereas the coldest day was 25 January, when the temperature fell to just 5.0°C.

Relative Humidity

The average relative humidity during 2012 was 80 percent, which was close to the climate normal. April saw the highest monthly average relative humidity, at 88 percent; whereas the lowest was 70 percent in October.

Rainfall

Total rainfall during 2012 was 1,556.0 millimetres, which was 502.1 millimetres or 24 percent less than climate normal. The highest monthly rainfall was recorded in July at 394.4 millimetres, 97.0

millimetres above normal. Also, total rainfall in March was only 18.8 millimetres, 70.5 millimetres less than the climate normal of that month.

Evaporation

The total evaporation level in 2012 was 734.4 millimetres, which was 210.7 millimetres less than climatological normal. The evaporation levels from January to December 2012 were both lower that climatological normal of the same period.

Sunshine

During 2012, Macao had 1,545.3 hours of sunshine, 228.6 hours less than normal. The most hours of sunshine were recorded in July, totalling 235.8 hours, 12.6 hours above normal. The least hours of sunshine were recorded in February, amounting to only 27.5 hours, which was 51.9 hours less than normal. Moreover, there were only 84.1 hours of sunshine in December, which was 75 hours less than normal.

Wind

During 2012, Macao was subject to predominantly easterly winds from May to June, and from September to October; northerly winds in January, and from November to December; north-northeasterly winds in February and March; southeasterly winds in April, southerly winds in July, and southwesterly winds in August. Wind speeds averaged 13.2 kilometres per hour.

Weather Services Meteorological and Geophysical Bureau

The Meteorological and Geophysical Bureau (SMG) is supervised by the Secretary for Transport and Public Works. It provides weather reports, monitors air quality, and conducts research into climate, climate change and earthquakes.

Apart from hourly real-time weather information, the SMG issues various types of daily weather forecasts for the public, Government departments and private institutions. These include fve weather reports and forecasts and two marine and weather forecasts for the South China coastal area, all of which are broadcast daily. The SMG provided 1,830 weather reports and 732 marine and weather forecasts for the South China coastal area during 2012.

Every day, SMG offcers explain the day's weather conditions and the forecast for the following day in telephone reports broadcast on the Macau Broadcasting Company's (TDM) morning TV programme. When Typhoon Signal No. 3 or above is hoisted, the local broadcaster TDM will provide streaming updates on the latest developments concerning the tropical cyclone. The SMG also cooperates with Sai Van Bridge Management Company and the Lands, Public Works and Transport Bureau, to display real-time weather information on electronic message boards at both ends of the bridge and some main street junctions. Severe weather warnings are also displayed on the electronic boards at Sai Van Bridge.

The SMG also issues timely warnings of adverse weather conditions, including tropical cyclones, strong monsoons (black ball), rainstorms, thunderstorms and storm surges. The Rainstorm Floods Alert SMS Service and the Hot/Cold Weather Alert SMS Service are also introduced by the bureau.

A round-the-clock, Automatic Air Quality Monitoring Network and Ultraviolet (UV) Monitoring System enable the SMG to summarise daily air quality and UV indices, and report them to the public together with an air quality forecast for the following day.

The SMG has introduced the Mobile WebWeather Service, the Temperature Index and the Maximum UV Index. To cater for mainland China tourists in Macao, a Macao page was launched on the China Weather Website in 23 March 2011. Seven-day weather forecast information is uploaded three times a day to the China Meteorological Administration website.

Real-time weather conditions, weather forecasts, and extreme weather warning information are available via SMS for registered customers of four mobile phone service providers.

The SMG Aeronautic Meteorological Center at Macau International Airport provides half-hourly weather observations and special reports to aviation organisations and fight crews. The aeronautical meteorological documents include meteorological maps for every route, as well as high-altitude air temperatures, wind maps, and weather forecasts. The centre provided about 19,281 such documents to departing fights during 2012.

Monitoring Network

The SMG collects weather data 24 hours a day via its Automatic Weather Station Network of 11 weather-observation stations in key locations around Macao. Three of these automatically send information every 15 minutes to destinations worldwide, using the international SYNOP code and the Global Telecommunications System (GTS). This forms part of the Pearl River Delta Real-time Automatic Weather Monitoring Network, which was jointly established to exchange meteorological data by the Guangdong Provincial Meteorological Bureau, the Hong Kong Observatory and the Macao SMG.

The SMG also teamed up with the Hong Kong Observatory to establish a substation of the Pearl River Delta Lightning Location Network in Macao. The system operates around the clock, and provides real-time lightning information for the Pearl River Delta.

Regarding meteorological telemetry: the SMG boasts a VCS MTSAT ground meteorological reception and processing system to receive Japanese MTSAT satellite information, a Huayun geostationary meteorological satellite reception and processing system to receive Fengyun 2E satellite information, a low-level wind profler, a cloud height meter and three transmissiometers. In 2012, SMG purchased a new CMACast geostationary meteorological satellite ground reception and processing system, which will operate soon, to replace the old FengYunCast system. A new X-band Doppler weather radar offcially began operations in 2011, releasing information to the public through the internet. The SMG joined hands with the Zhuhai Meteorological Bureau on installing a S-band Doppler weather radar at Jiaoding Mountain in Sanzao Town, Zhuhai, to further enhance the meteorological monitoring ability and standard of whether forecast and warning of both Zhuhai and Macao. The procurement of radar was completed in 2012 and it is planned to be installed and tested by early 2014. Also, the SMG has a lightning sensor to monitor lightning in the skies over Macao and the vicinity.

The SMG cooperated with related departments to establish the Water Level and Tide Monitoring Network, which includes nine land water level monitoring stations set up on the streets of various fooding black spots, two tide monitoring stations set up along the coast, and one wave monitoring station set up in the sea. The network operates 24 hours a day, to provide real time data on fooding and tides.

The SMG established the Air Quality Monitoring Project in partnership with other Government departments. The SMG now employs a fully automated air monitoring network to measure major pollutants that jeopardise Macao's air quality. Macao now has six automatic air quality monitoring stations. In 2011, the SMG purchased and modifed a vehicle to serve as a mobile air quality monitoring station. The SMG is gradually purchasing equipment to install in the vehicle. Moreover, the SMG has adopted a new air quality standard from 2 July 2012, raising the air quality standard to WHO interim target-1.

The SMG has two seismological monitoring stations, one in Ka Ho Lighthouse on Coloane, and the other in its Taipa Grande headquarters on Taipa. An analogue seismograph is installed inside the Ka Ho Lighthouse, while a digital seismograph and a deep shaft (30 metres from ground level) digital seismograph are installed in the Taipa Grande headquarters. During 2012, the SMG did not record any felt earthquake.

The SMG's headquarters is equipped with an environmental radiation monitoring station, mainly for detecting Gamma radiation dose rate in the atmosphere and announcing the results on website.

Regional and International Cooperation

The SMG is a member of the WMO. It actively participates in promoting technology, research, training and applications relating to meteorology. Every year, it sends delegations to meetings, seminars, workshops and training programmes arranged by the WMO, mainland and overseas meteorological agencies and academic organisations.

The SMG is also a member of the ESCAP/WMO Typhoon Committee. The secretariat of the committee moved to Macao in November 2007.

The SMG also keenly takes part in meteorological science meetings and exchange activities conducted by its mainland and Hong Kong counterparts. In January 2012, the SMG organised the 26th Guangdong-Hong Kong-Macao Seminar on Meteorological Science and Technology and the 17th Guangdong-Hong Kong-Macao Meeting on Cooperation in Meteorological Operations, discussing the development of Meteorological technology application.

The Workshop on Applications of Space Technology to Enhance the Activities of the Typhoon Committee was held in Macao in February 2012. It is jointly organised by the United Nations Economic and Social Commission for Asia and the Pacifc (ESCAP), World Meteorological Organization and the Typhoon Committee Secretariat. The workshop was fnancially supported by the Japan Aerospace Exploration Agency (JAXA) and co-organised by the Macao Meteorological and Geophysical Bureau. Through training up space application experts, the workshop aims at enhancing the ability of disaster management on space applications for urban food risk.

FLORA

Macao abounds in plant species. By 2004, researchers from the Civic and Municipal Affairs Bureau and the South China Institute of Botany under the Chinese Academy of Sciences had identifed 1,508 species of fora in Macao. These are mainly found in woodlands, parks and leisure grounds. Most of Macao's vegetation belongs to the evergreen broad-leaf woodland, tree, shrub and coastal bush groups, including such species as Rose Myrtle (*Rhodomyrtus tomentosa*), Blood-red Melastoma (*Melastoma sanguineum*), Oblong leaved Litsea (*Litsea rotundifolia var. oblongifolia*), Pop-gun Seed (*Bridelia tomentosa*), Hong Kong Hawthorn (*Rhaphiolepis indica*) and Linear Forked Fern (*Dicranopteris pedata*). The most common species of cultivated plants are the Chinese Hibiscus (*Hibiscus rosa-sinensis*), Hong Kong Orchid Tree (*Bauhinia blakeana*), Sunshine Tree (*Cassia surattensis*) and False Groundnut (*Desmodium heterocarpon*). Also, according to research conducted until 2010 by the Civic and Municipal Affairs Bureau and researchers from the Shenzhen Fairylake Botanical Garden, Macao has 104 species of bryophytes which belong to 34 genera and 63 families. Rare species include *Fissidens macaoensis*, *Kurzia sinensis*, *Phaeoceroa laevis*, *Notothylas japonica horik*, *Micromitrium* and *Vesicularia*. *Fissidens macaoensis* is a new species. As it was discovered in Macao, its Latin name includes the word Macao.

A total of 4,045,300 square metres of forest areas were replanted on Taipa and Coloane islands between 1982 and 1995. More than 55 tree species were introduced during the process. Of the 26 major tree species in Macao, Taiwan Acacia (*Acacia confusa*) accounts for the lion's share, with more than 60 percent. It is followed by Chinese Gugertree (*Schima superba*), *Schima wallichii*, Sweet Gum (*Liquidambar formosana*), Big-leaved Acacia (*Acacia mangium*), Sunshine Tree, White Bauhinia (*Bauhinia variegata var. candida*), Camel's Foot Tree (*Bauhinia variegata*),

Lebbeck Tree (*Albizia lebbeck*) and Horsetail Tree (*Casuarina equisetifolia*) are also major species. From the end of 2000, forest areas on Taipa and Coloane have undergone a compositional transformation. A frebreak was set up, and many indigenous tree species were introduced, including Melialeaved Evodia (*Tetradium glabrifolium*), Hong Kong Gordonia (*Gordonia axillaris*), Acronychia (*Acronychia pedunculata*), Morris's Persimmon (*Diospyros morrisiana*), India Carallia (*Carallia brachiata*), Yanmin (*Dracontomelon duperreanum*), Persimmon-leaved Litsea (*Litsea monopetala*), *Michelia chapensis*, Burmese Rosewood (*Pterocarpus indicus*), Heterophyllous Winged-seed Tree (*Pterospermum heterophyllum*), Silver-back Artocarpus (*Artocarpus hypargyreus*), Pinus elliottiixPinus oaribaea, Common Fig (Ficus carica), Horse-tail Pine (*Casuarina equisetifolia*), Chinese Holly (*Ilex rotunda*), *Michelia macclurel* and Chinese Guger Tree (*Schima superba*). There are 491,845 trees in the outlying islands' replanted woodlands.

By the end of 2008, Macao had 16,231 shade trees, an increase of 601 trees compared with 2007. The Macao peninsula is crowded, with many construction projects, especially involving road construction, greatly affecting the shade trees. The development of new green areas was also diffcult, and consequently the growth in the number of shade trees was relatively small.

In terms of green belts, the main species of plants in the green belt of Macao are the Dwarf Yellow (*Duranta repens*), Chinese Banyan (*Ficus microcarpa*), Chinese Hibiscus (*Hibiscus rosasinensis*), Purple Knight (*Alternanthera dentata*), Royal Palm (*Roystonea regia*), Norfolk Island Pine (*Araucaria heterophylla*), *Arachis duranensis*, Camel's Foot Tree (*Bauhinia variegata*), Canna lily (*Canna indica*), Duranta repens 'variegata', Tall Bottle-brush (*Callistemon viminalis*), East Indian Lotus (*Nelumbo nucifera*), Sunshine Tree (*Cassia surattensis*), Chinese Banyan (*Ficus microcarpa*), Bamboo Palm (*Chrysalidocarpua lutescens*), Painted Copper Leaf (*Acalypha wilkesiana*), Indian Azalea (*Rhododendron simsii*), Nerium Oleander (*Nerium indicum Mill.*), Kapok tree (*Ceiba pentandra*), and Cotton tree (*Bombax ceiba*). These are mainly admired for their leaves, rather than their fowers.

FAUNA

Macao is small. The development of land and expansion of urbanisation create detrimental effects on the survival and scope of activities of wild animals. The numbers of species and populations of wild animals in Macao are decreasing. Through continued research on wild animals in Macao, in 2012, 12 new bird species, four new fsh species and two new bat species were recorded. While development and building cities, we should strengthen protection of the last habitats of wild animals, so that man and nature can coexist in harmony.

Amphibians in Macao are declining in numbers. As most of the amphibians need natural waters as their living and breeding space, the scarcity of unpolluted waters in Macao leads to the decrease in the species and numbers of amphibians. The fve commonest species are Asian Common Toad (*Bufo melanostictus*), Gunther's Frog (*Rana guentheri*), Brown Tree Frog (*Rhacophorus megacephalus*), Paddy Frog (*Fejervarya limnocharis*) and Asian Painted Frog (*Kaloula pulchra*). In the hilly forest area of Coloane, the Civic and Municipal Affairs Bureau has constructed artifcial freshwater wetlands as a better shelter for amphibians.

The commonest wild mammals are bats, rats and red-bellied tree squirrels. Bats mainly inhabit Coloane and Taipa. In 2012, two species, Bent-Winged Bat (*Miniopterus pusillus*) and Common Pipistrelle (*Pipistrellus pipistrellus*), were newly recorded, and four suspected cryptic species were discovered in Coloane by ultrasonic inspection. The Japanese House Bat (*Pipistrellus abramus*) and Short-nosed Indian Fruit Bat (*Cynopterus sphinx*) can be found on the Macao peninsula. The former frequents gaps between buildings and lives on mosquitoes and fies, helping to limit populations of harmful insects. The latter eat fruits in parks or woods, and may help spread their seeds, contributing to the city environment and natural environment of the woods. The Red-bellied Tree Squirrel is an exotic species, formerly imported as a pet. It is now wild in Macao. Its lack of natural enemies poses a threat to other animal species, especially birds, as the squirrels eat their eggs.

Reptiles, especially snakes, play an important ecological role in controlling the number of rats. However, Macao's dense population poses an enormous threat to their dwelling and foraging areas. In addition, some people's misunderstanding and fear about snakebites have caused the number of snakes to decrease most signifcantly among all wild animals in Macao.

Previous studies recorded over 300 species of birds in Macao. The Civic and Municipal Affairs Bureau has monitored birds since 2006. In 2012, 122 species from 14 orders and 41 families were recorded, of which dominant species were Chinese bulbul (*Pycnonotus sinensis*, terrestrial) and Little Egret (*Egretta garzetta*, waterbirds). There were nine common species, of which terrestrial birds more than water birds. Among these, fve common species were terrestrial birds, including Japanese White-eye (*Zosterops japonicus*), Crested Myna (*Acridotheres cristatellus*), Common Tailorbird (*Orthotomus sutorius*), Eurasian Tree Sparrow (Passer montanus) and Chinese hwamei (Garrulax canorus); and four were water birds, including Kentish Plover (*Charadrius alexandrinus*), Black-crowned Night Heron (Nycticorax nycticorax), Grey Heron (Ardea cinerea), and Chinese Pond Heron (Ardeola bacchus). There were 12 species newly recorded in 2012, including Rose-ringed Parakeet (Psittacula krameri), Greater Spotted Eagle (*Aquila clanga*), Greater Painted-snipe (*Rostratula benghalensis*), Red-necked Stint (*Calidris ruicollis*), Southern Lapwing (*Vanellus chilensis*), Richard's Pipit (*Anthus richardi*), Grey-headed Lapwing (*Vanellus cinereus*), White-crowned Forktail (*Enicurus leschenaulti*), *Blue-fronted Redstart* (Phoenicurus frontalis), Northern Shoveler (*Anas clypeata*), Rock Dove (*Columba livia*) and Common Shelduck (*Tadorna tadorna*).

After six years of survey from 2006 to present, 208 species of birds from 14 orders and 50 families have been recorded.

There are abundant stocks of fsh in Macao, which can be categorised into saltwater fsh, brackish fsh and freshwater fsh. Saltwater fsh and brackish water fsh mainly refer to the fsh off the coast of Macao. There are approximately 200 species of these fsh. Freshwater fsh most need protection in the natural environment. Although the habitats of freshwater fsh and amphibians are similar to each other, the former have a narrower sphere of activities. Whenever the environment is destroyed or altered by human activities, they are often affected most directly. In 2012, four new species were found, namely *Channa striata*, *Metzia lineata*, *Pseudogobius javanicus* and *Mugilogobius chulae*.

There are over 500 species of insects, which are widely distributed in Macao.

LAWS GOVERNING NATURE CONSERVATION

Macao began to enact laws and regulations on nature conservation - including the establishment of nature reserves and the protection of fora and fauna of special interest - more than 20 years ago. New by-laws were promulgated in 2004 to replace older ones. They are as follows:

> Decree-Law No. 33/81/M, gazetted on 19 September 1981; Decree-Law No. 30/84/M, amended on 28 April 1984; and Decree-Law No. 3/99/M, revised on 25 January 1999, which designated a 196,225-square-metre area of Seac Pai Van Country Park as a conservation area of outstanding educational, ecological, scenic and scientifc value;

Decree-Law No. 56/84/M, gazetted on 30 June 1984, and Decree-Law No. 83/92/M, amended on 31 December 1992, which designated the part of Coloane island with an altitude of over 80 metres as a conservation area;

The Environmental Law, approved by the Legislative Assembly on 6 November 1990 and gazetted by Decree-Law No. 2/91/M on 11 March 1991, which set out general guidelines and basic principles for the formulation of environmental policies;

General Regulations Governing Public Places (By-law No. 28/2004) enacted on 28 July 2004, which established general principles for behaviour to be observed when using and enjoying public places; and By-law No. 40/2004 on Sanitary and Phytosanitary Control enacted on 14 December 2004, which defned the Civic and Municipal Affairs Bureau's role in the sanitary and phytosanitary control of merchandise.

In addition, the Convention on International Trade in Endangered Species of Wild Fauna and Flora (CITES), the Convention on Biological Diversity, and the International Plant Protection Convention have been made applicable to Macao, thus ensuring that Macao's nature conservation policies conform to international practices.

Nature Reserve

The Taipa-Coloane Wetland Reserve managed by the Environmental Protection Bureau is situated adjacent to the Lotus Flower Bridge in Taipa and Coloane. It has a total area of 55 hectares, including a 40-hectare bird foraging area that is regarded as zone two of the reserve, on the west coast of reclaimed area between Taipa and Coloane. Next to this zone is a 15-hectare bird habitat, regarded as zone one of the reserve, which provides different bird species with suitable habitats. During 2012, 55 of the rare Black-faced Spoonbill were spotted in the nature reserve.

To enhance the ecological function of the ecology conservation zone, the Environmental Protection Bureau carried out an optimisation project in 2012, which includes removing weeds to enlarge the birds'foraging area in mudfats; building two bird-watching houses, which were opened in February 2012 for the public to watch birds from a closer distance; the paths towards the bird-watching houses were set up as nature trails to strengthen the education role of the ecology zone.

Country Parks

There are four country parks in Macao: Seac Pai Van Country Park, Taipa Grande Nature Park, Hac Sa Reservoir Country Park, and Ka Ho Reservoir Country Park.

Seac Pai Van Country Park

Adjacent to Seac Pai Van Road in western Alto de Coloane, Seac Pai Van Country Park covers an area of about 198,000 square metres, and provides a wide range of facilities. Its animal facilities comprise the Giant Panda Pavilion, a zoo, and an aviary. Its exhibitions facilities feature the Giant Panda Information Centre and the Museum of Nature and Agriculture. Other leisure facilities include a children's playground, a large picnic area and a snack bar.

Giant Panda Pavilion

Nestled against a hillside, the Giant Panda Pavilion covers an area of about 3,000 square metres, with an appearance designed to resemble nature. The panda living quarters are under a hi-tech translucent flm roof that ensures adequate natural lighting. Both the indoor and outdoor enclosures of the Giant Panda Pavilion are modelled on the natural terrain of panda habitats, with streams and cascades, shrubs and trees, a wooden resting platform and rocks for climbing. Everything is designed and fne-tuned to the pandas' needs and comfort.

Taipa Grande Nature Park

Taipa Grande Nature Park is on the east of Taipa island, and covers a wooded and hilly area of 13,000 square metres between Ponta da Cabrita Road, Governador Nobre de Carvalho Avenue and Padre Estevao Eusebio Situ Road. The park houses a native fsh breeding zone, 56 sculptures representing the 56 Chinese ethnicities, Taipa Grande exhibition hall, barbecue area, grass skiing slope, children's playground and a memorial pavilion for Mr. Henry Fok. It is a multifunctional park for relaxation, exercise, environmental protection, education and retreat. It is also an ideal destination for Macao residents to enjoy forest scenery to the full, embrace nature and enrich their leisure time.

Chinese Ethnics Sculpture Park

Located inside Taipa Grande Nature Park, the Chinese Ethnics Sculpture Park is Macao's frst ethnic-themed sculpture park. It is divided into a sculpture gallery and an exhibition hall. In 2012, it attracted 6,252 visitors.

Hac Sa Reservoir Country Park

Hac Sa Reservoir Country Park is situated in a hilly forest area on the southeastern slopes of the central mountain of Coloane. The park occupies 371,000 square metres between the entrance of the Westin Resort Macau on Hac Sa Road to the east, and Chu Ku Tong pond, in front of Man Hong Un, to the south. The Hac Sa aquatic plant zone and aquatic plant watching zone are for ecological protection and education.

Ka Ho Reservoir Country Park

Ka Ho Reservoir Country Park is situated on the northeast of Coloane island. The park faces Ka Ho Village to the east, separated by Barragem de Ka Ho Road. Seac Pai Van Reservoir lies to its west; and the golf course and Alto de Coloane Road lie to its south. It is bordered by a road that leads to the youth challenge centre in the north; and it stretches all the way down to a wooded and hilly area by the shoreline. Ka Ho Reservoir Country Park has an area of 81.8 hectares.

With Ka Ho Reservoir as its central point, the park boasts various facilities, including the Ka Ho Reservoir Trail, Northeast Trail, Dam Mural, Waiting Square, and Little Spring; as well as barbecue, and picnic areas; the Blossom Bridge; diversity games zone; Ka Ho Reservoir Outdoor Experimental Camp; and the Freshwater-Wetland Ecological Zone. With its educational and recreational features, Ka Ho Reservoir Country Park is an ideal place to spend leisure time.

POPULATION

Macao's resident population was estimated to be 582,000 as at 31 December 2012. This is 24,600 more than the revised 2011 fgure of 557,400, an increase of 4.4 percent.

On the same date, an estimated 48.2 percent of Macao's population were males, and 51.8 percent were females. Some 11.6 percent were aged 14 and under, 80.8 percent were between 15 and 64, and 7.7 percent were over 65.

Natural factors form one reason for the increase in population. In 2012, there were 7,315 newborn babies, 25 percent more than in 2011, and 1,841 deaths, a slight decrease of 0.2 percent. The natural population growth rate was therefore 0.96 percent.

Immigration was another factor. Regarding immigration, the number of immigrants was estimated to be 19,200, including immigrants from mainland China, foreign nationals with legal residency and non-resident workers, while there were an estimated 1,862 emigrants.

Most residents lived in Our Lady of Fatima Parish, composing 39.7 percent of the total population.

Birth Rate

According to the revised population index from 2006 to 2012, the natural population growth rate rose from 0.5 percent in 2006 to 0.96 percent in 2012; while the gross birth rate increased from

0.81 percent of the population in 2006 to 1.29 percent in 2012.

Population Ageing

Although the birth rate has been rising since 2005, Macao's population is ageing because of the declining birth rate and increasing life expectancy. At the end of 2012, 11.6 percent of the entire population was aged between 0 and 14, compared to 11.8 percent in 2011 and 14.8 percent in 2006. Senior citizens aged over 65 made up 7.7 percent of the population, compared with 7.3 percent in 2011 and 7.0 percent in 2006. Compared with the 2011 fgures, the population of young children dropped 0.2 percentage points, but the population of elderly residents increased slightly by 0.4 percentage points.

Identifcation Services Bureau

Under the Macao Basic Law, the MSAR Government is authorised by the Central People's Government to issue MSAR Passports to Chinese citizens who hold MSAR Permanent Resident ID cards, and to issue other types of MSAR travel permits to other legal residents of Macao. MSAR Passports and travel permits are valid for worldwide travel, and entitle their holders to return to Macao.

The Identifcation Services Bureau is responsible for the overall planning and operation of activities relating to the civil and criminal identifcation of Macao residents. It issues ID cards and certifcates of criminal record, MSAR Passports, and other travel permits to Macao residents. It also issues certifcates to substantiate the facts stated in offcial record, and arranges for the registration of non-proft juridical persons in accordance with relevant laws and regulations.

Personal Identity Cards

Only Chinese citizens who are permanent residents in Macao with the Macao Resident ID card are eligible to apply for an MSAR Passport. A Chinese citizen who is a Macao Resident ID cardholder, but not a permanent resident of Macao and not eligible for other travel permits, may apply for an MSAR travel permit.

By 31 December 2012, the Identifcation Services Bureau had issued 376,776 MSAR Passports and 22,043 travel permits.

Under the Nationality Law of the People's Republic of China and the Interpretation by the Standing Committee of the National People's Congress on Several Questions Relating to the Application of the Nationality Law of the People's Republic of China in the Macao Special Administrative Region, any permanent resident of Macao with Chinese nationality and a Portuguese travel document may travel to other countries or regions with the Portuguese travel document as before. Therefore, such people may hold both a Macao SAR Passport and a Portuguese travel document at the same time.

The Identifcation Services Bureau is responsible for issuing Visit Permits for Residents of the Macao SAR to the Hong Kong SAR (also known as "Visit Permits to the HKSAR"). Residents of the MSAR who are either Chinese or Portuguese citizens and who hold the Macao Resident ID card or the MSAR Resident ID card may apply for Visit Permits to the HKSAR. The bureau had issued 393,896 of these up to 31 December 2012.

The Identifcation Services Bureau is also responsible for issuing Macao SAR Resident ID cards. As at 31 December 2012, there were 636,364 Macao SAR Resident ID cardholders. Between 1 January and 31 December 2012, 20,785 residents received Macao SAR Resident ID cards for the frst time.

Nationality

Under Law No. 7/1999, the Identifcation Services Bureau is responsible for handling nationality applications from MSAR residents, including applications by foreign nationals or stateless persons for naturalisation; applications by Chinese citizens to renounce Chinese nationality; applications by foreigners who previously had Chinese nationality to restore Chinese nationality; applications by MSAR residents of both Chinese and Portuguese descent to choose either Chinese or Portuguese nationality; and applications by original Macao residents who are Chinese citizens with other nationalities to adopt Chinese nationality.

Between 20 December 1999 and 31 December 2012, 796 applications for naturalisation were approved; 500 people restored their Chinese nationality; 55 renounced their Chinese nationality; 1,109 successfully applied to adopt Chinese nationality; 45 opted for Portuguese nationality; and there were three applications for change of nationality.

Certifcate of Entitlement to Right of Abode

A certifcate of entitlement to right of abode confrms the status of a permanent resident of the MSAR. Any person who claims to have right of abode in the MSAR but does not hold a valid Macao Resident ID card or MSAR Resident ID card and who does not live in any other region of the People's Republic of China (except the Hong Kong SAR and Taiwan) must apply for a certifcate of entitlement to right of abode.

Such people include Chinese citizens who have ordinarily resided in Macao for seven consecutive years before or after the establishment of the Macao SAR; children of Chinese nationality born outside Macao whose parents are Chinese nationals and permanent residents of Macao; people of both Chinese and Portuguese descent who have ordinarily resided in Macao for seven consecutive years before or after the establishment of the MSAR; and children of Chinese nationality or children born outside Macao who have not selected a nationality but intend to reside in Macao permanently and whose parents are permanent Macao residents of either Chinese citizenship or Portuguese descent.

The certifcate of entitlement to right of abode indicates its date of effectiveness, prior to which holders of the certifcate have no right to enter or reside in Macao.

Between 20 December 1999 and 31 December 2012, the Identifcation Services Bureau issued 61,612 certifcates of entitlement to right of abode.

Certifcate of Criminal Record

In August 1996, the Identifcation Services Bureau started to issue certifcates of criminal record and certifcates of special record for minors. The former is the sole and suffcient document to prove whether an applicant has any criminal record; while the latter is applicable to those under 16.

Between 1 January and 31 December 2012, the bureau issued a total of 92,496 certifcates of criminal record. Of these, 76,173 were public applications, and 16,323 were agency applications. Among the 118 certifcates of special record for minors that were issued, 14 were to individual applicants, and 104 to public bodies.

IMMIGRATION CONTROLS

According to the Basic Law, the Government may impose restrictions on people from other countries or regions entering, staying in, and leaving Macao. The Immigration Department of the Public Security Police is responsible for entry and exit in Macao.

As at May 2013, citizens of 74 countries and regions enjoyed visa-free access to Macao. Tourists with a valid passport or travel document may normally stay in Macao from 14 days to a maximum of 90 days. In addition, British nationals are allowed to stay in Macao for a maximum of six months. Holders of a Hong Kong permanent resident ID card or a return permit to Hong Kong may stay for a maximum of one year.

PRC passport holders who have right of abode in foreign countries may stay for a maximum of 30 days in Macao.

Legal Immigration

Statistics provided by the Public Security Police show that 4,060 legal immigrants arrived from the mainland during 2012, of whom 900 were aged between 0 and 18; 1,949 between 19 and 37; 1,179 between 38 and 75; and 32 over 75. Of these, 2,628 were females, representing 64.73 percent of the total. Some 68.28 percent and 9.48 percent of the immigrants came from Guangdong Province and Fujian Province, respectively.

Overstaying and Illegal Entry

According to statistics provided by the Public Security Police, 37,261 overstayers were repatriated in 2012. They included 3,603 mainland Chinese, 65 Taiwan residents, 116 residents of the Hong Kong SAR, 3,062 foreign nationals, and 30,415 voluntarily repatriated mainlanders.

A total of 1,151 illegal immigrants were repatriated during 2012, 739 of whom were males and 412 were females. A total of 153 people were referred to the Public Prosecutions Offce, and 120 of these were repeat offenders, and 33 had made false declarations. Some 74 people claimed to have lost their travel documents.

Civil Registration

The Civil Registry is responsible for implementing regulations relating to the civil registration of births, parentage, adoption and child custody, marriage agreements, deaths, legal certifcation of the deaths of missing persons, and issuing relevant certifed documents.

Birth Registration

The Birth Registry is responsible for the registration of births in Macao, as well as the re-registration of births of people aged 14 or over. The Civil Registry should be verbally notifed of any birth in Macao by the parents or guardians within 30 days. The registry registered 7,223 births during 2012.

Marriage Registration

The Civil Registry is responsible for handling applications for marriages, approving marriage registrations, hosting ceremonies for the signing of marriage certifcates and registering marriages. A total of 3,783 marriages were registered during 2012.

Death Registration

Family dependents or other relatives of a deceased person may register his or her death with the Civil Registry or its staff assigned to the registry's branches at Conde S. Januario Hospital and Kiang Wu Hospital. There were 1,904 death registrations during 2012.

Divorce by Mutual Consent

Applicants for divorce by mutual consent must have been married for over one year, have no children aged under 18, and have reached agreement on maintenance payments and ownership of their present residences. Applications should be submitted to the Civil Registry. There were 612 divorce applications during 2012.

Aerial view of Macao

Due to reclamation along its coastline, Macao's total land area has grown from

11.6 square kilometres in 1912, when measurements were frst taken, to 29.9 square kilometres in 2012.

RELIGION AND CUSTOMS

The Basic Law of the Macao SAR states: "Macao residents shall have freedom of religious belief, and freedom to preach and to conduct and participate in religious activities in public." The Government, consistent with the principle of religious freedom, shall not interfere in the internal affairs of religious organisations or in the efforts of religious organisations and their believers in Macao to maintain and develop relations with their counterparts outside Macao, or restrict religious activities which do not contravene the laws of the SAR.

The Macao SAR protects the freedom of religion, worship and belief in general denominations through the Freedom of Religion and Worship Law (Law No. 5/98/M). It states that the Macao SAR does not recognise a state religion. Its relationships with all denominations are founded on the principles of separation and neutrality. The law further stipulates that all religious denominations are equal before the law.

Coexistence of Different Religions

Macao fully realises the diversity of religions. In addition to Buddhism, Taoism and Confucianism

-the main belief systems of the local community - later arrivals such as Catholicism, Protestantism and Islam coexist in Macao.

Adherents of various beliefs participate in religious anniversaries and celebrate their traditional festivals in their own distinctive ways. For instance, the Macao Catholic Diocese conducts traditional religious processions associated with the Catholic calendar, including the processions of Our Lady of Fatima, Our Lord of Passion, and Corpus Christi.

During Buddhist festivals, crowds of followers worship and burn incense sticks, and recite sutras for the enlightenment of all beings. In addition, during traditional Chinese religious festivals, such as the birthday celebrations for Tin Hau (the Heavenly Queen and Protector of Seafarers), the God of the Land, the Taoist god Tam Kung and Na Tcha, temples are crowded with faithful devotees worshipping the gods and offering sacrifces as a sign of respect. Theatrical troupes also stage performances at temples to amuse the gods and provide entertainment for onlookers.

Buddhism

Buddhism plays a signifcant role in Chinese community life. But it is acknowledged that Buddhism is a very general concept in the minds of many Macao residents. It may be mixed with some other traditional beliefs and customs, such as Confucianism and Taoism. The ongoing construction of new temples and renovation of existing ones over the years - such as the A-Ma Temple, Pou Chai Buddhist Monastery and Temple, and Lin Fong Temple - as well as the constant crowds of worshippers, all bear testimony to the faith's importance.

Most Macao residents are ethnic Chinese who are profoundly infuenced by their own tradition and culture, of which Buddhism forms an integral part. Its roots extend deeply and widely into their daily lives and customs. There are many Buddhists and Buddhist communities in Macao. The most important of these is the Buddhist Association of Macau, which was established in 1997.

There are more than 40 Buddhist temples in Macao, as well as scores of village temples and houses dedicated to Buddhist deities. The majority of the temples, both large and small, are dedicated to Kun Iam (the Goddess of Mercy), Tin Hau or Kwan Tai (the God of War and source of righteousness).

Following the establishment of the Macao SAR Government, Buddha's Birthday, which falls on the eighth day of the Fourth Moon, was declared a public holiday.

Catholicism

The Macao Catholic Diocese was founded by decree of Pope Gregory XIII on 23 January 1576. As the frst Catholic missionary centre in the Far East, it was originally responsible for many regions, including China, Japan, Vietnam and the Southeast Asian coastal islands.

The frst bishop appointed to the Macao Catholic Diocese was the Jesuit Melchior Carneiro. Members of the Society of Jesus (Jesuits) had established a mission and a college in Macao by 1565. In the late 16th century, the standards of the latter's tertiary education were high enough to be recognised by European universities. Church of the Mother of God (commonly known as St Paul's Church), the Church of the Society of Jesus, was thrice destroyed by fre; the Ruins of St Paul's are the remnants of the blaze that occurred in 1835.

Franciscans, Augustinians, Dominicans, and Sisters of St Clare (who vowed to lead a hermetic life) all established missions in Macao during the 16th and 17th centuries.

Nowadays, the Macao Catholic Diocese is limited to the SAR itself. It has six parishes, three quasi-parishes and three cathedrals. There are also 18 freestanding churches of various sizes and 56 chapels within diocesan buildings.

According to fgures supplied by the Macao Catholic Diocese, Macao had 13,891 Catholic residents at the end of 2012. In addition, around 15,499 temporary residents of Macao were adherents, including Portuguese-speaking expatriates and their families, English-speaking people and their families from all over the world, Filipino domestic helpers and their families, and non resident workers from the mainland and other Asian countries. Altogether, there are around 29,390 Catholics in Macao.

The clerics registered in the Macao Catholic Diocese include one diocesan bishop, 18 priests and eight contributing priests. In addition, four priests from the Macao Catholic Diocese currently work in other dioceses.

There are also 58 priests and 28 brothers in male religious congregations that serve the community in Macao. In addition, there are 184 sisters and 110 dedicated voluntary workers.

Macao Catholic Diocesan statistics show that, in the 2011-2012 school year, it managed and maintained 31 educational institutions with 29,510 students, 1,934 of whom were in tertiary education, 12,670 in secondary schools, 9,802 in primary schools and 5,104 in kindergartens.

The Catholic Church also operates 23 social service agencies, including seven child-care centres, six convalescent homes for the elderly and sick, four rehabilitation homes for the physically and mentally handicapped, and six residential homes for students from single-parent families and/or who are experiencing personal problems. During the year, 1,602 people - 632 residents and 970 non-residents - benefted from the wide range of services provided by these institutions.

The Catholic Church is also engaged in other activities. It operates a bookshop, libraries, cultural and media affairs centres, a conference centre, social service centres, social welfare organisations, summer camps and retreats. It also publishes a few religious periodicals.

Protestantism

Macao is considered an important base for the introduction of Christianity to China in modern Protestant history. The religion was introduced to China during the Tang Dynasty, Yuan Dynasty and Ming Dynasty, a total of four times. Macao was involved in the last two introductions.

Robert Morrison was the frst missionary from the London Missionary Society to arrive in Macao, in 1807. He then opened the fourth chapter in the history of pioneering Christianity in China. He baptised Choi Kou in 1814, and made him the frst Chinese protestant. He led services in Macao and Guangzhou for 27 years, serving as a bridge for cultural exchanges between the West and China. In the 19th century, Protestant missionaries came mainly from Britain and America, and were engaged in local cultural and religious activities, becoming driving forces in modern China's healthcare, education, printing and publishing. In 1834, Robert Morrison died; his body lies in the Old Protestant Cemetery, beside the Luis de Camoes Garden.

After the Opium War, the missionary base in Macao was moved to Hong Kong and Shanghai. But Macao still played an active role in the development of Protestant churches in the Pearl River Delta area.

Entering the 20th century, a succession of Chinese Protestant churches were established, through the efforts of missionaries and returning Chinese believers. The Macau Baptist Church was established in 1904; the Chi Tou Church of the Church of Christ in China was established in 1906 at Hac Sa Beach; and Sheng Kung Hui (the Anglican Church) began their missionary activities in Macao in 1938. In the early 1950s, there were about fve Protestant churches. By the 1980s, the number of Protestant churches had increased to 20. During the 1990s, missionary organisations from Hong Kong and overseas arrived to establish branches, and further increased the number of Protestant churches to over 50 throughout Macao.

Today, major Protestant denominations in Macao include the Church of Christ in China, Baptist Church, Sheng Kung Hui (the Anglican Church), Sheun Tao Church, Christian and Missionary Alliance, Conservative Baptist Church, Assemblies of God, Church of the United Brethren in Christ, and the Evangelical Free Church. There are nearly 80 Protestant churches, with about 150 pastors and more than 8,000 believers. Some 4,400 believers currently attend Sunday worship each week.

Of the schools established by Protestants, four are secondary schools with primary and kindergarten sections; three are primary schools with kindergarten sections; one is a special education school; and there is one biblical institute. There are also several training centres and two bookshops operated by Protestant groups.

The Union of Evangelical Christian Churches and Associations in Macau was established in 1990, and comprises the Protestant churches and organisations. Its objectives are to strengthen links between Protestant organisations and enhance their development; and promote and organise local evangelising activities. Around 60 Protestant organisations are involved in social services covering underprivileged groups, young people, families, workers, charity, counselling services and education. They also serve other people in need, including prisoners, patients, drug addicts and street sleepers.

Islam

The Islamic Association of Macau was established in 1935. It has long planned to build a mosque and Islamic centre; and a blueprint for the Islamic centre was approved by the former Portuguese administration. According to the plan, the mosque will have a total area of 1,250 square metres and will be able to accommodate a congregation of 600.

Baha'i

The Baha'i Faith was introduced to Macao in 1953. Its administrative body - the Local Spiritual Assembly of the Baha'is of Macao - was established in 1958. Later, a local Baha'i Centre was set up in Taipa in 1984, and another local centre was set up in Coloane in 1988. An administrative body covering the entire territory - the National Spiritual Assembly of the Baha'is of Macao - was established in 1989, which also oversees the three local bodies of the Baha'is in Macao. Currently it has over 2,500 adherents.

The National Spiritual Assembly of the Baha'is of Macao established a school in Macao which includes a kindergarten, a primary school and a secondary school. It received a land grant from the Government in 2008 for campus expansion. Thus far, it has provided education to several thousand students, from many other countries.

Traditional Festivals

Macao is a city where Chinese and Western cultures coexist. Local Chinese, Portuguese and Macanese residents and other ethical minorities in Macao respect and usually celebrate each other's festivals. Macao's festivals are so colourful and cheerful that some are designated statutory and general holidays. Traditional Chinese celebrations include the Lunar New Year (also known as Chinese New Year or the Spring Festival), Qing Ming Festival, Buddha's Birthday, the Mid-Autumn Festival and Winter Solstice; while Easter, the Feast of the Immaculate Conception and Christmas are important local festivals derived from Western traditions.

Lunar New Year

The Lunar New Year is the most important festival for Chinese people. Macao residents usually perform religious ceremonies at home or in temples on the frst two days of the Lunar New Year. They visit friends and relatives, let off frecrackers and join in various celebrations. Civil servants, who are normally forbidden to enter casinos, are granted special permission to do so during the frst three days of the New Year. The incessant, ear-splitting noise of frecrackers and the red shreds of their wrappers last a whole week, creating a vibrant, joyful scene. These are the sights and sounds of Macao during Lunar New Year. In recent years, it has become increasingly popular for Macao residents to take family vacations during the Lunar New Year public holidays.

Qing Ming, Chong Yang Festivals and All Souls' Day

The Qing Ming and Chong Yang (Double Nine) festivals are occasions for people to commemorate their ancestors and visit their graves. They pay homage to the deceased, strengthen bonds with their relatives and perform flial duties. All Souls'Day, the traditional Christian festival to remember the deceased, is also a public holiday in Macao.

Buddha's Birthday

Buddha's Birthday is a special local festival in Macao. During the festival, Buddhist organisations in Macao usually organise many celebrations, including sutra recitations and "Bathing the Buddha" ceremonies to celebrate the birth of the Buddha. Some non-religious organisations, such as fshmongers' associations, also celebrate the festival. Drunken Dragon Dance performances and the distribution of "Dragon Boat Rice" are among the traditional activities staged at this time.

The Drunken Dragon Dance is an ancient custom that originated in neighbouring Zhongshan Municipality in Guangdong province, and has become a tradition among Macao's fshmongers. Through the dance, they show their team spirit and commitment to society. After much modifcation through the years, the Drunken Dragon Dance nowadays features only the head and tail of the Dragon. The performers are expected to drink as they dance; and people believe they can only perform well if they are drunk.

The Macao Drunken Dragon Dance was included in the Intangible Cultural Heritage List of Macao in 2009 and successfully inscribed on the List of National Intangible Cultural Heritage in 2011.

Dragon Boat Festival

The Dragon Boat Festival falls on the ffth day of the ffth month of the lunar calendar. It is a time for eating special dumplings and Dragon Boat Racing. Macao's Dragon Boat Races have a unique local favour, and have developed into an international competition. Many Westerners also participate, displaying their prowess.

Mid-Autumn Festival

Appreciating the moon's beauty while enjoying delicious mooncakes during the Mid-Autumn Festival is another Chinese tradition. Even before the day arrives, a joyous atmosphere builds up everywhere. Shops selling traditional mooncakes are packed with customers, as demand for them runs high. On the festival night, family members gather and enjoy reunions.

Feast of the Immaculate Conception

Macao is the only place in Asia where the Feast of the Immaculate Conception is a public holiday. Since 8 December 1854, Catholics in Macao have held celebrations on this day, seeking forgiveness of all their sins, and for their hearts to be cleansed.

Christmas

Christmas is the time when Christians all over the world celebrate the birth of Jesus. Macao is flled with a vibrant festive atmosphere at Christmas with its unique, European-style streets festooning with colourful lights and decorations, and Christmas carols wafting out from its churches.

Kun Iam Tong

Built in the late Ming Dynasty, the Kun Iam Tong Temple, also known as the Pou Chai Buddhist Monastery and Temple, is one of the three Buddhist monasteries in Macao. Enjoying a long history and situated on a large area of land built with splendid structures, Kun Iam Tong featured the ancient Chinese architectural style of Hui Fei, resembling ancient Chinese temples on famous mountains. It is well known worldwide, not only because of its history, but also as the venue for the signing of the Treaty of Wangxia between China and the United States in the 19th century.

History Macao Has Been Part of China Since Ancient Times

Historical records show that Macao has been Chinese territory since long ago. When Qinshihuang (the frst emperor of the Qin Dynasty) unifed China in 221BC, Macao came under the jurisdiction of Panyu County, Nanhai Prefecture. Administratively, it was part of Dongguan Prefecture in the Jin Dynasty (AD265-420), then Nanhai County during the Sui Dynasty (AD581-618), and Dongguan County in the Tang Dynasty (AD618-907). In 1152, during the Southern Song Dynasty, the Guangdong administration joined the coastal areas of Nanhai, Panyu, Xinhui and Dongguan Counties to establish Xiangshan County, thus bringing Macao under its jurisdiction.

Macao has been known variously. Besides Macao ("Aomen" in Chinese), it has also been called Haojing (Oyster Mirror), Jinghai (Mirror Sea), Haojiang, Haijing, Jinghu (Mirror Lake), Haojingao and Majiao. Haojing is the earliest name recorded in written documents.

The name "Aomen" frst appeared in 1564, in the following passage in Pang Shangpeng's *Memorandum to the Throne Concerning Long-Term Coastal Security*, which was presented to the Ming Emperor: "Xiangshan County in the south of Guangdong Province is a coastal area. It takes one day to travel from Yongmai to Haojingao. In Haojingao there are Nantai (South Tower) and Beitai (North Tower), two hills facing each other like two towers of a city gate. People call the place where the two hills stand Aomen (Gate to Ao). Aomen is surrounded by sea, and is only connected to the mainland at Zangge. It is a trading port where foreign ships and merchants anchor."

Aomen Jilue (Chronicles of Macao) by Yin Guangren and Zhang Rulin - the frst and second Qing offcials appointed to the place - which was published during the reign of Emperor Qianlong, records: "The name 'Haojingao' can be found in the documents of the Ming Dynasty. To the south of Haojingao lies Shizimen (Cross-Gate), where the sea runs both north-south and east-west between four island hills. Combining 'ao' from Haojingao and 'men' from Shizimen, people call the place 'Aomen'."

The earliest known written record of the name "Macau" in a foreign language is in a letter dated 20 November 1555.

In the 15th century, the Portuguese began to expand their trade to the Far East, taking control of several places in Africa and Asia. In 1553, claiming that they needed some land to air their soaked goods, the Portuguese gained permission from local Chinese offcials to stay temporarily on the Macao peninsula to carry out commercial activities. Around 1573, the Portuguese began paying land rent to the Chinese government. From then till the Opium War, for nearly 300 years, the Ming and subsequent Qing governments exercised sovereignty over Macao, levying taxes and implementing various controls.

The Ming and Qing Governments' Exercise of Sovereignty OverMacao

The Ming and Qing governments maintained irrefutable sovereignty over Macao, and under the principle of sovereignty exercised strict and comprehensive land, military, administrative, judicial and customs controls.

While exercising sovereignty over Macao in all aspects, the Ming and Qing governments used the strategy "let foreigners take charge of foreigners" to control the Portuguese in Macao. They did not directly interfere with the internal affairs of the Portuguese community, but allowed the Portuguese to exercise self-administration to keep their social and economic affairs in order. In 1583, the Portuguese in Macao were permitted to form a Senate to handle various issues concerning their community, on the understanding that they recognised overall Chinese sovereignty and that this autonomous organ was not politically independent.

The Portuguese Occupation of Macao and the Sino-PortugueseTreaty of Amity and Commerce

After the Opium War, the Chinese and British signed the Treaty of Nanking, stipulating the cession of Hong Kong to Britain. The Portuguese seized the opportunity to put forward various requests

-including exemption from the annual land rent - and gradually occupied Macao. In 1887, the Qing government was forced to sign the Sino-Portuguese Treaty of Amity and Commerce, under which the Portuguese obtained the right to permanently settle in Macao as well as control over the region. In 1928, the foreign affairs ministry of the then Kuomintang government offcially notifed the Portuguese side that it was abrogating the treaty.

The Signing of the Sino-Portuguese Joint Declaration

After the founding of the People's Republic of China in 1949, the Chinese government declared the abolition of all unequal treaties. In March 1972, China's Permanent Representative to the United Nations sent a letter to the UN Special Committee on Decolonization, stating the country's principled stand on the issues of Hong Kong and Macao. On 8 February 1979, when China and Portugal established diplomatic relations, the two governments reached the following agreement on the issue of Macao: Macao is a Chinese territory currently under Portuguese administration; the issue of Macao is a question left over from history, which will be settled through friendly consultation between the two governments when appropriate.

In 1984, as soon as the question of Hong Kong was solved, the issue of Macao was put on the agenda. June 1986 saw China and Portugal begin negotiations concerning the issue of Macao. After four rounds of talks, on 23 March 1987 the two governments reached a consensus on the entire text of the agreement and memorandum, thus bringing to a satisfactory conclusion of the Sino-Portuguese negotiations, which lasted eight months and 14 days. On the morning of 26 March 1987, the Joint Declaration of the Government of the People's Republic of China and the Government of the Portuguese Republic on the Question of Macao was initialled in the Great Hall of the People in Beijing, by Deputy Foreign Minister Zhou Nan, head of the Chinese government delegation, and his Portuguese counterpart, Ambassador Rui Medina.

The Sino-Portuguese Joint Declaration was offcially signed on 13 April 1987 in Beijing. A grand ceremony for the occasion was held in the Great Hall of the People. On behalf of their respective governments, the Premier of the State Council of the People's Republic of China, Zhao Ziyang, and the Prime Minister of the Portuguese Republic, Anibal Antonio Cavaco Silva, signed the Joint Declaration, which stated that China would resume the exercise of sovereignty over Macao from 20 December 1999 onwards. Deng Xiaoping attended the ceremony in person. The National People's Congress (NPC) of the People's Republic of China and the Portuguese parliament, the Assembly of the Republic, ratifed the Joint Declaration in June and December, respectively. On 15 January 1988, the Sino-Portuguese Joint Declaration came into effect, and Macao thus entered a transition period leading to the Handover.

The Enactment of the Basic Law and the Transition Period

In order to specify and legalise the basic principles and policies of the central government concerning Macao that were set forth in the Joint Declaration, the First Session of the Seventh NPC decided on 13 April 1988 to establish the Drafting Committee of the Basic Law of the Macao Special Administrative Region. On 5 September 1988, the list of members of the committee was approved at the Third Session of the Seventh NPC. It comprised experts and representatives from all walks of life, from both the mainland and Macao. For more than four years, the committee carried out extensive and painstaking investigations, consultations, democratic discussions and revisions, and fnally in January 1993, the Drafting Committee approved the draft of the Basic Law and the designs of the fag and emblem of the Macao Special Administrative Region.

On 31 March 1993, the First Session of the Eighth NPC passed the Basic Law of the Macao Special Administrative Region of the People's Republic of China, its annexes, and the designs of the fag and emblem of the Macao SAR. On the same day, President Jiang Zemin signed Presidential Decree No. 3, promulgating the Basic Law of the Macao Special Administrative Region, which was to come into effect when the Chinese government resumed the exercise of sovereignty over Macao on 20 December 1999.

The nearly 12-year period from 15 January 1988, when the Sino-Portuguese Joint Declaration came into effect, to 20 December 1999, when the central government resumed the exercise of sovereignty over Macao, was called the transition period. The Portuguese government prepared, in this period, for the handover of the government in 1999. Maintaining Macao's social stability, boosting economic development and creating favourable conditions for a smooth handover were the main tasks at that stage.

The Sino-Portuguese Liaison Group and the Sino-Portuguese Land Group, founded under the Sino-Portuguese Joint Declaration, resolved issues that arose during the transition period through negotiation. The two governments also reached agreement on the establishment of the Macau International Airport, the Bank of China becoming a Macao currency-issuing bank, and the amendment and renewal of the casino gaming franchise. Three key issues that had attracted much attention - the localisation of the civil service, the localisation of the law and the offcial status of the Chinese language - were also settled satisfactorily.

On 29 April 1998, the Second Session of the Ninth Conference of the Standing Committee of the NPC passed the list of members of the Preparatory Committee of the Macao Special Administrative Region. The Preparatory Committee was established in Beijing on 5 May 1998. One of its chief missions was to establish, in accordance with the NPC decision, a broadly representative Selection Committee comprising 200 members, all of them permanent residents of Macao, to select the frst Chief Executive of the Macao SAR. On 15 May 1999, in a secret ballot at the third plenary session of the Selection Committee for the First Government of the Macao SAR, Edmund Ho Hau Wah was elected the frst Chief Executive of the Macao Special Administrative Region of the People's Republic of China. On 20 May 1999, Zhu Rongji, Premier of the State Council, issued State Council Decree No. 264, appointing Edmund Ho Hau Wah as the frst Chief Executive of the Macao Special Administrative Region of the People's Republic of China, to assume offce on 20 December 1999.

Mandarin's House

The Mandarin's House was the family residence of the modern Chinese master Zheng Guanying (1842-1921). Zheng's world-famous book Shengshi Weiyan (Words of Warning in Times of Prosperity) was completed here. The house was probably built before 1869. The Government acquired the property rights to the house in 2001, and took eight years to repair and refurnish the building. In February 2010, the Mandarin's House was opened to the public.

First Prize -Playing Nazha -the Child Deity (CHAN MENG KAI),

Second Prize - Morning Exercise (KONG IU LAM),

Third Price - Fending Off (CHEONG KAM KA) and other winning entries.

GOVERNMENT AND POLITICAL SYSTEM

MACAO POLITICAL AND GOVERNMENT LEADERS

CHIEF EXECUTIVE

Chui Sai On

Mr Chui Sai On has been reappointed as the fourth-term Chief Executive of the Macao Special Administrative Region. After winning the election for the fourth-term Chief Executive on 31 August 2014, by receiving an overwhelming percentage of votes, Mr Chui was officially appointed by the State Council as the Chief Executive-elect of the fourth-term Chief Executive of the Macao SAR on 17 September. He received the Order of Appointment of the State Council from Premier Li Keqiang on 22 September, and assumed office on 20 December 2014.

Mr Chui was elected the third-term Chief Executive of the Macao SAR on 26 July 2009, also by receiving a high percentage of votes, and assumed office on 20 December of the same year.

Chui Sai On was born in Macao in 1957. His nationality is Chinese. After he had completed his secondary education at Ling Nam School in Macao, he continued his studies in the United States of America and graduated from the California State University of Sacramento with a bachelor degree in Community Health with honor. He then obtained his Master degree and Doctor degree of Public Health at the School of Public Health, University of Oklahoma, U.S.A.

He served as a lawmaker on the 5th Legislative Assembly from 1992-1996 and was both a member of the Council for Youth Affairs and the Environmental Committee. He was also the Principal of Kiang Peng School and the Kiang Peng Centre of Continuing Education for Professionals.

He played an active role in many community organizations in Macao. He was the Chief of Medical and Health Department of the Tung Sin Tong Charitable Institution and member of Management Board of the same Institution, Executive Director of Macao Kiang Wu Hospital Charitable Association, President of the Juvenile Staff Committee of Kiang Wu Hospital, Director of the Macao Eye Bank Fund, Honorary President of Macao Nursing Association, President of Macao Junior Chamber (1991), Honorary Life-Time President of Macao Junior Chamber of Commerce Senior Member Association, Chairman of the Supervisory Board of the Macao Association for the Mentally Handicapped, Vice-President of the Macao Management Association and Vice-President of the Association of the Natives of "San Wui" in Macao.

He was also a member of the Executive Committee of China Youth Federation and the Honorary Vice-President of Chinese Preventive Medicine Association.

In August 1999, he was appointed by the Central People's Government as the Secretary for Social Affairs and Culture of the Government of Macao SAR of the PRC. In the same year, he was also appointed as a member of the 1st Executive Council of the Macao SAR Government. On 4 December 2004, he was reappointed as the Secretary for Social Affairs and Culture for the second term of the Macao SAR Government.

While he was the Secretary for Social Affairs and Culture, he also held the following posts including President of Macao Health Reform Advisory Committee, President of Macao Healthy City Committee, President of AIDS Prevention and Control Commission, President of Education Committee, President of Youth Affairs Committee, President of Consultative Council of Culture, President of General Archives Committee, President of Macao Sports Committee, President of Committee on Social Welfare, President of Committee on Elderly Affairs, President of Narcotics Control Committee, President of Commission on Rehabilitation Affairs, President of Tourism Development Committee, Chairman of Macao Grand Prix Committee, President of Tourism Crisis Management Office, President of Coordinating Committee of Macao Special Administrative Region of the Support for the Reconstruction of the Zone Affected by the Earthquake in Sichuan, Coordinator of the Inter-departmental Working Group that Accompany and Support the Planning and the Execution of the Celebration of the 10th Anniversary of the Establishment of the Macao Special Administrative Region, Member of Science and Technology Committee, Macao S.A.R. Representative to the General Assembly of Shareholders & president of the General Assembly of Macao 4th East Asian Games Organising Committee, Ltd. (MEAGOC), President of the Consultative Council of the East Asian Games of the General Assembly of Macao 4th East Asian Games Organizing Committee, Ltd. (MEAGOC), President of the East Asian Games Broadcasting Council, Macao S.A.R. Representative to the General Assembly of Shareholders of the Macao 2nd Asian Indoor Games Organising Committee, Ltd. (MAIGOC) and Deputy-Chief Scout of Scout Association of Macao.

POLITICAL SYSTEMS

MACAO PEOPLE RULING MACAO AND A HIGH DEGREE OF AUTONOMY

The Government of the People's Republic of China resumed to exercise sovereignty over Macao on 20th December 2004 when the Special Administrative Region of Macao was established in accordance with the Article 31 of the Constitution of the People's Republic of China. In harmony with the principle of "one country, two systems", the previous capitalist system and way of lift shall remain unchanged for 50 years.

Macao people ruling Macao means the people of Macao governing Macao. The executive organ and the legislature of the Macao Special Administrative Region shall be composed of local residents of Macao. According to the Basic Law, the definition of Macao people refers to the permanent residents of the Macao Special Administrative Region, including the Chinese, Portuguese and other people who meet the qualifications of the Basic Law.

The Chief Executive, members of the Executive Council and the Legislative Council, the President of the Court of Final Appeal, the Procurator-General and principal officials of the Macao Special Administrative Region must be permanent residents of the Region. Some of these posts can only be assumed by the Chinese citizens among the permanent residents in Macao.

A high degree of autonomy means that China National People Congress (NPC)authorizes the Macao Special Administrative Region to exercise a high degree of autonomy in line with the Basic Law, and the Central Government will not interfere in the affairs that fall within the scope of autonomy of the Macao Special Administrative Region.

The high degree of autonomy to be exercised by the Region includes the administrative power, legislative power and independent judicial power including the power of final adjudication. But a high degree of autonomy does not mean complete autonomy. To safeguard China unification and uphold state sovereignty and territorial integrity, the Central government retains necessary power over the Macao Special Administrative Region. For instance, the Central People Government shall be responsible for the foreign affairs and defence relating to the Macao Special Administrative Region.

EXECUTIVE STRUCTURE

The Government of the Macao Special Administrative Region is the executive authority of the Macao Special Administrative Region. The Chief Executive is the head of the Government, and General Secretariats, Directorates of Services, Departments and Divisions are established in the Government of MSAR. The principal officials of the Macao Special Administrative Region shall be Chinese citizens who are permanent residents of the Region and have ordinarily resided in Macao for a continuous period of not less than fifteen years.

The Government of the Macao Special Administrative Region is responsible for formulating and implementing policies; conducting administrative affairs; conducting external affairs as authorised by the Central People's Government under the Basic Law; drawing up and introducing budgets and final accounts; introducing bills and motions and drafting administrative regulations; and designating officials to sit in on the meetings of the Legislative Council to hear opinions or to speak on behalf of the government.

The Government of the Macao Special Administrative Region must abide by the law and be accountable to the Legislative Council of the Region: it shall implement laws passed by the Council and already in force; it shall present regular policy addresses to the Council; and it shall answer questions raised by members of the Council.

THE CHIEF EXECUTIVE

The Chief Executive of the Macao Special Administrative Region is the head of the Macao Special Administrative Region and is accountable to the Central People's Government and the Macao Special Administrative Region.

The Chief Executive of the Macao Special Administrative Region shall be a Chinese citizen of not less than 40 years of age who is a permanent resident of the Region and has ordinarily resided in Macao for a continuous period of not less than 20 years. The Chief Executive is selected by election or through consultations held locally and is appointed by the Central People's Government. The term of office of the Chief Executive is five years and may serve for not more than two consecutive terms.

The Chief Executive is responsible for leading the government of the Macao Special Administrative Region; implementing the Basic Law and other laws which apply in the Macao Special Administrative Region; signing bills passed by the Legislative Council and promulgating laws; signing budgets passed by the Legislative Council and report the budgets and final accounts to the Central People's Government for the record; deciding on government policies and issuing executive orders; formulating the administrative regulations and promulgating them for implementation; nominating and reporting to the Central People's Government for appointment the Secretaries, Commissioner against Corruption, the Director of Audit, the leading members of the Police and the Customs and Excise, and recommending to the Central People's Government the removal of the above-mentioned officials; appointing part of the members of the Legislative Council; appointing or removing members of the Executive Council; nominating and reporting to the Central People's Government for appointment of the Procurator-General and recommending to the Central People's Government the removal of the Procurator-General; appointing or removing presidents and judges of the courts at all levels, procurators, holders of public office and, under certain circumstances, dissolving the Legislative Council.

THE EXECUTIVE COUNCIL

The Executive Council of the Macao Special Administrative Region is an organ for assisting the Chief Executive in policy-making. The Executive Council is presided over by the Chief Executive and meets at least once a month. Its members are appointed by the Chief Executive from among the principal officials of the executive authorities, members of the Legislative Council and public figures. The Executive Council is composed of seven to eleven persons. The Chief Executive may, as he or she deems necessary, invite other persons concerned to sit in on meetings of the Executive Council.

THE LEGISLATURE

The majority of the members of the Legislative Council of the Macao Special Administrative Region, which is composed of permanent residents of the Region, are elected. The term of office of the Legislative Council of the Macao Special Administrative Region is four years, except for the first term.

In the first term, the Legislative Council consists of 23 members, 8 of whom are returned through direct elections, 8 returned through indirect elections and 7 appointed by the Chief Executive. In the second term, which shall last until the year 2005, the Legislative Council shall be composed of 27 members, of whom 10 are returned through direct elections, 10 are returned through indirect elections and 7 appointed by the Chief Executive. In the third and subsequent terms, the Legislative Council shall consist of 29 members of whom 12 shall be returned through direct elections, 10 returned through indirect elections and 7 appointed by the Chief Executive.
The Legislative Council of Macao has a President and a Vice-President who are elected by and from among the members of the Legislative Council. The President and Vice-President of the Legislative Council are Chinese citizens who are permanent residents of the Macao Special Administrative Region and have ordinarily resided in Macao for a continuous period of not less than fifteen years.

The Legislative Council has powers to enact, amend, suspend or repeal laws; to examine and approve budgets introduced by the government; and to examine the report on audit introduced by the government.

The Legislative Council is also responsible for deciding on taxation according to government motions and approve debts to be undertaken by the government; and to receive and debate the policy addresses of the Chief Executive and to debate any issue concerning the public interests. Under certain circumstances, the Legislative Council may pass a motion to impeach the Chief Executive by a two thirds majority of all its members and report it to the Central People's Government for decision.

THE JUDICIARY AND LEGAL SYSTEMS

THE JUDICIARY

According to the Basic Law, the Macao Special Administrative Region (MSAR) has independent judicial power including the power of final adjudication. The courts of the MSAR exercise judicial power independently and are subordinated to nothing but the law.

The MSAR has Count of First Instance, Court of Second Instance and the Court of Final Appeal and the structure, powers and functions of the courts are established by law.
The Court of First Instance of the MSAR is the basic court including the Court of Criminal Examing Magistracy and the Administrative Court, which, if necessary, can be given special powers. The Basic Court has specialised, specific jurisdiction.

The judges of the courts of the MSAR at all levels are appointed by the Chief Executive on the recommendation of an independent commission composed of local judges, lawyers and eminent persons. Judges are chosen on the basis of their professional qualifications and qualified judges of foreign nationality may also be employed. Some Portuguese judges have remained working in the service of the Territory.

The Presidents of the courts of the MSAR at all levels are appointed by the Chief Executive from amongst the judges of the courts, and the President of the Court of Final Appeal must be Chinese citizen who is a permanent resident of the MSAR.

The Procuratorate of the MSAR exercises its procuratorial functions as vested by law, independently and free from any interference. The Procurator-General is nominated by the Chief Executive and appointed by the Central People's Government and must be Chinese citizen who is a permanent resident of the MSAR. Procurators are nominated by the Procurator-General and appointed by the Chief Executive. The structure, powers and operation of the procuratorate is prescribed by Law. At present, there are four experienced Portuguese procurators in the Procuratorate, one of whom is the Deputy Procurator-General.

MAGISTRATE TRAINING

The Faculty of Law of the University of Macao offers Law degree courses in Chinese and Portuguese, and also Master Degree Programs in Law and Politics. From 1991 to July 2004 academic year, around 110 students were graduated from the Faculty of Law.

The Magistrates Training Centre (MTC) was set up in 1994 as an independent institution organising and co-ordinating the training of new judges and employees of the Procuratorate. In accordance with the law in force, candidates for the course of the MTC must have a law degree recognised in Macao and must speak Chinese and Portuguese. 19 of the 35 candidates enrolled in the first three courses offered by the MTC were graduates of the University of Macao, ten were from universities in the People's Republic of China, five were from Portugal and one from Taiwan. The majority, 17 graduates, was from Macao.

At present, the average age of judges is 35 years old, while the average for procurators is 36. They have all completed and obtained the appropriate degree and attended the training course in the MTC, subsequently completing training in Macao's judiciary institutions.

The laws, decree-laws, administrative orders and other pieces of legislation previously in force in Macao have been retained apart from those that contravened the Basic Law of the Macao Special Administrative Region. In addition to the Basic Law, the laws applied in the MSAR include those previously in force in the territory approved by the Standing Committee of the National People's Congress and the Five Big Codes: the Criminal Code, the Code of Criminal Procedure, the Civil Code, the Code of Civil Procedure, and the Commercial Code, as well as the national laws contained in Annex III to the Basic Law.

PRINCIPAL OFFCIALS OF THE MACAO SAR

Chief Executive	Mr Chui Sai On
President of the Legislative Assembly	Mr Lau Cheok Va
President of the Court of Final Appeal	Mr Sam Hou Fai
Secretary for Administration and Justice	Ms Florinda Chan
Secretary for Economy and Finance	Mr Francis Tam Pak Yuen
Secretary for Security	Mr Cheong Kuoc Va
Secretary for Social Affairs and Culture	Mr Cheong U

Secretary for Transport and Public Works	Mr Lau Si Io
Public Prosecutor-General	Mr Ho Chio Meng
Commissioner Against Corruption	Mr Fong Man Chong
Commissioner of Audit	Mr Ho Veng On
Commissioner-General of the Unitary Police Service	Mr Jose Proenca Branco
Director-General of the Macao Customs Service	Mr Choi Lai Hang

MEMBERS OF THE EXECUTIVE COUNCIL OF THE MACAO SAR

The Executive Council is presided over by the Chief Executive.

Members of the Council: Ms Florinda Chan Mr Leong Heng Teng Mr Liu Chak Wan Mr Ma Iao Lai Mr Leonel Alberto Alves Mr Cheang Chi Keong Mr Leong Vai Tac Mr Chan Meng Kam Ms Ho Sut Heng Mr Wong Yue Kai

MEMBERS OF THE LEGISLATIVE ASSEMBLY OF THE MACAO SAR

Members (by Indirect Vote)

Mr Lau Cheok Va (President) Mr Ho Iat Seng (Vice-President) Mr Chui Sai Cheong (First Secretary) Mr Kou Hoi In (Second Secretary) Mr Fong Chi Keong Mr Cheung Lup Kwan Mr Cheang Chi Keong Mr Leonel Alberto Alves Mr Chan Chak Mo Mr Lam Heong Sang

Members (by Direct Vote)

Ms Kwan Tsui Hang Mr Au Kam San Mr Jose Maria Pereira Coutinho Mr Chan Meng Kam Mr Mak Soi Kun Mr Ho Ion Sang Mr Ng Kuok Cheong Mr Ung Choi Kun Ms Leong On Kei Mr Lee Chong Cheng Mr Chan Wai Chi Ms Chan Mei Yi

Members (Appointed by the Chief Executive)

Mr Tsui Wai Kwan Mr Chui Sai Peng Mr Lau Veng Seng Mr Tong Io Cheng Mr Vong Hin Fai Ms Ho Sio Kam Mr Sio Chi Wai

Committee Members of the Third Session of the Fourth Term Legislative Assembly

Executive Board
President: Mr Lau Cheok Va Vice-President: Mr Ho Iat Seng First Secretary: Mr Chui Sai Cheong
Second Secretary: Mr Kou Hoi In
Committee on Rules and Statutes
President: Mr Fong Chi Keong Secretary: Mr Vong Hin Fai Members: Mr Kou Hoi In
Mr Au Kam San
Mr Ung Choi Kun
Mr Lam Heong Sang
Mr Tong Io Cheng
First Standing Committee
President: Ms Kwan Tsui Hang

Secretary:	Mr Ung Choi Kun
Members:	Mr Kou Hoi In
	Mr Leonel Alberto Alves
	Mr Tsui Wai Kwan

	Mr Au Kam San
	Mr Sio Chi Wai
	Mr Ho Ion Sang
	Ms Chan Mei Yi

Second Standing Committee

President: Mr Chan Chak Mo Secretary: Mr Lee Chong Cheng Members: Mr Fong Chi Keong

Mr Chui Sai Cheong Mr Ng Kuok Cheong Mr Vong Hin Fai Mr Chan Meng Kam Ms Ho Sio Kam Mr Mak Soi Kun

Third Standing Committee

President: Mr Cheang Chi Keong Secretary: Mr Chui Sai Peng Members: Mr Cheung Lup Kwan

Mr Jose Maria Pereira Coutinho Ms Leong On Kei Mr Lau Veng Seng Mr Lam Heong Sang Mr Chan Wai Chi Mr Tong Io Cheng

FOLLOW-UP COMMITTEE FOR LAND AND PUBLIC CONCESSION AFFAIRS

President:	Ms Kwan Tsui Hang
Secretary:	Mr Kou Hoi In
Members:	Mr Leonel Alberto Alves
	Mr Tsui Wai Kwan
	Mr Au Kam San
	Mr Ung Choi Kun
	Mr Sio Chi Wai
	Mr Ho Ion Sang
	Ms Chan Mei Yi

Follow-up Committee for Public Finance Affairs

President: Mr Chan Chak Mo Secretary: Mr Lee Chong Cheng Members: Mr Fong Chi Keong

Mr Chui Sai Cheong Mr Ng Kuok Cheong Mr Vong Hin Fai Mr Chan Meng Kam Ms Ho Sio Kam Mr Mak Soi Kun

Follow-up Committee for Public Administration Affairs

President: Mr Cheang Chi Keong Secretary: Mr Chui Sai Peng Members: Mr Cheung Lup Kwan

Mr Jose Maria Pereira Coutinho Ms Leong On Kei Mr Lau Veng Seng Mr Lam Heong Sang

Mr Chan Wai Chi Mr Tong Io Cheng

POLITICS OF MACAU

Politics of Macau takes place in a framework of a political system dominated by the People's Republic of China, an own legislature, the Chief Executive as the head of government, and of a multi-party system. Executive power is exercised by the government.

MACAU AS PART OF THE PEOPLE'S REPUBLIC OF CHINA

In accordance with Article 31 of the Constitution of the People's Republic of China, Macau has Special Administrative Region status, which provides constitutional guarantees for implementing the policy of "one country, two systems" and the constitutional basis for enacting the Basic Law of the Macau Special Administrative Region. Although geographically part of Guangdong Province, the Macau Special Administrative Region is directly under the authority of the central government of the People's Republic of China in Beijing, which controls the foreign affairs and defence of Macau but otherwise grants the region "a high degree of authority." The Basic Law took force upon handover of sovereignty from Portugal on 20 December 1999, and is to remain in effect for fifty years (that is, until 2049).

Macau's seven deputies to the National People's Congress (NPC) are selected by an electoral conference; they attended their first session of the NPC in Beijing in March 2000. Previously, in December 1999, the NPC Standing Committee approved the membership of the NPC Committee for the Basic Law of the Macau Special Administrative Region, chaired by NPC Vice Chairman Qiao Xiaoyang, for a five-year term. Half of the ten members are from Macau, the others from mainland China. Macau also has representation on the National Committee of the Chinese People's Political Consultative Conference.

HEAD OF GOVERNMENT

Main office holders			
Office	Name	Party	Since
Chief of State (President of the PRC)	Xi Jinping	Communist Party of China	15 November 2012
Chief Executive	Fernando Chui Sai On	Non-partisan	20 December 2009

The Chief Executive of Macau is appointed by the People's Republic of China's central government after selection by an election committee, whose members are nominated by corporate bodies. The chief executive appears before a cabinet, the Executive Council, of between 7 and 11 members. The term of office of the chief executive is 5 years, and no individual may serve for more than two consecutive terms. The governor has strong policymaking and executive powers similar to those of a president. These powers are, however, limited from above by the central government in Beijing, to whom the governor reports directly, and from below (to a more limited extent) by the legislature.

In May 1999, Edmund Ho, a community leader and banker, is the first PRC-appointed chief executive of the Macau SAR, having replaced General de Rocha Viera on 20 December 1999. He was elected by the 200-member Chief Executive Selection Committee. Ho, born in Macau in 1955, was the first Chinese person to govern the region since the 1550s. Prior to 20 December 1999, Ho nominated major officials in the new government and carried out other transfer tasks. The executive branch of the Macau government has the following cabinet departments, each headed by a secretary: Administration and Justice, Economic and Financial Affairs, Security, Social Affairs and Culture, and Transport and Public Works. There also are two commissions, Against Corruption and Audit, and a chief public prosecutor. Upon Macau's reversion to China, the executive offices were moved from Macau Government House temporarily to the Banco Tai Fung

CHIEF EXECUTIVE OF MACAU

The **Chief Executive of Macau** is the head of the government of Macau, a special administrative region of the People's Republic of China and a former Portuguese overseas province governed by the Governor of Macau. Under the Basic Law of Macau, the CE's role is:

> ...be the head of the Macau Special Administrative Region and shall represent the Region. The Chief Executive of the Macau Special Administrative Region shall be accountable to the Central People's Government and the Macau Special Administrative Region in accordance with the provisions of this Law.

The current chief executive is Fernando Chui Sai On. His office is located at the Macau Government Headquarters, formerly the Governor's House (from 1883-1926) and the Governor's office (from 1926 to 1999). The CE has used this as his office since 2009.

POWERS OF THE CE OF MACAU

The powers of the CE of Macau are outlined in the region's Basic Law:

1. To lead the government of the Region;
2. To be responsible for the implementation of this Law and other laws which, in accordance with this Law, apply in the Macau Special Administrative Region;
3. To sign bills passed by the Legislative Council and to promulgate laws; To sign budgets passed by the Legislative Council and report the budgets and final accounts to the Central People's Government for the record;
4. To decide on government policies and to issue executive orders;
5. To formulate the administrative regulations and promulgate them for implementation;
6. To nominate and to report to the Central People's Government for appointment the following principal officials: Secretaries of Departments, Commissioner against Corruptions, Director of Audit, the leading members of the Police and the customs and excise; and to recommend to the Central People's Government the removal of the above mentioned officials;
7. To appoint part of the members of the Legislative Council;
8. To appoint or remove members of the Executive Council;
9. To appoint or remove presidents and judges of the courts at all levels and procurators in accordance with legal procedures;
10. To nominate and report to the Central People's Government for appointment of the Procurator-General and recommend to the Central People's Government the removal of the Procurator-General in accordance with legal procedures;
11. To appoint or remove holders of public office in accordance with legal procedures;
12. To implement the directives issued by the Central People's Government in respect of the relevant matters provided for in this Law;
13. To conduct, on behalf of the Government of the Macau Special Administrative Region, external affairs and Other affairs as authorized by the Central Authorities;
14. To approve the introduction of motions regarding revenues or expenditure to the Legislative Council;
15. To decide, in the light of security and vital interests, whether government officials or other personnel in charge of government affairs should testify or give evidence before the Legislative Council or its committees;

16. To confer medals and titles of honour of the Macau Special Administrative Region in accordance with law;
17. To pardon persons convicted of criminal offences or commute their penalties in accordance with law; and
18. To handle petitions and complaints.

ELECTION OF THE CE

The CE is selected by election or through consultations held locally and be appointed by the Central People's Government. The term of office of the Chief Executive shall be five years and may serve for not more than two consecutive terms.

RESIGNATION

Under Section 54 of the Basic Law, the CE can resign if:

1. When he or she loses the ability to discharge his or her duties as a result of serious illness or other reasons;
2. When, after the Legislative Council is dissolved because he or she twice refuses to sign a bill passed by it, the new Legislative Council again passes by a two-thirds majority of all the members the original bill in dispute, but he or she still refuses to sign it within 30 days; and
3. When, after the Legislative Council is dissolved because it refuses to pass a budget or any other bill concerning the overall interests of the Macau Special Administrative Region, the newly elected Legislative Council still refuses to pass the original bill in dispute.

Section 55 covers the temporary assignment of the role of the CE proceeding resignation.

EXTERNAL RELATIONS

In accordance with the Basic Law, the Macao Special Administrative Region may, using the name "Macao, China" maintain and develop relations, conclude and implement agreements with foreign states and regions and relevant international organisations in the appropriate fields, including economic, trade, financial and monetary, shipping, communications, tourism, cultural, science, technology and sports fields.

Macao, as a non-sovereign regional entity, maintains extensive close relations with various countries and regions in the world. Consequently, the MSAR government has representative offices in Portugal (Lisbon), and in Brussels (the seat of the European Union), and the Macao Government Tourist Office is represented in fourteen states and regions across the globe.
To date, over 57 countries have established consular services in Macao, including the consulate-general of Portugal. 37 consulates-general accredited to Hong Kong also cover the area of Macao, namely: Belgium, Uruguay, Germany, Sweden, Denmark, New Zealand, Canada, Austria, Norway, Switzerland, Finland, Nigeria, Israel, Spain, Holland, Japan, the United States of America, Italy, Korea, India, France, Chile, Poland, Malaysia, Russia, Singapore, Thailand, Czech, Bangladesh, Turkey, the Philippines, Samoa, Greece, Great Britain, Argentina, Pakistan and Australia.

There are twelve countries with consulates-general accredited to Hong Kong and which have, in the meantime, expanded their services to Macao: South Africa, Venezuela, Peru, Brazil, Colombia, Mexico, Saudi Arabia, the Bahamas, Laos, Hungary, Antigua and Barbados.

In addition to this, there are honorary consuls from ten countries appointed to Macao, namely Mali, France, Great Britain, Guinea, Mozambique, Peru, Bhutan, Surinam, Estonia and Guinea-Bissau.

For Macao, as a modern, international city, belonging to international organisations and conventions has assisted in maintaining its specific status within the international sphere, and developing relations abroad in the fields of the economy, trade, finance, air and maritime transport, culture, education, environmental protection and health.

Macao participates in 23 international governmental organisations as a full member, candidate or associate member. These include the World Trade Organisation, UNESCO, the International Maritime Organisation, the World Tourism Organisation, the World Health Organisation West Pacific Council, the World Meteorology Organisation, the Customs Co-operation Council, Interpol, the International Labour Organisation, the Universal Postal Union and the Asia-Pacific Economic and Social Committee.

Macao has three ways of participating in international organisations: by joining as a full member of such international organisations or conventions, taking responsibility in this case as an individual entity, for complying with the obligations and enjoying the international rights; by joining international organisations or conventions as a candidate, associate member or member with no voting rights, intervening in its own name and, in specific circumstances, accepting international duties and the right to enjoy international rights; participating as a member of the PRC delegation attending the meetings of international organisations, addressing issues relating to the MSAR using the name "Macao, China".

In July 1998, the issue of Macao remaining in non-governmental organisations was settled with the consensus reached by the Chinese and Portuguese sides of the Joint Liaison Group. As from that date, Macao has remained a member of 24 non-governmental organisations, most importantly, the European Telecommunications Standards Institute, the International Federation of the Family, the Standard Asian Association of Convention Visitors Bureau, the World Savings Banks Institute, the Union of Luso-Afro-American Capital Cities, the International Association of Labour Inspection, the Consumers International, and the International Federation of Library Associations and Institutions.
Currently around 158 international covenants and multilateral treaties are applied in Macao, covering the fields of civil aviation, customs and excise, countering drugs, the economic and financial, intellectual property, post and telecommunications, resources and the environment, human rights and maritime affairs amongst others.

In accordance with the provisions of the Basic Law, the articles applicable to Macao of the International Covenant on Civil and Political Rights, the International Covenant on Economic, Social and Cultural Rights and other international labour conventions remain in force in Macao. Other conventions and international covenants remain in force in the Macao Special Administrative Region, such as the Convention of the International Maritime Organisation, the Vienna Convention for the Protection of the Ozone Layer, the International Convention on Eliminating of all Forms of Racial Discrimination, the International Labour Convention on the Eliminating of all Forms of Discrimination in the Workplace, the International Convention on Eliminating all Forms of Discrimination against Women, the Convention on Children's Rights, the Convention against Torture and other Cruel, Inhumane or Degrading Treatment or Punishment and the Trade and Co-operation Agreement signed by Macao and the European Union.

MACAO'S RELATIONS WITH THE EUROPEAN UNION

Located in the Pearl River Delta economic zone, Macao is regarded as a southern gateway into the Chinese mainland. Its excellent geographical location, combined with its deep-rooted historical links with Europe, has made the city a trading point between China and the European Union.

EU-Macau relations are based on a Trade and Co-operation Agreement concluded on 14 December 1992, which came into effect on 1 January 1993. This agreement covers trade and industrial, scientific and technical co-operation. A Joint Committee meets annually to oversee the operation of the Agreement and devises ways of developing trade and co-operation. The agreement remained in force as usual after 20 December 1999.

The Commission's 1998 Communication "Building a Comprehensive Partnership with China" stated that EU policy was to support Macau's high degree of autonomy. This policy stems naturally from the EU's strong economic links and historical ties with Macau.

On 12 November 1999 the Commission adopted a Communication to the Council and the European Parliament, entitled "The EU and Macau: Beyond 2000" . In this communication the EU considers that the respect for the principles set out in the basic law of Macau and the full implementation of the concept "one country, two systems" guarantee the specific social, economic and cultural identity of Macau. The Commission committed itself to monitor the situation in the territory by issuing annual reports.

The Macau SAR has an Economic and Trade Office (METO) accredited to the European Union, which ensures a regular dialogue between the EU and Macau on areas under the new SAR's responsibility, such as trade, economic relations and co-operation.

On 15 March 2001 the Council of the European Union adopted a new visa regulation and the EU granted visa-free access to Macau SAR passport-holders as from 10 April 2001.

An EC-Macau re-admission agreement was finalized and initialled on the occasion of the 9th EC-Macau Joint Committee in Brussels, Belgium on 18 October 2002. It was signed on 13 October 2003 in Luxembourg by Commissioner Chris Patten and the Italian Minister of *Foreign Affairs* Franco Frattini on behalf of the EC, and by Florinda Chan, Secretary for Administration and Justice, on behalf of Macau. The EU-Macau Cooperation in the Legal Field Project was inaugurated on 3 December 2002, featuring a series of seminars and training programmes to be executed for a period of 48 months for judges, procurators, government lawyers and other legal practitioners of the Macau SAR.

Given its status as a separate customs territory as stated in the basic law, Macau continues to be treated by the EU as a separate entity for trade policy purposes. The EU was Macau's third largest trading partner and absorbed about 23% of its total exports, while 12% of Macau's imports came from the EU in 2003 (Macau trade statistics). Total bilateral trade between the EU and Macau reached €1 billion in 2002. Macau's trade surplus with the EU was €382 million (Eurostat). The EU was the third biggest investor in Macau after Hong Kong and the People's Republic of China with 25 firms investing in the SAR in 2001. Total investment stock amounted to over €400 million. Macau's membership in the World Trade Organization and liberal economic system offer favourable conditions for EU investments.

US RELATIONS WITH MACAU

In recognition of Macau's high degree of autonomy, the USA continues to treat Macau as a "special area" distinct from the People's Republic of China: e. g., the sanctions imposed on China after the June 1989 violence in Tiananmen Square do not apply to Macau. For the DV-Lottery, those who were born in Mainland China are not eligible to apply, whereas persons born in Macau are qualified.

The U.S. government supports Macau's autonomy by strengthening bilateral ties through the promotion of bilateral trade and investment, law enforcement cooperation, academic and cultural links, and high-level dialogue and visits.

After the September 11 attacks, Macau officials pledged full cooperation with U.S. and global efforts against terrorism. The legislature passed an anti-terrorism law in April 2002 that includes provisions that are consistent with the requirements of UN Security Council Resolution 1373.

ECONOMIC RELATIONS

Macau's clothes and textiles continued to enter the United States under quotas separated from those of China. Under the terms of a September 2000 bilateral Memorandum of Understanding, Macau and the US government cooperate in enforcing textile quotas and preventing illegal trans-shipment. The US continued periodic visits by U.S. Customs Textile Production Verification Teams to ensure compliance with Macau bilateral textile commitments.

The protection of intellectual property rights remains a priority issue on the U.S.-Macau bilateral economic agenda. Macau progress since 1999 in strengthening IPR laws, tightening controls over DVD and VCD manufacturing, and stepping up street-level IPR enforcement resulted in Macau being removed from USTR's Special 301 list in 2002. Macau's new customs service worked with U.S. industry associations and maintained high tempo operations to combat piracy .

U.S. investment in Macau, while small in the past, is expected to increase in coming years as the result of the 2002 awarding of two gaming concessions to consortia with U.S. interests. Though trade with Macau represents a small portion of U.S. trade, the United States was Macau's second largest trading partner after the People's Republic of China. U.S. exports to and imports from Macau in 2002 were USD $79 million and USD $1.2 billion, respectively. After the Macau government ended the 40-year-old gaming monopoly of the Sociedade de Turismo e Diversões de Macau (STDM) in February 2002, the government awarded concessions to three consortia, including two with significant U.S. investment. The restructuring of the gaming industry remains the centerpiece of Macau - efforts to improve its international reputation and become a Las Vegas-like gaming, convention, and family-oriented holiday destination. The possible new investment of USD $1.5-2.5 billion in the medium term will increase jobs and income and dramatically raise the U.S. business profile in Macau.

MACAO AND PORTUGAL

Due to historical reasons, Macao was under Portuguese administration. On the basis of friendly co-operation and guided by a spirit of understanding and mutual compromise, the governments of the People's Republic of China and Portugal reached consensus as to the question of Macao. On 13th April 1987 they signed the Sino-Portuguese Joint Declaration and Annexes, thereby resolving an historical legacy through peaceful means. Both countries agreed that the government of the People's Republic of China would resume sovereignty over Macao on 20th December 2004.

The presence of the Portuguese in Macao helped to develop close contacts with the European Union and Portuguese-speaking countries. After the Handover in 2004, Macao became the second special administrative region of the People's Republic of China, maintaining, nevertheless, its good trading and economic relations with the European Union. The Chief Executive's appointment of a delegate for the Macao Trade and Economic Representative Office to Portugal and for the Macao Economic and Trade Delegation in Brussels represents a further step in consolidating Macao's relations with Portugal and the European Union.

In 1992, Macao and the European Union signed a trade and co-operation agreement establishing a frame for bilateral relations in the fields of training, trade co-operation and preserving cultural heritage. The agreement came into force in 1993 and remains in force even after the establishment of the MSAR Government.

Pursuant to this agreement, a joint committee consisting of representatives from Macao and the European Union has met every year, alternately in Macao and in Brussels, with a view to stimulating co-operation projects defined by both sides. To date, seven sessions have been held, and the latest Joint Committee meeting enabled both sides to review the implementation of the Commission's Communication, "The European Union and Macao Beyond 2000", to exchange information concerning the introduction of the "Basic Law" of the MSAR and, finally, to look for ways of promoting and strengthening bilateral trade, investment and co-operation. With regard to the implementation of the recommendations in the Commission's Communication on EU-Macao relations, both sides commented favourably on the progress achieved.

The accreditation of the Macao Economic and Trade Office to the EU was successfully finalized. Trade relations have improved and new co-operation initiatives were initiated. These included the Regional Centre of Tourism, the EU Studies Institute and the EC Offshore Development Programme. In addition, both sides noted the progress made over the appointment of a Technical Co-operation Officer for Macao and discussed Macao's request for a legal co-operation assistance programme. The Macao authorities also presented further requests, which will need to be examined further. Finally, the EU and Macao authorities explored other areas where co-operation between the two sides could, on the basis of the existing EU instruments, develop further, like for instance in the field of science and technology or in the framework of EU's regional projects for Asia, such as Asia Link and Asia Invest.

THE MACAO INSTITUTE OF EUROPEAN STUDIES

Founded in 1995, the Macao Institute of European Studies is geared towards the fields of research, education and information, enhancing the awareness of Europe and providing information on the European Unions internal economy and legislation. The Institute organises meetings, seminars and other research activities, and it has entered into co-operation agreements with other similar institutions in Europe. It is also involved in studies leading to a greater understanding of the socio-economic status of the Asia-Pacific region, drafting reports and holding international congresses to discuss affairs of common interest to the Asia-Pacific region and the European Union.

EURO INFO-CENTRE

When it was established in 1992, the Euro Info-Centre was the first of its kind in Asia to have a direct link to over 250 information centres in Europe. These centres assist small to medium sized companies in obtaining information about Europe, particularly regarding the law or potential partnerships in the European Union and EFTA. Requests for information are handled through a computer system based in Brussels. Since it was established, the Euro Info-Centre has achieved major success in supplying the kind of information about Europe that businessmen in Macao, Hong Kong, the Pearl River Delta region and neighbouring areas require.

JUSTICE SYSTEM, PUBLIC ORDER AND IMMIGRATION

PUBLIC ORDER AND SECURITY

Macao is a peaceful, safe city with a much lower crime rate than many other cities around the world. Its citizens are well housed and adequately paid for their work. Taking into account the social situation and crime trends, the Government's security authorities adjust, deploy and execute relevant measures to effectively combat and prevent crime, safeguard the security of residents and their property, and maintain social stability and peace in accordance with the policy guidelines.

UNITARY POLICE SERVICE

The Unitary Police Service was formed as part of Macao's internal security system following the establishment of the MSAR Government. It began operating in October 2001, commanding and leading the operations of the Public Security Police and Judiciary Police. The service leads and coordinates the two bodies' operations by commanding them in the performance of their duties, coordinating all their criminal investigations, overseeing their operations, and evaluating the results of their actions. When considered necessary, the Unitary Police Service may intervene in police operations and directly coordinate and participate in joint actions. By strengthening its operational capability, the Unitary Police Service enhances its ability to combat crime, reduce crime rates, maintain public order, and ensure the safety of people and property.

The Unitary Police Service plans and advises on operations. It consists of six subsidiary units: the Offce of the Commissioner General, the Intelligence Analysis Centre, the Operations Planning Centre, the Administration and Finance Department, the Computer and Information Technology Unit and the Information and Public Relations Offce.

PUBLIC SECURITY POLICE

The Public Security Police is responsible for maintaining public order and social stability; preventing, investigating and combating crime; protecting public and private property; controlling illegal immigration; handling immigration; as well as controlling and monitoring vehicular and pedestrian traffc.

Affliated units of the Public Security Police include a Directorate and Interdepartmental Board, Resource Management Department, Information Department, Operations Department, Immigration Department, Traffc Department, Macao City Police Department, Taipa and Coloane Islands Police Department, Tactical Police Unit and Logistic Support and Services Division, as well as the Police School and Police Band.

At the end of 2012, the Public Security Police comprised 5,120 staff, with 4,248 personnel in service, 872 vacancies and 393 clerical staff.

OPERATIONS CONTROL CENTRE

The Operations Control Centre comes under the Operations Department of the Public Security Police. All 999 emergency calls from residents are routed to the centre, which classifes them and arranges for police offcers to visit the scene and take action. The Operations Control Centre received 422,285 emergency calls during 2012.

The centre also supervises traffc-monitoring systems. Video cameras installed on all sea bridges transmit images of traffc that enable its offcers to observe and control traffc fows. The Operations Control Centre is equipped with a computer-controlled video alarm system that can transfer video footage from crime scenes direct to the centre. This enables offcials to learn about a situation quickly, and respond to it.

POLICE TACTICAL UNIT

The Police Tactical Unit was established in 1979, and currently has 628 team members. Under the Police Tactical Unit, there are six special units – the anti-riot team, VIP and important facility protection unit, bomb-disposal team, police dog team, inspection and security team, and special operations team. They are responsible for the safety of important facilities, combating criminals – especially those using frearms, and taking action when there is serious violence, including instances of sniper attacks and hostage-taking.

JUDICIARY POLICE

The Judiciary Police is a criminal investigation police department under the supervision of the Secretary for Security, and it specialises in crime prevention and investigation. It also assists the judiciary and other Government departments in investigating criminal activities.

At present, the subsidiary units of the Judiciary Police are the Criminal Investigation Department; the Department for the Investigation of Gaming-related and Economic Crimes; the Intelligence and Support Department; the Forensic Science Department; the IT and Telecommunications Management Department; the Management and Planning Department; the Judiciary Police Training School; and the Interpol Macau, China (Sub-bureau of the Chinese National Central Bureau of ICPO – Interpol). At the end of 2012, the total number of permanent staff positions in the Judiciary Police was 1,356, and there were 1,045 serving staff.

In 2012, the Judiciary Police received 9,283 criminal cases, of which 4,556 were designated as investigations, 1,886 were preliminary investigations, 2,540 were investigations that had been requested and the other 301 were indictments. The investigations completed involved: three homicides, 23 illegal confnements, 32 extortion cases, 23 arson cases, 141 robberies, 1,800 thefts, 93 cases of drug traffcking, 142 cases of drug taking, 18 human traffcking cases, 17 cases of prostitution exploitation, six triad cases, 16 cases of criminal groups, 150 profteering and loansharking cases, 2,070 gambling-related cases, 249 cases of passing counterfeit currency (including using counterfeit credit cards), 210 fraud cases, 175 cases of computer or internet fraud, and two cases of phone fraud.

Judiciary Police School

The functions of the Judiciary Police School are to select and train personnel for special duties in the Judiciary Police, supervise trainees, publish promotional materials and organise publicity programmes.

Its training programmes include induction, in-service training and promotional training for inspectors and assistant inspectors, detectives and assistant criminologists handling criminal cases. In 2012, the school provided 88 courses totalling 2,672 teaching hours for 2,251 staff on induction training, in-service training, promotion-related training and joint programmes co-hosted with other institutions.

MACAO SUB-BUREAU, INTERPOL NATIONAL CENTRAL BUREAU, CHINA

The Interpol Macao, China (Sub-bureau of the Chinese National Central Bureau of ICPO – Interpol) carries out or assists in operations in Macao at the request of overseas Interpol offces. It issues international arrest warrants from Macao to Interpol's headquarters in France, releases relevant crime information, submits executable temporary detention requests in accordance with extradition procedures in other countries, and detains or helps to detain extraditable fugitives subject to Interpol international arrest warrants. Among its other functions are the detention of criminals or suspects repatriated to Macao, and the provision of advice on crime prevention and reduction. In addition, the sub-bureau exchanges materials concerning international crime, releases documents on police matters, and establishes cooperative relations with overseas public security authorities. At the same time, it receives, classifes, handles, issues and fles documents concerning international criminals.

CRISIS NEGOTIATION UNIT

Under the management and command of the Deputy Director responsible for criminal investigation and operations, the Crisis Negotiation Unit is designed to alleviate crises and disputes and minimise casualties and property losses by conducting negotiations. Members of the unit were drawn from various investigation departments and all participate on a voluntary, part-time basis. They become formal members of the unit after strict selection and training procedures. They also need to participate in regular drills and training. The members are called upon to serve as negotiators in emergency situations, such as advising on instances of suicide attempts and hostage taking.

In 2012, the Crisis Negotiation Unit handled 18 cases of suicide attempts and self-confnement, all of which were satisfactorily resolved. The unit also handled 15 cases from other administrative authorities, to assist in clearing illegal squatter houses or unlawful occupation of Government land.

MACAO PUBLIC SECURITY FORCES

The Macao Public Security Forces (FSM) consists of the Public Security Forces Affairs Bureau, Public Security Police Force, Fire Service and Academy of Public Security Forces. The FSM had a total of 6,348 members at the end of 2012, which includes 5,449 disciplined services staff and 899 clerical staff. It cooperates with the Unitary Police Service, Macao Customs Service, Judiciary Police and Macao Prison to form Macao's internal security system.

Public Security Forces Affairs Bureau (DSFSM)

The DSFSM is primarily responsible for ensuring administrative and fnancial resources management and providing technical support for every public security force and authority in Macao. Its subsidiary units include the Administrative Management Department, the Technical Support Department, and the Public Relations and Historical Archive Offce.

Recruitment

Recruitment of police offcers and fre service offcers comes under the central control of the DSFSM. The minimum academic entry requirement for police offcers and Fire Service offcers is senior high school level. Applicants must pass a full medical examination, a physical ftness test, a general knowledge test and a psychological test.

The following table shows details of the 2012 recruitment:

Training Programmes for FSM Police Cadets	Number of Applicants	Number of Students after Selection		
17th	1,076	Male 131	Female 19	Total 150
18th	1,064	137	25	162

After passing the training programme examinations, an eligible candidate can choose to become a police offcer or a fre service offcer. Also, clerical staff are recruited by the Public Security Forces Affairs Bureau (DSFSM). After examinations and assessments, successful applicants are allocated to various divisions of the Macao Public Security Forces (FSM).

Enquiries and Complaints

In 2012, the DSFSM received 116 cases, including 16 complaints, fve suggestions and opinions, 83 enquiries and three crime reports. A further nine cases were found to be unrelated to the FSM. Of the 16 complaints, nine concerned offcers and staff, three concerned traffc issues, two concerned service procedures, one concerned the environment and one concerned equipment and facilities.

Disciplinary Cases

The FSM requires rigorous disciplinary compliance from all its offcers. According to information provided by the FSM, during 2012 it handled 331 disciplinary cases involving 378 people, 285 of whom were in the Public Security Police, 40 in the Fire Service, two in the DSFSM and four in the Academy of Macao Public Security Forces. Most disciplinary actions were for minor offences. However, 12 Public Security Police offcers and one Fire Service offcer were disciplined for criminal offences.

FIRE SERVICE

The core functions of the Fire Service are to assist in cases of fre, fooding, building collapses, and other situations threatening life and property. It takes measures to prevent fres and provides assistance in emergency cases involving illness or danger. The Fire Service also participates in civil protection and emergency management. Its organisation currently consists of a Command Offce, Discipline Committee, Legal Advisors' Division, Command Support Offce, Resources Management Department, Personnel and Logistics Division, Technical Support Division, Macao Operations and Ambulance Division affliated to the Macao Operations Department, Islands' Operations and Ambulance Division affliated to the Islands' Operations Department, Fire Service School, Services Division and Airport Division.

At the end of 2012, the Fire Service had a staffng level of 1,173 posts, with 1,021 serving personnel and 144 vacancies. It has seven fre stations on the Macao peninsula, Taipa and Coloane islands: the Fire Service Headquarters and Sai Van Lake Station, Central Station, Areia Preta Station, Taipa Island Station, and Coloane Island Station, plus two stations at Macau International Airport.

The Fire Service responded to 38,524 incidents during 2012.

Appliances and Equipment

The Fire Service currently has 156 fre vehicles, including 16 large water pumps, fve 18-metre aerial ladder pumps, nine ladder platforms, six rescue units, two tenders equipped for high rescues, six rescue cushion tenders, two foam tenders, one hose foam carrier, 14 fre/ambulance motorcycles, 31 ambulances and six ambulance motorcycles.

Fire Fighting

In 2012, the Fire Service handled 25 medium-sized fres, 718 small fres, and 362 miscellaneous fres. Classifed by cause, 613 fre incidents were due to the careless disposal of embers, 94 were the result of electrical short circuits, 132 were accidental false alarms, two were deliberate false alarms, 17 were due to suspected arson and 247 were due to other causes. 161 people were injured in fres during the year.

OTHER EMERGENCY AND SPECIAL SERVICES

The Fire Service provides other accident, emergency and special services, such as handling gas leaks, emergency opening of doors and the rescue of people trapped in malfunctioning lifts, and suicide attempts. It assists the injured in industrial and traffc accidents, removes fallen objects, cleans roads, and deals with collapsed buildings or fallen trees, landslides and fooding. When needed, it also provides emergency and special services to Macau International Airport. In 2012, the Fire Service responded to 5,669 emergency calls concerning such incidents.

Ambulance Service

The Fire Service is also responsible for all emergency assistance work in Macao. Its emergency ambulance team comprises 796 paramedics. In 2012, the Fire Service responded to 31,750 emergency requests for ambulances, and dispatched ambulances on 35,592 occasions.

Fire Prevention

Under the Rules and Regulations on Fire Prevention and Safety, the Fire Service is responsible for monitoring the design of all new buildings and fre-prevention equipment. It also inspects older buildings and advises on improvements to fre-prevention facilities. In addition, it examines and monitors fre-prevention measures in shopping malls, factories, catering establishments, and various recreational and entertainment venues. In 2012, the Fire Service examined 2,043 construction plans, conducted 1,934 site inspections, performed 1,187 fre-fghting-equipment tests and undertook 2,118 fre-prevention and safety patrols. It handled 400 complaints about fre safety and awarded 30 quality certifcates for fre-prevention and fre-fghting equipment.

Academy of Macao Public Security Forces

The Academy of Macao Public Security Forces is a bureau-level unit under the Secretary for Security, and it is the tertiary educational institution responsible for training Macao's senior police offcers.

The academy's core function is to train offcers serving in different units of the FSM. Since its establishment, the academy has produced a large number of senior local police offcers and frefghters equipped with professional knowledge, skills and capabilities for the Macao Public Security Forces.

From 1995 to 2012, the academy trained 244 offcers in its Police/Fire Service Offcers'Training Programme. These graduates have now taken up leadership and directorate positions in different units of the FSM. At present, 73 people (including one exchange trainee from mainland China) are attending its 11th, 12th and 13th training programmes.

From 1991 to 2012, a total of 5,700 offcers attended the Training Programme for Police Cadets provided by the academy's Joint Training Centre.

Traffc Accidents

According to statistics provided by the Public Security Police, 14,688 traffc accidents occurred in Macao during 2012, resulting in 5,250 injuries and 18 fatalities.

Macao Customs Service

The Macao Customs Service (Macao Customs) was offcially inaugurated on 1 November 2001. A ceremony was held on 6 November 2001 to celebrate its establishment, and the formal inauguration of the Macao Customs Service Building. The Establishment Day of the Macao Customs Service has been commemorated on 6 November of every year since then.

Founded in accordance with the Basic Law, Macao Customs is an independently administered public authority. It is responsible for leading, implementing and monitoring measures related to customs policies, as well as policing duties related to customs affairs.

The duties of Macao Customs include preventing, tackling and eliminating customs fraud. It is also committed to curbing and stamping out unlawful traffcking. It helps to monitor external trade activities and contributes to protecting and enhancing Macao's international reputation. Macao Customs also safeguards intellectual property rights, as prescribed by law. It is dedicated to fulflling Macao's international obligations relating to customs matters and looking after the safety of people and property, as set out in the security policies of Macao. It also participates in civil protection preparedness, and special emergency operations.

Macao Customs has a Director-General, Deputy Director-General, Assistant Director-General, Operation Management Department, Checkpoint Enforcement Department, Intellectual Property Rights Department, Marine Enforcement Department, Information and Communication Technology Department, Internal Affairs Offce, and Finance and Administration Department.

In 2012, Macao Customs seized large quantities of illegal and smuggled contraband imports including 27.97 kilograms of ivory, 1.48 kilograms of turtles, 3.48 kilograms of deer antlers, 183,359.42 kilograms of meat and vegetables, 524.44 litres of alcoholic beverages, 810,368 cigarettes, 383 items of leather products related to protection of intellectual and industrial property rights, and 4,007 items of electronic and communications equipment and accessories.

Moreover, 15.49 grams of drugs were seized at border checkpoints, including psychoactive substances totalling 167,306.52 grams of powder, 592 pills and tablets and 1.44 litres of liquid.

Marine Supervision

The Macao Customs Fleet is responsible for patrolling Macao's coastal waters. With the cooperation of the Frontier Defence Offce of the Guangdong Provincial Public Security Department and other mainland China customs departments, it has strengthened its role in tackling organised illegal immigration and smuggling activities. In 2012, the Macao Customs Fleet and customs-related units in mainland China (such as the Frontier Defence Brigade of the Zhuhai Public Security Bureau) conducted 40 joint operations along the coast of Macao, to ensure order and safety at sea. The Macao Customs Fleet also conducted 43 joint sea patrols with the Macao Maritime Administration in the Inner Harbour and Outer Harbour to strengthen order and safety along the two harbour channels.

The Macao Customs Fleet currently has nine patrol vessels and 22 high-speed boats.

International Cooperation

Macao Customs is a member of the World Customs Organization (WCO). The service has participated in various operations with the World Customs Organization's Regional Intelligence Liaison Offce for Asia and the Pacifc as well as activities to prevent and combat crime related to terrorism, measures against human traffcking and activities to prevent and combat money laundering.

Handling Enquiries and Complaints

The Internal Affairs Offce, which is directly under the Director-General of Macao Customs, is responsible for handling reports, complaints and enquiries. During 2012, the offce received 370 reports from the public. The topics included intellectual property infringements, violation of external trade policies, violation of marine safety regulations, illegal immigration, illegal labour, and drug-related activities. In all, there were 72 complaints, concerning the conduct of customs offcers, service procedures, equipment and facilities, environment and noise pollution. It also handled 2,721 enquiries.

Civil Protection

Civil protection aims to prevent major loss of life and damage to property in the event of serious accidents, natural disasters and crises. It is jointly conducted by Government departments and public institutions, with the involvement of residents. Civil protection procedures can reduce casualties and save lives in dangerous situations.

The Action Coordination Centre makes suggestions and deploys manpower and material resources to coordinate and supervise a programme of measures to limit or prevent the effects of any serious accident, disaster or other catastrophe that occurs. It takes all necessary precautions to maintain basic services and normal living conditions for residents in the event of tropical storms or other abnormal situations.

Should a disaster occur, civil protection action will be carried out in phases, according to the nature of the disaster and the needs it creates in terms of rescue and other requirements. If necessary, Macao can be divided into two districts, the Macao peninsula and the islands area. Separate district action centres can be set up to carry out or coordinate activities under the overall command of the Action Coordination Centre headquarters.

The Public Security Forces, other Government departments, non-governmental organisations and private-sector companies jointly participate in civil protection. They include the Civil Protection Action Centre; Islands Area Action Centre; Fire Service; Public Security Police; Public Security Forces Affairs Bureau; Academy of Macao Public Security Forces; Public Security Coordination Offce; Judiciary Police; Macao Customs; Civil Aviation Authority; Maritime Administration; Conde

S. Januario Hospital; Education and Youth Affairs Bureau; Lands, Public Works and Transport Bureau; Government Tourist Offce; Meteorological and Geophysical Bureau; Government Information Bureau; Social Welfare Bureau; Housing Bureau; Civic and Municipal Affairs Bureau; Health Bureau; Transport Bureau; Companhia de Electricidade de Macau (CEM); Companhia de Telecomunicacoes de Macau (CTM); Kiang Wu Hospital; Macao Water Supply Company (SAAM); and Teledifusao de Macau (TDM).

MACAO PRISON

Located on Coloane island, the Macao Prison, formerly called Coloane Prison, was completed and became operational in 1990. After a few years, to meet special public security needs, construction of a Special Detention Centre located next to the Academy of Macao Public Security Forces on Coloane island and managed by the prison began in 1998. It was put into service in 1999, to house inmates requiring special supervision or custody. The nearby facility, formerly called the Coloane Youth Prison, is now a section for female inmates. The Coloane Prison was offcially renamed the Macao Prison when the Macao SAR was established on 20 December 1999.

Functions of the Prison

The prison is authorised to implement confnement and custodial sentences. The prison consists of nine buildings, six of which accommodate inmates. One of the buildings, situated next to the Academy of Macao Public Security Forces, is used to house inmates who are under special supervision or isolation in a special detention zone.

The prison has separate male and female sections. Each has its own sub-sections for inmates on remand and convicted inmates.

The prison can also set up special detention zones in other locations, for inmates who must be held under absolute or limited isolation regulations and special isolation security regulations.

With the approval of authorised Government offcials and in exceptional situations, the prison can provide protective custody for certain inmates.

Prison Population

The prison can accommodate a maximum of 1,341 inmates. As at 31 December 2012, it held 1,112 inmates: 238 were on remand and 874 were convicted.

		Number of inmates in the prison (as at 31 December 2012)
13%	18%	66%66% 3% Male Sentenced Prisoners 728 Female Sentenced Prisoners 205 Female Prisoners on Remand 33 Male Prisoners on Remand 146

Returning to Society

To implement its plan to assist inmates in returning to society, the prison provides education and occupational training. Inmates can apply to study according to their educational level, interests and needs.

Social Rehabilitation

The Social Rehabilitation Department under the Legal Affairs Bureau has three primary responsibilities: to provide rehabilitation services to adult inmates and to provide correctional services to rectify the behaviour of juvenile delinquents. It attempts to help clients reintegrate themselves into society and start new lives, and to help them get back on the right track.

As at 31 December 2012, the Social Rehabilitation Department had followed up on 1,161 cases, of which 811 concerned adults and 350 concerned minors.

Pre-sentencing reports

Reformatory for Juvenile Delinquents

Operating under the Legal Affairs Bureau, the Reformatory for Juvenile Delinquents takes in young people who have violated the law and who have been referred by the courts.

The reformatory is divided into separate areas for boys and girls, with counsellors working around-the-clock in each. There are also social workers, psychologists, occupational training tutors and teachers, providing academic and vocational training, personal and family counselling, as well as implementing social service schemes.

Inmates

The reformatory generally only accepts young people aged 12 to 16, but may extend its services to them until they reach 21. There were 17 boys and three girls in the reformatory at the end of 2012.

Police Dog Team

Established in October 1995, the Police Dog Team is under the Police Tactical Unit of the Public Security Police, and is responsible for patrolling, drug and explosive detection and rescue actions. Besides taking part in police actions to combat crime, police dogs also engage in public events, playing a unique role in enhancing police-community relations.

IMMIGRATION AND RESIDENCE - PRACTICAL INFORMATION

DOCUMENTS

Documents to be Used by Macao Residents for Entry to and Departure from Macao

1	Macao Resident Identity Card
2	Macao Special Administrative Region Passport
3	Macao Special Administrative Region Travel Permit
4	Visit Permit to the Hong Kong S.A.R.
5	Other valid passports or travel documents

ENTRY AND EXIT OF NON-RESIDENTS

I General Principle

Non-residents of the Macao Special Administrative Region are required to possess a valid passport and "entry permit" or "visa" for entry to Macao, except for people prescribed by certain law, administrative regulation or international law document.

II Immigration Control

The Immigration Department of the Macao Special Administrative Region keeps a record of the entry and departure of non-local residents on computer, as well as on their passport, travel document or other appropriate document, indicating the limit of stay granted in accordance with Administrative Regulation No.5/2003.

III Transfer and Transit

The transfer or transit of visitors who has no record made at any border and is not issued any "entry permit" at the Macao International Airport, at any immigration checkpoint, or during escort from one immigration checkpoint to another by the authorities is not considered as entry to the Macao Special Administrative Region.

Contacts Means of Different Border Checkpoints	Address:	Tel:	Fax:	Office Hours
Subdivision at Border Gate Checkpoint	Praça das Portas do Cerco, Macau	(853) 8980 0321	(853) 8980 0323	06:00 - 01:00 (next day)

IV Border Checkpoints

Subdivision at Hong Kong-Macao Ferry Terminal Checkpoint	Largo do Terminal Marítimo, Terminal Marítimo do Porto Exterior, Macau	(853) 8798 5327	(853) 8798 5304	24 hours
Subdivision at Macao International Airport Checkpoint	Avenida de Wai Long, Aeroporto Internacional de Macau, Taipa, Macau	(853) 8898 1317	(853) 2886 1162	24 hours
Subdivision at Cotai Checkpoint	Estrada Flor de Lótus, Posto	(853) 8898 9617	(853) 2887 0163	08H00 – 20H00 (cargos)

	Fronteiriço de Cotai, Taipa, Macau			24 hours (passengers)
Subdivision at Taipa Ferry Terminal Checkpoint	Estrada de Pac On, Taipa, Macau	(853) 8898 1501	(853) 8898 1510	24 hours
Subdivision at Interior Ferry Terminal Checkpoint	Rua das Lorchas, Macau	(853) 2893 9434	(853) 2893 9403	08H00 - 16H30
Subdivision at Zhuhai-Macao Cross-border Industrial Zone Checkpoint Note: Access with special permit for the zone	Avenida de Parque Industrial, Macau	(853) 2827 1327	(853) 8799 3330	00:00 - 07:00 (for mainland workers, students and Macao residents; no vehicles allowed) 24 hours (for pass holders)

V DOCUMENTS FOR ENTRY TO AND DEPARTURE FROM MACAO

(For details of the requirements to enter the Macao SAR, please see Section VI)

The following non-residents are entitled to enter and depart from the Macao Special Administrative Region if they possess the documents listed below:

1.A valid passport;

2.A One-way or Two-way Exit Permit or other travel documents issued by the authorities of the People's Republic of China;

3.A Hong Kong Permanent Identity Card or Re-entry Permit;

4.A Seaman's Identity Book issued by countries having ratified in the International Labour Organization Convention 108 of 13 May 1958;

5.A License or Crew Certificate (subject to travelling on duty only) issued under Annex 1 and 9 of the Convention on International Civil Aviation of 7 December 1944;

6.A travel document issued in accordance with Article 28 of the "Convention Relating to the Status of Refugees" of 28 July 1951, which was amended in the protocol of 31 January 1967;

7.Other documents as prescribed by law or international treaties which are applicable to the Macao Special Administrative Region;

8.Other valid travel documents;

9.Nationals or citizens of countries or territories which have reached an agreement with the Macao SAR on passport-free entry to and departure from the Macao Special Administrative Region.

(1)Holders of a valid "Non-Resident Worker's Permit" or "Special Stay Permit" of Macao are required to present the Permit as well when entering or departing from Macao;

(2)Except for the holders of documents listed in Point 6, all other document holders mentioned above in Part V are admissible to the Macao Special Administrative Region only on the condition that their document allows them to enter or re-enter any country or region;

(3)"One-way Exit Permit" holders and individuals who possess a travel document valid only for entering or returning to the Macao Special Administrative Region and preliminarily have their permanent residence status verified or declare possession of Residence Authorization are exempted from the requirement in (2);

(4)Under exceptional circumstances where proper reasons are given, other individuals can also be exempted from the requirement in (2);

(5)In cases specified in (3) and (4), individuals who intend to enter the Macao Special Administrative Region are required to possess prior permit or authorization granted for the purpose of entering the SAR, but One-way Exit Permit holders are not included.】

VI ENTRY REQUIREMENTS

1.The validity of the passport or travel document and entry or re-entry permit of other countries (or regions) upon the arrival of the visitor should meet the requirement stated in Term 1, Article 9 of Law No.5/2003 (i.e. The maximum limit of stay in the Macao Special Administrative Region granted to all individuals is restricted to 30 days before the expiry date of their passport or travel document and their entry or re-entry permit);
【Note: The above requirement is not applicable to mainland residents who possess permits issued by the authorities of the People's Republic of China, and exceptionally not applicable to individuals who intend to stay temporarily in Macao for proceeding to another destination and guarantee to have the authorization to enter or re-enter any country or region.】

2."Two-way Exit Permit" holders are required to possess a valid "exit endorsement";

3.Visitors are required to possess a valid onward or return ticket unless they can prove that they reside on the Mainland of China or in the Hong Kong Special Administrative Region. The exemption is not applicable to Chinese passport or Hong Kong Special Administrative Region passport holders who transit Macao to a third country or region;

4.Visitors are required to prove that they possess the vital resources of a minimum of MOP5000 for their expected period of stay in Macao;

5.Visitors who are not exempted from a visa and entry permit are required to:

i.Apply for an "Entry Permit" (aka "Visa-upon-arrival") at any of the border checkpoints of the Immigration Department of the Public Security Police upon arrival at Macao【Note: Starting from 1 July 2010, visitors from Bangladesh, Nepal, Nigeria, Pakistan, Sri Lanka and Vietnam are required to apply for a Macao visa in advance through a Chinese embassy or consulate. For details, please see "Application for Macao Visa through Chinese Embassy or Consulate"】; or

ii.Apply, by a representative, to the Immigration Department in advance for "Authorization to Enter and Stay"【Note: Refer to the "Authorization to Enter and Stay" Section for details】; or

iii.Apply for a "visa" of the Macao Special Administrative Region in advance through a Chinese embassy or consulate(visa sample).

6.Application for an "Entry Permit" (aka "Visa-upon-arrival")

A.Individuals who intend to enter the Macao Special Administrative Region but have not applied in advance to any Chinese embassy, consulate or diplomatic mission for a "visa" or the Macao Immigration Department for "Authorization to Enter and Stay" can apply for an "Entry Permit" (aka "Visa-upon-arrival") at the "Visa Room" of the border checkpoint when arriving at Macao. They will be granted "Authorization to Stay" for a maximum of 30 days once the application is approved.

B. Fees

Type	Fee
Individual	MOP100
Family Passport	MOP200
Children under the age of 12	MOP50
Groups comprised of at least 10 people organized by a single travel manager and presenting a collective travel document	MOP50 per head

C. Individuals who have paid the fee for an "Entry Permit" can enjoy multiple entries within the limit of stay granted (a maximum of 30 days) without making further payments.
Groups comprised of at least 10 people organized by a single travel manager and presenting a collective travel document

VII "VISA" AND "ENTRY PERMIT" EXEMPTION

1. Nationals of the following countries are exempted in accordance with the written instruction of the Chief Executive:

Albania	Iceland	New Zealand
Andorra	India	Norway
Australia	Indonesia	Philippines
Austria	Ireland	Poland
Belgium	Israel	Portugal
Bosnia and Herzegovina	Italy	Romania
Brazil	Japan	Russia
Brunei	Kiribati	Samoa
Bulgaria	Latvia	San Marino
Canada	Lebanon	Serbia
Cape Verde	Liechtenstein	Seychelles
Chile	Lithuania	Singapore
Croatia	Luxembourg	Slovakia
Cyprus	Macedonia	Slovenia
Czech	Malaysia	South Africa
Denmark	Mali	South Korea
Dominica	Malta	Spain
Egypt	Mauritius	Sweden
Estonia	Mexico	Switzerland
Finland	Moldova	Tanzania
France	Monaco	Thailand
Germany	Mongolia	Turkey

Greece	Montenegro	U.S.A.
Grenada	Namibia	United Kingdom
Hungary	Netherlands	Uruguay

2. Individuals specified in international treaties;

3.Holders of a "One-way Exit Permit", "Two-way Exit Permit", passport or other travel document issued by the authorities of the People's Republic of China;

4.Holders of a Hong Kong Identity Card, Hong Kong Permanent Identity Card or Re-entry Permit;

5.Chinese in possession of a valid document for entering and departing from Macao;

6.Individuals in possession of a travel document valid only for entering or returning to the Macao Special Administrative Region and preliminarily have their permanent residence status verified or declare possession of Residence Authorization;

7.Holders of a Seaman's Identity Book issued by countries having ratified in the International Labour Organization Convention 108 of 13 May 1958;

8.Holders of a License or Crew Certificate (subject to travelling on duty only) issued under Annex 1 and 9 of the Convention on International Civil Aviation of 7 December 1944;

9.Nationals and residents of the countries and regions which have reached an agreement with the Macao Special Administrative Region on passport-free entry to and departure from Macao;

10.Holders of a diplomatic or consular identity card issued by the Macao or Hong Kong Special Administrative Region Government;

11.Transit visitors who intend to enter the Macao Special Administrative Region for less than 48 hours for the purpose of travelling onward to another destination via the Macao International Airport;

12.Holders of a diplomatic passport;

13.Holders of a "Laissez-Passer" issued by the United Nations, provided they are travelling on duty;

14.Non-Portuguese in possession of a travel document issued by the Portuguese authorities;

15.Holders of a valid "Non-resident Worker's Permit" or "Special Stay Permit";

16.Individuals entering Macao before the expiry date of the "Temporary Authorization to Stay for Non-resident Workers" which is granted while pending the "Non-resident Worker's Identification Card";

17.Individuals entering Macao before the expiry date of the "Special Authorization to Stay" which is granted for study purpose or to the reuniting family of a non-resident worker;

18.Individuals entering Macao not later than the designated reporting date indicated on the "receipt" of the "Special Authorization to Stay" application or extension which is made for study purpose;

19.Individuals entering Macao before the expiry date of the "Extension of Stay" which is granted in accordance with Articles 11 and 12 of Administrative Regulation No.5/2003;

20.Individuals who have proof of having been granted Residence Authorization of the Macao Special Administrative Region;

21.Individuals entering Macao before the expiry date of the "Special Authorization to Stay" which is granted for the purpose of residence application;

22.Individuals granted "Visa" and "Entry Permit" exemption by the Chief Executive;

23.Under exceptional circumstances where proper reasons are given, individuals not meeting the legal requirements for entry or stay but granted Authorization to Enter and Stay in the Macao Special Administrative Region through the written instruction of the Chief Executive.

VIII Limit of Stay Granted upon Arrival

A. General Regulation

1. The maximum limit of stay in the Macao Special Administrative Region is restricted to 30 days before the expiry date of the passport or travel document and the entry or re-entry permit.

2. The above regulation is not applicable to mainland residents who possess permits issued by the authorities of the People's Republic of China, and exceptionally not applicable to individuals who intend to stay temporarily in Macao for proceeding to another destination and guarantee to have be admissible or re-admissible to any country or region.

B. Limit of Stay

1. Individuals who are not exempted from a "Visa" or "Entry Permit" will be granted Authorization to Stay for a maximum of 30 days upon arrival with a "Visa", "Entry Permit" or "Authorization to Enter and Stay". They can enjoy multiple entries within the 30 days without applying for another "Visa", "Entry Permit" or "Authorization to Enter and Stay".

2. Individuals exempted from a "Visa" or "Entry Permit":

Types of People	Limit of Stay
1. Holders of a valid passport or travel document	A maximum of 30 days
2. -- Holders of a passport issued by a European Union or Schengen Agreement member state (Austria, Belgium, Bulgaria, Czech, Denmark, Estonia, Finland, France, Germany, Greece, Hungary, Iceland, Ireland, Italy, Latvia, Liechtenstein, Lithuania, Luxembourg, Malta, Netherlands, Norway, Poland, Portugal, Romania, Slovakia, Slovenia, Spain, Sweden, Switzerland) -- Holders of a passport issued by Albania, Andorra, Bosnia and Herzegovina, Brazil, Cape Verde, Croatia, Dominica, Egypt, Grenada, Japan, Macedonia, Mali, Mauritius, Mexico, Moldova,	A maximum of 90 days

Mongolia, Montenegro, Serbia, South Korea, Tanzania.	
3. Holders of a passport issued by Brunei.	A maximum of 14 days
4. Holders of a passport issued by Cyprus, Israel, Lebanon, New Zealand.	A maximum of 3 months
5. British citizens holding a British passport	A maximum of 6 months
6. Holders of a Hong Kong Permanent Identity Card or a Re-entry Permit	A maximum of 1 year
7. Holders of a diplomatic passport, "Laissez Passer" issued by the United Nations, "diplomatic or consular identity card" issued by the Macao Special Administrative Region	No limit
8. Holders of a Seaman's Identity Book issued by countries having ratified in the International Labour Organization Convention 108 of 13 May 1958	The period the ship is berthed at a harbour in Macao
9. Holders of a License or Crew Certificate issued under Annex 1 and 9 of the Convention on International Civil Aviation of 7 December 1944	During the interval of service of the flight
10. Nationals and residents holding a passport issued by countries and regions which have reached a mutual visa-free agreement with the Macao Special Administrative Region	Not longer than the period stated in the agreement
11. Holders of a "Two-way Exit Permit" issued by the authorities of the People's Republic of China with a valid "Exit Endorsement to Macao"(1)	The period indicated in the endorsement, but not more than 90 days
12. Mainlanders holding a "Permit for Travelling to and from Taiwan" with an "Exit Endorsement to Taiwan"	A maximum of 7 days (no matter traveling to Taiwan via Macao or returning to the mainland via Macao)
13. Holders of a passport or travel document issued by the authorities of the People's Republic of China (with a flight ticket to and entry visa of a third country or region)	A maximum of 7 days (for transit)
14. Holders of a Hong Kong Special Administrative Region passport (with a flight ticket to and entry visa of a third country or region)	A maximum of 7 days (for transit)
15. Holders of a Macao "Non-resident Worker's Permit"(2)	Until the expiry date of the Permit (with multiple entries)
16. Individuals granted "Special Authorization to Stay" for study purpose or as reuniting family of a non-resident worker (in accordance with Article 8 of Law No. 4/2003)(2)	Until the expiry date of the Authorization (with multiple entries)
17. Individuals granted Extension of Stay in accordance with Articles 11 and 12 of Administrative Regulation No. 5/2003 (2)	Until the expiry date of the extended Authorization to Stay (with multiple entries)
18. Holders of a "Special Stay Permit"(2)	Until the expiry date of the Permit (with multiple entries)
19. Individuals granted "Special Authorization to Stay" in accordance with Term 6, Article 8 of Law No. 4/2003 for the purpose of residence application.	Until the expiry date of the Authorization (with multiple entries)

【 Note:

Holders of an endorsement with a comparatively longer limit of stay in Macao for work or study purpose should go to the Immigration Department in person and apply for an extension of stay before their endorsement expires if they intend to stay for more than 90 days. They will be regarded as overstayers if they do not apply for an extension while the "Authorization to Stay" granted upon arrival expires. In addition, if they renew their endorsement and are granted a new endorsement during their legal stay in Macao and before the expiry date of their current endorsement, they are required to go to the Immigration Department to extend their "Authorization to Stay" accordingly. Otherwise, they will also be regarded as overstayers.

2. In cases where the limit of stay granted upon re-entry extends beyond the expiry date of the "Non-Resident Worker's Permit", "Special Stay Permit", "Special Authorization to Stay" or "Extension of Stay", the Immigration Department will make the following arrangements:

(1) For individuals who do not enjoy the exemption specified in VII and choose to apply for an "Entry Permit", they are required to pay the fee for the "Entry Permit". When their relevant document/Authorization to Stay expires, they can then remain in Macao until the expiry date of the "Authorization to Stay" which is granted to visitors upon their arrival;

(2) For individuals who choose not to apply for an "Entry Permit", they can remain in Macao until the expiry date of their "Non-Resident Worker's Permit", "Special Stay Permit", "Special Authorization to Stay" or "Extension of Stay".】

C. Individuals making use of the Macao International Airport for transit to other destinations within 48 hours can enter and stay in Macao without a "Visa" or "Entry Permit" within this period.

IX Entry Refusal

A. Legal Reason

1. Non-residents are refused entry to the Macao Special Administrative Region for the following reasons:

(1) Having been deported;

(2) Interdicted from entering, staying at or transiting the Macao Special Administrative Region in accordance with the international law documents applicable to Macao;

(3) Interdicted from entering the Macao Special Administrative Region in accordance with the law.

2. Non-residents will be refused entry to the Macao Special Administrative Region for the following reasons:

(1) Attempting to evade the regulation on stay and residence and having frequent entries to the Macao Special Administrative Region within short intervals without appropriate justification;

(2) Having been sentenced to a penalty of freedom deprivation in or outside the Macao Special Administrative Region;

(3) Existence of strong indication of having committed or preparing to commit a crime;

(4) No guarantee of return to last port of embarkation, existence of sufficient reason to suspect the authenticity of the travel document, no possession of the vital resources for the expected

period of stay, no possession of transportation document necessary for return to last port of embarkation.

3. The power of entry refusal remains the competence of the Chief Executive; this power can be authorized to another person.

B. Transporter's Responsibility

1. If a sea or air transporter carries a passenger, seaman or crew member to the Macao Special Administrative Region who is refused entry, the transporter should immediately carry the person back to the first location where he or she boards a means of transport of the transport corporation. If it is not possible to carry the person back to the location, the transporter should carry him or her to the country or region where his or her travel document was issued.

2. If the transporter fails to remove the passenger, seaman or crew member who is refused entry in accordance with the above stipulation, it will be liable for all costs incurred by the person during his or her stay in the Macao Special Administrative Region, particularly accommodation expenses, costs of meals and health care expenses.

3. Airlines which carry inadmissible passengers and crew members to the Macao Special Administrative Region will be fined MOP10,000.00 per head, no matter whether the passengers and crew members are admissible afterwards, except if there is an indication under concrete circumstances that it is impossible to reasonably require the airlines to know the status of the passengers and crew members.

4. Payment for the above fine should be made within 10 days from the date of notification.

5. If the violator fails to voluntarily pay the fine in accordance with the above stipulation, the Immigration Department will send the notes of executory effect to the jurisdictional court for mandatory collection of the fine.

X Penalty for Overstaying

1. According to Administrative Regulation No. 14/2014 'Amendments to the Provision on Overstay in the 《Regulations of the Entry, Stay and Residence Authorization》', persons who still stay in the Macao SAR but not over 30 days after the expiry of the authorization granted is fined MOP500 per overdue day from 9/7/2014. The violators are required to pay the fine immediately after they are arrested or report themselves to the police. The above mentioned penalty regulation is not applicable to those who have overstayed in Macao within one year. Those will be considered to be illegal immigrants if they do not pay the fine and the penalty regulation is not applicable to them. Moreover, they cannot make any application for Residence Authorization, extension of Authorization to Stay and Authorization to Stay for Non-resident Workers within two years to the Immigration Department.

2. According to Law No. 6/2004, persons who are considered to be illegal immigrants will be deported and interdicted from entry to the Macao SAR for the period indicated in the deportation order.

XI Departure of Non-residents with Loss of Document

Service	Processing of Cases of Loss of Entry Identification Documents for Non-residents
Introduction (Service	Issue departure document to non-residents who have lost the

Coverage)	passport / travel document / identification document used for entry to Macao and do not have other document for departure
Service Provider	Foreigners Subdivision of the Immigration Department (during office hours) Investigation Subdivision of the Immigration Department (during non-office hours)
Other Entity / Agency	Police station/duty office of the Judiciary Police or the Public Security Police Force, China Travel Service (Macao) Ltd., Office of the Commissioner of the Ministry of Foreign Affairs of the PRC in the Macao SAR, Taipei Economic and Cultural Office in Macao
Application Location	Immigration Department
Office Hours	1. Foreigners Subdivision Mon to Thu: 9:00 – 17:45 Fri: 9:00 – 17:30 Closed on Sat, Sun and government holidays 2. Please call (853) 2872 5488 before applying to the Investigation Subdivision during non-office hours.
Enquiry Methods	In person: the above location Tel: (853) 2872 5488 Fax: (853) 8897 0300 Email: sminfo@fsm.gov.mo

Transactional Category	Issue (in our performance pledges)
Relevant Service (Relevant Information)	Report of Loss (Report of Loss of Document)
Target Groups and Application Eligibility	A. Target people: Non-residents who have lost the entry document and do not have other document for departure B. Requirement: Not in a lawfully restricted status [Note: Departure of persons who have lost their document and overstay will be arranged by the Investigation Subdivision of the Immigration Department.]
Application Approach	1. Simply a case of loss of document: They may go directly to the respective unit for report of 2. A case of loss of document involving criminal act (e.g.

	"Complaint Notification".
Necessary Documents	1. A completed declaration of the lost document; [Note: The form is available at the respective Subdivision and the website of the Public Security Police Force.] 2. "Report Testimonial" or "Complaint Notification" issued at a police department (for a case of loss of document involving criminal act); 3. Other documents certifying the person's identity (if any).
Charge (or Tax)	Free of charge
Time Needed	Within the same day
Quality Criterion	To issue a "Declaration of Loss of Document" to a resident of the Hong Kong Special Administrative Region: identity verifivation by the Hong Kong competent authorities - 3 hours [Please see Remark 3.] identity verifivation by our fingerprint system - 1 hour [Please see Remark 3. and 4.]
Remark	1. Procedure after obtaining the "departure document" 1) Hong Kong residents They are required to leave Macao by using the "departure document" before it expires (generally within 3 days). 2) Others A. To ensure successful entry to the original country/region, they are required to apply to the consulate/embassy or diplomatic mission of the original country/region in Macao before using the "departure document" to leave Macao, or apply to the consulate/embassy or diplomatic mission of B. Application for "return document" at Macao a. The person is required to apply to the department or organization concerned for a "return document" before the "departure document" expires (generally within 7 days), for example:

Type of Lost Document	Department/Organization Responsible for Reissue of Document
P.R.C. passport	Office of the Commissioner of the Ministry of Foreign Affairs of

b. If the "return document" is issued before the expiry of

before the two documents expire (subject to whichever document expires first). Otherwise, the person is required to extend the validity of the "departure document" at the respective unit until he/she is granted the "return document" and leaves Macao.

[Note: Persons who leave Macao or extend the validity of the "departure document" after it expires are considered to be overstayers.]

c. Both the "departure document" and the "return document" should be presented upon departure.

C. Application for "return document" at Hong Kong or Mainland China

a. The person should leave Macao before the "departure document" expires (generally within 7 days) and go to the consulate/embassy or diplomatic mission in Hong Kong or Mainland China to apply for a "return document". Otherwise, the person will be considered to be an overstayer;

b. Before going to Hong Kong or Mainland China, the person should contact the relevant consulate/ embassy and confirm the appointed date of application. Otherwise, the person will be subject to entry refusal;

[Note: If the appointed date of application is beyond the expiry of the "departure document", the person is required to extend the validity of the Document at the respective unit.]

c. If the person obtains the "return document" on the date of application and returns to Macao to take a flight, he/she is required to present the "return document" as well as the original "departure document" upon arrival at Macao. The authorities will grant him/her "Authorization to Stay" for a reasonable period of time based on the validity of the "return document" so that he/she can make arrangements for departure. However, if the person needs to collect the "return document" after he/she re-enters Macao, he/she is required to extend the validity of the original "departure document" with the relevant application receipt at the respective unit.

2. Penalty for overstay

1) According to Administrative Regulation No. 14/2014 'Amendments to the Provision on Overstay in the 《Regulations of the Entry, Stay and Residence Authorization》', persons who still stay in the Macao SAR but not over 30 days after the expiry of the authorization granted is fined MOP500 per overdue day from 9/7/2014. The violators are required to pay the fine immediately after they are arrested or report themselves to the police. The above mentioned penalty regulation is not applicable to those who have overstayed in Macao within one year. Those will be considered to be illegal immigrants if they do not pay the fine and the penalty regulation is not applicable to them.

	Moreover, they cannot make any application for Residence Authorization, extension of Authorization to Stay and Authorization to Stay for Non-resident Workers within two years to the Immigration Department. 2) According to Law No. 6/2004, persons who are considered to be illegal immigrants will be deported and interdicted from entry to the Macao SAR for the period indicated in the deportation order. 3. "Quality Criterion" refers to the time of processing required by service units (excluding time of waiting in a queue) calculated in the following manner: from the moment when the service unit received and confirmed that all the required documents had been correctly prepared. 4. For Hong Kong Residents who have registered for the Macao Automated Passenger Clearance System (e-Channel).
Attachments	Sample of "Loss of Document and Report Notification" Sample of "Declaration of Loss of Document"
Forms	Declaration of Loss of Hong Kong Identity Card Declaration of Loss of Australian Travel Document Declaration of Loss of Travel Document [Note: applicable to other types of document]
Legislations Website	1. General Principles of the System of Entry, Stay and Residence Authorization Law No. 4/2003 [B.O. no. 11 (I), 17/03/2003] 2. Regulations of Entry, Stay and Residence Authorization Administrative Regulation No. 5/2003 [B.O. no. 15 (I), 14/04/2003] 3. Amendments to the Stipulation on Overstay in the Regulations of Entry, Stay and Residence Authorization Administrative Regulation No. 14/2014 [B.O. no. 25 (I), 23/06/2014]

APPLYING FOR RESIDENCE IN MACAO S.A.R. REGULATIONS

I. DEPARTMENTS RESPONSIBLE FOR PROCESSING APPLICATIONS FOR RESIDENCE AUTHORIZATION

Persons who intend to apply for residence in Macao as an investor, managerial personnel or specialized technical personnel may make their application in accordance with Administrative Regulation No. 3/2005 to the Trade and Investment Promotion Institute (IPIM) (Address: 1/F, World Trade Centre, 918, Avenida da Amizade, Macao; Tel: (853) 2871 2055). After the application is approved, they need to apply to the Foreigners Subdivision of the Immigration Department for "Receipt of Residence Authorization / Residence Authorization Renewal" ("Residence Receipt"), with which they can apply to the Identification Bureau for a "Macao Non-Permanent Resident Identity Card".

Other persons who also intend to apply for residence in Macao may make their application in accordance with Law No. 4/2003 and Administrative Regulation No. 5/2003 to the relevant subdivision of the Immigration Department of the Public Security Police Force, depending on their status as indicated in the table below. After the application is approved, they will receive a "Residence Certificate" or a "Residence Receipt", with which they can apply to the Identification Bureau for a "Macao Non-Permanent Resident Identity Card".

<table>
<tr><th>Category of Applicant</th><th>Department</th><th>Document Issued</th><th>Office Hours / Inquiries</th></tr>
<tr><td>1. "P.R.C. Permit for Travelling to Hong Kong and Macao" holders from Mainland China</td><td rowspan="3">Residents Subdivision</td><td rowspan="3">Residence Certificate</td><td rowspan="4">Mon to Thu: 09:00-17:45
Friday: 09:00-17:30
(Tags dispensed until 17:00)
Closed on Sat, Sun and government holidays
Address: Immigration Department Office Building, Travessa Um do Cais de Pac On, Taipa, Macau
Tel: (853) 2872 5488
Fax: (853) 8897 0300
Email: sminfo@fsm.gov.mo
Online: Inquiry System of Progress of Application for 'Residence Authorization'</td></tr>
<tr><td>2. Minor children who are born outside the Macao S.A.R. and whose parents are Macao permanent residents / "P.R.C. Permit for Travelling to Hong Kong and Macao" holders granted residence in Macao</td></tr>
<tr><td>3. Persons of Portuguese Nationality</td></tr>
<tr><td>4. Others</td><td>Foreigners Subdivision</td><td>Receipt of Residence Authorization / Residence Authorization Renewal</td></tr>
</table>

Applicants belonging to Category 1 will make an appointment for the application upon entry through the Border Checkpoint at the Border Gate. Applicants of the other categories may make the application by approaching the subdivision concerned and waiting for their turn, or by using our Online Appointment System. Click here for online appointment.Upon completion of the application for Residence Authorization, the applicants belonging to Category 1 can choose collect the Residence Certificate at the Subsivision concerned or the Centro de Serviços da RAEM.

II. APPLICATION FOR RESIDENCE AUTHORIZATION THROUGH RESIDENTS

1. Application for Residence Authorization

1.1 Application and Necessary Documents

A. "P.R.C. Permit for Travelling to Hong Kong and Macao" holders from Mainland China

Upon completion of entry clearance, the interested person will receive a "notification letter" which notifies him/her to apply to the Residents Subdivision in person within 10 days for "Residence Authorization". Otherwise, the interested person will be fined MOP200 per overdue day; the maximum fine is limited to MOP5,000. The necessary documents to be submitted include:

【Note: The original should be exhibited for authentication if a copy is submitted】

1) A completed application form (format 6);

【Note: (1) Applicants under 18 years old should have their applications tendered and signed by the parent or guardian;
(2) The application form is available at the respective subdivision and the website of the Public Security Police Force.】

2) 2 copies of "P.R.C. Permit for Travelling to Hong Kong and Macao", and present the Arrival Card for this entry to Macao;
3) "Certificate of Criminal Record" of Macao issued within 90 days [Remark (2)];
4) Copy of national "Notarial Certificate of Criminal Record" of Mainland China issued within 6 months (if the interested person is 16 years old or above on the date of issue of the "P.R.C. Permit for Travelling to Hong Kong and Macao");
5) Copy of document of kinship between the interested person and his/her reuniting kindred in Macao (e.g. original Marriage Certificate, Notarial Marriage Certificate, Notarial Birth Certificate, Medical Certificate of Birth, Notarial Kinship Certificate, etc.);

【Note: (1) In cases of reunion between husband and wife, the interested person and his/her spouse residing in Macao should co-declare in written form the existence of marital relation and cohabitation. The declaration form is available at the respective subdivision and the website of the Public Security Police Force;
(2) For details, please see "Acceptance Standard for Necessary Documents in Application for Residence Authorization".】

6) Copy of the Macao Resident Identity Card of the reuniting kindred residing in Macao (the card holder should be present for the application);
7) Document indicating the interested person's address in Macao (e.g.: copy of water bill, electricity bill, phone bill, etc. of the last 3 months);
8) Other information requested by the authorities under special circumstances.

【Remark: (1)

Our staff will take a digital photo for the interested person at the respective subdivision. The interested person can choose to use the digital photo or his/her own recent photo (1.5-inch, full face, no-hat, white-background, coloured/black-and-white photo) on the residence document issued to him/her.

(3)(2) For details of the application procedures for a residence document at the Immigration Department and the Identification Bureau, please see "Guidelines for "P.R.C. Permit for Travelling to Hong Kong and Macao" Holders Entering the Macao S.A.R. and Applying for Residence Document" (Chinese version only)】

This certificate is required if the interested person is 16 years old or above on the day the application is submitted. This type of applicants may apply to the Identification Bureau for the certificate by presenting the "notification" granted upon entry or the receipt of the application for "Residence Authorization", together with the "P.R.C. Permit for Travelling to Hong Kong and Macao". To facilitate the application procedure, the applicants can first apply to the Identification Bureau and authorize the Bureau to send the certificate directly to the Immigration Department. Then they may apply to the Residents Subdivision for "Resident Authorization".

(3)

Applicants who have been verified by the Identification Bureau and are preliminarily eligible to be a permanent resident in Macao (with an "R" symbol

【Note: The processing time starts from the next working day after the service unit receives all the necessary documents and confirms nothing is missing】

Application by persons preliminarily eligible to be a permanent resident in Macao:	14:00 of the next working day ***【Note: The processing time starts from the moment after the service unit receives all the necessary documents and confirms nothing is missing】***	<performance pledge>

(6) For details of the application procedures for a residence document at the Immigration Department and the Identification Bureau, please see "Guidelines for "P.R.C. Permit for Travelling to Hong Kong and Macao" Holders Entering the Macao S.A.R. and Applying for Residence Document" (Chinese version only)】

B. Minor children who are born outside the Macao S.A.R. and whose parents are Macao permanent residents / "P.R.C. Permit for Travelling to Hong Kong and Macao" holders granted residence in Macao

The application should be tendered by the parent or guardian (or their legal representative) of the interested person. The necessary documents include:

【Note: ***(1)***
The original should be exhibited for authentication if a copy is submitted;

(2) If the interested person cannot appear at the Immigration Department, the parent / guardian or another representative should submit a recent photo of the interested person (1.5-inch, full face, no-hat, white-background, coloured/black-and-white photo);

(3) Unless the minor is represented by the parent, the representative should submit: a. a certified letter of authorization; b. a copy of his/her valid identification document.】

1) A completed application form (format 4); application form (format 9) is also required if the
   【Note: (1) The application form is available at the respective subdivision and the
2) Guarantee (format 5) signed by the guarantor for the purpose of undertaking the interested
   【Note: (1) The Guarantee template is available at the respective subdivision and the
3) Copy of the interested person's valid passport / travel document (bio data page and used
4) Copy of the interested person's birth certificate or equivalent document;
   【Note: For details, please see "Acceptance Standard for Necessary Documents in
5) Copy of the "Macao Permanent Resident Identity Card", "P.R.C. Permit for Travelling to

person's father and/or mother(the card holder should be present for the application);

6) If one of the interested person's parents is not a Macao resident, a written statement of that parent's consent and reason to let the child reside in Macao with the other parent should be submitted;

***【Note:** The above statement should contain the declarant's signature which is to be certified by the competent authorities. Otherwise, the declarant is required to sign the statement in the presence of the staff accepting the residence application and present the original of his/her identification document for verification.】*

7) "Certificate of Criminal Record" of Macao issued within 90 days (if the interested person is 16 years old or above on the day the application is submitted);

***【Note:** Application for the Certificate should be made to the Identification Bureau by presenting the application acceptance receipt of "Residence Authorization". The interested person may authorize the Bureau to send the Certificate directly to the Immigration Department.】*

8) Copy of national Certificate of Criminal Record issued by the competent authorities of the latest country or region of domicile (if the interested person is 16 years old or above on the day the application is submitted);

***【Note:** For details, please see "Acceptance Standard for Necessary Documents in Application for Residence Authorization".】*

9) Copy of document issued by the competent authorities of the interested person's country or region of domicile certifying he/she has continuously been residing in that place for at least two years just before applying for residence in Macao;

***【Remark:** (1) The above requirement is mainly applicable to Chinese who are originally residents of Mainland China but then emigrated to the Region of Taiwan or a foreign country and granted residence status there;*

(2) The 2-year residence should be counted from the day the residence status is officially granted and is subject to the actual residing period of two years at that place;

(3) The document should be a residence certificate or equivalent document issued by the competent authorities of the country or region in which the person resides. It can be presented in 2 or more certificates (e.g. Residents of the Region of Taiwan may submit their latest household registry transcript / household register and movement records of the Region of Taiwan as evidence of residence.)】

10) Copy of personal financial documents (e.g. employment certificate, bank book, payment receipt of revenue / sales tax of the reuniting kindred residing in Macao);

11) Proof of the interested person and his/her reuniting parent(s) habitually residing in Macao (e.g. proof of study of the interested person, employment certificate of the interested person's parents, etc);

12) Document indicating the interested person's residential address in Macao (e.g.: copy of water bill, electricity bill, phone bill, etc. of the last 3 months).

***【Note:** (1) Our staff will take a digital photo for the interested person at the respective subdivision. The interested person can choose to use the digital photo or his/her own recent photo (1.5-inch, full face, no-hat, white-background, coloured/black-and-white photo) on the residence document issued to him/her;*

permanent Resident Identity Card with the Residence Certificate issued by our department. After habitually residing in Macao for 7 consecutive years from the effective date of the Residence Authorization, they may apply to the Identification Bureau for a Macao Permanent Resident Identity Card. However, attention should be paid to Article 24 of the Administrative Regulation, which specifies the conditions causing the invalidation of the Residence Authorization, e.g. not habitually residing in Macao. To habitually reside in Macao and to meet the prerequisite for the Residence Authorization, the interested person and his/her reuniting parent(s) should make Macao a centre of living and reside in Macao for not less than 183 days per year starting from the effective date of the Residence Authorization. In addition, whenever they leave Macao, they should not be away for more than half a year. Otherwise, the Residence Authorization granted to the interested person may be invalidated.】

C. Persons of Portuguese nationality

The application can be made by the interested person or a legal representative by submitting the following:

【Note: (1) The original should be exhibited for authentication if a copy is submitted;
(2) If the interested person cannot appear at the Immigration Department, the parent / guardian or another representative should submit a recent photo of the interested person (1.5-inch, full face, no-hat, white-background, coloured/black-and-white photo);
(3) Unless the minor is represented by the parent, the representative should submit: a. a certified letter of authorization; b. a copy of his/her valid identification document.】

Basic Documents

1) A completed application form (format 4); application form (format 9) is also required if the application includes family members;

   【Note: (1) The application form is available at the respective subdivision and the website of the Public Security Police Force;
   (2) The reason for application or the interested person's intended activity in Macao should be stated in the application form.】

2) Declaration made in the reputation of the interested person to undertake to comply with the laws of the Macao Special Administrative Region (for applicants who are 18 years old or above);

   【Note: The Declaration template is available at the respective subdivision and the website of the Public Security Police Force】

3) Guarantee (format 5) signed by the guarantor for the purpose of undertaking the interested person's departure expenses;

   【Note: (1) The Guarantee template is available at the respective subdivision and the website of the Public Security Police Force;
   (2) The guarantor should be a permanent resident habitually residing in Macao or a bank.】

4) Copy of the interested person's valid Portuguese passport (bio data page and used pages only), and present the Arrival Card for this entry to Macao;
5) Copy of the interested person's birth certificate or equivalent document;

   【Note: For details, please see "Acceptance Standard for Necessary Documents in

Application for Residence Authorization".】

6) Copy of the Macao Resident Identity Card of the reuniting kindred residing in Macao (the card holder should be present for the application) (for cases of family reunion);
7) "Certificate of Criminal Record" of Macao issued within 90 days (if the interested person is 16 years old or above on the day the application is submitted and has resided / been residing in Macao);

   【Note: Application for the Certificate should be made to the Identification Bureau by presenting the application acceptance receipt of "Residence Authorization". The interested person may authorize the Bureau to send the Certificate directly to the Immigration Department.】
8) Copy of national Certificate of Criminal Record issued by the competent authorities of the latest country or region of domicile (if the interested person is 16 years old or above on the day the application is submitted);

   【Note: For details, please see "Acceptance Standard for Necessary Documents in Application for Residence Authorization".】
9) Copy of personal financial documents (e.g. employment certificate, bank book, payment receipt of revenue / sales tax of the reuniting kindred residing in Macao);
10) Document indicating the interested person's residential address in Macao (e.g.: copy of water bill, electricity bill, phone bill, etc. of the last 3 months).

Other documents (according to individual case)

Type of Application		**Necessary Documents**
	A. Reunion with spouse	Certificate of marriage (for details, please see "Acceptance Standard for Necessary Documents in Application for Residence Authorization")

	D. Reunion of grown-up child with parent(s) residing in Macao	1. Certificate of marital status of the grown-up child; ***【Note: For details, please see "Acceptance Standard for Necessary Documents in Application for Residence Authorization", but it is not necessary to submit a declaration of the husband and wife's claim to be maintaining marital relation if married.】*** 2. Identification document of the spouse and children (if any) if married; 3. Parent(s)' written statement of the status of the family member(s) (e.g. number of children, age, type of document in possession of, country of domicile, marital status, whether they are Macao residents or not, etc.).
	E. Reunion of parent(s) with child(ren) residing in Macao	1. Birth certificate of the child(ren) residing in Macao (for details, please see "Acceptance Standard for Necessary Documents in Application for Residence Authorization"); 2. Parents' certificate of marriage (for details, please see "Acceptance Standard for Necessary Documents in Application for Residence Authorization"); 3. Divorce certificate or spouse's death certificate if the parents are divorced or one of them is deceased (for details, please see "Acceptance Standard for Necessary Documents in Application for Residence Authorization"); 4. Document stated in D.3.
II. To be engaged in a professional post		1. Certificate of employment in Macao; 2. Certificate of the interested person's academic background or professional skill.
III. Previous connection with Macao		Proof of previous employment, education or living in Macao.

【Note: (1) Our staff will take a digital photo for the interested person at the respective
(2) Other information should be submitted upon request by the authorities
(3) According to Term 2, Article 22 of Administrative Regulation No. 5/2003,

Residence Authorization may not be approved.】

1.2 Application Approach

Fee	Payment Deadline	Consequence of Overdue Payment
Chinese: free Others: MOP100	The period specified in the notification letter mentioned in Point 1) (around 180 days from the date of issue of the letter)	Extinguishment of Residence Authorization application

1) After receiving the residence application of the persons listed in Points A, B and C, the authorities will issue an "application acceptance receipt", which includes the necessary documents that have not yet been submitted. The interested person (or the legal representative) should submit them within 180 days from the date the receipt is issued (or the date he/she is notified to supplement other documents). Otherwise, the authorities may announce the extinguishment of the application according to Article 103 of the Code of Administrative Procedure.
   If all the necessary documents are submitted, the interested person (or the legal representative) should come in person to complete the procedures or collect the "Residence Certificate" on the date specified on the receipt or by following the instructions on the receipt (e.g. to wait for a notification letter). When coming in person,
   (1) Present the application acceptance receipt;
   (2) Present the "P.R.C. Permit for Travelling to Hong Kong and Macao" or the valid passport / travel document / identification document used to apply for Residence Authorization;
   (3) The parent or guardian representing the minor child in the application should present his/her valid identification document and proof of their relationship; other legal representative should present a certified letter of authorization and his/her valid identification document;
   (4) Submit the "Non-resident Worker's Identification Card" (or the former "Non-resident Worker's Permit", also known as blue card) (if any) for cancellation.
   【Note: If the interested person is not able come to complete the procedure within 180 days after the appointed date or within the period specified in the notification letter regarding the approval of the "Residence Authorization" application (around 180 days from the date of issue of the letter), it may result in the extinguishment of the application and invalidation of the Residence Authorization.】
2) For approved application, the interested person (or the legal representative) will be issued a "Residence Certificate" after he/she pays the fee (Chinese nationals are exempted) within the period specified on the notification letter. For disapproved application, the interested person will receive a written notice of the content of the written instructions and the means to appeal.

3) After the Residence Authorization is granted, the statutory fee and the payment deadline are as follows:

4) While waiting for the result of the residence application, persons of Portuguese nationality and minor children who are born outside the Macao S.A.R. and whose parents are Macao permanent residents / "P.R.C. Permit for Travelling to Hong Kong and Macao" holders granted residence in Macao can apply to the Residents Subdivision for single or multiple extension of Authorization to Stay (by using an application form for extension of "Authorization to Stay", for detail, please see "Special Authorization to Stay" for Applicants of Residence Authorization) on the day they submit the residence application or on a later day by presenting the Application Acceptance Receipt.
5) When receiving the residence application of the applicants in Point B (minor children who are born outside the Macao S.A.R. and whose parents are Macao permanent residents / "P.R.C. Permit for Travelling to Hong Kong and Macao" holders granted residence in Macao) and Point C (persons of Portuguese nationality), the Immigration Department can deny part of or the whole application accordingly if the applicant's passport / travel document and return / re-entry permit is expiring in less than 30 days.

2. Application for Residence Authorization Renewal by Persons of Portuguese Nationality

2.1 Application and Necessary Documents

The application can be made by the interested person or a legal representative within 30 days before the expiry of the Residence Authorization by submitting the following:

【Note: (1) The original should be exhibited for authentication if a copy is submitted;
(2) If the interested person cannot appear at the Immigration Department, the parent / guardian or another representative should submit a recent photo of the interested person (1.5-inch, full face, no-hat, white-background, coloured/black-and-white photo);
(3) Unless the minor is represented by the parent, the representative should submit: a. a certified letter of authorization; b. a copy of his/her valid identification document.】

1) A completed application form for Residence Authorization Renewal ; application form (format 9) is also required if the application includes family members;

【Note: The application form is available at the respective subdivision and the website of the Public Security Police Force】

2) Copy of the interested person's valid Portuguese passport (bio data page only) and Macao Non-permanent Resident Identity Card;

3) Copy of the Macao Resident Identity Card of the reuniting kindred residing in Macao (the card holder should be present for the application) (for cases of family reunion);

4) Certificate of maintaining marriage / de facto marital relation (for cases including spouse / partner of marriage de facto or residence is granted on the basis of family reunion with spouse/partner of marriage de facto);

【Note: Applicants may apply to the Identification Bureau for the certificate first by presenting their Macao Resident Identity Card and authorize the Bureau to send the certificate directly to the Immigration Department. Then they may apply to the Residents Subdivision for "Residence Authorization" renewal by presenting the receipt issued by the Identification Bureau and other necessary documents.】

7) Copy of personal financial documents (e.g. employment certificate, bank book, payment receipt of revenue / sales tax of the interested person or his/her reuniting kindred residing in Macao);
8) Copy of water bill, electricity bill, phone bill, etc. of the last 3 months of the latest address (if the interested person has changed address).

【Remark: (1) Our staff will take a digital photo for the interested person at the respective subdivision. The interested person can choose to use the digital photo or his/her own recent photo (1.5-inch, full face, no-hat, white-background, coloured/black-and-white photo) on the residence document issued to him/her.

(2) Other information should be submitted upon request by the authorities under special circumstances.

(3) According to Term 2, Article 22 of Administrative Regulation No. 5/2003, renewal of the Residence Authorization depends on whether the application meets the prerequisites and requisites stipulated in Law No. 4/2003 and the above Administrative Regulation, especially whether the applicant (or the applicant and his/her reuniting kindred, or the applicant and the family members involved in the application and the reuniting kindred) habitually resides in Macao. In other words, they should make Macao a centre of living and reside in Macao for not less than 183 days per year starting from the effective date of the Residence Authorization. In addition, whenever they leave Macao, they should not be away for more than half a year. Otherwise, the applicant's (and the family members involved) application for renewal of Residence Authorization may not be approved.

Persons who have their final application for renewal of Residence Authorization approved should pay attention to the conditions causing the invalidation of the Residence Authorization specified in Article 24 of the above Administrative Regulation, e.g. not habitually residing in Macao and not meeting the prerequisite for the Residence Authorization. These persons (or their reuniting kindred) should continue to comply with the above stipulation of staying in Macao even during the 5th to 7th years of residence in Macao. Otherwise, their Residence Authorization may be invalidated.

(4) The interested person may still apply for renewal within 180 days after the expiry of the Residence Authorization, provided that he/she pays the fine (MOP20 per overdue day). Renewal depends on the submission of an application letter with reasonable justification and receipt of the fine payment. If no renewal application is made within this period, the Residence Authorization becomes invalid immediately and the duration accumulated for obtaining permanent resident status is forfeited, unless there is appropriate proof that the application is hindered for reasons of force majeure.】

2.2 Application Approach (Residence Authorization renewal for persons of Portuguese nationality)

1) After receiving the application, the authorities will issue an "application acceptance receipt", which includes the necessary documents that have not yet been submitted. The interested person (or the legal representative) should submit them within 180 days from the date the receipt is issued (or the date he/she is notified to supplement other documents). Otherwise, the authorities may announce the extinguishment of the application according to Article 103 of the Code of Administrative Procedure.

   If all the necessary documents are submitted, the interested person (or the legal representative) should come in person to complete the procedures on the date specified on the receipt or by following the instructions on the receipt (e.g. to wait for a notification letter). When coming in person,

   (1) Present the application acceptance receipt;

   (2) Present the valid Portuguese passport used to apply for Residence Authorization;

   (3) The parent or guardian representing the minor child in the application should present his/her valid identification document and proof of their relationship; other legal representative should present a certified letter of authorization and his/her valid identification document.

   【Note: If the interested person is not able come to complete the procedure within 180 days after the appointed date or within the period specified in the notification letter (around 180 days from the date of issue of the letter), it may result in the extinguishment of the application and invalidation of the Residence Authorization.】

2) For approved application, the interested person (or the legal representative) will be issued a "Residence Certificate" after he/she pays the stamp duty of MOP100 within the specified period. For disapproved application, the interested person will receive a written notice of the content of the written instructions and the ways to appeal.

3) Processing time: around 10 working days.

   【Note: The processing time will be different if certain necessary documents are not submitted, errors are found in the information provided or the application has to be submitted to the Secretary for Security for approval.】

III. APPLICATION FOR RESIDENCE AUTHORIZATION THROUGH FOREIGNERS SUBDIVISION

1. Application for Residence Authorization

1.1 Application and Necessary Documents

The application can be made by the interested person or a legal representative by submitting the following:

【Note: (1) The original should be exhibited for authentication if a copy is submitted;

(2) If the interested person cannot appear at the Immigration Department, the parent / guardian or another representative should submit a recent photo of the interested person (1.5-inch, full face, no-hat, white-background, coloured/black-and-white photo);

(3) Unless the minor is represented by the parent, the representative should submit: a. a certified letter of authorization; b. a copy of his/her valid identification document.】

Basic Documents

1) A completed application form (format 4); application form (format 9) is also required if the application includes family members;

   【Note: (1) The application form is available at the respective subdivision and the

website of the Public Security Police Force;

(2) The reason for application or the interested person's intended activity in Macao should be stated in the application form.】

2) Declaration made in the reputation of the interested person to undertake to comply with the laws of the Macao Special Administrative Region;

【Note: (1) If the applicant is 18 years old or above on the day the application is submitted;

(2) The Declaration template is available at the respective subdivision and the website of the Public Security Police Force.】

3) Guarantee (format 5) signed by the guarantor for the purpose of undertaking the interested person's departure expenses;

【Note: (1) The Guarantee template is available at the respective subdivision and the website of the Public Security Police Force;

(2) The guarantor should be a permanent resident habitually residing in Macao or a bank.】

4) Copy of the interested person's valid passport / travel document (bio data page and used pages only, and the Arrival Card for the latest entry to Macao) or identification document used for entry to and departure from Macao;

5) Copy of the interested person's birth certificate or equivalent document;

【Note: For details, please see "Acceptance Standard for Necessary Documents in Application for Residence Authorization".】

6) Copy of the Macao Resident Identity Card of the reuniting kindred residing in Macao (for cases of family reunion);

7) "Certificate of Criminal Record" of Macao issued within 90 days (if the interested person is 16 years old or above on the day the application is submitted);

【Note: Application for the Certificate should be made to the Identification Bureau by presenting the application acceptance receipt of "Residence Authorization". The interested person may authorize the Bureau to send the Certificate directly to the Immigration Department.】

8) Copy of national Certificate of Criminal Record issued by the competent authorities of the latest country or region of domicile (if the interested person is 16 years old or above on the day the application is submitted);

【Note: For details, please see "Acceptance Standard for Necessary Documents in Application for Residence Authorization".】

9) Copy of document issued by the competent authorities of the interested person's country or region of domicile certifying he/she has continuously been residing in that place for at least two years just before applying for residence in Macao [Remark (1)-(3)];

【Remark: (1) The requirement of submitting proof of 2-year residence overseas is mainly applicable to Chinese who are originally residents of Mainland China but then emigrated to the Region of Taiwan or a foreign country and granted residence status there;

(2) The 2-year residence should be counted from the day the residence status is officially granted and is subject to the actual residing period of two years at that place;

(3) The document should be a residence certificate or equivalent document issued by the competent authorities of the country or region in which the person resides. It can be presented in 2 or more certificates (e.g. Residents of the Region of Taiwan may submit their latest household registry transcript / household register and movement records of the Region of Taiwan as evidence of residence.)】

10) Copy of personal financial documents (e.g. employment certificate, bank book, payment receipt of revenue / sales tax of the interested person or his/her reuniting kindred residing in Macao);
11) Document indicating the interested person's residential address in Macao (e.g.: copy of water bill, electricity bill, phone bill, etc. of the last 3 months).

Other Documents (depending on the case type)

Type of Application	Necessary Documents
A. Reunion with spouse	Certificate of marriage ***(for details, please see "Acceptance Standard for Necessary Documents in Application for Residence Authorization")***
B. Reunion with partner of marriage de facto	Certificate of no marriage, divorce or marriage de facto ***(for details, please see "Acceptance Standard for Necessary Documents in Application for Residence Authorization")***
C. Reunion of minor child with parent(s) residing in Macao	1. If one of the interested person's parents is not a Macao resident, a written statement of that parent's consent and reason to let the child reside in Macao with the other parent should be submitted; 2. Proof of the minor child studying in Macao (if any). ***【Note: The above statement should contain the declarant's signature which is to be certified by the competent authorities. Otherwise, the declarant is required to***
D. Reunion of grown-up child with parent(s) residing in Macao	1. Certificate of marital status of the grown-up child; ***【Note: For details, please see "Acceptance Standard for Necessary Documents in Application for Residence Authorization", but it is not necessary to submit a declaration of the husband and wife's claim to be maintaining marital relation if married.】*** 2. Identification document of the spouse and children (if any) if
E. Reunion of parent(s) with child(ren) residing in Macao	1. Birth certificate of the child(ren) residing in Macao ***(for details, please see "Acceptance Standard for Necessary Documents in Application for Residence Authorization")***; 2. Parents' certificate of marriage ***(for details, please see***

	2. Parents' certificate of marriage ***(for details, please see "Acceptance Standard for Necessary Documents in Application for Residence Authorization")***; 3. Divorce certificate or spouse's death certificate if the parents are divorced or one of them is deceased ***(for details, please see "Acceptance Standard for Necessary Documents in Application for Residence Authorization")***; 4. Document stated in D.3.

【Note: (1) Our staff will take a digital photo for the interested person at the respective subdivision. The interested person can choose to use the digital photo or his/her own recent photo (1.5-inch, full face, no-hat, white-background, coloured/black-and-white photo) on the residence document issued to him/her;

(2) Other information should be submitted upon request by the authorities under special circumstances】

1.2 Application Approach

1) The Immigration Department can deny part of or the whole application accordingly if the interested person's passport / travel document and return / re-entry permit is found to be expiring in less than 30 days when he/she submits the application;

2) After receiving the residence application, the authorities will issue an "application acceptance receipt", which includes the necessary documents that have not yet been submitted. The interested person (or the legal representative) should submit them within 180 days from the date the receipt is issued (or the date he/she is notified to supplement other documents). Otherwise, the authorities may announce the extinguishment of the application according to Article 103 of the Code of Administrative Procedure.

If all the necessary documents are submitted, the interested person (or the legal representative) should come in person to complete the follow-up procedures by following the instructions on the receipt (e.g. to wait for a notification letter):

A. For approved application, the interested person should pay the fee stated in Point 4) below and collect the "Residence Receipt" as soon as he/she receives the notification letter from the authorities. When coming in person, he/she should:

the application meets the prerequisites and requisites stipulated in Law No. 4/2003 and the above Administrative Regulation, especially whether the applicant (or the applicant and his/her reuniting kindred, or the applicant and the family members involved in the application and the reuniting kindred) habitually resides in Macao. In other words, they should make Macao a centre of living and reside in Macao for not less than 183 days per year starting from the effective date of the Residence Authorization. In addition, whenever they leave Macao, they should not be away for more than half a year. Otherwise, the applicant's (and the family members involved) application for renewal of Residence Authorization may not be approved.】

B. For disapproved application, the interested person will receive a written notice of the content of the written instructions and the means to appeal.

3) While waiting for the result of the residence application, the interested person can apply to the Foreigners Subdivision for single or multiple extension of Authorization to Stay (by using an application form for extension of "Authorization to Stay", for detail, please see "Special Authorization to Stay" for Applicants of Residence Authorization) by presenting the Application Acceptance Receipt.

4) After the Residence Authorization is granted, the statutory fee and the payment deadline are as follows:

Fee	Payment Deadline	Consequences of Overdue Payment
Residency tax: MOP20,000 (Remark)	Within 20 days from the date the interested person signs to acknowledge the notification of Residence Authorization approval (No extension is allowed except for reasons of force majeure.)	- Invalidation of Residence Authorization - Interdiction of application for Residence Authorization for 2 years
Service charge: (Chinese) MOP100 (Others) MOP200	The period specified in the notification letter (around 180 days from the date of issue of the letter)	- Extinguishment of Residence Authorization application

【Remark: (1) Persons listed below are exempted from the residence tax of MOP20,000 by law:

a. Chinese citizens;
b. Portuguese citizens;
c. Reuniting kindred of Macao residents;
d. Persons exempted from the fee by international treaties;
e. Staff recruited from outside by the public administrative authorities of the Macao SAR, or staff recruited from outside to provide service at enterprises which are adjudicated public works or which are concessionaires of public services;
f. Buyers and promissory buyers of an immovable of the Macao SAR. The promissory buyers should provide proof of having fulfilled the contract within 180 days from the payment deadline of the respective fee.

(2) If the Residence Authorization includes persons other that the reuniting kindred of the interested persons mentioned in Point (1), the fee to be paid by the applicant will be doubled;

(3) Interested persons other than those mentioned in Point (1) can be exempted from the fee under exceptional circumstances where reasonable justifications are given.】

2. Application for Residence Authorization Renewal

2.1 Application and Necessary Documents

The application can be made by the interested person or a legal representative within 30 days before the expiry of the Residence Authorization by submitting the following:

【Note: (1) The original should be exhibited for authentication if a copy is submitted;
(2) If the interested person cannot appear at the Immigration Department, the parent / guardian or another representative should submit a recent photo of the interested person (1.5-inch, full face, no-hat, white-background, coloured/black-and-white photo);
(3) Unless the minor is represented by the parent, the representative should submit: a. a certified letter of authorization; b. a copy of his/her valid identification document.】

1) A completed application form for Residence Authorization Renewal; application form (format 9) is also required if the application includes family members;

【Note: The application form is available at the respective subdivision and the website of the Public Security Police Force.】

4/2003 and the above Administrative Regulation, especially whether the applicant (or the applicant and his/her reuniting kindred, or the applicant and the family members involved in the application and the reuniting kindred) habitually resides in Macao. In other words, they should make Macao a centre of living and reside in Macao for not less than 183 days per year starting from the effective date of the Residence Authorization. In addition, whenever they leave Macao, they should not be away for more than half a year. Otherwise, the applicant's (and the family members involved) application for renewal of Residence Authorization may not be approved.

Persons who have their final application for renewal of Residence Authorization approved should pay attention to the conditions causing the invalidation of the Residence Authorization specified in Article 24 of the above Administrative Regulation, e.g. not habitually residing in Macao and not meeting the prerequisite for the Residence Authorization. These persons (or their reuniting kindred) should continue to comply with the above stipulation of staying in Macao even during the 5th to 7th years of residence in Macao. Otherwise, their Residence Authorization may be invalidated.

(4) The interested person may still apply for renewal within 180 days after the expiry of the Residence Authorization, provided that he/she pays the fine (MOP20 per overdue day). Renewal depends on the submission of an application letter with reasonable justification and receipt of the fine payment. If no renewal application is made within this period, the Residence Authorization becomes invalid immediately and the duration accumulated for obtaining permanent resident status is forfeited, unless there is appropriate proof that the application is hindered for reasons of force majeure.】

2.2 Application Approach

1) After receiving the application, the authorities will issue an "application acceptance receipt", which includes the necessary documents that have not yet been submitted. The

If all the necessary documents are submitted, the interested person (or the legal representative) should come in person to complete the procedures on the date specified

(1) Present the application acceptance receipt;

(2) Present the valid passport / travel document / identification document used to apply for Residence Authorization renewal;

(3) The parent or guardian representing the minor child in the application should present his/her valid identification document and proof of their relationship; other legal

A. For approved application, the interested person should come to pay the fee (Chinese: MOP100, Others: MOP200) and collect the "Residence Receipt" within the specified

【Note: If the interested person is not able to collect the "Residence Receipt" in person (because he/she has to be fingerprinted on the Receipt) within

may result in the extinguishment of the application and invalidation of the Residence Authorization.】

B. For disapproved application, the interested person will receive a written notice of the content of the written instructions and the ways to appeal.

2) Processing time: around 18 working days.

【Note: The processing time will be different if certain necessary documents are not submitted, errors are found in the information provided or the application has to be submitted to the Secretary for Security for approval.】

IV. MAJOR LAWS OF EXAMINATION AND APPROVAL OF APPLICATION FOR RESIDENCE AUTHORIZATION

(Residence applications processed according to Law No. 4/2003 and Administrative Regulation No. 5/2003)

1. Term 2, Article 9 of Law No. 4/2003 stipulates that:

To grant the above authorization (Residence Authorization), the following should be considered in particular:

A. Previous criminal crimes, confirmed incompliance against the laws of the Macao SAR or the conditions specified in Article 4 of Law No. 4/2003 (as shown below):

2. Term 3, Article 9 of Law No. 4/2003 stipulates that:

Habitual residence of the interested person in the Macao SAR is a condition for maintaining the Residence Authorization.

3. Term 1, Article 10 of Law No. 4/2003 stipulates that:

The following are the requisites for granting Residence Authorization, but they do not cast any prejudice to the documents specified in the complementary regulation (i.e. Administrative Regulation No. 5/2003):

A. Payment of the fee for Residence Authorization as specified in the complementary regulation (i.e. MOP20,000 specified in Article 29 of the Regulation);

4. Term 2, Article 10 of Law No. 4/2003 stipulates that:

Payment of the fee specified in Paragraph A above (i.e. MOP20,000) is a condition for the Residence Authorization to come into effect.

5. Term 3, Article 10 of Law No. 4/2003 stipulates that:

Chinese citizens residing in Mainland China can be granted Residence Authorization in the Macao SAR only if they possess the document issued by the competent authorities in China for this purpose.

Chinese citizens residing in Mainland China can be granted Residence Authorization in the Macao SAR only if they possess the document issued by the competent authorities in China for this purpose.

6. **Article 11 of Law No. 4/2003 stipulates that:**
   A. The Chief Executive can, for humanitarian reasons or under exceptional circumstances where reasonable justifications are given, grant Residence Authorization by waiving the requisites and conditions stipulated in this law and the procedures specified in the complementary regulation.
   B. After the above exemption is granted, persons other than those specified in the relevant written instructions cannot request the same exemption on the basis of being in the same situation or having more reasonable justifications.

V. MAJOR LAWS OF EXAMINATION AND APPROVAL OF APPLICATION FOR RESIDENCE AUTHORIZATION RENEWAL

(Residence applications processed according to Law No. 4/2003 and Administrative Regulation No. 5/2003)

1. **Term 2, Article 22 of Administrative Regulation No. 5/2003 stipulates that:**
   Residence Authorization Renewal depends on whether the presuppositions and requisites stipulated in the principle law (Law No. 4/2003) and the administrative regulation (Administrative Regulation No. 5/2003) are met.
2. **Term 3, Article 9 of Law No. 4/2003 stipulates that:**
   Habitual residence of the interested person in the Macao SAR is a condition for maintaining the Residence Authorization.

VI. ACCEPTANCE STANDARD FOR NECESSARY DOCUMENTS IN APPLICATION FOR RESIDENCE AUTHORIZATION

1. **Certificate of marriage / de facto marital relation** (certificate of no marriage / marriage / divorce and declaration)

Status	Type of Application	Place of Marriage	Requirement
		(1) Macao SAR	Certificate of latest Macao marriage registration issued within 3 months + declaration of the interested person and his/her spouse (claiming to be maintaining marital relation and cohabiting)
		(2) Mainland China	A. Residence application by "P.R.C. Permit for Travelling to Hong Kong and Macao" holders: Original marriage certificate or notarial
		(3) Hong Kong SAR	Original marriage certificate or true copy of marriage certificate (issued within 6 months) archived at the office of the Registrar in Hong Kong + declaration of the interested person and his/her spouse (claiming to be maintaining marital relation and cohabiting)

		(3) Hong Kong SAR	Original marriage certificate or true copy of marriage certificate (issued within 6 months) archived at the office of the Registrar in Hong Kong + declaration of the interested person and his/her spouse (claiming to be maintaining marital relation and cohabiting)
		(4) Region of Taiwan	Original marriage certificate + household registry transcript / household register of the Region of Taiwan (bearing the marriage registration) issued within 6 months + declaration of the interested person and his/her spouse (claiming to be maintaining marital relation and cohabiting)
		(5) Philippines	Certificate of marriage registration ("certified by diplomatic representation") issued by the National Statistics Office within 6 months + declaration of the interested person and his/her spouse (claiming to be maintaining marital relation and cohabiting)
		(6) Others	A. In cases where the marriage registration system is the same as that in Macao (e.g. Angora, Cape Verde, etc.): Certificate of latest marriage registration ("certified by diplomatic representation") issued within 6 months + declaration of the interested person and his/her spouse (claiming to be maintaining marital relation and cohabiting) B. In other cases: Original marriage certificate ("certified by diplomatic representation" within 6 months) + declaration of the interested person and his/her spouse (claiming to be maintaining marital relation and cohabiting)

Status	Type of Application	Place of Marriage	Requirement

Marriage Residence Authorization Renewal (1) Macao SAR

Certificate of latest Macao marriage registration issued within 3 months + declaration of the interested person and his/her spouse (claiming to be maintaining marital relation and cohabiting)

(2) Philippines

A. Certificate of marriage registration ("certified by diplomatic representation") issued by the National Statistics Office within 6 months + declaration of the interested person and his/her spouse (claiming to be maintaining marital relation and cohabiting)

B. If it is not possible to present the certificate specified in Point A., a request to submit another document can be made and it can be changed to → declaration of the interested person, his/her spouse and 2 witnesses (claiming to be maintaining marital relation and cohabiting)

(3) Others

A. In cases where the marriage registration system is the same as that in Macao (e.g. Angora, Cape Verde, etc.):

(i) Certificate of latest marriage registration ("certified by diplomatic representation") issued within 6 months + declaration of the interested person and his/her spouse (claiming to be maintaining marital relation and cohabiting)

(ii) If it is not possible to present the certificate specified in Point A. (i), a request to submit another document can be made and it can be changed to → declaration of the interested person, his/her spouse and 2 witnesses (claiming to be maintaining marital relation and cohabiting)

B. In other cases:
Declaration of the interested person, his/her spouse and 2 witnesses (claiming to be maintaining marital relation and cohabiting)

Marriage de facto (in accordance with Article 1472 of the Civil Code)

Residence Authorization /

A. Declaration of the interested person, his/her spouse and 2 witnesses (claiming the interested person and his/her partner have been cohabiting voluntarily like husband and wife for at least two years)

B. "Certificate of no marriage" issued within 6 months by the competent authorities of the place of origin (or issued within 3 months in Macao) if both parties have never been married ("certification by diplomatic representation" is required if the certificate is issued in a place other Mainland China, the Macao SAR, the Hong Kong SAR and the Region of Taiwan)

C. Certificate of marriage dissolution if any party had married before:

(i) Issued in the Macao SAR: Certificate of marriage registration bearing the marriage dissolution record (issued within 3 months)

(ii) Issued in the Hong Kong SAR: Divorce certificate (affixed with a confirmation stamp of the competent authorities of Hong Kong within 6 months)

(iii) Issued in the Region of Taiwan: Original divorce certificate + household registry transcript / household register of the Region of Taiwan bearing the divorce record (issued within 6 months)

(iv) Issued in Mainland China: Notarial divorce certificate (issued within 6 months)

(v) Issued in other places: Certificate "certified by diplomatic representation" within 6 months

D. Death certificate of the original spouse if any party is a widow/widower (for details, please see the requirements for death certificate)

	Residence Authorization Renewal	/	Declaration of the interested person, his/her spouse and 2 witnesses (claiming the interested person and his/her partner are still cohabiting voluntarily like husband and wife)

2. Birth / adoption / death certificate and certificate of criminal record

Type of Certificate	Place of Birth / Adoption / Death	Requirement
Birth / Adoption / Death Certificate 【The requirement that the birth certificate with "*" should be issued or certified within 6 months is directed at cases where the birth certificate is required to serve as proof of kindred and cases where the personal information declared before by the interested person is different from that declared in this application】	(1) Macao SAR	Certificate of birth registry / adoption / death issued by the Macao Civil Affairs Registry (within 3 months)
	(2) Mainland China	Notarial birth* / adoption / death certificate issued by the competent authorities of the Mainland China (within 6 months)
	(3) Hong Kong SAR	Certificate of birth registry* / adoption / death issued by the competent authorities of Hong Kong (within 6 months)
	(4) Region of Taiwan	Original birth / adoption / death certificate + household registry transcript / household register of the Region of Taiwan bearing the birth* / adoption / death record (issued within 6 months)
	(5) Others	Birth* / adoption / death certificate issued by the competent authorities of the country ("certified by diplomatic representation" within 6 months)
Certificate of Criminal Record Issued in Latest Place of Domicile 【within 6 months】	(1) Mainland China	"Notarial Certificate of No Criminal Conviction" or "Notarial Certificate of Criminal Record" issued by the competent authorities of the Mainland China
	(2) Hong Kong SAR	"Certificate of No Criminal Conviction" issued by the Hong Kong Police Headquarters
	(3) Region of Taiwan	"Police Criminal Record Certificate" issued by the Police of the Region of Taiwan
	(4) Others	National certificate of criminal record issued by the competent authorities of the country ("certified by diplomatic representation")

*【Remark: (1) The declaration listed in Table 1 serving as proof of (maintaining) marriage or de facto marital relation should contain the declarant's signature which is to be certified by the competent authorities of Macao or another country/region. Otherwise, the interested person, his/her spouse (or partner of marriage de facto) and the two witnesses are required to come **in person**, sign the declaration in the presence of the staff accepting the application and present the original of their*

identification document for verification.

(2) The service unit will provide the template of the declaration listed in Table 1.

(3) The service unit will only collect the copies of the above documents, but the originals have to be exhibited for authentication.

(4) The international practice of having the above foreign documents (not including those of the Mainland China, the Hong Kong SAR and the Region of Taiwan) "certified by diplomatic representation" (or "certified by consular representation") in order to ensure its authenticity is not applicable in the following situations:

i. The document comes with the Apostille certification concluded by the Hague Convention (the Apostille certificate should be issued within 6 months. For details, please see the Hague Convention Abolishing the Requirement for Legalization for Foreign Public Documents, 5 October 1961 at the website: http://www.hcch.net);

ii. The document is issued by a country which has certification-free agreement with Macao (e.g. according to the legal and judicial assistance agreement with Portugal and East Timor, documents and translations issued or certified by the court or competent authorities of these two countries require no certification as long as they are affixed with an official stamp.).

(5) The current procedure of "certification by diplomatic representation" of civil registration certificates issued by the Philippine authorities is as follows:

i. The competent department issuing the certificate verifies the document;

ii. A consular official of the Ministry of Foreign Affairs of the Philippines issues an "Authentication Certificate" to certify that the document is truly issued by the competent authorities of the country;

iii. The Philippine consulate in Macao or the Chinese Embassy in the Philippines certifies the authenticity and legality of the signature of the above Philippine official.

(6) The requirement that foreign documents are accepted only if they are issued within 6 months is stipulated in Article 28 of Macao Law No. 5/98/M.】

VII. PROCEDURES OF APPLICATION FOR AUTHORIZATION TO STAY AND RECEIPT OF RESIDENCE AUTHORIZATION FOR RESIDENCE AUTHORIZATION APPLICATIONS THROUGH MACAO TRADE AND INVESTMENT PROMOTION INSTITUTE

A. Service unit: Foreigners Subdivision of the Immigration Department/ Centro de Serviços da RAEM (Application for " Receipt of Residence Authorization " after renewal application of Residence Authorization is approved only)

B. Charge (or Tax): Free of charge

C. Application approach and procedure

1. Application for Residence Authorization

1.1 Procedure of Application for "Special Authorization to Stay" (35 minutes)

1) Persons who have submitted an application for Residence Authorization to the Macao Trade and Investment Promotion Institute ("IPIM") according to Administrative Regulation No. 3/2005 and need to extend their stay in Macao may come in person

【***Note: i. Unless the minor is represented by the parent, the representative***

his/her valid identification document.

ii. The original should be exhibited for authentication if a copy is submitted.】

(1) A completed application form;

【Note: The application form is available at the respective subdivision and the website of the Public Security Police Force】

(2) A completed "Declaration of Identity";

【Note: i. The Declaration template is available at the respective subdivision and the website of the Public Security Police Force;

ii. The interested person is required to sign the Declaration in the presence of the staff accepting the application for verification. If he/she is not able to show up, the signature on the (completed) Declaration will be authenticated by the competent authorities, or the Declaration is to be completed by a legal representative. The latter should also submit a certified letter of authorization, a copy of the interested person's birth certificate, certificate of marital status (not applicable to unmarried applicants) and a document indicating the interested person's residential address in Macao. To avoid any delay in the issue of the "Residence Receipt" due to incomplete or incorrect information, it is necessary to complete the Declaration with accurate personal information.】

(3) A copy of the interested person's valid passport / travel document (bio data page and observation pages only) or identification document used to apply for "Residence Authorization";

(4) 2 copies of the "Declaration" issued by IPIM (certifying that the application for Residence Authorization is under examination).

2) All 10 fingers of the interested person have to be fingerprinted (applicable to applicants who come in person and applicants under 5 years old are exempted).

3) Applicants who meet the requirements will be granted a maximum of 9 months of "Special Authorization to Stay".

4) Documents (1), a copy of document (3) specified in Point 1) and a copy of the "declaration" issued by IPIM are required if the "Special Authorization to Stay" has to be extended. Generally, the application for extension will be processed according to the "Quality Criterion".

【Note: For details, please see "Special Authorization to Stay" for Applicants of Residence Authorization.】

1.2 Procedure of Application for "Residence Receipt" after Residence Authorization is granted (7 working days of processing time)

1)

Persons who have applied for "Special Authorization to Stay" before

【Note: When collecting the "Residence Receipt", the original of the above document should be exhibited for authentication.】

The application can be made by the interested person or a legal representative by submitting the following:

(3) A recent 1.5-inch, full face, no-hat, white-background photo or digital photo taken free of charge at the Immigration Department;

【Note: i. Unless the minor is represented by the parent, the representative should submit: a. a certified letter of authorization; b. a copy of

(4) Application form of change of personal information or notification of change of address, together with supporting documents such as birth certificate, certificate of marital status or document indicating the residential address, if there is any change in the personal information or address of the interested person.

(1) Copy of the "Approval Notification of Residence Authorization" issued by IPIM;

2) Persons who have never applied for "Special Authorization to Stay"

(2) Copy of the interested person's valid passport / travel document (bio data page

(1) Besides documents (1) – (3) listed in Point 1) of Section 1.2, a completed

(2) *Copy of the interested person's valid passport / travel document (bio data page and observation pages only) or identification document used to apply for "Residence Authorization";*

【Note: When collecting the "Residence Receipt", the original of the above document should be exhibited for authentication.】

(3) *A recent 1.5-inch, full face, no-hat, white-background photo or digital photo taken free of charge at the Immigration Department;*

(4) *Application form of change of personal information or notification of change of address, together with supporting documents such as birth certificate, certificate of marital status or document indicating the residential address, if there is any change in the personal information or address of the interested person.*

2) Persons who have never applied for "Special Authorization to Stay"

(1) *Besides documents (1) – (3) listed in Point 1) of Section 1.2, a completed "Declaration of Identity" should also be submitted;*

【Note: i. The Declaration template is available at the respective subdivision and the website of the Public Security Police Force;

ii. The interested person is required to sign the Declaration in the presence of the staff accepting the application for verification. If he/she is not able to show up, the signature on the (completed) Declaration will be authenticated by the competent authorities, or the Declaration is to be completed by a legal representative. The latter should also submit a certified letter of authorization, a copy of the interested person's birth certificate, certificate of marital status (not applicable to unmarried applicants) and a document indicating the interested person's residential address in Macao. To avoid any delay in the issue of the "Residence Receipt" due to incomplete or incorrect information, it is necessary to complete the Declaration with accurate personal information.】

(2) *All 10 fingers of the interested person have to be fingerprinted (applicable to applicants who come in person and applicants under 5 years old are exempted).*

3) Processing of application

(1) *After receiving the above documents, the authorities will issue an "application acceptance receipt", which includes information such as the date of collection of the "Residence Receipt";*

(2) *After confirmation of receipt of the residence approval letter from IPIM to the Public Security Police Force and the accuracy of the necessary documents and information, the authorities will prepare the "Residence Receipt". The interested person is required to collect the Receipt in person (because he/she has to be fingerprinted on the Receipt).*

(3) *If any error is found in the information during investigation, the authorities will notify the interested person to supplement relevant supporting documents (e.g. birth certificate, marriage certificate, divorce certificate or death certificate of spouse). Therefore, the "Residence Receipt" can only be issued after all necessary documents are submitted and all irregularities are fixed.*

2. Application for Residence Authorization Renewal

2.1 Procedure of Application for "Residence Receipt" after Residence Authorization is renewed (7 working days of processing time)

1) The interested person should submit the renewal application to IPIM before the expiry of Residence Authorization. After receiving the approval notification from IPIM, the interested person or a legal representative may apply for "Residence Receipt" by submitting:

【Note: i.

should submit: a. a certified letter of authorization; b. a copy of his/her valid identification document.

ii. If the interested person cannot appear at the Immigration Department, the parent / guardian or another representative should submit a recent photo of the interested person (1.5-inch, full face, no-hat, white-background, coloured/black-and-white photo);

iii. The original should be exhibited for authentication if a copy is submitted.】

(1) Copy of the "Approval Notification of Residence Authorization Renewal" issued by IPIM;

(2) Copy of the interested person's valid passport / travel document (bio data page and observation pages only) or identification document used to apply for "Residence Authorization" renewal;

【Note: When collecting the "Residence Receipt", the original of the above document should be exhibited for authentication.】

(3) A recent 1.5-inch, full face, no-hat, white-background photo or digital photo taken free of charge at the Immigration Department;

(4) Application form of change of personal information or notification of change of address, together with copies of supporting documents such as birth certificate, certificate of marital status or document indicating the residential address, if there is any change in the personal information or address of the interested person.

2) Processing of application

(1) After receiving the above documents, the authorities will issue an "application acceptance receipt", which includes information such as the date of collection of the "Residence Receipt";

(2) After confirmation of receipt of the renewal approval letter from IPIM to the Public Security Police Force and the accuracy of the necessary documents and information, the authorities will prepare the "Residence Receipt". The interested person is required to collect the Receipt ***in person*** *(because he/she has to be fingerprinted on the Receipt)*

D. Effective date of Residence Authorization For details, please see Point 1 in Section IX

E. Expiry of "Residence Receipt" For details, please see Point 2 in Section IX

F. Expiry of Residence Authorization stated in the "Residence Receipt"
Determined by the competent authorities but no longer than 3 years as stipulated by law

G. Application for "Macao Permanent Resident Identity Card" For details, please see Point 3 in Section IX

H. Change of address For details, please see Point 4 in Section VIII

I. Applicants may make the application by approaching the subdivision concerned and waiting for their turn, or by using our Online Appointment System.

VIII. REMINDER AFTER APPROVAL OF RESIDENCE AUTHORIZATION THROUGH RESIDENTS SUBDIVISION

1. Expiry of "Residence Certificate"

"Residence Certificate" is valid for 90 days from the date of issue. Within this period, the applicant can apply to the Identification Bureau for a "Macao Non-Permanent Resident Identity Card" (persons who have been verified preliminarily by the Bureau to be eligible to be a permanent resident in Macao, i.e. persons whose "P.R.C. Permit for Travelling to Hong Kong and Macao" bears an "R" symbol, may apply to the Bureau for a "Macao Permanent Resident Identity Card"). If no application is made within this period, the "Residence Authorization" will be invalid. Applicants have to apply to the Residents Subdivision for "Residence Authorization" again.

2. Expiry of Residence Authorization stated in the "Residence Certificate"

Target People	Expiry
1. "P.R.C. Permit for Travelling to Hong Kong and Macao" holders	No expiry
2. Minor children who are born outside the Macao S.A.R. and whose parents are Macao permanent residents / "P.R.C. Permit for Travelling to Hong Kong and Macao" holders granted residence in Macao	No expiry
3. Persons of Portuguese nationality	1 year from the date of approval for persons granted Residence Authorization 2 years from the expiry of the last Residence Authorization for persons granted Residence Authorization renewal

Remark*: Only persons of Portuguese nationality are required to apply for Residence Authorization renewal at the Immigration Department.

3. Application for "Macao Permanent Resident Identity Card"

1) After collecting a "Macao Non-Permanent Resident Identity Card" from the Identification Bureau, persons listed in Point 1 (not including those who have been verified preliminarily by the Identification Bureau to be eligible to be a permanent resident in Macao, i.e. persons whose "P.R.C. Permit for Travelling to Hong Kong and Macao" bears an "R" symbol) and Point 2 of the above table do not have to apply to the Immigration Department for Residence Authorization renewal. They can apply to the Identification Bureau for a "Macao Permanent Resident Identity Card" after residing in Macao consecutively for 7 years from the date of approval of the Residence Authorization application.
2) If the persons listed in Point 1 have been verified preliminarily by the Identification Bureau to be eligible to be a permanent resident in Macao, they do not have to apply to the Immigration Department for Residence Authorization renewal. They can apply directly to the Identification Bureau for a "Macao Permanent Resident Identity Card" by presenting the "Residence Certificate" issued to them upon approval of their Residence Authorization application.
3) Persons of Portuguese nationality are required to apply to the Immigration Department for Residence Authorization renewal. They also need to apply to the Identification Bureau for a new "Macao Non-Permanent Resident Identity Card" by presenting the "Residence Certificate" issued to them upon each approval of renewal application. They can apply to the Bureau for a "Macao Permanent Resident Identity Card" after they are granted residence in Macao for 7 consecutive years.

【Note: If the persons listed in Point 2 of the above table and the persons of Portuguese nationality are not recognized as a "Macao permanent resident" by the Identification Bureau for not habitually residing in Macao, their Residence Authorization becomes invalid according to Article 24 of Administrative Regulation No. 5/2003. If they intend to continue residing in Macao, they have to apply to the relevant department for Residence Authorization again.】

4. Changing of Address

Articles 27 and 33 of Administrative Regulation No. 5/2003 stipulates that:

- If there is any change of address, persons who are granted Residence Authorization should notify the Immigration Department within 30 days from the date of occurrence;

notify the Immigration Department within 30 days from the date of occurrence;

- Persons who do not notify the authorities of the change of address will be fined MOP1,000;
- Recidivists will be fined double;
- Recidivism means the same offence is repeated within 1 year from the date of last offence.

【Note: For details, please see "Notice of Change of Address" (Chinese version / Portuguese version only).】

5. Renewal of Residence Authorization after Expiry

Renewal of Residence Authorization after its expiry incurs a fine of MOP20 per overdue day. **(Article 36 of Administrative Regulation No. 5/2003)**

The interested person may still apply for renewal within 180 days after the expiry of the Residence Authorization by paying the above fine. If no renewal application is made within this period, the Residence Authorization becomes invalid immediately and the duration accumulated for obtaining permanent resident status is forfeited, unless there is appropriate proof that the application is hindered for reasons of force majeure. **(Article 23 of Administrative Regulation No. 5/2003)**

IX. REMINDER AFTER APPROVAL OF RESIDENCE AUTHORIZATION THROUGH FOREIGNERS SUBDIVISION

1. Effective date of Residence Authorization

Type of Case	Effective Date
1. MOP20,000 residence tax is mandatory	Date of payment or date of exemption
2. The above residence tax is waived by law	Date of approval by written instructions (unless remarks are stated in the written instructions)

2. Expiry of "Residence Receipt"

1) "Residence Receipt" is valid for 60 days from the date of issue. Within this period, the applicant can apply to the Identification Bureau for a "Macao Non-Permanent Resident Identity Card". If no application is made within this period, the "Residence Receipt" will be invalid. According to Item 3, Term 1, Article 31 of Administrative Regulation No. 5/2003, the fee for the reissue of a "Residence Receipt" at the Immigration Department is MOP200. However, if the "Residence Receipt" is lost, damaged, stolen or expires and reasonable
2) Expiry of Residence Authorization stated in the "Residence Receipt"

Upon approval of the residence application, the interested person will be granted Residence Authorization which expires in 1 year in principle from the effective date. He/she has to apply to the Foreigners Subdivision of the Immigration Department for renewal within 30 days before its expiry date. Each renewed Residence Authorization expires in 2 years.

e.g.: If the interested person is granted Residence Authorization on 1 January 2005 and the Residence Authorization is renewed every 2 years, the expiry of the Residence

Date of Approval by Written Instructions	Expiry Date
1 January 2005 (approval of application)	31 December 2005
Date of approval of renewal application*	31 December 2007
Date of approval of renewal application*	31 December 2009

Date of approval of renewal application*	31 December 2009
Date of approval of renewal application*	31 December 2011

* The date of approval of the renewal application depends on the date the interested person submits the renewal application and the time for examination by the authorities

3. Application for "Macao Permanent Resident Identity Card"

The interested person has to apply to the Immigration Department for Residence Authorization renewal and apply to the Identification Bureau for a new "Macao Non-Permanent Resident Identity Card" by presenting the "Residence Receipt" issued to him/her upon approval of the renewal application. He/she can apply to the Bureau for a "Macao Permanent Resident Identity Card" after he/she is granted residence in Macao for 7 consecutive years.

【Note: If the interested person is not recognized as a "Macao permanent resident" by the Identification Bureau for not habitually residing in Macao, his/her Residence Authorization becomes invalid according to Article 24 of Administrative Regulation No. 5/2003. If he/she intends to continue residing in Macao, he/she has to apply to the relevant department for Residence Authorization again.】

4. Change of Address For details, please see Point 4 in Section VIII

5. Renewal of Residence Authorization after Expiry For details, please see Point 5 in Section VIII

AUTHORIZATION TO ENTER AND STAY

Service	Authorization to Enter and Stay
Introduction (Service Coverage)	Visitors who are not exempted from a visa or entry permit [Note: For details, please see 'Persons Exempted from "Visa" or "Entry Permit"'.] and do not wish to apply for an entry permit (aka "visa-upon-arrival") at the moment they arrive at Macao may appoint a representative to apply to the Immigration Department in advance for "Authorization to Enter and Stay" if no Chinese consulate/embassy or diplomatic representation is located at their place of residence for pre-arrival visa application.
Service Provider	Foreigners Subdivision of the Immigration Department
Application Location	Immigration Department Office Building, Travessa Um do Cais de Pac On, Taipa, Macao
Office Hours	Mon to Thu: 9:00 – 17:45 (Tags dispensed until 17:00) Fri: 9:00 – 17:30 (Same as above) Closed on Sat, Sun and government holidays
Enquiry Methods	In person: the above address Tel: (853) 2872 5488 Fax: (853) 8897 0300 Email: sminfo@fsm.gov.mo

APPLICATION

Transactional Categories	Application
Relevant Service	Entry and Departure of Non-residents
	Extension of "Authorization to Stay"

(Relevant Information)	Extension of "Authorization to Stay" Application for Macao Visa through Chinese Embassy or Consulate Certificate 1. Statement to prove the applicant is in application procedure 2. Certificate to prove the document is copied from the applicant's dossier 3. Certificate issued according to the information in archives
Target Groups and Application Eligibility	Visitors who are not exempted from a visa or entry permit
Application Approach	1. Interested person or a legal representative applying to the Chief Executive through the Immigration Department 2. The legal representative should submit the following: (1) A certified letter of authorization; (2) A copy of his/her valid identification document.
Documents to be Presented	Unless otherwise noted, the original should be exhibited for authentication if a copy is submitted; The copy should be authenticated if the original cannot be exhibited.
Required Documents	Documents to be submitted according to purpose of visit: A. For the purpose of study at a higher institute: 1. A completed application form (format 1); application form 2. Copy of the bio data page of a valid passport/travel document; 3. Document of financial status (e.g. bank statement, bank book of savings account, tax receipt, etc.); 4. Admission document issued by a higher institute in Macao; 5. Reservation document of return flight (if the program taken by the student lasts for less than 6 months). 6. 2 recent 1.5-inch, full-face, no-hat, white-background, coloured or black-and-white photos of the interested person. B. For the purpose of work: 1. A completed application form (format 1); application form 2. Copy of the bio data page of a valid passport/travel document; 3. Copy of employment approval document issued by the Macao 4. 2 recent 1.5-inch, full-face, no-hat, white-background, coloured or black-and-white photos of the interested person.

<table>
<tr><td></td><td>
4. 2 recent 1.5-inch, full-face, no-hat, white-background, coloured or black-and-white photos of the interested person.
C. For the purpose of stay as family of non-resident workers:
1. A completed application form (format 1); application form (format 9) is also required if the application includes family members; [Note: The application form is available at the Subdivision concerned and the website of the Public Security Police Force.]
2. Copy of the bio data page of a valid passport/travel document;
3. Copy of approval notification (i.e. the letter notifying the non-resident worker's reuniting family of the granting of "Special Authorization to Stay"). [Note: The original of this document is not required.]
4. 2 recent 1.5-inch, full-face, no-hat, white-background, coloured or black-and-white photos of the interested person.
D. For the purpose of group tour:
1. Guarantee issued by the travel agency responsible for the group tour and the traveler list;
2. Information of the local travel agency organizing the group tour;
3. Copy of the bio data page of all travelers' valid passport/travel document.
4. 2 recent 1.5-inch, full-face, no-hat, white-background, coloured or black-and-white photos of the interested person.
E. For other purposes (e.g. individual travel, family visit, stay as dependant, residence, etc.):
1. A completed application form (format 1); application form (format 9) is also required if the application includes family members; [Note: The application form is available at the Subdivision concerned and the website of the Public Security Police Force.]
2. Copy of the bio data page and used inside pages of a valid passport/travel document;
3. Document of financial status (e.g. bank statement, bank book of savings account, tax receipt, employment certificate, etc.);
4. Document of transportation to Macao and accommodation arrangement (e.g. round-trip air ticket and hotel reservation receipts, etc.);
5. Proof of purpose of visit (e.g. copy of residence/stay document or Macao Identity Card of kindred in Macao, document of kinship, etc.);
6. Bio data page of travel document that has been used for entry to Macao (if any);
7. Valid entry visa or residence visa/permit of other countries or regions (if any).
8. 2 recent 1.5-inch, full-face, no-hat, white-background, coloured or black-and-white photos of the interested person.
</td></tr>
<tr><td>Charge (or Tax)</td><td><table><tr><td>Type</td><td>Charge</td></tr></table></td></tr>
</table>

<table>
<tr><td></td><td><table><tr><td>Individual</td><td>MOP100</td></tr><tr><td>Family Passport</td><td>MOP200</td></tr><tr><td>Children under the age of 12</td><td>MOP50</td></tr><tr><td>Groups comprised of at least 10 people organized by a single travel manager and presenting a collective travel document</td><td>MOP50 per head</td></tr></table></td></tr>
<tr><td>Time Needed</td><td>Approximately 15 working days [Note: It varies case by case.]</td></tr>
<tr><td>Remark</td><td>1. The "Authorization to Stay" granted in a document in format 2 should be used within 120 days from the date it is granted. Otherwise, the Authorization will expire. The holder may stay in Macao for the period specified in the Authorization (generally 30 days from the date of entry).
2. The holder is entitled to multiple entries within the limit of stay granted upon entry and do not have to apply for another visa or "entry permit" (aka "visa-upon-arrival").</td></tr>
<tr><td>Attachments</td><td>Application form for "Authorization to Enter and Stay"(Format 1)
Family Members of Applicant (format 9)
Sample of "Authorization to Enter and Stay"
Sample of "Entry Permit" (aka "visa-upon-arrival")
Sample of Macao visa</td></tr>
<tr><td>Legislations Website</td><td>1. General Principles of the System of Entry, Stay and Residence Authorization
Law No. 4/2003 [B.O. no. 11 (I), 17/03/2003]
2. Regulations of Entry, Stay and Residence Authorization
Administrative Regulation No. 5/2003 [B.O. no. 15 (I), 14/04/2003]
3. Amendments to the Stipulation on Overstay in the Regulations of Entry, Stay and Residence Authorization
Administrative Regulation No. 14/2014 [B.O. no. 25 (I), 23/06/2014]</td></tr>
</table>

APPLICATION FOR MACAO VISA THROUGH CHINESE EMBASSY OR CONSULATE

<table>
<tr><td>Service</td><td>Application for Macao Visa through Chinese Embassy or Consulate</td></tr>
<tr><td>Introduction (Service Coverage)</td><td>1. Visitors who are not exempted from a "visa" and "entry permit"
2. Starting from 1 July 2010, visitors from the following 6 countries
1. Bangladesh
2. Nepal
3. Nigeria
4. Pakistan</td></tr>
</table>

	4. Pakistan 5. Sri Lanka 6. Vietnam
Service Provider	Embassy and consulate of the People's Republic of China
Other Entity / Agency	Immigration Department
Application Location	Embassy and consulate of the People's Republic of China
Office Hours	Please refer to the website of Chinese embassies and consulates
Enquiry Methods	Please refer to the website of Chinese embassies and consulates

Transactional Category	Application
Relevant Service (Relevant Information)	Entry and Exit of Non-residents Extension of "Authorization to Stay" Authorization to Enter and Stay
Target Groups and Application Eligibility	Visitors who are not exempted from a visa and entry permit
Application Approach	Interested person applying through a Chinese embassy or consulate
Documents to be Presented	Depending on the requirement of the Chinese embassy or consulate The original should be exhibited for authentication if a copy is submitted
Required Documents	Documents to be submitted according to purpose of visit: A. For the purpose of study at a higher institute: 1. A completed application form; [Note: The application form is available at the respective Subdivision and the website of the 2. Copy of the bio data page of a valid passport/travel document; 3. Document of financial status (e.g. bank statement, bank book of savings account, tax receipt, etc.); 4. Admission document issued by a higher institute in Macao; 5. Reservation document of return flight (if the program taken by the student lasts for less than 6 months). B. For the purpose of work: 1. A completed application form; [Note: The application form is available at the respective Subdivision and the website of the 2. Copy of the bio data page of a valid passport/travel document; 3. Copy of employment approval document issued by the Macao authorities (i.e. the application or renewal application of C. For the purpose of stay as family of non-resident workers: 1. A completed application form; [Note: The application form is available at the respective Subdivision and the website of the

	available at the respective Subdivision and the website of the Public Security Police Force.] 2. Copy of the bio data page of a valid passport/travel document; 3. Copy of approval notification (i.e. the letter notifying the non-resident worker's reuniting family of the granting of "Special Authorization to Stay"). [Note: The original of this document is not required.] D. For the purpose of group tour: 1. Letter of guarantee by the travel agency organizing the tour group and name list of the tour members; 2. Information of the local travel agency organizing the group tour; 3. Copy of the bio data page of all travelers' valid passport/travel document. E. For other purposes (e.g. individual travel, family visit, stay as dependant, residence, etc.): 1. A completed application form; [Note: The application form is available at the respective Subdivision and the website of the Public Security Police Force.] 2. Copy of the bio data page and used inside pages of a valid passport/travel document; 3. Document of financial status (e.g. bank statement, bank book of savings account, tax receipt, employment certificate, etc.); 4. Document of transportation to Macao and accommodation arrangement (e.g. round-trip air ticket and hotel reservation receipts, etc.); 5. Proof of purpose of visit (e.g. copy of residence/stay document or Macao Identity Card of kindred in Macao, document of kinship, etc.); 6. Travel documents affixed with Macao entry and exit stamps (if any); 7. Valid entry visa or residence visa/permit of other countries or regions (if any).
Supplementary Document	Depending on the requirement of the Chinese embassy or consulate
Charge (or Tax)	1. Application fee: USD30 2. Additional charge: (1) Communication fee of relating to the Macao Immigration Department: USD20 (2) Express: USD20 (3) Extra express: USD30
Time Needed	Normal: 5 working days (applications that do not have to be related to the Macao Immigration Department) Express: 3 working days (only applications that do not have to be related to the Macao Immigration Department)
	Extra express: Same day or next working day (only applications that do not have to be related to the Macao Immigration Department)

	Extra express: Same day or next working day (only applications that do not have to be related to the Macao Immigration Department) [Note: Processing time starts after all necessary documents are properly submitted.]
Remark	1. Types of Macao visa: (1) Diplomatic visa; (2) Official visa; (3) Ordinary visa. 2. Expiry of Macao visa: (1) Valid for 1 entry within 3 months, 14 days of stay per entry; (2) Valid for 2 entries within 3 months, 14 days of stay per entry; (3) Valid for multiple entries within 6 months, 14 days of stay per entry.
Attachment	Sample of Macao visa
Form	Application Form for Macao visa
Legislations Website	1. General Principles of the System of Entry, Stay and Residence Authorization Law No. 4/2003 [B.O. no. 11 (I), 17/03/2003] 2. Regulations of Entry, Stay and Residence Authorization Administrative Regulation No. 5/2003 [B.O. no. 15 (I), 14/04/2003] 3. Amendments to the Stipulation on Overstay in the Regulations of Entry, Stay and Residence Authorization Administrative Regulation No. 14/2014 [B.O. no. 25 (I), 23/06/2014] 4. Stipulation of application for pre-arrival visa by nationals of certain countries Chief Exective's Written Instruction No. 165/2010 [B.O. no. 22 (I), 31/05/2010]

EXTENSION OF "AUTHORIZATION TO STAY"

Service	Extension of "Authorization to Stay"
Introduction (Service Coverage)	Non-residents are required to apply for "ordinary extension" or "exceptional extension" according to Articles 11 and 12 of Administrative Regulation No. 5/2003 if they wish to extend their "Authorization to Stay".
Service Provider	Foreigners Subdivision of the Immigration Department
Application Location	Immigration Department Office Building, Travessa Um do Cais de Pac On, Taipa, Macao
Office Hours	Mon to Thu: 9:00 – 17:45 (Tags dispensed until 17:00) Fri: 9:00 – 17:30 (Same as above) Closed on Sat, Sun and government holidays
Enquiry Methods	In the above address Tel: (853) 2872 5488 Fax: (853) 8897 0300

	Fax:	(853) 8897 0300
	Email:	sminfo@fsm.gov.mo
	Online:	Inquiry system of Progress of Application for Extension of "Authorization to Stay"

Ordinary Extension (for less than 90 days)	**Exceptional Extension**

Transactional Category	Application (in our performance pledges)
Relevant Service (Relevant Information)	Authorization to Enter and Stay Application for Macao Visa through Chinese Embassy or Consulate "Special Authorization to Stay" for Non-resident Students Certificate
Target Groups and Application Eligibility	A. Target People Individuals who need to extend their "Authorization to Stay" for not more than 90 days B. Requirement Meeting the stipulations relevant to the system of entry, stay
Application Approach	1. The interested person or a legal representative making the application 5 days before the expiry of the "Authorization to Stay"; 2. The legal representative should submit the following: 1) A certified letter of authorization:
Document Must be Presented	The original should be exhibited for authentication if a copy is submitted
Required Documents	1. A completed application form; 2. Copy of the interested person's valid passport/travel

	identification document used for stay in Macao; 3. Document which can confirm the justification for the application (e.g. document of kinship between the interested person and his/her kindred in Macao, medical certificate, Macao identity card of a kindred in Macao, etc.).
Charge (or Tax)	Free of charge
Quality Criterion	1 working day [Please see Remark 3.]
Remark	1. The interested person is required to bring along his/her valid passport / travel document / identification document based 2. Penalty for overstay 1) According to Administrative Regulation No. 14/2014 'Amendments to the Provision on Overstay in the 2) According to Law No. 6/2004, persons who are considered to be illegal immigrants will be deported and 3. "Quality Criterion" refers to the time of processing required by service units (excluding time of waiting in a queue)

	confirmed that all the required documents had been correctly prepared.
Form	Application Form for Extension of Authorization to Stay
Legislations Website	1. General Principles of the System of Entry, Stay and Residence Authorization Law No. 4/2003 [B.O. no. 11 (I), 17/03/2003] 2. Regulations of Entry, Stay and Residence Authorization Administrative Regulation No. 5/2003 [B.O. no. 15 (I), 14/04/2003] 3. Amendments to the Stipulation on Overstay in the Regulations of Entry, Stay and Residence Authorization Administrative Regulation No. 14/2014 [B.O. no. 25 (I), 23/06/2014]

"SPECIAL AUTHORIZATION TO STAY" FOR NON-RESIDENT STUDENTS

Service	"Special Authorization to Stay" for Non-resident Students
Introduction (Service Coverage)	1. Mainland students who intend to take a higher education program at a higher institute in Macao are required to apply for "Special Authorization to Stay" (aka "Authorization to Stay - student type") and renewal of the Authorization according to Terms 1-4, Article 8 of Law No. 4/2003 in order to legally stay in Macao for study. 2. Students from other countries/regions and studying at a higher institute in Macao may apply for "Special Authorization to Stay" (aka "Authorization to Stay - student type") and renewal of the Authorization according to Terms 1-4, Article 8 of Law No. 4/2003 if the limit of stay granted in the original "Authorization to Stay" is not long enough for them to legally stay in Macao for study.
Service Provider	Foreigners Subdivision of the Immigration Department
Application Location	Immigration Department Office Building, Travessa Um do Cais de Pac On, Taipa, Macao
Office Hours	Mon to Thu: 9:00 – 17:45 (Tags dispensed until 17:00) Fri: 9:00 – 17:30 (Same as above) Closed on Sat, Sun and government holidays
Enquiry Methods	In person: the above address Tel: (853) 2872 5488 Fax: (853) 8897 0300 Email: sminfo@fsm.gov.mo Online: Inquiry System of Progress of Application for "Special Authorization to Stay" for Non-resident Students

Application	Renewal	Cancellation

Relevant Service (Relevant Information)	Extension of "Authorization to Stay" Certificate 1. Statement to prove the applicant is in application procedure 2. Certificate to prove the document is copied from the applicant's dossier 3. Certificate of record of "Special Authorization to Stay" for foreign students 4. Certificate issued according to the information in archives
Target Groups and Application Eligibility	I. Target Group Non-resident students taking a higher education program in Macao II. Application Eligibility 1. Meeting the stipulations relevant to the system of entry, stay and residence authorization in Macao (e.g. 1. Meeting the stipulations relevant to the system of entry, stay and residence authorization in Macao and 2. Not in a lawfully restricted status. [Note: For reference, please see 'Remark']) 2. Admitted to a higher institute in Macao 3. Limit of stay granted in original "Authorization to Stay" not long enough for the student to legally stay in Macao until the program ends.
Application Approach	1. Mainland Students: Mainland students holding a "P.R.C. Permit for Travelling to and from Hong Kong and Macao" are required to apply for "Authorization to stay - student type" as soon as they enter Macao with "Type D – Stay" endorsement and within the limit of stay granted upon their first entry (a maximum of 90 days). [For details, please see Point I in "Remark"] 2. Students from other countries/regions: They should make the application in person 20 days before the expiry of the "Authorization to Stay".
Documents to be Presented	The original should be exhibited for authentication if a copy is submitted
	I. Documents to be submitted: 1. A completed application form for "Special Authorization to Stay"; II. Follow-up procedure: 1. After submitting all the necessary documents and receiving a "receipt", the interested person (or institute representative) is required to come for inquiry of the application result on the date specified on the "receipt". For inquiry of the progress of the application, the interested person may refer to 'Inquiry System of

and the "endorsement" for book style "P.R.C. Permit for Travelling to and from Hong Kong and Macao" users), and the copy of Arrival Card for the latest entry to Macao;

(2) Students from other countries/regions – A copy of a valid passport/travel document (bio data page only), and the Arrival Card for the latest entry to Macao.

II. Follow-up procedure:

1. After submitting all the necessary documents and receiving a "receipt", the interested person (or institute representative) is required to come for inquiry of the application result on the date specified on the "receipt". For inquiry of the progress of the application, the interested person may refer to 'Inquiry System of Progress of Application for "Special Authorization to Stay" for Non-resident Students' on our website. He/she can

2. Individual application:

   (1) The interested person is required to bring along the following documents for inquiry of the application result:

   A. Application acceptance receipt

   B. Valid passport/travel document or "P.R.C. Permit for Travelling to and from Hong Kong and Macao" (together with "Type D – Stay" endorsement)

3. Group application by institute:

The institute can make the application on behalf of the students so that their visits to the Immigration Department can be minimized. The procedure is as follows:

(1) The institute sends an official letter to the respective Subdivision, providing the personal information of the institute representative;

(2) When making the application, the institute representative is required to:

	[Note: If the institute adopts the approach of group application to facilitate the students, it should supervise the whole procedure, ensuring that its representative can collect all the documents of the students concerned and submit them to the respective Subdivision, as well as returning the documents to the respective student upon completion of the procedure.]
Charge (or Tax)	Free of charge
Processing Time	30 days [Note: It is time from the next working day following the day when the service unit received and confirmed that all the required documents had been correctly prepared.]
	I. Time limit for application for "Authorization to Stay - student type" by mainland students 1. Starting from 8 February 2010, mainland students holding a "P.R.C. Permit for Travelling to and from Hong Kong and Macao" are required to apply for "Authorization to Stay - student type" as soon as they enter Macao with 2. Mainland students who entered Macao with "Type D – Stay" endorsement before 8 February 2010 but have not applied for (or completed the application procedure of) "Authorization to Stay - student type" are also required to [Note: Students who do not apply to the Foreigners Subdivision within their limit of stay or on the date specified in the notification letter issued at the border checkpoint will be considered to be overstayers and liable to penalty.] II. Expiry of "Slip of Authorization to Stay - student type" 1 For program of studies that lasts for less than a year: The "Slip of Authorization to Stay - student type" will expire on the last day of the program 2. For program of studies that lasts for more than a year until a date before December 31 of the following year: The "Slip of Authorization to Stay - student type" will expire on the last day of the program 3 For program of studies that lasts for more than a year until a date after December 31 of the following year: [Note: (1) The expiry date of the above "Authorization to Stay - student type" should not exceed that of the "P.R.C. Permit for Travelling to and from Hong Kong and Macao" and "Type D – Stay" endorsement of mainland students. For other students, the expiry date of the above "Authorization to Stay - student type" is restricted to 30 days before the expiry of their passport/travel document and entry/return permit (Article 9 of Administrative Regulation No. 5/2003). (2) Students whose passport / travel document or "P.R.C. Permit for Travelling to and from Hong Kong and Macao" (together with the "Type D – Stay" endorsement) expires earlier and so are not granted "Authorization to Stay - student type" that expires as mentioned above are required to submit copies of the relevant documents to the Foreigners Subdivision for reposition (i.e. issuing the "Slip of Authorization to Stay - student type" which expires as mentioned above) as soon as they finish renewing the document.] III. Extension of stay If a student needs to continue his/her stay in Macao for personal reason after completing the program, he/she may apply for extension of the "Authorization to Stay". [For details, please see the extension section] IV. Multiples entries 1. Students can enjoy multiple entries before the expiry of the temporary "Authorization to Stay" or "Authorization to Stay - student type" granted by our Department. (1) Persons who are exempted from a "visa" or "entry permit" [for details, please see Section VII of "Entry and Departure of Non-residents"] are allowed to stay until the expiry of that "Authorization to Stay" whenever they re-enter Macao, except for persons

expire on December 31 of the following year [Application for renewal is required. For details, please see the Renewal Section of "Special Authorization to Stay" (for Non-resident Students)]

[Note:

(1) The expiry date of the above "Authorization to Stay - student type" should not exceed that of the "P.R.C. Permit for Travelling to and from Hong Kong and Macao" and "Type D – Stay" endorsement of mainland students. For other students, the expiry date of the above "Authorization to Stay - student type" is restricted to 30 days before the expiry of their passport/travel document and entry/return permit (Article 9 of Administrative Regulation No. 5/2003).

(2) Students whose passport / travel document or "P.R.C. Permit for Travelling to and from Hong Kong and Macao" (together with the "Type D – Stay" endorsement) expires earlier and so are not granted "Authorization to Stay - student type" that expires as mentioned above are required to submit copies of the relevant documents to the Foreigners Subdivision for reposition (i.e. issuing the "Slip of Authorization to Stay - student type" which expires as mentioned above) as soon as they finish renewing the document.]

III. Extension of stay

If a student needs to continue his/her stay in Macao for personal reason after completing the program, he/she may apply for extension of the "Authorization to Stay". [For details, please see the extension section]

IV. Multiples entries

1. Students can enjoy multiple entries before the expiry of the temporary "Authorization to Stay" or "Authorization to Stay - student type" granted by our Department.

(1) Persons who are exempted from a "visa" or "entry permit" [for details, please see Section VII of "Entry and Departure of Non-residents"] are allowed to stay until the expiry of that "Authorization to Stay" whenever they re-enter Macao, except for persons

2. Mainland students who submit an application for "Authorization to Stay - student type" will have their "P.R.C. Permit for Travelling to and from Hong Kong and Macao" be granted a temporary "Authorization to Stay". Upon approval of their application, "Authorization to Stay

| | Macao" be granted a temporary "Authorization to Stay". Upon approval of their application, "Authorization to Stay - student type" will be granted. These students can enjoy multiple entries until the expiry of that "Authorization to Stay".
V. Reminders to students granted "Authorization to Stay - student type"
1. Class attendance should meet the institute requirement, or it may result in invalidation of the "Authorization to Stay - student type".
2. If the student drops out, suspends schooling or finishes his/her studies early, he/she will have to:
(1) Leave Macao on or before the first government working day following the completion of the school leaving procedure.
(2) Cancel his/her original "Special Authorization to Stay" in person at the Foreigners Subdivision of our Department and apply for ordinary "Authorization to Stay" for the purpose of extension of stay and single departure from Macao during office hours on the first government working day following the completion of the school leaving procedure, in case he/she needs to extend his/her limit of stay in Macao.
(3) Become an "overstayer" in case he/she remains in Macao on and after the second government working day following our receipt of the formal notification from the higher institute. Unless he/she possesses a valid 'endorsement', he/she is likely to be refused re-entry to Macao.
For example: Student A completes the school leaving procedure on 2 January 2015 (Friday). He/she should leave Macao on or before 5 January 2015 (Monday). If not, he/she becomes an 'overstayer' starting from 6 January 2015 (Tuesday). If Student A needs to extend his/her limit of stay in Macao, he/she should cancel the original "Special Authorization to Stay" in person at our Foreigners Subdivision and apply for ordinary "Authorization to Stay" during office hours on 5 January 2015 (Monday).
3. If the student intends to transfer to another higher institute, he/she should also cancel the "Authorization to Stay - student type" as mentioned above at the Foreigners Subdivision and apply for new "Authorization to Stay - student type" before the expiry of the ordinary "Authorization to Stay" by submitting proof of enrollment for a new program.
VI. Penalty for overstay
1. According to Administrative Regulation No. 14/2014 'Amendments to the Provision on Overstay in the 《Regulations of the Entry, Stay and Residence Authorization》', persons who still stay in the Macao SAR but not over 30 days after the expiry of the authorization |

	granted is fined MOP500 per overdue day from 9/7/2014. The violators are required to pay the fine immediately after they are arrested or report themselves to the police. The above mentioned penalty regulation is not applicable to those who have overstayed in Macao within one year. Those will be considered to be illegal immigrants if they do not pay the fine and the penalty regulation is not applicable to them. Moreover, they cannot make any application for Residence Authorization, extension of Authorization to Stay and Authorization to Stay for Non-resident Workers within two years to the Immigration Department. 2. According to Law No. 6/2004, persons who are considered to be illegal immigrants will be deported and interdicted from entry to the Macao SAR for the period indicated in the deportation order.
Form	Application Form for Special Authorization to Stay
Legislations Website	1. General Principles of the System of Entry, Stay and Residence Authorization Law No. 4/2003 [B.O. no. 11 (I), 17/03/2003] 2. Regulations of Entry, Stay and Residence Authorization Administrative Regulation No. 5/2003 [B.O. no. 15 (I), 14/04/2003] 3. Amendments to the Stipulation on Overstay in the Regulations of Entry, Stay and Residence Authorization Administrative Regulation No. 14/2014 [B.O. no. 25 (I), 23/06/2014]

"SPECIAL AUTHORIZATION TO STAY" FOR REUNITING KINDRED OF NON-RESIDENT WORKERS

Service	"Special Authorization to Stay" for Reuniting Kindred of Non-resident Workers
Introduction (Service Coverage)	Application for "Special Authorization to Stay" to reuniting kindred of non-resident workers specified in Term 5, Article 8 of Law No. 4/2003, as well as renew and cancel the Special Authorization.
Service Provider	Non-resident Workers Subdivision of the Immigration Department
Other Entity / Agency	Human Resources Office
Application Location	Immigration Department Office Building, Travessa Um do Cais de Pac On, Taipa, Macao
Office Hours	Mon to Thu: 9:00 – 17:45 (Tags dispensed until 16:30) Fri: 9:00 – 17:30 (Same as above) Closed on Sat, Sun and government holidays
Enquiry Methods	In the above address Tel: (853) 2872 5488 Fax: (853) 8897 0300 Email: sminfo@fsm.gov.mo Website: Inquiry System of Progress of Application for "Special

	resident Workers

Transactional Category	Application
Relevant Service (Relevant Information)	Non-resident Worker's Identification Card ("Non-resident Worker's Card" for short) Certificate 1. Statement to prove the applicant is in application procedure 2. Certificate to prove the document is copied from the applicant's dossier 3. Certificate of limit of stay granted in "Authorization to Stay" 4. Other certificates issued based on information in dossier
Target Groups and Application Eligibility	A. Target People Non-resident workers and their reuniting kindred B. Requirement 1. Non-resident workers meeting the stipulation in Term 5, Article 8 of Law No. 4/2003, i.e. with specific qualification and beneficial to the Macao SAR; 2. Reuniting kindred of non-resident workers meeting the stipulation: (1) relevant to the system of entry, stay and residence authorization in Macao (e.g. 1. in possession of a valid passport / travel document / identification document for entry to and departure from Macao; and 2. not in a lawfully restricted status); (2) in Article 2 of Administrative Regulation No. 5/2003, belonging to any of the following category: i. spouse; ii. individual having de facto marital relation and fulfilling the requirement specified in Article 1472 of the Civil Code; iii. first-level lineal ascendants of the non-resident worker and his/her spouse; iv. first-level lineal minor descendants and adopted minors of the non-resident worker and his/her spouse; v. minors and consanguinities proved to be supported by the non-resident worker.
Application Approach	Applicant 1. Non-resident worker; 2. Reuniting kindred of a non-resident worker who are planning to stay in Macao; 3. Legal representative of the above two types of applicant. [Note: The representative should submit: 1. a certified letter of authorization; 2. a copy of his/her valid identification document (the original should be exhibited for authentication).]

	Macao SAR" are eligible. Besides, it takes a relatively long period for examination as we have to consult the Human Resources Office. Therefore, in order to avoid any inconvenience aroused from the limited validity of the "Authorization to Stay" granted to visitors, the reuniting kindred concerned should come to Macao only after the "Special Authorization to Stay" is granted.
Documents to be Presented	The original should be exhibited for authentication if a copy is submitted
Application Procedures and Necessary Documents	A. After a non-resident worker is granted "Temporary Authorization to Stay for Non-resident Workers", the respective Subdivision will start to accept applications for "Special Authorization to Stay" by his/her reuniting kindred. The following documents should be submitted: 1. A completed application form for "Special Authorization to Stay"; 2. Declaration signed by the non-resident worker to express consent to the application (if the application is made by the dependant of the non-resident worker); 3. Copy of "Non-resident Worker's Identification Card" <"Non-resident Worker's Card" for short> / "Revenue Receipt" / "Authorization to Stay for Non-resident Workers" application form which passes the primary examination; 4. 2 copies of the non-resident worker's valid passport / travel document / P.R.C. Permit for travelling to and from Hong Kong and Macao ("Two-way Exit Permit" for short) (bio data page only and the inside page containing "Type D-Stay endorsement" for

	Workers" application form which passes the primary examination; (2) Copy of the spouse's valid passport / travel document / "Two-way Exit Permit" (Bio data page only and the inside page containing "Type D-Stay endorsement" for "Two-way Exit Permit" holders, while the electric "Two-way Exit Permit" in card type holders shall also submit the back copy containing "Type D-Stay endorsement") or identification document used for entry to and departure from Macao; (3) Copy of pay slip or equivalent document of the last 3 months (if the non-resident worker is hired through unnamed "employment authorization"). B. After all the necessary documents are submitted, the Subdivision will issue an "Application Acceptance Receipt" to the applicant. The applicant can come or use the 'Inquiry System of Progress of Application for "Special Authorization to Stay" for Reuniting Kindred of Non-resident Workers' for inquiry of the progress and result of the application on the date specified on the "Receipt" for inquiry of the progress and result of the application. The Subdivision also send the application result through SMS to persons who have chosen this service. C. If the application is approved, the reuniting kindred is required to go to the Subdivision for fingerprinting (persons under 5 years old are exempted) and submit the following: 1. Reuniting kindred's valid passport / travel document / "Two-way Exit Permit" (Bio data page only and the inside page containing "Type D-Stay endorsement" for "Two-way Exit Permit" holders, while the electric "Two-way Exit Permit" in card type holders shall also submit the back copy containing "Type D-Stay endorsement") or identification document used for entry to and departure from Macao and a copy of it; 2. 2 recent colour photos of 1.5-inch, full face, no-hat, white-background. D. Upon completion of the procedure specified in Point C, the reuniting kindred will immediately be granted "Special Authorization to Stay".
Charge (or Tax)	Free of charge
Time Needed	Approximately 50 days (Processing time starts from the first working day after the service unit receives all the necessary documents and confirms nothing is missing)
Remark	A. Generally, the expiry of the "Special Authorization to Stay" granted to the reuniting kindred is the same as that of the "Authorization to Stay for Non-resident Worker" (and of the "Non-resident Worker's Card"). However, the "Special Authorization to Stay" granted to minor reuniting kindred expires on the day he/she becomes an adult.

<table>
<tr><td></td><td>C. After the Subdivision receives the notification letter of employment termination or employment authorization revocation, the relevant "Authorization to Stay for Non-resident Worker" (including the "Non-resident Worker's Card") and the reuniting kindred's "Special Authorization to Stay" will be revoked (even though the Authorization is not expiring). Under such circumstances, if the non-resident worker and his/her reuniting kindred continue to stay in Macao without getting another "Authorization to Stay", they will be considered to be overstaying starting from the day following the revocation of the original "Authorization to Stay".
Therefore, as soon as the non-resident worker acknowledges the employment termination or employment authorization revocation, he/she should go to the Subdivision immediately with his/her reuniting kindred for certain cancellation procedure. Upon completion of the procedure, they will be granted another "Authorization to Stay" for departure arrangement for not more than 10 days (if necessary).
D. The dependants of a non-resident worker are prohibited from working in Macao (except otherwise stipulated in the law).

E. Penalty for overstay

1. According to Administrative Regulation No. 14/2014 'Amendments to the Provision on Overstay in the《 Regulations of the Entry, Stay and Residence Authorization》', persons who still stay in the Macao SAR but not over 30 days after the expiry of the authorization granted is fined MOP500 per overdue day from 9/7/2014. The violators are required to pay the fine immediately after they are arrested or report themselves to the police. The above mentioned penalty regulation is not applicable to those who have overstayed in Macao within one year. Those will be considered to be illegal immigrants if they do not pay the fine and the penalty regulation is not applicable to them. Moreover, they cannot make any application for Residence Authorization, extension of Authorization to Stay and Authorization to Stay for Non-resident Workers within two years to the Immigration Department.
2. According to Law No. 6/2004, persons who are considered to be illegal immigrants will be deported and interdicted from entry to the Macao SAR for the period indicated in the deportation order.
F. Once non-resident workers / reuniting kindred of non-resident workers / "Special Stay Card" holders changed the valid passport / travel document / "Two-way Exit Permit" / identification document, have to update the related information in the executing Subdivision.</td></tr>
<tr><td>Attachment</td><td>"Acceptance Standard for Documents"</td></tr>
<tr><td>Forms</td><td>Application Form for Renewal of "Special Authorization to Stay" for Reuniting Kindred of Non-resident Workers</td></tr>
</table>

	Format A2 (to use for declare and sign by applicant and his/ her spouse/ de facto marital partner, as well as sign by two attesters.) Format B1 (to use for declare and sign by applicant or his/ her spouse/ de facto marital partner.) Format B2 (to use for declare and sign by applicant and his/ her spouse/ de facto marital partner.)
Legislations Website	1. Law of the Employment of Non-resident Workers Law No. 21/2009〔 B.O. no. 43 (I), 27/10/2009.〕 2. Regulation of the Law of the Employment of Non-resident Workers Administrative Regulation No. 8/2010〔 B.O. no. 16 (I), 19/04/2010.〕 3. Approval of the Design of the Non-resident Worker's Identification Card Chief Executive's Written Instruction No. 197/2010〔 B.O. no. 27 (I), 05/07/2010.〕 4. Regulation of Prohibition of Illegal Employment Administrative Regulation No. 17/2004〔 B.O. no. 24 (I), 14/06/2004.〕 5. General Principles of the System of Entry, Stay and Residence Authorization Law No. 4/2003〔 B.O. no. 11 (I), 17/03/2003.〕 6. Regulations of Entry, Stay and Residence Authorization Administrative Regulation No. 5/2003〔 B.O. no. 15 (I), 14/04/2003.〕 7. Amendments to the Stipulation on Overstay in the Regulations of Entry, Stay and Residence Authorization Administrative Regulation No. 14/2014〔 B.O. no. 25 (I), 23/06/2014.〕 8. Law of Illegal Immigration, Illegal Stay and Deportation Law No. 6/2004〔 B.O. no. 31 (I), 02/08/2004.〕

NON-RESIDENT WORKER'S IDENTIFICATION CARD ("NON-RESIDENT WORKER'S CARD" FOR SHORT)

Service	Non-resident Worker's Identification Card
Introduction (Service Coverage)	To issue, renew, reissue, replace and cancel "Non-resident Worker's Identification Card" ("Non-resident Worker's Card" for short) for non-residents who are employed by Macao employers with valid "employment authorization" ("non-resident workers" for short) and non-residents who engage in activities for their own benefits in Macao ("self-employed" for short).

	the Human Resources Office's 'employment authorization'. This is because we had been issuing the "Non-resident Worker's Card" based on the information indicated in their 'employment authorization' and we should ensure the consistency between the information in their 'employment authorization' and that in the fields of employing entity and occupation on the "Non-resident Worker's Card". [Location of the Fields of Employing Entity and Occupation] 2. Therefore, if an employer (or employee) requests both Chinese and Portuguese languages or the other official language (e.g. request for Portuguese while the 'employment authorization' is in Chinese) to be printed in the fields of employing entity and occupation on the "Non-resident Worker's Card" while the Human Resources Office's 'employment authorization' shows the information in only one language (Chinese or Portuguese), the employer should make the request to the Human Resources Office first and have the 'employment authorization' updated before we proceed accordingly.
Service Provider	Non-resident Workers Subdivision of the Immigration Department
Other Entity / Agency	Human Resources Office
Application Location	Immigration Department Office Building, Travessa Um do Cais de Pac On, Taipa, Macao
Office Hours	Mon to Thu: 9:00 – 17:45 (Tags dispensed until 16:30) Fri: 9:00 – 17:30 (Same as above) Closed on Sat, Sun and government holidays
Enquiry Methods	In person: the above address Tel: (853) 2872 5488 Fax: (853) 8897 0300 Email: sminfo@fsm.gov.mo Website: • Inquiry System of Progress of Application for "Authorization to Stay for Non-resident Workers" in the Preliminary and Initial Examination Phases (Applicable to non-professional workers and domestic helpers from the Mainland of China) http://www.fsm.gov.mo/psp/sm/tnr/enq.asp • Inquiry System of Date of Collection of "Non-resident Worker's Identification Card" http://www.fsm.gov.mo/psp/sm/tnr2/enq.asp • Inquiry System of Progress of Application for Renewal of "Authorization to Stay for Non-resident Workers" (Applicable to non-professional workers and domestic helpers from the Mainland of China) http://www.fsm.gov.mo/psp/sm/tnr3/enq.asp • Inquiry System of Archived Digital Copy of Non-resident Worker's Identification Card https://www.fsm.gov.mo/PSP/ImageQuery/Default.aspx • Inquiry System of Invalidity of "Employment Authorization" (Article 12 of Law No. 21/2009) http://www.fsm.gov.mo/psp/tnr4/enq.asp

Online Appointment	Professional workers and domestic helpers (from countries and regions other than Mainland China) may take the application by using our Online Appointment System. Click here for online appointment.

Transactional Category	Issue
Relevant Service (Relevant Information)	"Special Authorization to Stay" for Reuniting Kindred of Non-resident Workers Certificate 1. Declaration of application in process 2. Certificate of document copied from dossier 3. Certificate of China resident's employment status in Macao 4. Certificate of limit of stay granted in "Authorization to Stay" 5. Other certificates issued based on information in dossier Registration for Automated Passenger Clearance System (e-Channel) for Non-residents
Target Groups and Application Eligibility	A. Target Groups "Non-resident workers", their employers and the "self-employed" B. Application Eligibility 1. Employers possessing valid "employment authorization"; 2. "Non-resident workers" and the "self-employed" meeting the stipulation relevant to the system of entry, stay and residence authorization in Macao (e.g. 1. in possession of a valid passport/travel document/identification document for entry to and departure from Macao; and 2. not in a lawfully restricted status).
Application Approach	Applicant: 1. Application for "Non-resident Worker's Card" can be made by any one of the following persons or entities: (1) Employer; (2) Licensed employment agency appointed by the employer; [Note: For details, please see the Labour Affairs Bureau's website at http://www.dsal.gov.mo/.] (3) "Self-employed"; (4) Legal representative of persons listed in Points (1) and (3). [Note: The legal representative should submit the following: 1. A certified letter of authorization; 2. Copy of his/her valid identification document (the original should be exhibited for authentication).]
Documents to be Presented	The original should be exhibited for authentication if a copy is submitted
Application Procedures and Necessary Documents	I. Professional, non-professional workers and domestic helpers from Mainland China A. Preliminary Examination 1. The following documents should be submitted to the Subdivision concerned: (1) A completed application form for "Authorization to Stay for Non-resident Workers" (from Mainland China) ("application form" for short) and 2 copies of it;

	(2) 2 recent colour photos of 1.5-inch, full face, no-hat, white-background; (3) Copy of the written instruction and official notification regarding the "employment authorization". For the person who employs domestic helper, the following documents are required to submit: (1) Copy of the joint statement of labour cooperation; (2) Copy of employer's valid identification document (the employer's signature on the copy of his/her identification document is required if he/she is also a non-resident worker or a "Special Stay Permit" holder). 2. The applicant may inquire about the result through the "Inquiry System of Progress of Application for "Authorization to Stay for Non-resident Workers" in the Preliminary and Initial Examination Phases (applicable to non-professional workers and domestic helpers from Mainland China)", or by presenting the "receipt of application" in person (or through the employer or employment agency) to the Subdivision around 5 working days after the above documents are properly submitted. If the application is approved, the applicant is required to collect from the Subdivision the preliminarily approved "application form" and the relevant copies, with which he/she can apply to the border control department in the Mainland for a "P.R.C. Permit for Travelling to and from Hong Kong and Macao" (hereafter call "Two-way Exit Permit" for short) and an endorsement for the "non-resident worker". Then the applicant may proceed to the formal examination procedures. B. Formal Examination 1. After the Preliminary Examination result is out, the Subdivision concerned will conduct a detailed examination of the application. The "non-resident workers" should go to the Subdivision concerned in person for inquiry of the examination result after he/she enters Macao with "Two-way Exit Permit" and "type (D) Stay Endorsement". 2. If it is approved, the application for "Authorization to stay for the Non-resident Workers" can enter Final Examination directly. (1) The "non-resident workers" should go to the

	iv. A completed "Declaration of Identification"; v. Copy of other certificates or documents (specifically named in the "employment authorization" written instruction). (2) Upon completion of the procedure, the Subdivision will issue a "Revenue Receipt" and grant "Authorization to Stay for Non-resident Workers" (which expires on the same date as that of the "Non-resident Worker's Identification Card", hereafter called "Non-resident Worker's Card" for short). C. In special situations, the application for "Authorization to Stay for Non-resident Workers" cannot enter Final Examination but has to be further examined in Initial Examination. 1) Initial Examination 2) Final Examination (1) The Subdivision concerned will conduct a detailed examination of the application and make a final decision before the "Temporary Authorization to Stay for Non-resident Workers" expires. (1) The following documents should be submitted to the i. Approved "application form" and a copy of it; (2) After submission of the above documents: i. For non-professional workers and domestic helpers: (3) After entering Macao, the "non-resident worker" may (2) The "non-resident worker" should go to the Subdivision in person for inquiry of the result on the expiry date of the Authorization (or the date specified by the authorities). If the application is approved, the "non-resident worker" is required to be fingerprinted, pay the application fee and submit the following: i. The approved "application form"; ii. 1 recent colour photo of 1.5-inch, full face, no-hat, white-background; iii. A completed "Declaration of Identification. 3) Upon completion of the procedure, the Subdivision will issue a "Revenue Receipt" and grant "Authorization to Stay for Non-resident Workers" (which expires on the same date as that of the "Non-resident Worker's Identification Card").

	legally until the Authorization expires. 2) Final Examination (1) The Subdivision concerned will conduct a detailed examination of the application and make a final decision before the "Temporary Authorization to Stay for Non-resident Workers" expires. (2) The "non-resident worker" should go to the Subdivision in person for inquiry of the result on the expiry date of the Authorization (or the date specified by the authorities). If the application is approved, the "non-resident worker" is required to be fingerprinted, pay the application fee and submit the following: i. The approved "application form"; ii. 1 recent colour photo of 1.5-inch, full face, no-hat, white-background; iii. A completed "Declaration of Identification. 3) Upon completion of the procedure, the Subdivision will issue a "Revenue Receipt" and grant "Authorization to Stay for Non-resident Workers" (which expires on the same date as that of the "Non-resident Worker's Identification Card"). D. There are the following situations after the Non-resident's Working Permit has been approved, 1) While applying the Non-resident Worker's Identification Card, the non-resident holds electric "Two-way Exit Permit" in card type, who authorized to use the fingerprint information, is available to use the E-channel with the above document. 2) While applying the Non-resident Worker's Identification Card, the non-resident holds electric "Two-way Exit Permit" in card type, who did not authorize to use the fingerprint information, is not available to use the E-channel with the electric "Two-way Exit Permit" in card type. But Non-resident Worker can bring along the original of "Two-way Exit Permit" and the revenue receipt and come in person to the designated locations within office hours to Register for Automated Passenger Clearance System (e-Channel), then the E-channel is available to use with the above document after granted the Non-resident Worker's Identification Card. 3) Non-resident workers not belong to the above point 1) and 2), can bring along the original of "Two-way Exit Permit" and the revenue receipt, then the E-channel is available to use with a registered "Two-way Exit Permit" or Non-resident Worker's Identification Card. [For details, please refer to "Registration for Automated Passenger Clearance System (e-Channel) for Non-residents"] E. Card Collection On the date of collection specified on the "Revenue Receipt",

the applicant may bring along the Receipt and go to the Subdivision to collect the "Non-resident Worker's Card". The applicant may learn about the progress or status of the card issue by referring to the "Inquiry System of the Date of Collection of the "Non-resident Worker's Identification Card"" or by calling our hotline at (853) 2872 5488.

II. Professional and non-professional workers and domestic helpers from countries and regions other than Mainland China

A. Formal Examination

B. Final Examination

Initial Examination:

(1) The Subdivision concerned will conduct a detailed examination of the application and make a final decision before the "Temporary Authorization to Stay for Non-resident Workers" expires.

(2) The "non-resident worker" should go to the Subdivision in person for inquiry of the result on the expiry date of the Authorization (or the date specified by the authorities). If the application is approved, the "non-resident worker" is required to be fingerprinted, pay the application fee and submit the following:

i. Copy of the approved "application form";

ii. 1 recent colour photo of 1.5-inch, full face, no hat, white background;

(1) The following documents should be submitted to the executing Subdivision:

iii. A completed "Declaration of Identification".

(3) Upon completion of the procedure, the Subdivision will issue a "Revenue Receipt" and grant "Authorization to Stay for Non-resident Workers" (which expires on the same date as that of the "Non-resident Worker's Identification Card").

i. A completed application form for "Authorization to Stay for Non-resident Workers" (from countries and regions other than Mainland China) (hereafter called the "application form" for short) and a copy of the bio data page of the non-resident workers

C. After the Non-resident's Working Permit has been approved, the non-resident worker can bring along the original of the valid identification document which is used to apply the Working Permit and the revenue receipt and come in person to the designated locations within office hours to Register for

	ii. For professional workers and domestic helpers: Initial Examination of the application is instantaneously conducted. If the application is approved, the initially approved "application form" will be returned instantaneously. (3) After entering Macao, the "non-resident worker" may apply to the Subdivision for "Temporary Authorization to Stay for Non-resident Workers" in person (or through the employer or employment agency) with the "application form" and a valid identification document. Then the "non-resident worker" can remain and temporarily work in Macao legally until the Authorization expires. B. Final Examination (1) The Subdivision concerned will conduct a detailed examination of the application and make a final decision before the "Temporary Authorization to Stay for Non-resident Workers" expires. (2) The "non-resident worker" should go to the Subdivision in person for inquiry of the result on the expiry date of the Authorization (or the date specified by the authorities). If the application is approved, the "non-resident worker" is required to be fingerprinted, pay the application fee and submit the following: i. Copy of the approved "application form"; ii. 1 recent colour photo of 1.5-inch, full face, no-hat, white-background; iii. A completed "Declaration of Identification". (3) Upon completion of the procedure, the Subdivision will issue a "Revenue Receipt" and grant "Authorization to Stay for Non-resident Workers" (which expires on the same date as that of the "Non-resident Worker's Identification Card"). C. After the Non-resident's Working Permit has been approved, the non-resident worker can bring along the original of the valid identification document, which is used to apply the Working Permit and the revenue receipt and come in person to the designated locations within office hours to Register for Automated Passenger Clearance System (e-Channel). [For details, please refer to "Registration for Automated Passenger Clearance System (e-Channel) for Non-residents"]. D. Card Collection On the date of collection specified on the "Revenue Receipt", the applicant may bring along the Receipt and go to the Subdivision to collect the "Non-resident Worker's Card". The applicant may learn about the progress or status of the card issue by referring to the "Inquiry System of the Date of

Collection of the "Non-resident Worker's Identification Card"" or by calling our hotline at (853) 2872 5488.

III. Self-employed

A. Formal Examination

1. Initial Examination

(1) The following documents should be submitted to the Subdivision concerned:

i. A completed application form for "Authorization to Stay for Non-resident Workers" ("self-employed" who engage in activities for their own benefits) (hereafter called the "application form" for short) and a copy of it (the bio data page of the non-resident worker's document used for entry to Macao has to be copied to the blank space on the right side of the "application form");

ii. Copy of the written instruction and official notification regarding the "employment authorization";

	iii. A completed "Declaration of Identification". (3) Upon completion of the procedure, the Subdivision will issue a "Revenue Receipt" and grant "Authorization to Stay for Non-resident Workers" (which expires on the same date as that of the "Non-resident Worker's Card") (4) After approved the non-resident stay permit, "self-employed" can bring along the original of valid identification document and the revenue receipt and come in person to the designated locations within office hours to Register for Automated Passenger Clearance System (e-Channel). [For details, please refer to "Registration for Automated Passenger Clearance System (e-Channel) for Non-residents"] 3. Card Collection On the date of collection specified on the "Revenue Receipt", the applicant may bring along the Receipt to the Subdivision to collect the "Non-resident Worker's Card". The applicant may learn about the progress or status of the card issue by referring to the "Inquiry System of the Date of Collection of the "Non-resident Worker's Identification Card"" or by calling (853) 2872 5488
Charge (or Tax)	"Non-resident Worker's Card": MOP100
Time Needed	A. Professional and non-professional workers and the domestic helpers from Mainland China 1. Examination ※General Situation B. Professional and non-professional workers and domestic helpers from countries and regions other than Mainland China 1. Formal Examination (1) Initial Examination: non-professional workers – C. "Self-employed" 1. Formal Examination: Initial Examination – within the same day;

	situation) 2. Issue: approximately 45 to 60 days
Remark	I. Date of issue and expiry of "Non-resident Worker's Card" A. Date of Issue: Same as that of the "Revenue Receipt" B. Date of Expiry: Correspondent with the limit approved by the Secretary for Economy and Finance or the II. Languages Used in the Fields of Employing Entity and Occupation on the "Non-resident Worker's Card" 1. The information regarding the employing entity and occupation on the "Non-resident Worker's Card" will be printed exactly in the languages (Chinese / Portuguese, or Chinese and Portuguese) indicated in the Human Resources III. Penalty for overstay 1. According to Administrative Regulation No. 14/2014 'Amendments to the Provision on Overstay in the 《 Regulations of the Entry, Stay and Residence Authorization》', persons who still stay in the Macao SAR but 2. According to Law No. 6/2004, persons who are considered to be illegal immigrants will be deported and interdicted from entry to the Macao SAR for the period indicated in the deportation order.

	2. According to Law No. 6/2004, persons who are considered to be illegal immigrants will be deported and interdicted from entry to the Macao SAR for the period indicated in the deportation order. IV. Once non-resident workers / reuniting kindred of non-resident workers / "Special Stay Card" holders changed the valid passport / travel document / "Two-way Exit Permit" / identification document, have to update the related information in the executing Subdivision.
Forms	1. Application Form for "Authorization to Stay for Non-resident Workers" (from Mainland China) 2. Application Form for "Authorization to Stay for Non-resident Workers" (from countries and regions other than Mainland China) 3. Application Form for "Authorization to Stay for Non-resident Workers" ("self-employed" who engage in activities for their own benefits)
Legislations Website	1. Law of the Employment of Non-resident Workers Law No. 21/2009〔 B.O. no. 43 (I), 27/10/2009〕 2. Regulation of the Enforcement of Law of the Employment of Non-resident Workers Administrative Regulation No. 8/2010〔 B.O. no. 16 (I), 19/04/2010〕 3. Approval of the Design of the Non-resident Worker's Identification Card Chief Executive's Written Instruction No.197/2010〔 B.O. no. 27 (I), 05/07/2010〕 4. Regulation of Prohibition of Illegal Employment Administrative Regulation No.17/2004〔 B.O. no. 24 (I), 14/06/2004〕 5. General Principles of the System of Entry, Stay and Residence Authorization Law No. 4/2003〔 B.O. no. 11 (I), 17/03/2003〕 6. Regulations of Entry, Stay and Residence Authorization Administrative Regulation No. 5/2003〔 B.O. no. 15 (I), 14/04/2003〕 7. Amendments to the Stipulation on Overstay in the Regulations of Entry, Stay and Residence Authorization Administrative Regulation No. 14/2014〔 B.O. no. 25 (I), 23/06/2014〕 8. Law of Illegal Immigration, Illegal Stay and Deportation Law No. 6/2004〔 B.O. no. 31 (I), 02/08/2004〕 9. Amendments to Law No. 21/2009 "Law of the Employment of Non-resident Workers" Law No. 4/2013〔 B.O. no. 16 (I), 15/04/2013〕

PROCESSING OF CASES OF LOSS OF ENTRY IDENTIFICATION DOCUMENTS FOR NON-RESIDENTS

Service	Processing of Cases of Loss of Entry Identification Documents for Non-residents

Introduction (Service Coverage)	Issue departure document to non-residents who have lost the passport / travel document / identification document used for entry to Macao and do not have other document for departure
Service Provider	Foreigners Subdivision of the Immigration Department (during office hours) Investigation Subdivision of the Immigration Department (during non-office hours)
Other Entity / Agency	Police station/duty office of the Judiciary Police or the Public Security Police Force, China Travel Service (Macao) Ltd., Office of the Commissioner of the Ministry of Foreign Affairs of the PRC in the Macao SAR, Taipei Economic and Cultural Office in Macao
Application Location	Immigration Department
Office Hours	1. Foreigners Subdivision Mon to Thu: 9:00 – 17:45 Fri: 9:00 – 17:30 Closed on Sat, Sun and government holidays 2. Please call (853) 2872 5488 before applying to the Investigation Subdivision during non-office hours.
Enquiry Methods	In person: the above location Tel: (853) 2872 5488 Fax: (853) 8897 0300 Email: sminfo@fsm.gov.mo

Transactional Category	Issue (in our performance pledges)
Relevant Service (Relevant Information)	Report of Loss (Report of Loss of Document)
Target Groups and Application Eligibility	A. Target people: Non-residents who have lost the entry document and do not have other document for departure B. Requirement: Not in a lawfully restricted status [Note: Departure of persons who have lost their document and overstay will be arranged by the Investigation Subdivision of the Immigration Department.]
Application Approach	1. Simply a case of loss of document: They may go directly to the respective unit for report of document loss and application for a "departure document" ("Loss of Document and Report Notification" for residents of Mainland China and "Declaration of Loss of Document" for others) at the same time. 2. A case of loss of document involving criminal act (e.g. document is stolen or robbed of): The person is required to report the loss of document in person at a police department and then apply to the respective unit for a "departure document" ("Loss of Document and Report Notification" for residents of Mainland China and "Declaration of Loss of Document" for others) with a "Report Testimonial" or "Complaint Notification".

<table>
<tr><td>Necessary Documents</td><td>1. A completed declaration of the lost document;
[Note: The form is available at the respective Subdivision and the website of the Public Security Police Force.]
2. "Report Testimonial" or "Complaint Notification" issued at a police department (for a case of loss of document involving criminal act);
3. Other documents certifying the person's identity (if any).</td></tr>
<tr><td>Charge (or Tax)</td><td>Free of charge</td></tr>
<tr><td>Time Needed</td><td>Within the same day</td></tr>
<tr><td>Quality Criterion</td><td>To issue a "Declaration of Loss of Document" to a resident of the Hong Kong Special Administrative Region:
identity verifivation by the Hong Kong competent authorities - 3 hours [Please see Remark 3.]
identity verifivation by our fingerprint system - 1 hour [Please see Remark 3. and 4.]</td></tr>
<tr><td>Remark</td><td>1. Procedure after obtaining the "departure document"
1) Hong Kong residents
They are required to leave Macao by using the "departure document" before it expires (generally within 3 days).
2) Others
A. To ensure successful entry to the original country/region, they are required to apply to the consulate/embassy or diplomatic mission of the original country/region in Macao before using the "departure document" to leave Macao, or apply to the consulate/embassy or diplomatic mission of the original country/region in Hong Kong or Mainland China after leaving Macao, for reissue of a passport or for a single-entry travel document (aka "return document");
B. Application for "return document" at Macao
a. The person is required to apply to the department or organization concerned for a "return document" before the "departure document" expires (generally within 7 days), for example:
<table>
<tr><th>Type of Lost Document</th><th>Department/Organization Responsible for Reissue of Document</th></tr>
<tr><td>P.R.C. passport</td><td>Office of the Commissioner of the Ministry of Foreign Affairs of the PRC in the Macao SAR</td></tr>
<tr><td>P.R.C. Permit for Travelling to and from Hong Kong and Macao</td><td>China Travel Service (Macao) Ltd.</td></tr>
<tr><td>Travel Document of the Region of Taiwan</td><td>Taipei Economic and Cultural Office in Macao</td></tr>
<tr><td>Philippine passport</td><td>Philippine Consulate in Macao</td></tr>
</table>
b. If the "return document" is issued before the expiry of "departure document", the person should leave Macao before the two documents expire (subject to whichever</td></tr>
</table>

	document expires first). Otherwise, the person is required to extend the validity of the "departure document" at the respective unit until he/she is granted the "return document" and leaves Macao. [Note: Persons who leave Macao or extend the validity of the "departure document" after it expires are considered to be overstayers.] c. Both the "departure document" and the "return document" should be presented upon departure. C. Application for "return document" at Hong Kong or Mainland China a. The person should leave Macao before the "departure document" expires (generally within 7 days) and go to the consulate/embassy or diplomatic mission in Hong Kong or Mainland China to apply for a "return document". Otherwise, the person will be considered to be an overstayer; b. Before going to Hong Kong or Mainland China, the person should contact the relevant consulate/ embassy and confirm the appointed date of application. Otherwise, the person will be subject to entry refusal; [Note: If the appointed date of application is beyond the expiry of the "departure document", the person is required to extend the validity of the Document at the respective unit.] c. If the person obtains the "return document" on the date of application and returns to Macao to take a flight, he/she is required to present the "return document" as well as the original "departure document" upon arrival at Macao. The authorities will grant him/her "Authorization to Stay" for a reasonable period of time based on the validity of the "return document" so that he/she can make arrangements for departure. However, if the person needs to collect the "return document" after he/she re-enters Macao, he/she is required to extend the validity of the original "departure document" with the relevant application receipt at the respective unit. 2. Penalty for overstay 1) According to Administrative Regulation No. 14/2014 'Amendments to the Provision on Overstay in the 《Regulations of the Entry, Stay and Residence Authorization》', persons who still stay in the Macao SAR but not over 30 days after the expiry of the authorization granted is fined MOP500 per overdue day from 9/7/2014. The violators are required to pay the fine immediately after they are arrested or report themselves to the police. The above mentioned penalty regulation is not applicable to those who have overstayed in Macao within one year. Those will be considered to be illegal immigrants if they do not pay the fine and the penalty regulation is not applicable to them. Moreover, they cannot make any application for Residence Authorization, extension of Authorization to Stay and

	Authorization to Stay for Non-resident Workers within two years to the Immigration Department. 2) According to Law No. 6/2004, persons who are considered to be illegal immigrants will be deported and interdicted from entry to the Macao SAR for the period indicated in the deportation order. 3. "Quality Criterion" refers to the time of processing required by service units (excluding time of waiting in a queue) calculated in the following manner: from the moment when the service unit received and confirmed that all the required documents had been correctly prepared. 4. For Hong Kong Residents who have registered for the Macao Automated Passenger Clearance System (e-Channel).
Attachments	Sample of "Loss of Document and Report Notification" Sample of "Declaration of Loss of Document"
Forms	Declaration of Loss of Hong Kong Identity Card Declaration of Loss of Australian Travel Document Declaration of Loss of Travel Document [Note: applicable to other types of document]
Legislations Website	1. General Principles of the System of Entry, Stay and Residence Authorization Law No. 4/2003 [B.O. no. 11 (I), 17/03/2003] 2. Regulations of Entry, Stay and Residence Authorization Administrative Regulation No. 5/2003 [B.O. no. 15 (I), 14/04/2003] 3. Amendments to the Stipulation on Overstay in the Regulations of Entry, Stay and Residence Authorization Administrative Regulation No. 14/2014 [B.O. no. 25 (I), 23/06/2014]

11."SPECIAL AUTHORIZATION TO STAY" FOR APPLICANTS OF RESIDENCE AUTHORIZATION

Service	"Special Authorization to Stay" for Applicants of Residence Authorization
Introduction (Service Coverage)	According to Item 6, Article 8 of Law No. 4/2003, before the result of the application for Residence Authorization is out, the interested person may apply to the Immigration Department for "Special Authorization to Stay" (aka "Visa for Residence Application"). The Authorization can be extended for more than once.
Service Provider	Foreigners Subdivision or Residents Subdivision of the Immigration Department (depending on which Subdivision accepts and processes the application for Residence Authorization)
Application Location	Immigration Department Office Building, Travessa Um do Cais de Pac On, Taipa, Macao
Office Hours	Mon to Thu: 9:00 – 17:45 (Tags dispensed until 17:00) Fri: 9:00 – 17:30 (Same as above) Closed on Sat, Sun and government holidays
Enquiry Methods	In the above address Tel: (853) 2872 5488

	Tel: (853) 2872 5488 Fax: (853) 8897 0300 Email: sminfo@fsm.gov.mo
Online Appointment	Click here for online appointment

Transactional Category	Application and Renewal (in our performance pledges)
Relevant Service (Relevant Information)	Applying for Residence in Macao S.A.R.
Target Groups and Application Eligibility	A. Target Groups Persons who have applied to the Immigration Department of the Public Security Police Force or the Trade and Investment Promotion Institute (hereinafter called "IPIM") for Residence Authorization and need to extend their limit of stay in Macao before the application result is out. B. Application Eligibility (1) Meeting the stipulations relevant to the system of entry, stay and residence authorization in Macao; (e.g. A. In possession of a valid passport / travel document / identification document for entry to and departure from Macao; and B. Not in a lawfully restricted status.) (2) Limit of stay granted in the original "Authorization to Stay" not long enough for the interested person to wait till the application result is out.
Application Approach	1. The interested person or a legal representative making the application within 7 days before the expiry of the "Authorization to Stay"; 2. The parent or guardian making the application on behalf of a minor child should present his/her valid identification document and proof of their relationship; other representative should present a certified letter of authorization and his/her valid identification document.
Documents to be Presented	The original should be exhibited for authentication if a copy is submitted
Required Documents	A. For "Residence Authorization" applications submitted to the Immigration Department (a) Application 1. Making the application together with the application for "Residence Authorization" (1)

Submit the reverse side of a completed "Application Form for Residence Authorization" (format 4)

2. Making the application separately

	(1) Submit a completed application form; [Note: The "application form" is available at the Subdivision concerned and the website of the Public Security Police Force] (2) Submit a copy of the interested person's valid passport / travel document (bio data page and observation pages only) or identification document used to apply for "Residence Authorization"; (3) Present the "application acceptance receipt". (b) Renewal (1) Submit a completed application form; [Note: The "application form" is available at the Subdivision concerned and the website of the Public Security Police Force] (2) Submit a copy of the interested person's valid passport / travel document (bio data page and observation pages only) or identification document used to apply for "Residence Authorization"; (3) Present the "application acceptance receipt". B. For "Residence Authorization" applications submitted to IPIM (a) Application (1) Submit a completed application form; [Note: The "application form" is available at the Subdivision concerned and the website of the Public Security Police Force] (2) A completed "Declaration of Identity"; [Note: a. The Declaration template is available at the Subdivision concerned and the website of the Public Security Police Force; b. The interested person is required to sign the Declaration in the presence of the staff accepting the application for verification. If he/she is not able to show up, the signature on the (completed) Declaration will be authenticated by the competent authorities, or the Declaration is to be completed by a legal representative. The latter should also submit a certified letter of authorization, a copy of the interested person's birth certificate, certificate of marital status (not applicable to unmarried applicants) and a document indicating the interested person's residential address in Macao.] (3) Submit a copy of the interested person's valid passport / travel document (bio data page and observation pages only) or identification document used to apply for "Residence Authorization"; [Note: The document used for entry to Macao should be presented as well] (4) Submit 2 copies of the "Declaration" issued by IPIM to prove that the application for Residence Authorization is being processed.

	(b) Renewal (1) Submit a completed application form; [Note: The "application form" is available at the Subdivision concerned and the website of the Public Security Police Force] (2) Submit a copy of the interested person's valid passport / travel document (bio data page and observation pages only) or identification document used to apply for "Residence Authorization"; [Note: The document used for entry to Macao should be presented as well] (3) Submit a copy of the "Declaration" issued by IPIM to prove that the application for Residence Authorization is being processed.
Charge (or Tax)	Free of charge
Quality Criterion	35 minutes [Please see Remark 3.]
Remark	1. The interested person is required to be legally staying in Macao while the application is being processed, otherwise the Immigration Department may refuse to accept the application. 2. Penalty for overstay (1) According to Administrative Regulation No. 14/2014 'Amendments to the Provision on Overstay in the 《Regulations of the Entry, Stay and Residence Authorization》', persons who still stay in the Macao SAR but not over 30 days after the expiry of the authorization granted is fined MOP500 per overdue day from 9/7/2014. The violators are required to pay the fine immediately after they are arrested or report themselves to the police. The above mentioned penalty regulation is not applicable to those who have overstayed in Macao within one year. Those will be considered to be illegal immigrants if they do not pay the fine and the penalty regulation is not applicable to them. Moreover, they cannot make any application for Residence Authorization, extension of Authorization to Stay and Authorization to Stay for Non-resident Workers within two years to the Immigration Department. (2) According to Law No. 6/2004, persons who are considered to be illegal immigrants will be deported and interdicted from entry to the Macao SAR for the period indicated in the deportation order. 3. "Quality Criterion" refers to the time of processing required by service units (excluding time of waiting in a queue) calculated in the following manner: from the moment when the service unit received and confirmed that all the required documents had been correctly prepared.
Forms	Application Form for Extension of Stay Declaration of Identity
Legislations Website	1. General Principles of the System of Entry, Stay and Residence

	Law No. 4/2003 [B.O. no. 11 (I), 17/03/2003] 2. Regulations of Entry, Stay and Residence Authorization Administrative Regulation No. 5/2003 [B.O. no. 15 (I), 14/04/2003] 3. Amendments to the Stipulation on Overstay in the Regulations of Entry, Stay and Residence Authorization Administrative Regulation No. 14/2014 [B.O. no. 25 (I), 23/06/2014]

REISSUE OF "RECEIPT OF RESIDENCE AUTHORIZATION / RESIDENCE AUTHORIZATION RENEWAL"

Service	Reissue of "Receipt of Residence Authorization / Residence Authorization Renewal" ("Residence Receipt")
Introduction (Service Coverage)	Persons who are granted a "Residence Receipt" by the Immigration Department may apply for reissue of the document if it is lost, damaged, stolen or has expired.
Service Provider	Foreigners Subdivision of the Immigration Department
Other Entity / Agency	Identification Bureau, police station / duty office of the Judiciary Police or the Public Security Police Force
Application Location	Immigration Department Office Building, Travessa Um do Cais de Pac On, Taipa, Macao
Office Hours	Mon to Thu: 9:00 – 17:45 (Tags dispensed until 17:00) Fri: 9:00 – 17:30 (Same as above) Closed on Sat, Sun and government holidays
Enquiry Methods	In person: the above address Tel: (853) 2872 5488 Fax: (853) 8897 0300 Email: sminfo@fsm.gov.mo

Transactional Category	Reissue (with performance pledge)
Relevant Service (Relevant Information)	Applying for Residence in Macao S.A.R.
Target Groups and Application Eligibility	Persons whose "Receipt of Residence Authorization / Residence Authorization Renewal" ("Residence Receipt" for short) is lost, damaged, stolen or has expired and hence need to apply for reissue of the document
Application Approach	1. The interested person or his/her legal representative applies to the respective Subdivision during office hours. 2. In case of loss or theft, the interested person should first report the case to the police and then apply for reissue with the "Report 3. The legal representative should submit: (1) A certified letter of authorization; (2) A copy of his/her valid identification document.

4. The interested person should collect the "Receipt of Residence Authorization" in person as he/she is required to be fingerprinted

	Authorization" in person as he/she is required to be fingerprinted on the "Receipt".
Documents to be Presented	The original should be exhibited for authentication if a copy is submitted
Necessary Documents	1. An application letter with reasonable justification [Note: The "application letter" template is available at the respective Subdivision and the website of the Public Security Police Force]; 2. Copy of the interested person's valid passport/travel document (bio data page only) or identification document used for application for "Residence Authorization" (or renewal of "Residence Authorization"); *3. "Report Testimonial" or "Complaint Notification" issued at a police department (in case of loss or theft).
Supplementary Document	Documents/information marked with "*"
Charge (or Tax)	1. Reasonable justification given: MOP50; 2. Reasonable justification not given: MOP200.
Quality Criteria	by 12:00 of the next working day [Please see Remark 3.]
Remark	1. According to Article 25 of Administrative Regulation No. 5/2003, the "Residence Receipt" should be used to apply to the Identification Bureau for a Macao Identity Card before its expiry (within 60 days). 2. "Report Testimonial" and "Complaint Notification" can be submitted later as supplementary document. 3. "Quality Criterion" refers to the time of processing required by service units (excluding time of waiting in a queue) calculated in the following manner: from the moment when the service unit received and confirmed that all the required documents had been correctly prepared.
Attachment	Sample of "Receipt of Residence Authorization/Residence Authorization Renewal"
Form	Declaration/Application Letter
Legislations Website	1. General Principles of the System of Entry, Stay and Residence Authorization Law No. 4/2003 [B.O. no. 11 (I), 17/03/2003] 2. Regulations of Entry, Stay and Residence Authorization Administrative Regulation No. 5/2003 [B.O. no. 15 (I), 14/04/2003] 3. Amendments to the Stipulation on Overstay in the Regulations of Entry, Stay and Residence Authorization Administrative Regulation No. 14/2014 [B.O. no. 25 (I), 23/06/2014]

REISSUE OF "RESIDENCE CERTIFICATE"

Service	Reissue of "Residence Certificate"
Introduction (Service Coverage)	Persons who are granted a "Residence Certificate" by the Immigration Department may apply for reissue of the document if it is lost, damaged or stolen before its expiry (valid for 90 days).
Service Provider	Residents Subdivision of the Immigration Department

Other Entity / Agency	Identification Bureau
Application Location	Immigration Department Office Building, Travessa Um do Cais de Pac On, Taipa, Macao
Office Hours	Mon to Thu: 9:00 – 17:45 (Tags dispensed until 17:00) Fri: 9:00 – 17:30 (Same as above) Closed on Sat, Sun and government holidays
Enquiry Methods	In person: the above address Tel: (853) 2872 5488 Fax: (853) 8897 0300 Email: sminfo@fsm.gov.mo

Transactional Category	Reissue (in our performance pledges)
Relevant Service (Relevant Information)	Application for Residence in the Macao SAR
Target Groups and Application Eligibility	Persons whose "Residence Certificate" is lost, damaged or stolen before its expiry (valid for 90 days) and hence need to apply for reissue of the document
Application Approach	1. The interested person or his/her legal representative applies to the respective Subdivision during office hours. 2. In case of loss or theft, the interested person should first report the case to the police and then apply for reissue with the case reporting certificate. 3. The legal representative should submit: (1) A certified letter of authorization; (2) A copy of his/her valid identification document (the original should be exhibited for authentication).
Documents to be Presented	The original should be exhibited for authentication if a copy is submitted
Required Documents	Applying in person 1. An application letter with reasonable justification [Note: The "application letter" template is available at the respective Subdivision and the website of the Public Security Police Force]; 2. "Report Testimonial" or "Complaint Notification" issued at a police department (in case of loss or theft); 3. Copy of the interested person's "P.R.C. Permit for Travelling to Hong Kong and Macao" or valid passport / travel document (bio data page only) or identification document used for entry to and departure from Macao. Applying by representative 1. A certified letter of authorization; 2. Copy of representative's valid identification document; 3. All the necessary documents to be submitted when "applying in person".
Charge (or Tax)	1. Chinese: free of charge; 2. Others: MOP100
Quality Criteria	By 16:00 of the next working [Please see Remark 2.]

Remark	1. Interested persons under 18 years old should have their applications tendered by the parent or guardian, who is required to submit a copy of his/her identification document. The guardian should also submit a copy of the proof of relationship with the interested person. 2. "Quality Criterion" refers to the time of processing required by service units (excluding time of waiting in a queue) calculated in the following manner: from the next working day following the day when the service unit received and confirmed that all the required documents had been correctly prepared.
Attachment	Sample of "Residence Certificate"
Form	Declaration / Application Letter
Legislations Website	1. General Principles of the System of Entry, Stay and Residence Authorization Law No. 4/2003 〔B.O. no. 11 (I), 17/03/2003〕 2. Regulations of Entry, Stay and Residence Authorization Administrative Regulation No. 5/2003 〔B.O. no. 15 (I), 14/04/2003〕 3. Amendments to the Stipulation on Overstay in the Regulations of Entry, Stay and Residence Authorization Administrative Regulation No. 14/2014 〔B.O. no. 25 (I), 23/06/2014〕

RE-ENTRY CERTIFICATE

Service	Re-entry Certificate
Introduction (Service Coverage)	Macao residents who need to prove that they are admissible to the Macao Special Administrative Region after their short stay at another country or region may apply for a "Re-entry Certificate".
Service Provider	Foreigners Subdivision of the Immigration Department
Application Location	Immigration Department Office Building, Travessa Um do Cais de Pac On, Taipa, Macao
Office Hours	Mon to Thu: 9:00 – 17:45 (Tags dispensed until 17:00) Fri: 9:00 – 17:30 (Same as above) Closed on Sat, Sun and government holidays
Enquiry Methods	In person: the above address Tel: (853) 2872 5488 Fax: (853) 8897 0300 Email: sminfo@fsm.gov.mo

Transactional Category	Application
Target Groups and Application Eligibility	Macao residents who need to prove to the country or region which they intend to visit that they are allowed to return to Macao
Application Approach	1. To apply in person or by a legal representative to the Subdivision concerned during office hours 2. The legal representative should submit the following: (1) A certified letter of authorization; (2) A copy of his/her valid identification document.

Documents to be Presented	The original should be exhibited for authentication if a copy is submitted
Required Documents	1. A completed application form for Re-entry Certificate; 2. A copy of interested person's valid Macao Identity Card AND travel document; 3. Document certifying the reason for application; *4. 2 photos of 1.5-inch, full face, no-hat, white-background, coloured/black-and-white.
Supplementary Documents	The above document/information marked with "*"
Charge (or Tax)	MOP100
Time Needed	Approximately 10 working days [Note: It is timed from the next working day the service unit receives all the necessary documents and confirms nothing is missing.]
Remark	A. Validity of Re-entry Certificate: 1. For permanent residents: The validity is generally 1 year, but it may reach 5 years under special circumstances with reasonable justification. 2. For non-permanent residents: The maximum validity can be the same as that of the "Residence Authorization" and is limited to 2 years. B. Extension of validity: 1. The validity of a "Re-entry Certificate" can only be extended under exceptional circumstances where reasonable justifications are given. 2. In any circumstances, the exceptional extension of the validity of a "Re-entry Certificate" cannot be used as an excuse for any failure to duly renew the "Residence Authorization" within the statutory time.
Attachment	Sample of "Re-entry Certificate"
Form	Application Form for Re-entry Certificate
Legislations Website	1. General Principles of the System of Entry, Stay and Residence Authorization Law No. 4/2003 [B.O. no. 11 (I), 17/03/2003] 2. Regulations of Entry, Stay and Residence Authorization Administrative Regulation No. 5/2003 [B.O. no. 15 (I), 14/04/2003

NOTIFICATION OF CHANGE OF ADDRESS

Service	Notification of Change of Address
Introduction (Service Coverage)	According to Article 27 of Administrative Regulation No. 5/2003, persons granted "Residence Authorization" are required to notify the Immigration Department of any change of address within 30 days from the date of change. Failure to do so will incur a penalty.
Service Provider	Foreigners or Residents Subdivision of the Immigration Department (subject to the Subdivision that processed the residence application)
Application Location	Immigration Department Office Building, Travessa Um do Cais de Pac On, Taipa, Macao
Office Hours	Mon to 9:00 17:45 (Tags dispensed until 17:00)

	Thu: Fri: 9:00 – 17:30 (Same as above) Closed on Sat, Sun and government holidays
Enquiry Methods	In person: the above address Tel: (853) 2872 5488 Fax: (853) 8897 0300 Email: sminfo@fsm.gov.mo

Transactional Category	Update/Change of Information
Target Groups and Application Eligibility	Persons granted "Residence Authorization"
Application Approach	To notify the Immigration Department of the change of address in person, by a legal representative or by post.
Documents to be Presented	The original should be exhibited for authentication if a copy is submitted
Required Documents	A. Notifying in person or by post: 1. Notification of Change of Address signed by the interested person; 2. Document indicating the new address (e.g.: copy of water bill, electricity bill, phone bill, etc. of the last 3 months); 3. Copy of interested person's Macao Resident Identity Card. B. Submitting documents by third party: 1. Documents 1-3 listed in Point A; 2. Copy of third party's identification document. C. Notifying by legal representative: 1. Documents 1-3 listed in Point A (Notification of Change of Address to be signed by the representative); 2. A certified letter of authorization; 3. Copy of representative's identification document.
Charge (or Tax)	Free of charge
Time Needed	1. Notifying in person: within the same day 2. Notifying by post: the day the Subdivision receives the letter
Remark	Penalty for unreported change of address: Persons who fail to notify the change of address as stipulated in Article 27 of Administrative Regulation No. 5/2003 will be fined MOP1000 according to Article 33 of the Regulation. Recidivists will be fined double the amount.
Forms	Notification of Change of Address (Chinese version) Notification of Change of Address (Portuguese version)
Legislations Website	Regulations of Entry, Stay and Residence Authorization Administrative Regulation No. 5/2003 [B.O. no. 15 (I), 14/04/2003]

CHANGE OF PERSONAL INFORMATION

Service	Change of Personal Information
Introduction (Service Coverage)	A. Persons who need to change the personal information (e.g. their

<table>
<tr><td></td><td>authorization.
<table>
<tr><th>Department</th><th>Application Item</th></tr>
<tr><td>Residents Subdivision</td><td>1. Application for "Residence Authorization"
(1) "P.R.C. Permit for Travelling to Hong Kong and Macao" holders from Mainland China;
(2) Persons of Portuguese nationality (including applications for renewal of "Residence Authorization");
(3) Minor children who are born outside Macao and whose parents are Macao permanent residents or holders of a "P.R.C. Permit for Travelling to Hong Kong and Macao".</td></tr>
<tr><td>Foreigners Subdivision</td><td>1. Application for "Residence Authorization" (beyond the service scope of the Residents Subdivision and the Trade and Investment Promotion Institute);
2. Application for Exceptional Extension of Authorization to Stay;
3. Application and renewal of "Special Authorization to Stay" for Foreign Students;
4. Application for "Residence Receipt" (persons granted residence authorization by the Trade and Investment Promotion Institute).</td></tr>
<tr><td>Non-resident Workers Subdivision</td><td>1. Application, renewal, reissue or replacement of "Non-resident Worker's Identification Card";
2. Application, renewal or reissue of "Special Stay Permit";
3. Application and renewal of "Special Authorization to Stay" for Reuniting Kindred of Non-resident Workers.</td></tr>
</table>
B. Persons who are applying or are going to apply for renewal of "Residence Authorization", "Authorization to Stay" or residence / stay permit may make an application for change of personal information at the same time.</td></tr>
<tr><td>Service Provider</td><td>Immigration Department
- Foreigners Subdivision
- Residents Subdivision
- Non-resident Workers Subdivision</td></tr>
<tr><td>Other Entity / Agency</td><td>Identification Bureau</td></tr>
<tr><td>Application Location</td><td>Immigration Department Office Building, Travessa Um do Cais de Pac On, Taipa, Macao</td></tr>
<tr><td>Office Hours</td><td>Mon – Thu: 9:00 – 17:45 (Tags dispensed until 16:30 at the Non-resident Workers Subdivision and until 17:00 at the other</td></tr>
</table>

	Fri: 9:00 – 17:30 (same as above) Closed on Sat, Sun and government holidays
Enquiry Methods	In person: the above address Tel: (853) 2872 5488 Fax: (853) 8897 0300 Email: sminfo@fsm.gov.mo

Transactional Category	Change of Information
Target Groups and Application Eligibility	Persons granted any type of residence or stay authorization (e.g. "Residence Authorization", Exceptional Extension of Authorization to Stay") and persons issued any type of certificate or document (e.g. "Residence Receipt", "Residence Certificate", "Non-resident Worker's Identification Card", "Special Stay Permit", etc.)
Application Approach	To apply in person or by a legal representative [Note: The legal representative is required to submit: 1. A certified letter of authorization; 2. Copy of his/her valid identification document (the original should be exhibited for authentication).]
Documents to be Presented	The original should be exhibited for authentication if a copy is submitted
Required Documents	1. Application form with reasonable justification [Note: The "application" form is available at the Subdivision concerned and the website of the Public Security Police Force.]; 2. Copy of interested person's valid identification document; 3. Proof supporting the application justification.
Charge (or Tax)	Free of charge
Time Needed	Varies case by case
Remark	According to the current laws of Macao, persons who make a false declaration of personal information or submit false documents will be subject to imprisonment.
Form	Application Form for Change of Personal Information
Legislations Website	1. Law of Illegal Immigration, Illegal Stay and Deportation Law No. 6/2004〔B.O. no. 31 (I), 02/08/2004〕 2. Criminal Code Decree No. 58/95/M〔B.O. no. 46 (I), 14/11/1995〕

STATEMENT OF TRAVEL TO HKSAR

Service	Statement of Travel to HKSAR
Introduction (Service Coverage)	The "Statement" is a one-off special certificate issued to Macao residents who are not eligible for a travel document which entitles them to travel to Hong Kong but need to go there in an emergency
Service Provider	Residents Subdivision of the Immigration Department
Other Entity / Agency	Centro Hospitalar Conde de São Januário
Application Location	Immigration Department Office Building, Travessa Um do Cais de Pac On, Taipa, Macao
Office Hours	Mon to Thu: 9:00 – 17:45 (Tags dispensed until 17:00)

	Fri: 9:00 – 17:30 (Same as above) Closed on Sat, Sun and government holidays
Enquiry Methods	In person: the above address Tel: (853) 2872 5488 Fax: (853) 8897 0300 Email: sminfo@fsm.gov.mo

Transactional Category	Application (in our performance pledges)
Relevant Service (Relevant Information)	Certificate 1. Statement to prove the applicant is in application procedure 2. Certificate to prove the document is copied from the applicant's dossier 3. Certificate issued according to the information in archives
Target Groups and Application Eligibility	Macao residents who are not eligible for a travel document which entitles them to travel to Hong Kong but need to go there in an emergency (e.g. attending family funeral, seeking medical treatment, visiting critically-ill relative, summoned by a consulate or a court in Hong Kong, etc.)
Application Approach	The interested person (or a representative) and his/her guarantor (a Macao permanent resident) going to the Residents Subdivision together for application
Documents to be Presented	The original should be exhibited for authentication if a copy is submitted
Required Documents	1. A completed application form for the Statement; 2. Copy of the interested person's Macao Identity Card; 3. Proof of urgent need to travel to Hong Kong; 4. Other relevant proof or document; 5. 3 photos of 1.5-inch, full face, no-hat, white-background, coloured / black-and-white; 6. Copy of guarantor's Macao Identity Card. [Note: In case of travelling to Hong Kong for medical treatment, the document listed above in Point 3 refers to an official letter from the Centro Hospitalar Conde de São Januário and a medical certificate issued by a doctor.]
Charge (or Tax)	Free of charge
Quality Criteria	By 15:00 of the next working day [Please see Remark 3.]
Remark	1. In case of travelling to Hong Kong for visiting a patient or for a 2. In case of travelling to Hong Kong for medical treatment, the 3. "Quality Criterion" refers to the time of processing required by

	correctly prepared.
Attachment	Sample of "Statement of Travel to HKSAR"
Forms	Application Form for Statement of Travel to HKSAR

CERTIFICATE

Service	Certificate
Introduction (Service Coverage)	1. Issue certificate of personal movement record to persons who had gone through immigration clearance at any of the border checkpoints in Macao; 2. Issue certificate of personal record in dossier or fingerprint authentication to persons who had made or are making applications to the Immigration Department of the Public Security Police Force.
Service Provider	Immigration Department
Application Location	1. Certificate of personal movement record: (1) Reception desk at Immigration Department Office Building, Travessa Um do Cais de Pac On, Taipa, Macao (2) Centro de Serviços da RAEM, Rua Nova da AreiaPreta N.° 52 (3) At Self-Service Kiosk (applicable only to Macao Resident) 2. Other certificate / declaration: (1) Immigration Department Office Building, Travessa Um do Cais de Pac On, Taipa, Macao (2) Centro de Serviços da RAEM, Rua Nova da AreiaPreta N.° 52 (except of Type B Certificate)
Office Hours	1. Immigration Department Office Building Mon to Thu: 9:00 – 17:45 (Tags dispensed until 16:30 at the Non-resident Workers Subdivision and until 17:00 at the other Subdivisions) Fri: 9:00 – 17:30 (Same as above) Closed on Sat, Sun and government holidays 2. Centro de Serviços da RAEM Mon to Fri: 9:00 – 18:00 Closed on Sat, Sun and government holidays
Enquiry Methods	In person: the above address Tel.: (853) 2872 5488 Fax: (853) 8897 0300 Email: sminfo@fsm.gov.mo

Transactional Category	Application (in our performance pledges)
Target Groups and Application Eligibility	1. Statement to prove the applicant is in application procedure (Type A Statement): Persons who are making an application to the Immigration Department and have a dossier opened; 2. Certificate to prove the fingerprints are collected from the applicant (Type B Certificate): Persons who need to use this certificate to apply for a document which is required in the 3. Certificate to prove the document is copied from the applicant's dossier (Type C Certificate): Persons who have made or are making an application to the Immigration Department and have a

<table>
<tr>
<td></td>
<td>
dossier (Type C Certificate): Persons who have made or are making an application to the Immigration Department and have a dossier opened;
4. Certificate of record of "Special Authorization to Stay" for foreign students (Type D Certificate): Foreign students who had studied or are studying at a higher institute in Macao and are granted "Special Authorization to Stay".
5. Certificate of China resident's employment status in Macao (Type E Certificate): China residents who lose their "P.R.C. Permit for Travelling to and from Hong Kong and Macao".
6. Certificate of limit of stay granted in "Authorization to Stay" (Type F Certificate): For persons who need this certificate to prove to a public department or private organization in Macao that they are granted valid "Authorization to Stay" by the relevant unit of our Department.
7. Other certificates issued based on information in dossier (Type G Certificate): Persons who have made or are making an application to the Immigration Department and have a dossier opened;
8. Certificate of personal entry and exit movement record: Persons who had gone through immigration clearance at any of the border checkpoints in Macao. [Refer to remark 1. for details]
List of statements and certificates available for persons who have made or are making an application to the Immigration Department:
<table>
<tr><th>Services</th><th>A</th><th>B</th><th>C</th><th>D</th><th>E</th><th>F</th><th>G</th></tr>
<tr><td>Authorization to Enter and Stay</td><td>✓</td><td></td><td>✓</td><td></td><td></td><td></td><td>✓</td></tr>
<tr><td>Extension of "Authorization to Stay"</td><td>✓</td><td></td><td>✓</td><td></td><td>✓</td><td>✓</td><td>✓</td></tr>
<tr><td>Non-resident Worker's Identification Card</td><td>✓</td><td></td><td>✓</td><td></td><td>✓</td><td>✓</td><td>✓</td></tr>
<tr><td>"Special Authorization to Stay" for Reuniting Kindred of Non-resident Workers</td><td>✓</td><td></td><td>✓</td><td></td><td></td><td>✓</td><td>✓</td></tr>
<tr><td>"Special Authorization to Stay" for Non-resident Students</td><td>✓</td><td></td><td>✓</td><td>✓</td><td></td><td>✓</td><td>✓</td></tr>
<tr><td>Residence Authorization</td><td>✓</td><td>✓</td><td>✓</td><td></td><td></td><td></td><td>✓</td></tr>
<tr><td>"Special Authorization to Stay" for Applicants of Residence Authorization</td><td>✓</td><td></td><td></td><td></td><td></td><td></td><td>✓</td></tr>
<tr><td>Special Stay Permit</td><td>✓</td><td></td><td>✓</td><td></td><td></td><td>✓</td><td>✓</td></tr>
<tr><td>Statement of Travel to HKSAR</td><td>✓</td><td></td><td>✓</td><td></td><td></td><td></td><td>✓</td></tr>
<tr><td>Re-entry Certificate</td><td>✓</td><td></td><td>✓</td><td></td><td></td><td></td><td>✓</td></tr>
</table>
</td>
</tr>
<tr>
<td>Application Approach</td>
<td>
1. Type B Certificate: to apply in person;
2. Others: to apply in person or by a legal representative.
[Note: The legal representative is required to submit:
□ A certified letter of authorization;
□ Copy of his/her valid identification document (the original should be exhibited for authentication).]
</td>
</tr>
<tr>
<td>Documents to be Presented</td>
<td>The original should be exhibited for authentication if a copy is submitted</td>
</tr>
<tr>
<td>Required Documents</td>
<td></td>
</tr>
</table>

	[Note: □ The template of the "application letter" is available at the Subdivision concerned and the website of the Public Security Police Force □ The application letter should contain: (1) the applicant's personal information; (2) the fact to be certified; (3) the purpose the certificate/declaration serves.] 2. Copy of applicant's valid identification document; 3. Copy of the travel document used for entry/exit the Macao SAR during the period stated in the application (application for "Certificate of Personal Movement Record" only).
Charge (or Tax)	1. Declaration: free of charge; 2. Certificate: MOP15 for the first page, MOP5 per following page (including copies of the documents in the interested person's dossier).
Time Needed	Certificate of limit of stay granted in "Authorization to Stay": 16:00 of the next working day
Quality Criteria	1. Statement to prove the applicant is in application procedure: 2 hours [Refer to remark 2.1) for details] 2. Certificate to prove the fingerprints are collected from the applicant: 3 hours [Refer to remark 2.1) for details] 3. Certificate to prove the document is copied from the applicant's dossier: 2 working days [Refer to remark 2.2) for details] 4. Certificate of record of "Special Authorization to Stay" for foreign students: 2 working days [Refer to remark 2.2) for details] 5. Certificate of China resident's employment status in Macao: by 16:00 on the next working day [Refer to remark 2.1) for details] 6. Other certificates issued based on information in dossier: 3 working days [Refer to remark 2.2) for details] 7. Certificate of personal entry and exit movement record: 3 working days [Refer to remark 2.2) for details]
Remark	1. We started to register the movement records of passengers electronically from January 1994. Therefore, certification of movement records registered before January 1994 cannot be provided. 2. "Quality Criterion" refers to the time of processing required by service units (excluding time of waiting in a queue and postage time for documents sent by mail) calculated in the following manner: 1) from the moment when the service unit received and confirmed that all the required documents had been correctly prepared. 2) from the next working day following the day when the service unit received and confirmed that all the required documents had been correctly prepared.
Forms	Declaration / application form Application Form for "Certificate of China Resident's Employment Status in Macao" (chinese version) Application Form for "Certificate of personal entry and exit movement record"
Legislations Website	Approval of Stamp Duty Regulation, Tax Rate and Payment Method

	Law no. 17/88/M〔B.O. n.° 26, de 27/06/1988〕

REGISTRATION FOR AUTOMATED PASSENGER CLEARANCE SYSTEM (E-CHANNEL) FOR NON-RESIDENTS

Service	Registration for Automated Passenger Clearance System (e-Channel) for Non-residents
Introduction (Service Coverage)	After successful completion of the registration for the Automated Passenger Clearance System, the registered travel document entitles the following persons to use the e-channels at the Border Gate, Hong Kong-Macao Ferry Terminal, Taipa Ferry Terminal, Macao International Airport and Cotai checkpoints for immigration clearance.
Registration Location and Time	**Registration Location** — **Registration Time** Border Checkpoint at the Hong Kong-Macao Ferry Terminal (Arrival Hall) — 8:00 – 00:00 Border Checkpoint at the Taipa Ferry Terminal (Arrival Hall) — 8:00 – 00:00 Border Checkpoint at the Border Gate (Arrival Hall) — 9:00 – 23:00 Immigration Department Office Building at Pac On — 9:00 – 17:00 (no lunch break but closed on Sat, Sun and government holidays)
Enquiry Methods	In person: Immigration Department Office Building, Travessa Um do Cais de Pac On, Taipa, Macao Tel: (853) 2872 5488 Fax: (853) 8897 0300 Email: sminfo@fsm.gov.mo

Registration for e-Channel for 'Non-resident Workers and their Dependants/Holders of "Special Stay Permit"/ Non-resident Students'	Registration for e-Channel for 'Hong Kong Permanent Residents'	Registration for e-Channel for 'Residents of Mainland China'

Transactional Category	Registration
Target Groups and Application Eligibility	- Holders of a valid "Non-resident Worker's Identification Card" and their dependants - Holders of a valid "Special Stay Permit" - Students possessing valid "Temporary Authorization to Stay" (aka "red stamp") or "Special Authorization to Stay" (aka "green stamp").

	3. Original "Receipt" of application for "Special Authorization to Stay" for Non-resident Students (aka "student visa") . Note: 1) "Non-resident Worker's Identification Card", "Special Stay Permit" or "Special Authorization to Stay" holders can still use the conventional channels for immigration clearance no matter their fingerprint templates have been captured or not in the registration process. 2) Minors aged 11 to 17 are required to be accompanied by a parent or guardian, and produce the birth certificate of the applicant and the identification document of the accompanying parent or guardian for registration. (If accompanied by a guardian, the proof of legal relationship should also be provided.)
Charge (or Tax)	Free of charge

ENTRY AND EXIT PROCEDURES FOR MACAO RESIDENTS

Service	Entry and Exit Procedures for Macao Residents	
Introduction (Service Coverage)	1. After receiving the identity card (and the boarding pass during departure at the airport) from a Macao resident, the immigration officer at the border checkpoint immediately examines the card and verifies the identification of the holder. The officer would also input the resident's bio data to the computer either manually or through the Optical Character Reader. The identity card will be returned to the resident after it is confirmed that the information is correct. 2. Immigration officers conduct a preliminary examination of any Macao resident who fails to present an identity card or travel document upon entry or return to Macao because his/her identification document is lost or stolen outside Macao. Immigration officers also compose an application letter for verification of identity and capture fingerprints for the resident, whose entry will be permitted after the Immigration Department verifies his/her identity through the database shared by the Identification Bureau.	
Service Provider	Border checkpoints of the Immigration Department	
Office Hours	Border Checkpoint at the Border Gate	06:00 - 01:00 (next day)
	Border Checkpoint at the Interior Harbour	08:00 - 16:30
	Border Checkpoint at COTAI	08:00 - 20:00 (cargos) 24 hours
	Border Checkpoint at the Hong Kong - Macao Ferry Terminal	24 hours
	Border Checkpoint at the Macao International Airport	24 hours
	Border Checkpoint at the Taipa Ferry Terminal	24 hours
	Border Checkpoint at the Zhuhai-Macao Cross-border Industrial Zone	

	□ 00:00 - 07:00 (for mainland workers, students and Macao residents; no vehicles allowed) □ 24 hours (for pass holders)
Enquiry Methods	In person: Immigration Department Office Building, Travessa Um do Cais de Pac On, Taipa, Macao Tel: (853) 2872 5488 Fax: (853) 8897 0300 Email: sminfo@fsm.gov.mo

Transactional Category	Exit / entry inspection procedures for Macao residents (Non-automated channel) (in our performance pledges)
Relevant Service (Relevant Information)	Certificate - Certificate of personal entry and exit movement record
Required Documents	1. Valid Macao Identity Card; 2. Boarding pass (for departure at the Macao International Airport).
Charge (or Tax)	Free of charge
Quality Criteria	10 seconds [Please see Remark]
Remark	"Quality Criterion" refers to the time of processing required by service units (excluding time of waiting in a queue) calculated in the following manner: 1. From the moment when the service unit received the document; 2. Based on each document (excluding the procedure of checking more than one document or proof at Macau International Airport Border Checkpoint and Zhuhai-Macao Cross Border Industrial Zone Border Checkpoint).

ENTRY CLEARANCE PROCEDURE FOR HOLDERS OF A PRC PERMIT FOR TRAVELLING TO HONG KONG AND MACAO

Service	Immigration Clearance for Holders of a "PRC Permit for Travelling to Hong Kong and Macao"
Introduction (Service Coverage)	After receiving the "PRC Permit for Travelling to Hong Kong and Macao" from the applicant, the immigration officer at the Border Gate Checkpoint immediately examines the Permit and verifies the Permit holder. Then the officer enters the holder's bio data to the computer either manually or through the Optical Character reader. After confirming the information, the officer completes the entry clearance procedure and returns the Permit to the holder, together with a "notification". An appointment will also be made to facilitate the holder in his or her application for Residence Authorization at the Residents Subdivision located at the Immigration Department Office Building.
Service Provider	Border Control Subdivision at the Border Gate
Office Hours	6:00 – 1:00 (of the next day)
Enquiry Methods	In Immigration Department Office Building, Travessa Um do Tel: (853) 2872 5488

	Tel: (853) 2872 5488 Fax: (853) 8897 0300 Email: sminfo@fsm.gov.mo

Transactional Category	Immigration Clearance for Holders of a "PRC Permit for Travelling to Hong Kong and Macao" (in our performance pledges)
Relevant Service (Relevant Information)	Applying for Residence in Macao SAR – Application for Residence Authorization through Residents Subdivision Certificate – Certificate of Personal Movement Record
Target Groups & Application Eligibility	Holders of a "PRC Permit for Travelling to Hong Kong and Macao"
Necessary Documents	Valid "PRC Permit for Travelling to Hong Kong and Macao"
Charge (or Tax)	Free of charge
Quality Criteria	20 minutes [Please see Remark]
Remark	"Quality criteria" refers to the time of processing (excluding the time of waiting in a queue) and is calculated in the following manner: from the moment when the service unit receives the document.

AMENDMENTS OF "AUTORIZATION TO STAY" GRANTED TO NON-RESIDENTS UPON ENTRY

Service Name	Amendments of "Autorization to Stay" granted to non-residents upon entry
Introduction (Service Coverage)	Non-residents who are granted incorrect limit of stay may apply for amendment at the Investigation Subdivision.
Service Provider	Investigation Subdivision of the Immigration Department
Application Location	Immigration Department Office Building, Travessa Um do Cais de Pac On, Taipa, Macao
Office Hours	Mon to Thu: 9:00 – 17:45 (Tags dispensed until 16:30) Fri: 9:00 – 17:30 (Same as above) Closed on Sat, Sun and government holidays
Enquiry Methods	In person: the above address Tel: (853) 2872 5488 Fax: (853) 8897 0300 Email: sminfo@fsm.gov.mo

Transactional Category	Application (in our performance pledges)
Relevant Service (Relevant Information)	Certificate - Certificate of personal movement record
Target Groups and Application Eligibility	Non-residents who are granted incorrect limit of stay upon entry and need to have it amended
Application Approach	Applicant should apply to the Subdivision concerned in person
Required Document	Original of the travel document used for entry to Macao
Charge (or Tax)	Free of charge

Quality Criteria	26 minutes【 Please see Remark】
Remark	"Quality Criterion" refers to the time of processing required by service unit (excluding time of waiting in a queue) calculated in the following manner: from the moment when the service unit received and confirmed that all the required documents had been correctly prepared.

REISSUE OF "ARRIVAL CARD" / "SLIP OF AUTHORIZATION TO STAY"

Service	Reissue of "Arrival Card" / "Slip of Authorization to Stay"
Introduction (Service Coverage)	Reissue of "Arrival Card" / "Slip of Authorization to Stay" to non-residents who have lost
Service Provider	Police Station No.1, No.2 and No.3 Taipa Police Station and Airport Police Division (Police Reception at the airport terminal) Foreigners Subdivision and Non-resident Workers Subdivision of the Immigration Department Investigation Subdivision of the Immigration Department
Application Location	1. Police Station No.1 (Calçada do Gamboa, Instalações do Departamento Policial de Macau) 2. Police Station No.2 (Avenida de Almirante Lacerda, Macau) 3. Police Station No.3 (Praceta de 1 de Outubro, Entrada Principal do Comando da PSP, 1º. Piso, Macau) 4. Taipa Police Station (Rua de Tai Lin, n.º 141, Taipa, Macau) 5. Airport Police Division (Res do chão do Areporto International de Macau) 6. Investigation Subdivision, Foreigners Subdivision and Non-resident Workers Subdivision of the Immigration Department (Immigration Department Office Building, Travessa Um do Cais de Pac On, Taipa, Macao)
Office Hours	1. Police Station, Taipa Police Station and Investigation Subdivision of the Immigration Department: 24 hours 2. Foreigners Subdivision and Non-resident Workers Subdivision of the Immigration Department Mon to Thu: 9:00 – 17:45 (Tags dispensed until 16:30 at the Non-resident Workers Subdivision and until 17:00 at the other Subdivisions) Fri: 9:00 – 17:30 (Same as above) Closed on Sat, Sun and government holidays
Enquiry Methods	In person: Immigration Department Office Building, Travessa Um do Cais de Pac On, Taipa, Macao Tel: (853) 2872 5488 Fax: (853) 8897 0300 Email: sminfo@fsm.gov.mo

Transactional Category	Application
Target Groups and Application Eligibility	Non-residents who have lost the "Arrival Card" / "Slip of Authorization to Stay"

Application Approach	In person
Documents to be Presented	The original travel document used to apply for the relevant "Authorization to Stay"
Charge (or Tax)	Free of charge
Time Needed	Within the same day

STRATEGIC ECONOMIC AND BUSINESS INFORMATION

MACAO ECONOMY - BASIC INFORMATION AND DEVELOPMENTS

The **economy of Macau** has remained one of the most open in the world since its handover to China in 1999. Apparel exports and gambling-related tourism are mainstays of the economy. Since Macau has little arable land and few natural resources, it depends on mainland China for most of its food, fresh water, and energy imports. Japan and Hong Kong are the main suppliers of raw materials and capital goods. Although Macau was hit hard by the 1997–98 Asian financial crisis and the global downturn in 2001, its economy grew approximately 13 % annually on average Macau is a full Member of the World Trade Organization. Public Security has greatly improved after handover to People's Republic of China. With the tax revenue from the profitable gambling industry, the Macau government is able to introduce the social welfare program of 15 years of free education to all Macau citizens.

During the first three quarters of 2007, Macau registered year-on-year GDP increases of 31.4%.

A rapid rise in the number of mainland visitors due to China's easing of travel restrictions, increased public works expenditures, and significant investment inflows associated with the liberalisation of Macau's gaming industry drove the five-year recovery. The budget also returned to surplus after 2002 because of the surge in visitors from China and a hike in taxes on gambling profits, which generated about 70% of government revenue. The Hong Kong dollar is itself a reserve currency for the Macanese pataca, which is pegged at the official rate of around 1 Hong Kong dollar to 1.03 Macanese pataca

Macau was a barren fishing village with a population of about 400 before the Portuguese arrived in the 16th century, during the Age of Discovery.

In 1535, the Portuguese traders obtained by bribing the right to anchor ships in Macau harbours and engage in trading activities. Portuguese and Chinese merchants flocked to Macau, and it quickly became an important regional trading center in Portugal's lucrative trade along three major routes: Macau-Malacca-Goa-Lisbon, Guangzhou-Macau-Nagasaki and Macau-Manila-Mexico. However, with the decline of Portugal as a world power in the 17th and 18th centuries, the trading routes were challenged by other powers such as the Dutch and the British. After China ceded Hong Kong to the British in 1842, Macau's position as a major regional trading center declined further still because larger ships were drawn to the deep water port of Victoria Harbour. In an attempt to reverse the decline, from 1848 to the early 1870s Macau engaged in the infamous trade of coolies (slave labourers) as a transit port, shipping locals from southern China to Cuba, Peru, and other South American ports to work on plantations or in mines.

Fishing re-emerged as a dominant economic activity in Macau as it lost its position as a regional trading center. In the early 1920s, over 70% of Macau's 84,000 residents were engaged in fishing.

Meanwhile, some other businesses started to develop, such as matches, firecrackers, incense and fishing-boat building. But the most notable was the gambling business. Gambling was first legalised in the 19th century in an attempt to generate revenues for the government. The first casino monopoly concession was granted to the Tai Xing Company in 1937. The company was, however, too conservative to fully exploit the economic potential of gambling. The industry saw a major breakthrough in 1962 when the government granted the *Sociedade de Turismo e*

Diversoes de Macau (STDM), a syndicate jointly formed by Hong Kong and Macau businessmen, the monopoly rights to all forms of gambling. The STDM introduced western-style games and modernised the marine transport between Macau and Hong Kong, bringing millions of gamblers from Hong Kong every year.

In the 1970s Macau also saw a rapid development in its manufacturing sector. With Macau's low-cost operating environment and its surplus quotas under the Multi Fiber Arrangement (MFA), many Hong Kong industrialists established textile and garment manufacturing bases in Macau. At its golden age in the 1980s, the manufacturing sector accounted for about 40% of Macau's GDP; textiles and garments accounted for about 90% of Macau's total visible exports. However, the manufacturing sector has experienced a gradual decline since the early 1990s due to phasing out of the MFA quota system and the rising labour costs relative to mainland China and Southeast Asian countries

Although Macao has a relatively small economy, it pursues an open economic policy. It is one of the two international free ports in China. Goods, capital, foreign exchange and people fow freely in and out of Macao. As a separate customs territory, it boasts one of the lowest tax regimes in the region. Macao is integrated with the global economy and maintains traditional and special economic ties with the European Union (EU) and Portuguese-speaking countries. Consequently, Macao plays a relatively important role in the regional economies and is an important gateway and bridge linking mainland China with international markets.

MAJOR ECONOMIC INDICATORS

GDP at current prices: 348.216 billion patacas GDP (chain volume): 303.951 billion patacas GDP per capita at current prices: 611,300 patacas Median monthly earnings of employed population:

11,300 patacas Narrow money supply (M1): 47.519 billion patacas (at year-end) Broad money supply (M2): 374.431 billion patacas (at year-end) Residents' deposits: 366.762 billion patacas (at year-end) Inflation rate (Composite CPI): 6.11 percent Total merchandise imports and exports

Total imports: 70.928 billion patacas Total exports: 8.16 billion patacas Inbound and outbound container movements by land: 30,681 tonnes Inbound and outbound container movements by sea: 207,280 tonnes Seaborne container throughput: 119,927 TEUs Air cargo movements: 27,794 tonnes Inbound commercial flights: 19,285

TOURISM

Visitor arrivals: 28,082,300 By sea: 11,484,800 By land: 14,829,700 By air: 1,767,800

Hotel occupancy: 83.1 percent Per-capita spending of visitors (excluding gaming): 1,864 patacas

LONG-TERM DEVELOPMENT

Administrative Priorities of the MSAR Government

Looking back over the past year, we have strictly abided by the Basic Law of Macao, continued to follow the prpinciples of “One country, two systems”, “Macao people governing Macao” and a high degree of autonomy, and pragmatically opened up new opportunities with an eagerness to forge ahead. With the strong support of the central government and the concerted efforts of the MSAR Government and Macao people, we have overcome both internal and external diffculties, leading to steady development in society, politics, the economy and culture. Certainly, we recognise that there remains room for improvement in the Government's administration, and are also aware of the various issues that affect society. Therefore we continue to strive to enhance our administration and seek solutions to our problems.

In 2013, to realise the various policy objectives, we will make progress over time and will intensify scientifc policy-making; continue to improve public administration operations, live out the spirit of accountability, and govern in accordance with the law; strengthen our efforts to foster integrity and in auditing; safeguard social justice; fully protect the freedom of the press; pay heed to the voices of the public; design policies that are scientifc and forward-looking; and work hard towards realising our sound development plan.

ECONOMIC DEVELOPMENT TRENDS

Although Macao has a relatively small economy, it pursues an open economic policy. It is one of the two international free ports in China. Goods, capital, foreign exchange and people fow freely in and out of Macao. As a separate customs territory, it boasts one of the lowest tax regimes in the region. Macao is integrated with the global economy and maintains traditional and special economic ties with the European Union (EU) and Portuguese-speaking countries. Consequently, Macao plays a relatively important role in the regional economies and is an important gateway and bridge linking mainland China with international markets.

FINANCIAL INDUSTRY

The fnancial industry in Macao underwent rapid development towards the end of the 1980s. Following 20 years of growth and refnement, Macao now boasts a sophisticated and open fnancial system with unique characteristics in the region. The Monetary Authority supervises Macao's fnancial industry.

Macao's fnancial institutions consist of banks, insurance companies, fnancial companies, fnancial intermediaries, bureaux de change, cash remittance companies, non-banking credit agencies and the representative offces of overseas fnancial institutions. As at 31 December 2012, among fnancial institutions authorised to operate in Macao there were 29 banks (including the Government-owned Postal Savings Offce), 23 insurance companies, one pension-fund management company, one fnance company, two fnancial intermediary companies, 12 bureaux de change, six bureaux de change counters, two cash remittance companies, one non-banking credit agency and one representative offce of an overseas fnancial institution.

THE BANKING SYSTEM

The primary legislation regulating Macao's fnancial industry, the Financial System Act, was promulgated in 1993, and focuses on measures to strengthen risk management. In particular, it emphasises strict requirements on operators, and monitors the suitability of major shareholders and managers, and new operating risks. The act also introduced a new monitoring system based on fnancial institutions and their subsidiaries. The act takes into account the recommendations of the Basel Committee on Banking Supervision and lessons learnt from the EU's experience in harmonising banking legislation, while drawing on the experiences of countries and territories whose fnancial systems are similar to those of Macao.

In accordance with the Financial System Act, the Chief Executive of the MSAR may, on an individual basis, approve the registration of credit institutions in Macao, the establishment of branches of overseas credit institutions, the setting-up of branches or representative offces outside Macao by locally registered credit institutions, and the establishment of fnancial intermediaries and other fnancial institutions in Macao, after considering the advice of the

Monetary Authority. However, this provision does not include companies regulated by special laws.

In addition, under Decree-Law No. 58/99/M of 18 October 1999, the Offshore Service Law, the Chief Executive of Macao, may, on the advice of the Monetary Authority, grant permission for the establishment of offshore fnancial institutions.

At the end of 2012, the 29 banks in Macao owned assets with a total value of 796.2 billion patacas, and hired 5,348 employees at their 188 headquarters and branches. Total deposits in Macao's banking system amounted to 540.6 billion patacas, while loans totalled almost 407 billion patacas – the loan-to-deposit ratio being 75.3 percent.

When classifed by source of origin, the banking system of Macao - excluding the Government-operated Macao Postal Savings – has just one bank registered with local capital, with the other 27 currently operating banks being either branches or subsidiaries of overseas banking groups. Foreign capital mainly comes from seven countries and regions: mainland China, Portugal, the United States, the United Kingdom, Singapore, Taiwan and Hong Kong.

The operations of Macao's banks now make extensive use of computer software and hardware. With the popularity of electronic banking, inter-bank ATMs are now found all over Macao, serving customers of different banks. Additionally, certain banks offer 24-hour banking services via channels including mobile phones and the Internet.

Notwithstanding their relatively rapid development in recent years, Macao's banks have continued to achieve new heights in terms of fnancial results, thanks to their strong business tradition, prudent operations, and stringent regulation. Macao's banks also boast healthy capital, full liquidity and quality assets, keeping the whole banking system safe and reliable.

THE INSURANCE INDUSTRY MARKET

At the end of 2011, some 23 insurance companies were permitted to conduct business in Macao.

Of these, 11 were life insurance companies and the other 12 were engaged in non-life insurance. Classifed by their origins, eight of these companies were local, and the other 15 were branches of overseas companies. In addition, one fund-management company was authorised to conduct pension-fund business in the SAR. At the end of 2012, Macao's insurance industry employed 459 people. There were 3,364 authorised insurance intermediaries: 2,266 individual agents, 1,016 salespersons, 69 corporate agents, and 13 insurance brokers.

In 2012, total insurance premium income was 5.4 billion patacas, 23.8 percent more than in 2011. Life insurance premium income accounted for 69.4 percent of the insurance market's total income, with the remaining 30.6 percent coming from non-life insurance. Life insurance premiums totalled 3.7 billion patacas, up by 19.1 percent from the previous year. Non-life insurance premiums totalled 1.7 billion patacas, representing an increase of 35.9 percent.

At the end of 2012, seven life insurance companies and one pension-fund management company were providing private pension fund management services. So far, 46 pension funds have been established under the Legal Framework for Private Pension Funds, of which fve are closed-end and 41 are open-end funds. To date, more than 780 private pension fund schemes have been established by businesses or self-employed individuals, benefting a total of more than 100,000 employees. The assets of the managed funds totalled about 8.5 billion patacas.

Supervision and Regulation of the Insurance Industry

In Macao, the duty to supervise, coordinate and inspect insurance activities rests with the Chief Executive, with the Monetary Authority authorised to perform these functions.

The Macao Insurance Law, the Legal Framework for Private Pension Funds, and the Insurance agents and Brokers Law have been formulated to regulate insurance companies, private pension fund management companies, and insurance intermediaries, respectively.

Compulsory Insurance

There are six categories of compulsory insurance in Macao, all of which require uniform policy wording and tariff rates. The compulsory insurance categories include: motor vehicle (third-party risks) insurance, employees' compensation insurance, professional liability insurance for travel agents, public liability insurance relating to the installation of publicity and advertising objects, third party liability for pleasure boats, and civil liability insurance for lawyers.

Insurance Intermediaries Quality Assurance Scheme

To raise the overall level of professionalism of insurance intermediaries, it is required that all applicants must pass a qualifcation examination before obtaining an intermediary licence and conducting insurance business in Macao. In 2012, a total of 3,320 candidates sat the insurance intermediary qualifcation examination, with a pass rate of 86 percent.

To better protect customer interests and ensure that all intermediaries possess basic product knowledge, it became mandatory from 1 July 2011 for all intermediaries intending to sell investmentlinked insurance products to pass a qualifying examination. However, intermediaries who had obtained life insurance licences before this date were granted a two-year transition period before they had to meet the requirement. The transition period ended on 30 June 2013. At the end of 2012, a total of 1,024 candidates had sat for the qualifying examination with a pass rate of 82 percent.

To further safeguard customer interests, the Monetary Authority has enacted various rules that set standards for data disclosure methods and procedures for insurance companies. The rules include detailed explanations of the cooling-off period specifc to life insurance policies, and the rights and interests concerned, as well as various guidelines regarding life insurance.

THE CONSTRUCTION AND REAL ESTATE INDUSTRY

As Macao's economy rebounded soon after the Handover, the local property industry entered a new stage of development.

The average sales price for residential units in 2012, calculated in terms of usable foor area, was 57,362 patacas per square metre, 38.4 percent higher than the previous year's fgure of 41,433 patacas. The average prices per gross foor area for residential units on the Macao peninsula, Taipa and Coloane were 52,573 patacas, 64,494 patacas and 80,981 patacas per square metre, respectively.

The corresponding sales price of industrial units was 20,812 patacas per square metre, up by 73.4 percent from a year earlier. The average sales price of offce space was 46,320 patacas per square metre, up by 32.1 percent from a year earlier. In 2012, construction began on buildings totalling a gross foor area of 304,376 square metres, 17.1 percent less than in the previous year. These buildings, when completed, will provide 1,592 residential units, 1,029 car parking spaces and 355 motorcycle parking spaces.

Buildings completed in 2012 (including expansion) providing 2,558 units with a total area of 1,568,470 square metres, representing a 34.9 percent increase compared with 2011. Among them, 2,443 were residential units, up 1.2-fold year on year, 4,236 car parking spaces and 1,468 motorcycle parking spaces.

In 2012, the number of recorded residential transactions involving payment of property transfer stamp duty was 25,419, down eight percent year on year, with a total transaction value of 100.91 billion patacas, up 32.3 percent. Among them, 9,520 units were new building units within the real estate tax waiver period (representing 37.5 percent of the total), involving a total transaction value of 52.42 billion patacas.

A total of 16,917 residential units changed hands in 2012 (of which 4,527 were uncompleted units), 2,205 less than in 2011. Among them 12,435 were located in the Macao peninsula, 3,440 in Taipa and 1,042 in Coloane. The total value of transaction was 74.23 billion patacas, 26.1 percent higher than the fgure in 2011. The numbers of shops, offces and industrial building units bought and sold during the year were 2,189, 783 and 246 respectively. For parking spaces, 5,122 transactions were recorded.

In 2012, prices of construction materials rose steadily. The price index of construction materials for residential buildings rose by 3.5 percent year on year to 120.1. The price indices for sand and concrete rose by 22.6 percent and 21.2 percent respectively.

The average daily wage of a construction worker in 2012 decreased by 2.1 percent year on year to 565 patacas, however, the average daily wage of local construction workers increased by 9.7 percent over the past year to 670 patacas. The real wage index for construction workers, discounted for infation, was 88.4, down 6.9 percent on the previous year. The real wage index of local construction workers, however, increased by 2.4 percent to 99.9.

INDUSTRIAL LICENCES

Under Decree-Law No. 11/99/M dated 22 March 1999, all assembly and processing manufacturing enterprises licensed under Decree-Law No. 55/97/M dated 9 December 1997 and listed in Category D of the frst revised edition of the Macao Industries Classifcation Index must apply for industrial licences from the Economic Services Bureau. Under Article 11 of Decree-Law No. 11/99/M, it is strictly prohibited to carry out the above activities in residential buildings.

Applications for industrial licences are classifed as "general system" (for industrial buildings), “special system” or “special activities”. A non-special activities licence for a general-system operation in an industrial building costs 500 patacas. The fees for special-system (not located in industrial buildings) or special-activity licences are calculated according to the foor area, and they range from 700 patacas to 4,500 patacas.

In 2012, the Economic Services Bureau issued fve general-system industrial licences and 17 special system/special activities industrial licences. In addition, 11 general-system industrial unit licences and 32 special-system/special-activity industrial unit licences were issued, 34 industrial licences and 86 industrial unit licences were revoked, and 126 industrial licences were reissued due to the transfer, removal or merger of industrial establishments, or because information relating to them had changed.

Certifcates of Origin

Certifcates of Origin (CO) may be applied for from the Economic Services Bureau. These are used to prove to a third party that exports have been suffciently assembled and processed in Macao, and are thus classifed as products originating in Macao.

There are four types of COs: the Certifcate of Origin, the Generalised System of Preferences (GSP) Certifcate of Origin, the Certifcate of Origin (Foreign Products) and the CEPA Certifcate of Origin. The frst is a general document used for customs clearance. The second is used for customs clearance in importing countries and regions that use GSP. The third is used to prove that Macao was not the origin of products re-exported via Macao. The fourth is used for goods of Macao origin that enjoy zero tariff and other incentives under CEPA.

In 2012, the Economic Services Bureau issued 8,881 COs, for exports primarily destined for the United States and the EU. Exports to the United States accounted for 41.8 percent of the total; exports to the EU for 26.6 percent. The bureau also issued 19 GSP Certifcates of Origin; 73.7 percent of these were for exports to the EU. It also issued 465 CEPA certifcates of origin.

Certifcates of Macao Service Supplier

To enjoy the incentives and benefts under CEPA, all Macao enterprises that conform to Annex 5 of CEPA and all regulations in supplementary protocols are required to apply to the Economic Services Bureau for a Certifcate of Macao Service Supplier. From 1 January 2004, when CEPA was implemented, to 31 December 2012, the Economic Services Bureau issued 429 Certifcates of Macao Service Suppliers.

Export and Import Licences

Licences for Export and Import are regulated by External Trade Law (Law No. 7/2003). Under the law, any natural person or legal person may engage in external trade activities, provided the Government holds evidence that they have fulflled their tax obligations, particularly those involving business tax and excise duty. Macao exercises minimal controls over import and export activities that are consistent with its international obligations, and considerations of environmental, sanitary, safety and security issues.

The laws and regulations that currently govern imports and exports include:

Law No. 7/2003 of the External Trade Law; Regulatory By-law No. 28/2003 on External Trade Operations;

Executive Order No. 452/2011 (Table of goods for self use or self consumption; Exportation Table and Importation Table; and table of goods requiring health quarantine/plant quarantine);

Decree-Law No. 45/86/M on regulations applicable to Macao under the Convention on International Trade in Endangered Species of Wild Fauna and Flora (CITES);

Law No. 4/99/M of the Excise Duty Regulations amended by Law No. 8/2008 on 25 August, Law No. 7/2009 on 25 May and Law No. 11/2011 on 19 December;

Decree-Law No. 62/95/M about the formulation of policies and measures on the Control and Reduced Use of Ozone-Depleting Substances and its related regulations;

Executive Order No. 425/2009 setting a limit on the annual import of HCFCs, in Table C of Executive Order No. 78/GM/95, issued on 4 December; and

Decree-Law No. 51/99/M regulating commercial or industrial activities concerning computer programs, audiovisual products, and other relevant regulations.

According to law, licences for commodities that are subject to the special regime, listed in Exportation Table A and Importation Table B (contained in Executive Order No. 452/2011), must be applied for in advance, regardless of the type of import or export. These licences are issued by authorised institutions. The Economic Services Bureau is authorised to issue such licences.

Regulated exported goods include:

Textiles and garments; Species regulated by the Convention on International Trade in Endangered Species of Wild

Fauna and Flora (CITES);

Ozone-depleting substances;

CD ROM production facilities;

Weapons, ammunition and related parts and accessories; and

Pharmaceutical items and medicines, and certain chemicals.

Regulated imported goods include:

Drinks with alcohol concentrations of at least 30 percent by volume, and tobacco;

Motor vehicles; Species regulated by the Convention on International Trade in Endangered Species of Wild Fauna and Flora (CITES);

Ozone-depleting substances;

CD ROM production facilities and materials;

Live animals, meat and seafood, eggs and certain milk products;

Pharmaceutical products and drugs, and certain chemicals;

Weapons, ammunition and related parts and accessories;

Infammable explosives; and

Certain telecommunication transmitters and receivers.

Since applications for export licences for textile and garment products were frst processed electronically in the fourth quarter of 2000, the Economic Services Bureau has been stepping up its efforts to electronically process applications for import and export licences. Since the introduction of the pilot scheme for electronically processing the import licence applications of some products in 2004, the number of applications for electronic services increased gradually from 2005 to 2012, with product categories expanding to include cigarettes, alcohol, motor vehicles, and air conditioners.

In 2012, the Economic Services Bureau issued 6,548 export licences and 32,107 import licences.

PROTECTION OF INTELLECTUAL PROPERTY RIGHTS

The Intellectual Property Department of the Economic Services Bureau is responsible for managing and enforcing laws relating to intellectual property rights; handling registration affairs relating to industrial property rights, including registration of trademarks, business names and logos; patents for inventions; utility patents, designs/new prototypes, semiconductor product topographies, places of origin / geographical indicators and awards. It is also responsible for updating and recording any remarks, extensions and acts of termination relating to industrial property rights. In addition, the department registers copyright and other related rights collectively managed by relevant organisations. The Macao Customs Service is responsible for enforcement of legislation and implementation of punitive measures regarding intellectual property rights, to enhance fair competition and combat counterfeiting, thus promoting compliance with intellectual property rights and authorship regulations.

Intellectual Property Rights System

The Copyright and Related Rights Code and the Industrial Property Law are currently the two major pieces of legislation related to intellectual property rights in Macao.

Copyright and Related Rights Code

In Macao, copyright is regulated by the 27 April 1966 Decree-Law No. 46980, published in the Government Gazette on 8 January 1972. Law No. 4/85/M was then promulgated on 25 November 1985 and supplemented by Decree-Law No. 17/98/M promulgated on 4 May 1998. On 16 August 1999 the Copyright and Related Rights Law (Decree-Law No. 43/99/M) was gazetted and came into effect on 1 October of the same year, protecting copyright under clearly defned terms. The regulation provides full protection for works of literature, drama, music and art, movies and television broadcasting, as well as all original productions, and it fulfls the requirements of Trade Related Intellectual Property Rights formulated by the WTO.

To comply with the international protection standards arising from the special features of the modern information society, in 2012 the Government amended the Copyright and Related Rights Law approved by Decree-Law No. 43/99/M to produce Law No. 5/2012, which came into effect on 1 June in the same year. The amended Copyright and Related Rights Law enhances the rights and protection of copyright holders, art workers and producers, providing them with the rights of Internet transmission, distribution and commercial lease. At the same time, the law also adequately modifes the relevant criminal penalty to further protect copyright in a digital environment. Together, these measures more closely aligned Macao's copyright system with the latest international protection standards.

In Macao, copyright is an inherent right. A piece of work, whether issued, published, used or operated, already lends copyright to the author upon completion, allowing the author to enjoy related legal protection, even without registration. In general, copyright in Macao expires 50 years after the death of the author, including for works issued or published after death. However, the period of protection of individual pieces of work varies, depending on their type.

THE INDUSTRIAL PROPERTY RIGHTS SYSTEM

The current Industrial Property Law was promulgated on 13 December 1999 and came into effect on 6 June 2000, replacing the previous rules and regulations. It was only then that Macao had its own industrial property rights laws and was able to completely fulfl its international duties. The Industrial Property Law offers protection in the following eight areas: patents, including invention patents and utility patents; certifcates of complementary protection for drugs and herbal medicines; topology maps of semiconductor products; industrial designs and new industrial products; trademarks; the names and logos of business establishments; places of origin and geographical indications; and awards.

Trademark Registration

Any trademarks that fulfl the requirements of the Industrial Property Law may be registered in Macao, but registration is not compulsory. Trademark registration is geographical: trademark regulations in the Macao SAR protect only trademarks issued locally. Separate applications must be made in other countries and regions for protection there.

In 2012, the Intellectual Property Department of the Economic Services Bureau accepted 9,581 applications for trademark licences, an increase of 11.54 percent on the 8,590 applications processed in 2011. Applications were mainly from mainland China, the United States, Hong Kong, Macao, Japan and British Virgin Islands. As at 31 December 2012, the Economic Services Bureau had received a cumulative total of 87,336 applications.

Patent Registration

Since 7 June 2000, all applications for patents – including invention patents and utility patents, designs and new products – may be submitted directly to the Economic Services Bureau.

The Economic Services Bureau and the State Intellectual Property Offce (SIPO) signed the Cooperation Agreement on Intellectual Property between the State Intellectual Property Offce and the Economic Services Bureau of the Macao SAR on 24 January 2003. They agreed to extend the applicability of SIPO patent approvals to Macao. The effective period of this agreement was extended for fve years from 2008.

In 2012, the Economic Services Bureau accepted 239 applications for patent extensions for inventions, 82 patent registration applications, and applications for registration of 167 designs and new products. These applications were mainly from Switzerland, Japan, the United States, Macao and mainland China. As at 31 December 2012, the Economic Services Bureau had received a cumulative total of 966 applications for patent extensions for inventions, 1,309 applications for patents and applications for the registration of 1,033 designs and new products.

SME Assistance Programme

Supporting the development of small and medium-sized enterprises (SMEs) has always been a focal point for the Government's policy. In 2003, in response to the prevailing socio-economic situation, three enterprise-fnance programmes were introduced.

Under the SME Assistance Programme introduced in May 2003, the Government provided enterprises with interest-free loans to improve business, enhance operating capacity and mitigate impacts from SARS. During the past few years, Macao's economy has grown rapidly. To meet the increasing demands arising from development, in November 2006 the scheme was revised, and the maximum amount of fnancial aid was increased from 200,000 patacas to 300,000 patacas. Upon a new revision in February 2009, the maximum amount was further increased to 500,000 patacas.

In March 2012, another revision increased the maximum amount to 600,000 patacas. As at the end of December 2012, a total of 7,005 applications had been received, of which 6,223 were approved, involving total fnancial aid amounting to 1.481 billion patacas (These fgures include the fnancial aid applications by businesses affected by Severe Typhoon Hagupit in 2008). The enterprises that received loans are mainly engaged in retailing, construction and public works, Chinese restaurants and hotels, wholesale, public services, social welfare and private services, as well as real estate and company services.

The SME Credit Assurance Scheme was launched in August 2003. The scheme is designed to assist enterprises in obtaining bank loans for business development. The MSAR Government provides eligible enterprises with credit guarantees of up to 50 percent of a bank loan up to 1.5 million patacas. The scheme was revised in June 2009, with the maximum credit guarantee rate raised to 70 percent, and the maximum credit guarantee amount raised to 3.5 million patacas. From the scheme's commencement to the end of December 2012, the Government received 308 applications, involving a total loan amount of 748 million patacas; of which 295 applicants obtained Government credit guarantees totalling 492 million patacas. Most applicants were from the construction and public works sector, followed by retailing, wholesaling, imports and exports, real estate, company services, textiles, garments and leather manufacturing.

The SME Special Credit Assurance Programme was introduced in August 2003. Its aim is to assist enterprises to carry out special projects. Under the fnancing scheme, the Government provides banks with a maximum of 100 percent credit guarantee for the eligible enterprises. The maximum credit is one million patacas. Since the scheme's implementation at the end of December 2012, the Government has received 69 applications, involving a total credit guarantee of 55.037 million patacas, of which 56 applicants obtained 100 percent credit guarantees from the Government, with a total value of 45.73 million patacas. Most of the approved enterprises are engaged in retail, followed by wholesale, paper, printing and publishing, imports and exports, textiles, garments and leather manufacturing, restaurants and hotels.

LABOUR REGULATIONS

The Labour Relations Law (Law No. 7/2008) is the legal basis of industrial relations. It defnes the rules and regulations on working hours, working at night and on shifts, weekly rest days, mandatory holidays, annual leave, absence from work, maternity leave, remunerations, termination of employment, contract types, administrative infractions, and procedures and penalties for minor contraventions. The law further protects and balances the legal interests and rights of employers and employees alike. Law No. 21/2009, the Law on Employment of Non-Resident Workers, and its relevant supplementary rules further implemented the Framework Law on Employment Policy and Workers' Rights, reaffrming that when employing non-resident workers, the employer must assure employment priority for local employees, and ensure equal rights, working conditions and benefts for local and non-resident workers.

In view of the characteristics of Macao's industries and social needs, the Labour Affairs Bureau studied several laws concerning labour relations, including the System of Part-time Work, Workplace Sub-contract Management System and Maritime Labour Convention, as well as Decree Law No. 40/95/M, Employees' Compensation Insurance Ordinance, and Decree Law No. 32/94/M, System for Approvals of Recruitment Agency Licences.

LABOUR RELATIONS

The Labour Inspection Department under the Labour Affairs Bureau provides consultancy services on labour regulations to local citizens free of charge, accepts and mediates in labour-relations or work accident disputes, and monitors enterprises' compliance with labour regulations. To effectively curb illegal employment, the Labour Inspection Department, the Public Security Police, and the Macao Customs Service jointly or independently carried out regular or non-regular inspections, according to their authority.

In 2012, the Labour Inspection Department provided 5,251 consultations about labour regulations to enquirers visiting the offce. Among the individuals who sought assistance, 76.8 percent were employees and 23.4 percent were employers. Most enquiries were from the community, social and individual services in terms of industry, as well as from families hiring domestic helpers. Topics of consultation were mainly dismissal compensation, prior notice period and annual leaves, which accounted for 14.3 percent, 12.4 percent and 10.4 percent of all enquires. There were 38,247 enquiries via telephone.

A total of 2,016 complaints from 3,907 employee enquiries were handled, 25.3 percent fewer than in 2011. Most involved wages (16.3 percent), overtime compensation (11.5 percent) and weekly leave (8.6 percent). By industry, most complainants were from construction, followed by group, social and individual services, each accounting for 28.9 percent, and accommodation, western and Chinese restaurants and establishments of similar nature (19.7 percent).

The 8,363 complaints settled in 2012 involved 9,020 employee enquiries and 3,009 workplaces; 619 transcripts were prepared. Among the identifed illegalities concerning employment disputes, 1,433 cases involved creditor's rights – mainly regarding wages, reduction of basic remuneration and suspension of work. Of all breaches of law, 1.2 percent were cases in which the employer paid the employee's claim without resorting to compiling transcripts of evidence; the remaining cases were resolved through the compilation of evidence transcripts or litigation in court.

Creditors' rights arising from employment disputes, industrial accidents and occupational diseases totalled 55.64 million patacas, involving 6,293 employees. Industrial accidents, wage compensation and reduction of basic remuneration accounted for 60.0 percent, 15.8 percent and 7.0 percent of these cases, respectively.

In 2012 the Labour Inspection Department received notifcations of 87 cases of agreement on lowering basic remuneration, involving 292 local employees, and seven non-resident employees. After investigations, one case was fled as alleged contravention of the Labour Relations Law, involving one person.

The Labour Inspection Department received 233 copies of employment contracts for the under-aged, involving 838 individuals aged over 16 but below 18, and six aged over 14 but below 16. After verifcation, 31 cases were fled as alleged contraventions against the Labour Relations Law, involving 59 persons.

In its efforts to combat illegal employment, the Labour Affairs Bureau fled 709 cases of illegal employment, in accordance with the Regulation on the Prohibition of Illegal Employment and the Law on Employment of Non-resident Workers and its relevant supplementary laws. After investigation, 743 offenders were penalised for breaches of the law, with fnes imposed totalling 8.24 million patacas. In these cases, 264 non-local residents were found working for others in the MSAR without permits. Also, 171 non-local residents were found to be engaged in activities for their own beneft. Individuals in the two groups were fned a total of 5.64 million patacas.

Under the Law on Employment of Non-resident Workers and rules related to non-resident worker accommodation rights stipulated in Executive Order No. 88/2010, 27 cases regarding the accommodation rights of non-resident workers were initiated and 40 inspections were carried out in 2012.

Human Resources Offce

The Human Resources Offce (HRO) was established under Executive Order No. 116/2007. Its main duties are:

To collect and analyse all information related to the local labour market and its changes. The administration will rely on this information when making decisions on matters that concern the employment of non-resident employees;

To recommend measures on the employment of non-resident employees, for consideration by senior offcials;

To accept applications for the employment of non-resident employees, and to compile these applications into dossiers;

To work with other public departments to jointly enforce laws related to the employment of non-resident employees; and

To enforce labour laws and implement related policies with the Labour Affairs Bureau.

Employment of Non-resident Employees

The Government imports non-resident labour on the main premise that the employment and labour rights of local employees are not harmed. As such, the employment of non-resident employees is merely a measure to overcome local manpower shortages, whilst ensuring the continuous and stable development of Macao's economy. Since its establishment on 28 May 2007, the HRO has rigorously analysed each application to take on non-resident employees. During 2012, it received 37,591 applications for work permits for professionals, non-professionals, domestic helpers, non-resident workers and activities for personal interest, including importation of non-resident employees, renewal of permits, transfer of employees, statements of objection, and petitions.

Of these applications, 15,368 were for non-professional employees, 3,732 were for professional employees and 18,451 were for domestic helpers. Also, there were 40 applications for work permits to engage in activities for the applicants' personal interest. At the end of 2012, there were 110,552 employees with non-resident ID cards in Macao.

Consumer Council

The Consumer Council is responsible for providing comments on consumer protection policies to be implemented by the Government, and driving various efforts to protect consumers' rights.

Establishment of Cooperative Networks

In 1997, the council became a full member of Consumers International. It subsequently signed cooperation agreements with the Consumer Protection Bureau of Portugal , the Instituto Nacional del Consumo (National Consumer Institute) of Spain, the Consumers Association of Singapore, and Consumers' Foundation, Chinese Taipei (CFCT). It also formed an alliance network with consumer protection units in the "9 +2" PPRD region. In October 2009, the Consumer Council announced a declaration of cooperation together with 22 consumer protection agencies in Hong Kong and a number of cities in mainland China, to establish the Urban Alliance for the Protection of Consumer Rights. For over ten years, the council has been a signatory to cooperation agreements regarding the protection of consumers' rights, along with 42 mainland, Hong Kong and Taiwan consumer protection units, including the Guangdong Consumer Council, Shandong Provincial Consumers Association, Fujian Province Commission of Consumers, Beijing Consumers Association, Shanghai Commission for the Protection of Consumers' Rights and Interests, Chongqing Commission for the Protection of Consumers' Rights and Interests, Zhejiang Provincial Consumers Association, Tianjin Consumers Association, Zhuhai Municipal Consumer Council and Shenzhen Consumer Council. In these networks, the signatories exchange relevant information and undertake various cooperative programmes.

Reception Services

At the end of 2011, the Consumer Council moved its Iao Hon Offce to the Government Integrated Service Centre in Areia Preta. In March 2013, the Consumer Council moved its head offce to 3rd5th foors, Clementina A. L. Ho Building, No. 26 Avenida de Horta e Costa. In addition, consumers can fle complaints and submit enquiries to the Consumer Council via e-mail.

Consumer Arbitration Centre

The Consumer Arbitration Centre was established in 1998 with an aim of resolving minor disputes that occur within the territory, and which do not involve more than 50,000 patacas, through mediation, conciliation and arbitration.

Businesses that value their reputations and wish to resolve potential customer disputes are invited to apply for membership.

By 2012, 1,261 active companies had joined the Consumer Arbitration Centre. They included Chinese and western pharmaceutical businesses, department stores, supermarkets, catering companies, jewellery and timepiece shops, insurance agencies, laundry and dyeing companies, beauty and ftness centres, mobile telephone companies, computer products companies, travel agencies and real estate agencies.

THE GAMING INDUSTRY

To meet the real needs of sustainable development of Macao, the Government continues to implement and modify measures to regulate the scope and pace of the gaming industry's expansion. With the objective of increasing the industry's competitiveness, the Government stringently limits the numbers of new casinos, gaming tables and slot machines. It also strengthens supervision of the gaming industry to facilitate appropriate, gradual and healthy development of the industry, and promotes responsible gambling.

According to statistics provided by the Statistics and Census Service and the Gaming Inspection and Coordination Bureau, gaming tax revenues continued to set new records in 2012, totalling

113.378 billion patacas, 13.76 percent above the 2011 fgure of 99.656 billion patacas. The gaming industry's gross income was 305.235 billion patacas, up by 16.97 percent from 260.958 billion patacas in 2011.

THE HISTORY AND VARIETY OF GAMING IN MACAO

With a history stretching back over three centuries, gaming is one of Macao's oldest industries. Legal gaming businesses in Macao currently include games of chance, interactive gaming, parimutuels (betting on animal races) and lotteries. MSAR Law No. 16/2001, Gaming Industry Regulatory Framework, states that games of chance are gambling games with results that depend completely or mainly on the player's luck. Since such games must be played in casinos or other licensed venues, they are usually known as casino games. Games of chance form the biggest sector of Macao's gaming industry. Gross revenues in this area rose to 304.139 billion patacas in 2011,

12.74 percent more than the previous year's fgure of 267.867 billion patacas, and accounted for 99.64 percent of the industry's gross takings.

The laws and regulations governing gaming allow the following types of games to be played in casinos: Baccarat, Blackjack, Boule, Dice/Craps, Big-and-Small, 12-number game, Fan-tan, FishPrawn-Crab dice game, Lucky 13-card game, Mahjong, Baccarat Mahjong, Chinese Dominoes Mahjong, Pachinko (Japanese pinball game), Chinese Dominoes (Pai Gow), Chinese Dominoes with two stones, Three-card poker, Five-card poker, Roulette, Sap I Chi (or 12-card game), Super Pan Nine game, Taiwanese Dominoes, Three-card Baccarat, Wheel of Fortune, Football Poker, Stud Poker, Tombola, Slot Machines, Q Poker, Casino Challenge, Makccarat, Texas Poker, Fortune 3 Card Poker, Fortune 8, Dragon/Phoenix and Omaha Poker.

Three signifcant changes occurred in Macao's gaming industry during the 20th century. The most important and far-reaching of these was the establishment of a syndicate jointly formed by Hong Kong and Macao businessmen Stanley Ho Hung Sun, Henry Fok Ying Tung, Teddy Ip Tek Lei and Ip Hon in 1961 to enter an open bid for a casino gaming licence. The syndicate's successful bid subsequently led to the founding of Sociedade de Turismo e Diversoes de Macau (STDM) in 1962, which replaced the Tai Heng Entertainment Corporation that had held a gaming monopoly for the previous 24 years. STDM's exclusive casino gaming concession was renewed four times in the following four decades, and ended only on 31 March 2002.

Under its franchise concession contract, STDM paid a special gaming tax to the Government. Its rate was revised many times; but as of 2001, it was 31.8 percent of the company's gross revenue. Meanwhile, the concessionaire was required to invest in major infrastructure developments, and fulfl an obligation to beneft the Macao community. Prior to Macao's return to the motherland, the highest-ever annual casino gaming gross revenue was only around 17.78 billion patacas – a much lower fgure than those seen in more-recent years.

Horse racing and dog racing are also legal gaming activities in Macao, and they are categorised as pari-mutuels. According to the defnition in MSAR Law No. 16/2001, Gaming Industry Regulatory Framework, pari-mutuels are animal races or sports on which bets are placed, and the winners share the pooled bets in accordance with their stakes and after the deduction of commissions, charges and taxes.

In fact, the histories of horse racing and dog racing in Macao can be traced back at least as far as 1842 and 1932, respectively, although repeated suspensions and resumptions of racing have occurred, due to changing economic conditions. At present, the Macau Jockey Club (MJC) operates Macao's horseracing activities; while the Macau (Yat Yuen) Canidrome Co. organises dog races.

To create more favourable conditions for the development of horse racing and dog racing in Macao, the Government granted approval in August 2003 for related franchise operators to accept online bets via the Internet. At present, the MJC has approval to simulcast and accept bets on races in Hong Kong, Singapore and Malaysia. In 2010, approval was granted to simulcast races in South Africa.

In 2012, there was a decrease in gross revenue from horse racing in Macao, with the fgure dropping 19.4 percent over the previous year, while gross income from dog racing decreased by 31.6 percent.

In addition to casino gaming, horse racing and dog racing, many other gaming activities are popular in Macao. The most popular of these are sports lotteries.

Sports lotteries are operated by Macau Slot Co. (Macau Slot). The Government granted the company a franchise to conduct football betting in 1998 and basketball betting in 2000. Since 1987, Macau Slot has also held the franchise to operate instant lottery tickets, which were launched in Macao in 1984.

Pacapio, a kind of Chinese lottery, is one of the oldest lottery formats in Macao. Pacapio tickets are printed with the frst 80 Chinese characters from a book called The Thousand-Character Classic. Formerly, the 20 winning characters were picked at random by a pigeon, later they were decided by a ball-draw system. From the late 1990s onwards, the drawing of pacapio was computerised, and it subsequently became known as "Computer Pacapio". Since April 2004, the Government has also allowed betting on pacapio via telephone or the Internet. The Wing Heng Lottery Company currently holds the concession for operating Chinese lotteries.

Gross revenue from sports lotteries, instant lotteries and pacapio accounted for only 0.18 percent of Macao's gross gaming income during 2012.

Macao's long heritage and rich variety of gaming activities has brought it worldwide renown as a tourism and gaming destination.

DECISIVE LIBERALISATION AND TIMELY CONTROL

The gaming monopoly franchise system enjoyed a long history in Macao after it was introduced in the 1930s. In 1982, the Legislative Assembly passed Law No. 6/82/M stipulating that the operation of casino gaming activities would be subject to a monopoly franchise or special concession system. Under the special concession system, concessions were granted to a maximum of four concessionaires. In 1986, the Legislative Assembly passed Law No. 10/86/M, which partially revised Law No. 6/82/M. The amendment stipulated that a maximum of three concessionaires would in future be granted gaming concessions. It indicated that the then administration was considering ending the casino gaming monopoly, though this move was not implemented at the time.

After the establishment of the MSAR, the Government decided to end the franchise contract when it expired on 31 December 2001. In order to bring new momentum to Macao's gaming sector and the entire economy, appropriate competition and modern operating and management models were to be introduced. The Government also expected the new arrangements to create more job opportunities and lay solid foundations for Macao's sustainable development.

The Macao Gaming Committee was established in July 2000, under the chairmanship of the Chief Executive, in order to look into the future approach to developing the gaming industry.

In late August 2001, the Legislative Assembly approved Law No. 16/2001, Gaming Industry Regulatory Framework. As well as clearly defning "casino" and "gaming", the framework spelt out regulations governing the number of concessions, conditions and processes for open bidding, and operating models and qualifcations of shareholders and concessionaires, as well as issues concerning gaming tax and contributions to charity.

The Chief Executive signed the by-law for Open Bidding for Casino Concessions: the Contract and the Required Qualifcations and Financial Strength of Bidders and Concessionaires (By-law No. 26/2001) on 26 October 2001. The by-law stipulated that a bidding committee comprising no fewer than three members be established. It also determined the nature of premiums and the payment method.

On 30 October 2001, the Casino Concessions Committee responsible for coordinating work related to the tender invitation and bidding was established by Executive Order. The eight-member committee is chaired by the Secretary for Economy and Finance, Francis Tam Pak Yuen. The bidding process offcially began on 2 November. After a series of procedures including an international tender invitation and tender evaluation, the Chief Executive issued an Executive Order on 8 February 2002 granting provisional casino concessions to Galaxy Casino Company (Galaxy), Wynn Resorts (Macau) (Wynn), and Sociedade de Jogos de Macau (SJM).

In 2002, the Government signed a Concession Agreement on Operating Games of Luck and Other Games in Casinos in the Macao Special Administrative Region with SJM on 28 March, with Wynn on 24 June, and with Galaxy on 26 June. The 18-year concession contract with SJM is valid from 1 April 2002 to 31 March 2020, while the 20-year concession contracts with Wynn and Galaxy are both valid from 27 June 2002 to 26 June 2022. All three concessionaires must pay a special gaming tax of 35 percent. Additionally, SJM must annually contribute 1.6 percent of its gross gaming revenue to a Government-appointed public foundation for promoting, developing and conducting research regarding cultural, academic, charitable and other relevant activities; plus another 1.4 percent to bodies supporting urban development, tourism and social security. Wynn and Galaxy must likewise contribute 1.6 percent of their gross gaming revenues to the foundation, as well as contribute 2.4 percent of gross gaming revenues to bodies supporting urban development, tourism and social security.

The successful granting of the new casino concessions indicates that Macao's gaming industry has entered a new era. Under the contracts, the three concessionaires were to invest a combined total of at least 17.54 billion patacas by the end of 2009.

According to Law No. 16/2001, a maximum of three casino gaming concessions can be granted. However, after granting licences to three operators, the Government agreed to allow Galaxy, SJM and Wynn to each grant a gaming sub-concession to one other operator, to meet Macao's changing needs. Thus, a "3+3" market structure was formed.

In December 2002, the Government and Galaxy agreed to amend its concession contract. The Venetian Group was authorised to operate casino gaming in Macao under a sub-concession. With the permission of the Government, in April 2005 SJM signed a sub-concession contract with MGM Grand Paradise (hereinafter referred to as MGM), and in September 2006 Wynn signed a contract with Melco PBL Gaming (Macau) (hereinafter referred to as Melco PBL).

As a result, there are now six licensed gaming companies in Macao, each of which enjoys the right to autonomously operate casino gaming businesses as an independent legal person. On April 2002, SJM, a subsidiary of STDM, became the frst new concessionaire to open for business.

The opening-up of the gaming market has greatly added to the development of Macao's economy. After the gaming industry had grown rapidly for several years, the Government found the time was right to review the present conditions and future development. On 22 April 2008, the Chief Executive announced new measures for the gaming industry, and decided the number of gaming licences would not be increased in the foreseeable future. In February 2010, the Government restructured the Macao Gaming Committee; it is now chaired by the Chief Executive. The committee is responsible for formulating relevant policies for development of the gaming industry, monitoring the industry's development and operation, and drawing up regulations and guidelines.

One new casino was opened in 2012. At the end of the year, there were 35 casinos operating in Macao, of which 20 belonged to SJM, four to the Venetian Group, six to Galaxy, one to Wynn, three to Melco PBL, and one to MGM.

By the end of 2012, the numbers of gaming tables increased from 5,302 to 5,485, a 3.45 percent rise over the previous year, while the number of slot machines increased from 16,056 to 16,585,

3.29 percent more than the previous year.

At the end of 2012, there were 2,144 vacant gaming jobs, representing a year-on-year decrease of 130 vacancies. Vacancies for dealers decreased by 295 to 1,209; vacancies for cage cashiers, pit bosses, casino foor persons and betting service operators increased by 195 to 393.

By year end, there were 54,835 gaming industry employees, representing a year-on-year increase of 9.2 percent.

Categorised by occupation, there were 23,895 dealers, representing an increase of 6.9 percent; 14,696 cage cashiers, pit bosses, casino foor persons and betting service operators, representing an increase of 8.9 percent; 6,177 casino waiters, slot machine attendants, security guards and CCTV surveillance staff, representing an increase of 11.5 percent.

At the end of 2012, the average monthly wage for full-time paid employees in the industry (excluding incentive bonuses and rewards) was 18,040 patacas, an increase of 7.9 percent compared with the 2011 fgure. The average monthly wage of dealers was 15,990 patacas, 8.8 percent higher than in the previous year. The average monthly wage of cash cashiers, pit bosses, casino foor persons and betting service operators was 21,890 patacas, representing an increase of 5.4 percent. The average monthly wage of casino waiters, slot machine attendants, security guards and CCTV surveillance staff increased by 11.4 percent, to 12,180 patacas.

Legal Regulations Refned and Junket Commissions Capped

To regulate gaming and related activities more effectively in the wake of changes in the industry, the Government has formulated and promulgated a series of laws and regulations since 2001. They included laws to regulate gaming promoters and gaming-related loans.

The gaming promotion system can be traced back to the 1930s. Since the 1980s, gaming promoters have made great contributions to Macao's gaming sector. However, they had no legal status until the passage of Law No. 16/2001. This law defnes a gaming promoter as a person who promotes casino games and provides players with services such as transportation, accommodation, catering and entertainment, in return for commissions or other rewards from gaming concessionaires.

By-law No. 6/2002 is the main provision for regulating casino gaming promotion activities. When the by-law was promulgated in 2002, it was named the By-law on the Qualifcations and Regulations for Casino Gaming Promoters. In August 2009, as amended by By-law No. 27/2009, it was renamed the By-law on the Regulation of Casino Gaming Promotion Activities. It includes detailed requirements for mandatory qualifcations and the liabilities of promoters, licensing processes and registration of promoters with gaming concessionaires. The by-law strictly regulates the mandatory qualifcations of gaming promoter licence applicants, as well as gaming promoters who serve a company or individual business owner.

Under the by-law, only persons granted a gaming promoter's licence by the Gaming Inspection and Coordination Bureau (DICJ) are permitted to engage in gaming promotion activities. Gaming promoters must conduct their businesses in accordance with contracts signed in triplicate with related concessionaires. These contracts must be in writing, and the signatures they bear must be notarised immediately. Copies of contracts must also be submitted to the DICJ. The Government began to accept applications for gaming promoter licences on 7 June 2004. By the end of 2012, a total of 232 such licences had been issued. Of these, 202 were issued to companies and 30 to individuals. In 2012, the DICJ continued to strengthen the process of reviewing the qualifcations of these two types of gaming promoters, to monitor the capacity and fnancial strength of the licensees.

Gaming promoters may select partners according to their business needs. However, the eligibility of their partners is subject to the DICJ's examination and approval.

As a result of more aggressive market competition, the price war in junket commissions increased the operating costs of VIP rooms in casinos, thus reducing their profts. The resulting vicious competition has hindered the normal development of the gaming industry. To maintain market order and effective regulation of the industry, the Government decided to set a cap on junket commissions, for safeguarding the healthy development of the gaming industry.

On 21 May 2008, the Government held the frst joint meeting with the management of the six casino operators, to discuss the cap on junket commissions. After negotiations in several meetings, the Government and the industry operators reached a consensus to cap junket commissions at 1.25 percent. In August 2009, the Government promulgated By-law No. 27/2009, to amend By-law No. 6/2002 concerning the regulations of the commissions or other rewards to gaming promoters. The Secretary for Economy and Finance, Francis Tam, then signed an order to set the upper limit on the junket commissions for gaming promoters from gaming concessionaires; in September, the Secretary signed Order No. 83/2009 to cap junket commissions of gaming promoters at 1.25 percent of bets, and require each gaming concessionaire to submit a monthly report to the DICJ.

Following promulgation of the by-laws, the Government continues to maintain communications, discussions and reviews with the gaming concessionaires and other industry operators. The Government will also listen to opinions from all parties, and introduce more refned and detailed guidelines. The amended by-law came into force on 1 December 2009.

Gaming promoters are legally obliged to pay tax at a rate of fve percent on commissions they collect from concessionaires, and other remuneration they receive.

The Government is also making efforts to regulate gaming-related loan activities. The Law on Regulating Credit Related to Gaming and Betting in Casinos or Other Gaming Venues (Law No. 5/2004) was passed by the Legislative Assembly in May 2004, and came into force on 1 July the same year. It stipulates that only concessionaires and sub-concessionaires are authorised to conduct credit-related business. In addition, gaming promoters and management companies are also allowed to conduct such business provided they have already signed relevant contracts with a concessionaire or sub-concessionaire. The credit provided in accordance with this law is regarded as statutory debt. The law also states principles and conditions governing the signing of contracts, credit activities and other related matters. It defnes the granting of credit as being transfer of the ownership of casino gaming chips to a third party when the lender is not immediately compensated by a monetary payment. It also clearly defnes different types of money.

The enactment of the Law on Regulating Credit Related to Gaming and Betting in Casinos or Other Gaming Venues is a signifcant step forward in regulating the development of Macao's gaming industry.

The Gaming Inspection and Coordination Bureau (DICJ) Restructuring Supervisory Departments to Reinforce Functions

To ensure the effective regulation of the gaming industry, it is essential to enact relevant laws and regulations, as well as establish effcient administrative and regulatory institutions. From the formation of the Gaming Inspection Committee in the 1960s right up to the establishment of the DICJ after the Handover, the functions and effectiveness of supervision in this area have been continuously strengthened. Since the liberalisation of the gaming industry, the Government has restructured the DICJ under By-law No. 34/2003.

The DICJ provides guidance and assistance to the Chief Executive on the formulation and implementation of the economic policies for the operations of casino games of fortune or other ways of gaming, pari-mutuels and gaming activities offered to the public. Its major responsibilities include the following:

INSPECTING THE ASSESSMENT OF GROSS GAMING REVENUE

The Concession Agreement on Operating Games of Luck and Other Games in Casinos in the Macao Special Administrative Region stipulates that each concessionaire is liable to pay a certain percentage of its gross gaming revenue in the form of gaming tax. Thus, relevant departments attach great importance to supervising the accounting of gross gaming revenue. Since such activities take place in casinos and their cashiers' offces, the DICJ stations inspectors in them to audit their accounts.

Ensuring the Observance of Laws and Regulations in Casinos

In accordance with relevant laws, the DICJ is responsible for monitoring the daily operations of casinos, including the collection of money and chip boxes, tip boxes, calculation of chips, the banker's fund, and various types of chips. It also inspects activities on gaming tables, and mediates in disputes between individuals and between gaming concessionaires and members of the public. Incidents such as thefts in casinos or at gaming tables, misconduct by dealers, disputes, fghting and the ejection of unwelcome persons occur frequently.

Analysing Changes in Gaming Operations

The DICJ must give its approval before any changes may be made to gaming operations. The usual practice is for a concessionaire to submit a plan for the proposed changes in its operations, and for the Inspection of Games of Fortune Department to study the proposal and comment on its feasibility and appropriateness. The most common scenarios are changes in maximum bet amounts, in the initial fow on gaming tables, in the numbers of gaming tables, in the operating hours of gaming tables, in the use of new chips, and the introduction of new slot machines.

Pre- and Post-activity Inspection

All pari-mutuels and lottery activities are inspected by the DICJ, which conducts inspections before, during and after each event. In addition, after an event the concessionaire must submit reports and data to the DICJ.

Preventing, Eliminating and Punishing Illegal Gambling

The DICJ uses the following measures to prevent, eliminate and punish illegal gambling activities: cooperation with other Government departments and community groups to educate teenaged students and the general public via promotional campaigns; collection of information about illegal gambling activities through a variety of channels, and referral of relevant data to the police for further action if investigations confrm such activities have taken place; and identifcation and administrative punishment of individuals involved in illegal gambling in accordance with Law No. 8/96/M.

A total of 245 people were found to be involved in illegal gambling during 2012, a decrease of 19.1 percent on the previous year's fgure. Of these, 93 percent were Macao residents who were involved mainly in mahjong games. The DICJ would continue to educate the public, to stringently combat and prevent illegal gambling.

MONITORING SALES OF LOTTERY TICKETS AND LUCKY DRAWS

The DICJ receives applications for approval of the sale of lottery tickets and lucky draws. Permits for these are issued once the approval process has been completed. It also monitors the entire operation of such activities.

REGISTERING AND INSPECTING THE QUALIFCATIONS OF GAMING PROMOTERS

Under the By-law on the Regulation of Casino Gaming Promotion Activities (By-law No. 6/2002), the DICJ is responsible for examining the qualifcations of applicants for gaming promoter licences. Gaming promoters can only operate if they possess such a licence. Their business activities are also monitored by the DICJ once their licence has been issued.

As for the registration of gaming promoters, a total of 232 licences were issued in 2012, representing an increase of 5.9 percent on the fgure of 2011. Of these, 202 were issued to legal entities and 30 were issued to individuals. The DICJ continued to enhance the review of the qualifcations of these two types of gaming promoters, to monitor the capacity and fnancial strength of the licensees.

With regard to the supervision of the implementation of the cap on junket commissions, in 2011 the bureau completed the second round of inspections of the six casino concessionaires. It also continued to improve the detailed report on payments related to junket commissions and related audit procedures, to ensure that junket commissions paid by the concessionaires did not exceed the stipulated upper limit.

REGULAR ACCOUNT AUDITING

The DICJ's Audit Department is responsible for regular audits of accounting data provided by the accounting systems of casino concessionaires. The department also verifes the implementation of contracts between the Government and concessionaires, especially the fulfment of payments specifed in contracts.

Establishing a Gaming Activities Database

The Research and Investigation Department is responsible for collecting, analysing and processing all information related to the activities of licensed gaming operators and their fnancial indicators, in order to create and continuously update a database about the major activities of licensed gaming operators. Besides compiling fnancial forecasts about gaming activities, the department supervises and investigates the fnancial background and eligibility of gaming-related companies on a day-to-day basis.

In 2012, the DICJ continued to improve the mechanism of gaming regulations, amend relevant laws and regulations to improve the internal structure of the gaming industry and enhance the competitiveness of the Macao gaming industry in the international market. Additionally, the DICJ was committed to preventing problem gambling, promoting responsible gambling and reducing the negative effects of the gaming industry on society. Its efforts can be summarised as follows:

The DICJ continued to cooperate with government departments and organisations, including the Social Welfare Bureau and the University of Macau, to organise various activities and publicity campaigns to promote responsible gambling, and established a trial version of responsible gambling information kiosks with these two parties.

To enforce Law No. 10/2012, the DICJ inspected casinos for clear notices stating that individuals under 21 years old are prohibited from entering since the law came into effect. DICJ inspectors are stationed at venues to provide necessary assistance to casino staff on checking the age of casino visitors.

From 1 November 2012, self-exclusion and third-person exclusion were made effective. The DICJ kept close contact with casino operators to improve the application process and provide assistance to individuals in need. At the end of December 2012, the DICJ had received 30 applications, which were mainly for self-exclusion.

To comprehensively monitor the air quality of casinos and safeguard the health of frontline staff, the DICJ joined hands with other government departments such as the Health Bureau and the Lands, Public Works and Transport Bureau for a strict and thorough assessment of applications for smoking space in casinos, to ensure the smoking area does not exceed 50 percent of that of gambling space. The DICJ also held regular meetings and communicated with the six casino operators regarding the guidelines on casino smoking areas, in preparation for enforcement of the guidelines from 1 January 2013 onward.

To strengthen auditing and technology advancement, the DICJ set up CCTV rooms in fagship casinos of every operator and stationed inspectors to monitor the cashiers' offces. Moreover, personnel were sent to gambling concessionaires to carry out feld auditing regarding the requirements stipulated in the Minimum Internal Control Requirements, including the implementation of the cap on junket commissions.

To implement and promote the Macau Central Monitoring Systems Technical Standard, the DICJ set up specifc monitoring rooms to improve regulation of slot machines.

The money laundering control procedures submitted by the gaming concessionaires under Directive No. 2/2006, were reviewed on a regular basis, and amended and updated in accordance with changes in the operating modes of different gaming concessionaires and technological developments. The Summary Report on Large Transactions was further analysed and examined, while relevant information was gathered and transferred to the Financial Intelligence Offce for further case analysis, fling and investigation.

8. With regard to inspection of pari-mutuels, close monitor over gaming data of pari-mutuels and lotteries was retained. The DICJ spared no effort in coordination regarding replacement and improvement of betting systems of gaming companies and studying of the revision of law, including sports lotteries-football betting regulations.

Chinese Dominoes Mahjong Three-card Poker Fish-Prawn-Crab Three-card Baccarat Pachinko Tombola Wheel of Fortune Live Multi Game Football Poker Stud Poker Q Poker Casino War Dice/craps Makccarat Texas Poker Fortune 3 Card Poker Fortune 8 Dragon Phoenix

Enhancing competitiveness of the gaming industry

At the end of 2012, there were 35 casinos operating in Macao. The Government continues to implement and modify measures to regulate the scope and pace of the gaming industry's expansion, to enhance the industry's competitiveness and strengthen supervision of gaming to facilitate appropriate, gradual and healthy development of the industry.

TOURISM SECTOR DEVELOPMENTS

Tourism is the backbone of Macao's economy. With the long-term goal of building Macao as a world tourism and leisure centre, the government department responsible for tourism development started adjusting tourism policies and measures in accordance with Macao's new positioning, and promoted sustainable and healthy development of the tourism industry in areas including marketing and promotion, tourism planning, products and events, tourism industry management, and training and quality control.

Overview of Tourism in Macao Major Markets

According to the Statistics and Census Service, the total number of tourists visiting Macao in 2012 was 28,082,292, a slight increase of 0.3 percent over the 2011 fgure. During 2012, Macao's tourism maintained steady growth. Despite uncertainties in the global economy resulting in fewer visitors from several major tourist sources, the performance of new emerging markets was satisfactory.

In 2012, the 10 major source markets of visitors were:

Country / Region	No. of Visitors	Percentage (%)
Mainland China	16,902,499	60.2%
Hong Kong	7,081,153	25.2%
Taiwan	1,072,052	3.8%
Korea	444,773	1.6%
Japan	395,989	1.4%
Malaysia	301,802	1.1%
Philippines	283,881	1.0%
Thailand	231,295	0.8%
Indonesia	209,084	0.7%
Singapore	205,692	0.7%

In 2012, Greater China (mainland China, Hong Kong and Taiwan) comprised 89.2 percent of the total market, and the international market comprised 10.8 percent. Mainland China continued to be the largest market for visitors to Macao, with the number of visitors increasing by 4.6 percent over the 2011 fgure. They accounted for 60.2 percent of the total number of visitors, and 7,131,914 (42.2 percent) of them travelled to Macao under the Facilitated Individual Travel (FIT) scheme. Hong Kong and Taiwan were the second and third largest markets for visitors to Macao, respectively; the numbers of visitors from these regions decreased by 6.6 percent and 11.8 percent, respectively, compared with the fgures in 2011.

In 2012, there was a signifcant increase in the number of Thai tourists, up by 17.8 percent over the fgure in 2011. Thailand became the eighth largest source of tourists, compared to tenth in the previous year. There was a large drop in numbers of Singaporean tourists, down by 26.7 percent over the 2011 fgure. As a result, Singapore was ranked tenth among sources of tourists.

Despite the slowdown in the global economy, Macao tourism sustained its 2011 momentum. Certain individual markets with great potential recorded considerable growth, especially Russia. In 2012, 26,844 Russian tourists visited Macao, a 62.6 percent increase over the 2011 fgure. During the year, there were 3,026,588 tourists from international markets, 0.5 percent more than in 2011.

THE HOTEL INDUSTRY

According to Macau Government Tourist Offce (MGTO) statistics, at the end of 2012, Macao had a total of 69 star-rated hotels and 33 guesthouses.

The total number of guests who occupied hotel rooms in Macao during 2012 was 9,541,397, a 10.8 percent increase over the 2011 fgure. The average year-round hotel occupancy rate dropped from 84.1 percent in 2011 to 83.1 percent in 2012. The average length of stay was 1.4 nights, a decrease of 0.13 nights compared with the 2011 fgure.

TRAVEL AGENCIES

At the end of 2012, there were 169 licensed travel agencies in Macao, 12 (7.6 percent) more than in 2011. A total of 1,643 people held tourist guide licences issued by the MGTO, an increase of 125 (8.2 percent) compared with the 2011 fgure. The language abilities of these tourist guides span Cantonese, Putonghua, English, Portuguese, German, Japanese, Korean, Thai, French, Spanish, Russian, Indonesian, Hokkien and Chaozhouese.

In 2012, 9,122,332 tourists visited Macao on package tours, an increase of 21.0 percent over 2011. Most package tourists (6,521,675) came from mainland China, an increase of 18.9 percent over the 2011 fgure. The second and third-largest sources of package tourists were Taiwan and Hong Kong, at 784,386 and 417,127, respectively.

In 2012, a total of 430,065 Macao residents joined outbound group tours. Of these, 319,270 (74.2 percent) headed for mainland China. Korea and Taiwan were the second and third most-popular tourism destinations for Macao residents, with Korea attracting 29,703 visitors or 6.9 percent of the total, and Taiwan attracting 21,285 visitors or 4.9 percent of the total. A total of 861,152 residents used travel agent services without joining package tours, which is 31.2 percent more than in 2011.

MACAU GOVERNMENT TOURIST OFFCE

The functions of the Macau Government Tourist Offce (MGTO) include assisting the formulation and implementation of local tourism policies; enhancing development and diversity of the tourism industry; and monitoring tourism and related business and issuing licences, in order to realise the Government's overall tourism objectives.

To promote Macao, the MGTO has set up representative offces in many countries and territories throughout the world, including Hong Kong, Japan, South Korea, Singapore, Malaysia, India, Indonesia, German-speaking countries, France, the United Kingdom and Ireland, the United States, Russia, Australia and New Zealand. Macao's tourism industry is also actively promoted by the Tourism Section of the Offce of the Macao Special Administrative Region in Beijing, the Macau Economic and Cultural Offce in Taiwan, the Macao Economic and Trade Offce to the European Union in Belgium, and the Macau Tourism Promotion and Information Center in Portugal.

The MGTO has participated in large scale promotional events in Australia, the United States and Guangdong. After the visa-free access agreement between the MSAR and Russian governments came into effect, the MGTO planned to set up its representative offce in Russia in 2013, to strengthen the promotion of Macao.

BUSINESS TOURISM

To promote Macao as a business tourism destination, the MGTO continued to participate in relevant international expos held overseas. Incentive programmes also continued, to encourage the industry to further engage in overseas marketing. In 2012, the MGTO jointed hands with the Economic Services Bureau and the Macao Trade and Investment Promotion Institute to participate in overseas expos to promote Macao's meetings, incentives, conventions and exhibition (MICE) industry and related incentive measures and policies.

The MGTO launched its incentive travel stimulation programme to attract overseas companies to choose Macao as a destination for their incentive travel, enhance cooperation between the local industry and international buyers and organisations, and help raise the quality of the local industry to international levels. In 2012, 39 applications for the programme were accepted, involving 28,242 participants.

INDUSTRY MANAGEMENT

In 2012, the legislative procedures for the bill on the amendments to the law governing travel agents and tour guides commenced. The bill on the amendments to the law governing the hotel and catering industries was also under the drafting process.

After the law on Prohibition of Illegal Provision of Accommodation came into effect in 2010, the MGTO has been joining hands with homeowners' councils and social groups in combating illegal provision of accommodation. The MGTO has also received and transferred complaints through the 2833 3000 hotline, via the Internet, in person and by post.

In 2012, the inter-departmental task force conducted 238 joint operations and the MGTO undertook 2,441 inspections.

During the year, the MGTO processed 2,131 cases regarding licence applications. Moreover, it conducted 1,780 inspections of the establishments, industries and tourist spots under its administration.

During 2012, the MGTO held four training sessions to improve service quality of tourism and related businesses. A total of 132 participants received training; retail industry employees were the frst target group.

REGIONAL AND INTERNATIONAL COOPERATION

In 2012, the MGTO facilitated the signing of Cooperation Agreement on Quality and Honest Macau Tour between Macao and Shenzhen, safeguarding market order.

The MGTO represented the Government to participate as a core leadership member in international organisations such as the United Nations World Tourism Organization (UNWTO), the Pacifc Asia Travel Association, the Tourism Working Group of the Asia-Pacifc Economic Cooperation, the Asian Association of Convention and Visitor Bureaus, the International Congress and Convention Association and the World Tourism Cities Federation.

The MGTO established supportive measures for Portuguese-speaking countries, including provision of training to government offcials of these countries, and provided project subsidies to Mozambique and East Timor in accordance with the UNWTO Sustainable Tourism - Eliminating Poverty Initiative.

Handling Tourist Comments

In 2012, the MGTO received 633 complaints concerning retail services, gaming establishments, restaurants, travel agencies, hotels, transport, frauds, and others relating to public entities.

MGTO hotline 2833 3000 is a phone enquiry service that is manned 24 hours per day. It also provides recorded travel information, giving assistance and responses to enquiries, and receiving opinions and complaints from tourists and Macao residents. The hotline is operated in Cantonese, Putonghua, English, Portuguese and Japanese. It received 29,871 calls during 2012.

Information Counters

The MGTO has 10 information counters, which are at major ports and tourist attractions in Macao (the Border Gate, the Outer Harbour Ferry Terminal, Edif Ritz Largo do Senado, Guia Lighthouse, Macau International Airport, Macau Fisherman's Wharf and Taipa Ferry Terminal), and major ports in Hong Kong (Shun Tak Centre and Hong Kong International Airport), providing up-to-date tourism information and assistance to tourists. In 2012, MGTO's information counters in Macao and Hong Kong offered assistance to 1,389,437 visitors, an increase of one percent over the 2011 fgure.

Tourism Training

Tourism and related industries account for a signifcant proportion of Macao's total workforce. The Government attaches great importance to training people employed in the tourism sector; it offers training courses for various tourism-related professionals through the Institute for Tourism Studies.

The Institute of Tourism Studies

Established in 1995, the Institute for Tourism Studies (IFT) is a public tertiary education institute affliated to the Secretariat for Social Affairs and Culture, and is the frst educational institution to be granted the TedQual Certifcation by the UNWTO. The IFT offers degree and professional programmes in a wide range of tourism-related disciplines, such as hotel services, tourism, cultural heritage, conventions and exhibitions, retail and marketing, leisure and entertainment, sports and recreation, cultural and creativity, and culinary arts. The institute also cooperates with renowned overseas colleges and training institutions to offer advanced management courses. In addition, the IFT has been commissioned by the Government and other institutions to conduct policy research on tourism planning and development.

To meet the human resources demands of the tourism sector and complement the sector's future development, IFT's degree programmes admitted 439 students during the 2011/2012 academic year. During the academic year, a total of 1,452 students enrolled in degree programmes in culinary arts management, tourism business management, heritage management, hotel management, tourism event management, and tourism retail and marketing management. IFT also established evening degree programmes in hotel management and tourism event management with Chinese as the medium of instruction. As for non-degree education, there were 18,180 students enrolled in various professional and continuing education courses.

The IFT has established relationships with universities and related institutions in numerous countries and regions, including mainland China, the Asia Pacifc Region, Europe and North America. This international network facilitates academic and cultural exchanges, and promotes overseas internships, faculty and student exchanges and "train-the-trainer" programmes. For details, please refer to ie@IFT. http://www.ift.edu.mo/Content/Uploads/IFT/doc/Networking/ IE Brochure.pdf.

TOURISM RESOURCES

Boasting a brilliant and fascinating history encompassing 400 years of cultural exchanges between China and the West, Macao has a unique appeal to tourists. Its scenery is embellished with tourist treasures of all types, including picturesque dwellings constructed in traditional styles and ancient temples built during the Ming and Qing dynasties, buildings with Southern European architectural features, baroque-style churches and impressive contemporary structures.

Churches Ruins of St Paul's

Macao's most famous landmark is the Ruins of St Paul's, the surviving facade of St Paul's Church. Designed by a Spanish Jesuit, construction of the original church began in 1602, and it was completed between 1637 and 1640. St Paul's Church has been destroyed by fre three times but fortunately its precious facade remained standing after the blaze. The facade has since been repaired many times, and it is now generally known as the Ruins of St Paul's.

St Paul's Church is a delicate mixture of European Renaissance and Eastern architectural styles. The Museum of Sacred Art and Crypt was built at the location of the church, and houses collections paintings, sculptures and ceremonial decorations from churches and abbeys.

The Chapel of Our Lady of Guia

Originally built in 1622, the Chapel of Our Lady of Guia is the oldest building on Guia Hill. A project to enlarge it was carried out in 1637 and was completed in 1638. The Portuguese dedicated the church to the protector of seafarers. The interior preserves features that were common in 17th century Portuguese abbeys. In 1996, a mural was discovered inside the church, a rarity in the churches of southern China.

St. Anthony's Church

The oldest church in Macao, St Anthony's Church, was built by the Society of Jesus between 1558 and 1560. Catholics regard St Anthony as the patron saint of marriage, so locals also call it the "Wedding Church".

St. Augustine's Church

St Augustine's Church was built in 1591. It is one of the oldest churches in Macao. The church underwent considerable changes and assumed its present form when it was restored in 1874.

St Dominic's Church

St Dominic's Church stands on part of the former site of St Dominic's Convent. In 1587, Spanish friars built the original church, which was dedicated to Our Lady of the Rosary. It was initially built of camphor wood and then restructured with stucco bricks and cream-coloured stones. The architecture is in Portuguese style, which was popular in the Orient in the 17th and 18th centuries.

In the main chapel stands a statue of Our Lady of Fatima, from which the Parade of the Virgin commences on 13 May each year. Believers march to Penha Hill to commemorate the Virgin Mary's appearance in Fatima, Portugal.

There is a museum of sacred art inside the chapel. The collection includes religious items of artistic value, as well as scriptures and carved wooden representations of saints.

In recent years, major international concerts held inside the church have imbued it with an even more profound sense of culture.

St Lawrence's Church

St Lawrence's is one of Macao's most famous large churches. Built in the middle of the 16th century, it has undergone several restorations, and its present construction was completed in 1846. The Portuguese, who were great mariners and navigators, believed that St Lawrence offered protection and bestowed the gift of the wind.

Hermitage of Our Lady of Hope

The Hermitage of Our Lady of Hope, also called St Lazarus's Church, was Macao's cathedral until the present one was built. It was also the frst cathedral built after the establishment of the

Macao Diocese. Whenever a new bishop arrived in Macao to take up offce, he frst had to come to St Lazarus's Church to receive his crosier before he could exert his power. Consequently, this church is especially holy among Catholics in Macao. The present structure of St Lazarus's Church remains as it was in 1885.

The Cathedral

The Cathedral was built in 1576 and was originally a simple wooden structure. Between 1844 and 1850, Catholic parishioners collected donations to rebuild the church and enlarge it to its present size.

Many major events in the Church's calendar centre on the Cathedral, especially during Easter. In addition to the procession of Our Lord of Passion, a solemn parade takes place on Good Friday and special masses are held on Easter Sunday.

Fortresses Mount Fortress

Mount Fortress is one of Macao's major tourist attractions. Work on its construction began in 1617, during the reign of Emperor Shenzong of the Ming Dynasty, and it was completed in 1626. Mount Fortress was originally used by the Church to protect the clergymen of St Paul's Church from pirate attacks. It was later turned into a military installation. In the past, the fortress stood high above the city centre of Macao, and it was regarded as an important part of its defensive fortifcations. It has now become a heritage site and witness to history.

Mount Fortress occupies about 8,000 square metres. The ancient fortress tower was once an offce of the Society of Jesus. It was also used as the offce of the Macao Meteorological and Geophysical Bureau, and it has since been rebuilt as the Museum of Macao. At the entrance, a stone carving records the fort's military successes in defending the city against invasions.

Mong Ha Fortress

Construction of Mong Ha Fortress began in 1849. It covers an area of 650 square metres. The fortress was once a barracks for African Portuguese soldiers stationed in Macao, and was called "Black Ghost Fortress". After the former Portuguese administration withdrew its Macao garrison during the 1970s, the barracks were abandoned. In the 1980s, Mong Ha Fortress was renovated and became the Government-owned Tourism School, now known as the Institute for Tourism Studies.

St Francis Fortress

St Francis Fortress was constructed in 1622. In 1584, Spanish clergymen built St Francis Convent on the site behind the fortress; subsequently, the convent was converted into a barracks. In the 20th century, after Portuguese soldiers withdrew from Macao, the barracks became the headquarters of the security forces in charge of the Marine Police, Public Security Police and Fire Service.

Guia Fortress

Guia Fortress occupies about 800 square metres. Its construction began in 1622, and it was expanded from 1637 to 1638. It was formerly valued for military purposes, because of its position overlooking the entire peninsula. It was therefore classifed as a restricted military area until 1976, when the Portuguese army left. It was then turned into a tourist spot, and its appearance has been kept intact until now.

The Chapel of Our Lady of Guia was built in the fortress in 1622. Adjacent to the hermitage is the 13-metre-high Guia Lighthouse, which was built in 1864, and is one of the oldest lighthouses in the Far East. It resumed service in 1910 and has been guiding seamen ever since, with a visibility of 25 nautical miles from Macao. When a typhoon approaches, typhoon signals are hoisted on the side of the lighthouse to warn nearby residents.

Barra Fortress

Barra Fortress, also called Pousada de S. Tiago Fortress or Sai Van Fortress, was built in 1622. It was an important fortress for protecting Macao's Inner Harbour. Inside the castle is the Chapel of St James. In 1981, the castle was converted into a hotel, while retaining its old characteristics.

Three Ancient Grand Temples

Macao's famous grand temples are the A-Ma Temple, Pou Chai Buddhist Monastery and Temple, and Lin Fong Temple. Many visitors are attracted to these temples, because of the different generations and backgrounds they represent, and because of the gods to whom they are dedicated.

A-Ma Temple

The A-Ma Temple is one of the most famous tourist attractions in Macao and the oldest of Macao's three ancient grand temples.

Built in the Ming Dynasty, the A-Ma Temple was originally called the "A-Ma Pavilion" or "Tin Hau (Heavenly Queen) Temple" by local people. The entire temple consists of four main structures: the Stone Hall, the Main Hall, the Hong Ren Hall and the Kun Iam Pavilion. This ancient structure is distinguished by its traditional Chinese cultural characteristics.

Between Hong Ren Hall and Kun Iam Pavilion, there are many stone inscriptions along the cliff path written by celebrities, statesmen, poets and scholars and engraved in different calligraphic styles.

Pou Chai Buddhist Monastery and Temple

Built in the late Ming Dynasty, Pou Chai Buddhist Monastery and Temple is also called Kun Iam Tong Temple. The Buddhist monastery is built in the ancient Chinese architectural style of Hui Fei, resembling ancient Chinese temples on famous mountains. The frst large hall in the monastery is dedicated to the Three Precious Buddhas, the second to the Buddha of Longevity, and the third to Kun Iam. Besides the large halls, there are also some other buildings, such as the western hall, the eastern hall, the backyard garden, and so forth. Such a large Buddhist temple complex is unusual in Macao and Hong Kong.

Many collections of paintings, items of calligraphy and antiques by famous masters are housed in the temple. They include the works of Gao Jianfu, a famous painter of the Ling Nan (Guangdong and Guangxi areas) school, and his student Guan Shanyue; Chen Gongyin, who ranked among the three great poets in Ling Nan; and the famous scholar Zhang Taiyan; as well as inscriptions by ancient celebrities such as Mi Fu, Dong Qichang, and Liu Yong. The unequal Treaty of

Wanghia between the United States of America and the Qing regime of China was signed in the temple garden.

Lin Fong Temple

Built in the Ming Dynasty, Lin Fong Temple is one of the most famous temples in Macao. Formerly named the "Tin Fei Temple", Lin Fong is a comparatively small monastery and temple dedicated to Tin Hau. Since the Qing Dynasty, it has been expanded and renovated from time to time, and it has gradually been expanded to its present size.

Today, the main Lin Fong temple is for worshipping Kun Iam and Tin Hau; whereas other gods are worshipped in the Kun Iam Hall, Wu Di Hall, Ren Shou Hall, Shen Nong Hall, Yi Ling Hall, Cang Xie Hall, Ju Yong Hall, Jin Hua Hall and Dou Mu Hall.

In the middle of the 19th century, Lin Zexu, a Qing Dynasty imperial commissioner, received Portuguese offcials in Lin Fong Temple during his temporary residence in Macao.

As well as the three ancient grand temples, there are many other old temples in Macao, such as the Na Tcha Temple, Hong Kung Temple, Tam Kung Temple, Yeok San Buddhist Monastery, Chu Lam Chi Buddhist Monastery, Sam Po Temple, Po Tai Buddhist Monastery, Lin Kai Temple, Pak Tai Temple and Tin Hau Temple.

Cybernetic Fountains

Macao has a cybernetic fountain at Nam Van Lake. The fountain comprises various spouts and lights for fountain shows. The Civic and Municipal Affairs Bureau schedules two musical fountain shows and laser fountain shows on Saturdays and Sundays. More shows are staged during special festivals, such as New Year's Day, Chinese New Year, the Mid-Autumn Festival and Christmas.

Macau Tower

The Macau Tower Convention and Entertainment Centre, which was funded and constructed by the Sociedade de Turismo e Diversoes de Macau, offcially opened on 19 December 2001 as Macao's new signature landmark. Soaring 338 metres high, the Macau Tower was the tenth-highest freestanding tower in the world and the eighth-highest in Asia when it was completed.

The main observation level is 223 metres above the ground, and consists of four foors. Two foors accommodate an indoor viewing deck, cafe, revolving restaurant and outdoor viewing deck. The indoor viewing deck provides visitors with panoramic views of up to 55 kilometres.

The multifunction convention and entertainment centre integrated with the tower also has four foors containing exhibition and conference facilities.

A-Ma Statue

Located at the top of the Alto de Coloane, the A-Ma Statue is the tallest white marble statue of this goddess in the world. Constructed from 120 white marble boulders and completed on 28 October 1998, it is 19.99 metres in height. The face is carved from a single white marble boulder, and the statue weighs 500 tonnes.

International Sports and Cultural Events

Macao hosts a variety of international sports and cultural events throughout the year. These play an important role in promoting Macao, enhancing its international profle and attracting tourists and visitors.

Macau Grand Prix

The Macau Grand Prix began in 1954, and was originally an amateur sports event for Macao motor racing fans. Today, it has become a major event for the world's leading racing teams.

Every year in late November, world-class drivers and thousands of visitors fock to Macao to join the world's only street track event that includes both a formula touring car race and a motorcycle race.

The Formula Three race of the Macau Grand Prix is the premier event, drawing national championship racers from throughout the world to compete for the honour of frst prize.

Grand Prix street track riders and motorcycle superstars such as Ayrton Senna, Michael Schumacher, David Coulthard, Jenson Button, Kevin Schwantz, Carl Fogarty, Didier de Radigues and Ron Haslam have competed at the Guia Circuit.

Macao International Marathon

The Macao International Marathon seeks to foster sports development, enhance international friendship and promote Macao's sports and tourism industry to the world.

The Macao International Marathon is held every December and is the largest track-and-feld event in Macao. The route circles the Macao peninsula and crosses to Taipa and Coloane islands, and has a total length of 42.195 kilometres. Marathon competitors come from all over the world, and include athletes from Macao and Hong Kong as well as famous international track-and-feld stars.

Macao International Fireworks Display Contest

The Macao International Fireworks Display Contest is recognised throughout the world. It attracts numerous prominent freworks companies and is attended each year by large numbers of tourists and Macao residents. The contest provides an opportunity for Macao to showcase its tourism industry and reputation.

The frst Macao International Fireworks Display Contest was held in 1989, and was contested by just fve teams, from Portugal, Japan, mainland China and Taiwan. The contest has gradually become a major annual tourism event, attracting high standard freworks companies from countries and regions such as mainland China, the Philippines, Thailand, Taiwan, Japan, South Korea, Australia, the United Kingdom, Switzerland, France, Germany, Portugal and Spain. The Macao International Fireworks Display Contest is usually held between September and October each year, on the seafront near the Macau Tower.

Other major sports events and cultural activities held in Macao include the FIVB World Grand Prix, the Macao Open (Golf Tournament), the annual Macao International Dragon Boat Races, the Macao Arts Festival in March, the Macao International Music Festival in October, and Macau Food Festival.

Culinary Delights

Since Chinese and Western cultures coexist in Macao, it offers food that blends culinary infuences from around the world. Different cuisines can be sampled throughout the area, and tourists may taste the regional dishes of Beijing, Shanghai, Sichuan, Guangdong and Taiwan to their heart's content. They can also enjoy authentic cuisines from Portugal, Italy, France, Japan, India, Vietnam, Korea, Brazil and Thailand.

Regarded as one of the world's unique cuisines, Macanese cuisine is actually a distillation of the culinary arts of Portugal, Africa, India, Malaysia and mainland China's Guangdong Province. Bacalao balls, African chicken, spicy prawns, Portuguese chicken, stewed duck with herbs, stewed knuckle with red beans, stuffed crab shells, and grilled sardines are celebrated delicacies in Macao.

Macao specialties also include almond cakes, egg rolls, crackers, peanut candy, chicken-shaped pastries, dried preserved fruits and various dried meats. Tourists love to buy these snacks as gifts for relatives and friends, or for their own enjoyment. Pastry houses and snack shops cluster along Almeida Ribeiro Avenue to the Auto Novo Alley, Sao Paulo Road and around the old district on Taipa island.

Grand Prix Museum

The Grand Prix Museum was inaugurated on 18 November 1993 to commemorate the 40th anniversary of the Macao Grand Prix. More than 20 racing cars, including formula racing cars and motorcycles driven over the years, and accessories used by famous champions, are exhibited.

CULTURE AND SPORT

Eastern and western cultures have co-existed in Macao for over 400 years. A wide variety of cultural traditions, languages, values, religious beliefs, and customs have all existed side by side and infuenced one another. Out of this melting pot, a regional culture unique to Macao has gradually developed into its present richness. Macao's culture is thus a diverse mixture, with traditional Chinese culture as its heart, and it has assimilated Western, particularly Portuguese, cultural infuences in perfect harmony.

Following its policy of promoting Chinese culture while preserving the unique pluralistic cultural heritage of Macao, the Government has hosted various cultural and artistic activities invited art troupes from the mainland and overseas, as well as Macao, to perform. These have created opportunities for audiences to learn more about the history, society, and culture of different regions, as well as enhancing cultural exchange and the quality of cultural life of Macao's residents.

CULTURAL AFFAIRS BUREAU

The Cultural Affairs Bureau is a Government department that sets out the Government's key objectives in cultural matters.

The bureau is responsible for protecting cultural heritage, giving guidance on aesthetic appreciation, supporting community organisations, nurturing talent in arts and culture, developing local cultural industries, as well as organising cultural entertainment programmes, such as concerts, exhibitions, seminars, music classes, dance and drama courses, the Macao Youth Music Competition, Macao International Music Festival, Macao Arts Festival and the Macao Annual Visual Arts Exhibition. It also provides subsidies and research bursaries to support the publication of research and advanced studies about the arts.

CULTURAL AND CREATIVE INDUSTRIES

In 2010, the bureau established the Department for the Promotion of Cultural and Creative Industries, to proactively promote cultural and creative industries and so boost their development - including through promoting and exhibiting cultural and creative products; conducting studies of the cultural and creative industries; formulating a policy framework and measures for the development of the cultural and creative industries; and collecting information on local cultural and creative industries. At present, information in the database is used in business matching, and selecting cultural and creative institutions and companies to participate in local and overseas activities and fairs, to foster Macao's culture and creativity.

The 23rd Macao Arts Festival

The 23rd Macao Arts Festival was held from 1 May to 2 June and featured 33 programmes with over 130 performances and two visual arts exhibitions. More than 17,500 tickets were sold, representing a take-up of 92.5 percent.

Festival participants included top performing troupes and artists from the United Kingdom, Argentina, Spain, Portugal, Italy, France, the United States, mainland China, Hong Kong and Macao, among which more than half were local. Among all the wonderful shows, a new historical Peking Opera Su Wu of the Han Dynasty was staged by the China National Peking Opera Company at the opening ceremony, and broadcast live nationwide through the Chinese opera channel of China Central Television (CCTV). The many overseas troupes employed traditional and advanced techniques in their performances, including the experimental theatre When We Meet Again, Landscapes and the Planet of the Beetlebuns by the British troupes, and the unprecedented interactive recording device Congregation at Tap Seac Square.

A variety of performances ranging from Cantonese opera, dance, drama, and music to environmental theatre were staged by local troupes including Macao Kaifong Cantonese Opera Children's Troupe, Hiu Kok Drama Association, Theatre Farmers, Macao Youth Repertory Theatre, D6ci Papiayam Di Macau, Theatre Horizon, Macao Little Mountain Arts Association, Black Sand Theatre, Macao Youth Dance Group of Macao Conservatory, Macanese musician Lei Vai Fan and Soda-City Experimental Workshop Arts Association, many of which made imaginative use of Macao's historical buildings in their shows.

The 26th Macao International Music Festival

The 26th Macao International Music Festival was held from 5 October to 7 November, with a total of 23 programmes including operas, musicals, orchestra performances, contemporary music, pop music, choir performances with jazz music and chamber music. A total of 12,967 tickets were sold, representing a take-up of 91 percent. A few concerts were also broadcast live and recorded by China National Radio, the festival media partner, effectively promoting the festival brand.

The grand opening of the festival was graced by Broadway musical Peter Pan. Other programmes included Italian opera Tosca and comic opera La Serva Padrona. Famous musical groups and musicians performing in the festival included the San Francisco Symphony, world renowned violinist Vadim Repin, the Kodnly Quartet from Hungary, the English Concert, the Legendary Count Basie Orchestra from the USA, Kaunas State Choir from Lithuania, Tai Chi Band from Hong Kong, Haya Band from Inner Mongolia and female Portuguese singers Teresa Salgueiro and Aurea.

Parade through Macao, Latin City

Since 2011, the Cultural Affairs Bureau has organised the Parade through Macao, Latin City to celebrate the Handover. The theme and slogan of the 2012 event were "Peace, Love and Cultural Integration" and "An annual celebration for the entire city - VIVA!". Performing troupes from Latin-speaking countries and regions and 40 local troupes, with a total of about 2,000 people, joined the parade, attracting an audience of more than a hundred thousand, who watched in person or via the live television broadcast.

The Fresh Fish Traders Association of Macao and Macau "Casa de Portugal", performed exquisitely in the parade and were invited to participate in the annual Nice Carnival Parade held in France in February 2013.

Macao Orchestra

During the year the Macao Orchestra presented 75 concerts, attended by 39,171 people.

Macao Chinese Orchestra

The Macao Chinese Orchestra is a professional Chinese Orchestra under the Cultural Affairs Bureau. There are currently 42 musicians in the orchestra.

In 2012, the orchestra gave 50 concerts and performances, attracting a total audience of 17,700 people.

Macao Youth Music Competition

The annual Macao Youth Music Competition, organised by the Cultural Affairs Bureau, aims to promote the development of culture and art in Macao, and to provide valuable opportunities for performance, learning and the exchange of experience. Through musical competitions, many prize winners have already entered into the music profession, while the number of music students wishing to continue professionally is increasing steadily.

The 30th Macao Youth Music Competition took place from 22 June to 17 July, during which competitions were held in 24 categories including Chinese and Western Instrumental Solo, Trio, Quartet, Quintet, Chamber Music, Vocal Solo, Ensemble Singing and Chorus, and attracting 1,272 competitors and 2,586 spectators.

Visual Arts Exhibition

The Visual Arts Exhibition organised by the Cultural Affairs Bureau aims to showcase outstanding art from around the world, stimulate creativity among Macao artists, appreciate various types of visual artworks with the public, and promote arts exchange.

Cultural Information Platform

The website of the Cultural Affairs Bureau (www.icm.gov.mo) and mobile site (m.icm.gov.mo) provide cultural services information regarding cultural activities, performances, exhibitions, heritage protection, promotion of arts education, and academic research. There are affliated websites for cultural facilities including the Macao Central Library, Macao Historical Archives, Macao Conservatory, Museum of Macau, and the Tap Seac Gallery. Also provided is detailed information on cultural events such as the Macao Arts Festival, the Macao International Music Festival, and Parade through Macao, Latin City. In 2012, the website received 2,863,727 visits. Furthermore, Macao Heritage Net (www.macauheritage.net) and Macao Art Net (www.macauart.net) are two of Macao's most important cultural information platforms.

To promote information exchange in the local cultural and creative industries, and increase community understanding of the cultural and creative industry and its development, the Cultural Affairs Bureau launched a website on the Macao Cultural and Creative Industry (www.macaucci.com) in August 2011. In 2012, the website received 152,912 visits.

Macao Conservatory

A subsidiary of the Government's Cultural Affairs Bureau, the Macao Conservatory is a public educational institution that provides lower secondary education, vocational education of higher secondary level in dance, music and drama. The Conservatory comprises a School of Dance, School of Music, and School of Drama. It is a local education institute that trains competent professionals in the performing arts, and strives to discover and nurture local performing arts talents. Additionally, the conservatory offers the public a range of training courses in various performing arts disciplines. It regularly organises various dance performances, concerts and drama performances, giving its students the opportunity to display their skills and gain stage experience. It currently has over 2,000 students and more than 120 teachers.

Protection of Architecture, Scenic Spots and Cultural Heritage

To safeguard Macao's heritage and enable it to shine in all its unique glory, Decree-Laws Nos. 56/84/M and 83/92/M, were passed and gazetted in 1984 and 1992, respectively. These specify that all buildings of historical signifcance or artistic value must be renovated in accordance with offcially approved plans. Macao currently has 128 such heritage sites, which are classifed into fve categories: Monuments, Buildings of Architectural Interest, Classifed Complexes, Classifed Sites and Protected Areas. They are distributed across the Macao peninsula, Taipa and Coloane. Various conservation measures have been formulated for each category. The Government sets great store by the signifcance of Macao's architectural heritage. It has established clear policies on the protection, renovation, restoration, and compilation of a list of heritage sites in Macao, all of which are characterised by unique multicultural diversity and harmony.

Protecting cultural heritage has always been one a priority of the Government. In 2005, the Historic Centre of Macao was inscribed on the World Heritage List, further advancing heritage protection work in Macao. In 2006, through Executive Order No. 202/2006, the area of heritage protection was further expanded.

Intangible Cultural Heritage

In recent years, the conservation of intangible cultural heritage has been a matter of concern. The Convention on Safeguarding Intangible Cultural Heritage passed by the United Nations Educational, Scientifc and Cultural Organization came into effect in Macao in September 2006. During the same year, Cantonese Opera and Chinese herbal tea were jointly nominated by Guangdong, Hong Kong and Macao, which later became the frst batch of intangible cultural heritage inscribed on the National List of Intangible Cultural Heritage in 2007. In June 2008, "Wood carving - Macao's religious fgure carving" was among the second batch added to the National List of Intangible Cultural Heritage, which signifed the frst successful independent application made by Macao for inscription on the national list.

In September 2009, Cantonese Opera was offcially inscribed onto the UNESCO Representative List of the Intangible Cultural Heritage of Humanity as a result of a joint application by Guangdong, Hong Kong and Macao.

In May 2011, "Cantonese Naamyam (Singing and Narrative Songs)", "Macao Taoist Ritual Music" and "Festival of the Drunken Dragon", applied for by Macao independently, were among the third batch inscribed on the National List of Intangible Cultural Heritage. In June 2012, Mazu (A Ma) Belief and Customs, Na Tcha Belief and Customs, Macanese Gastronomy, and Macanese Theatre (Theatre in Patun) were also added to the List of Macao Intangible Cultural Heritage.

By the end of 2012, a total of 10 items from Macao had been included in the List of Macao Intangible Cultural Heritage, six in the National List of Intangible Cultural Heritage, and one in the UNESCO Representative List of the Intangible Cultural Heritage of Humanity.

Research Bursaries

Academic Research Grant Regulations aim to encourage forward-looking and innovative research projects conducive to the understanding of Macao, and of the relationship between Macao and other regions in the humanities feld. The bursary for each project has been increased, varying from 110,000 patacas to 180,000 patacas. Applications may be submitted at any time throughout the year.

From 2006 to the end of 2012, a total of 46 people received the bursaries.

Macao Central Library

Founded in 1895, the Macao Central Library is under the Cultural Affairs Bureau. It comprises the Macao Central Library (main branch), Sir Robert Ho Tung Library, Library of the Civic and

Municipal Affairs Bureau Building, Ilha Verde Library, Mong Ha Library, Red Market Library, Coloane Library and mobile libraries. Currently the largest public library network in Macao, it houses a collection of 800,000 books and 35,000 multimedia items.

Major services provided by the Macao Central Library include: processing applications for reader cards, lending book materials, providing current and back issues of newspapers and periodicals, advising readers on Macao information, providing access to broadband Internet, making microflms, maintaining an online e-resources database, and photocopying of materials. Publishers can apply for an ISBN, ISSN or International Standard Recording Code (ISRC) through the ISBN Centre in the library.

To highlight the many facets of Macao's libraries and promote the use of their resources for educational purposes, every year the central library hosts a range of activities that encourage reading and on how to use library services. It also receives group visits.

Libraries Managed by the Civic and Municipal Affairs Bureau

The Civic and Municipal Affairs Bureau manages a number of libraries, including Wong Ieng Kuan Libraries located in Dr Sun Yat Sen Municipal Park, Luis de Camoes Garden, Areia Preta Urban Park and in Taipa, Ho Yin Garden Library, S. Lourenco Library and Children's Library in Areia Preta Urban Park.

These libraries purchase books and periodicals according to the needs of the people living in their districts. They also regularly host storytelling, thematic lectures, flm sessions, and reading camps.

In 2012, the libraries managed by the Civic and Municipal Affairs Bureau organised 745 reading promotion activities, attracting 19,072 participants. During the year, the seven community libraries under the bureau received 757,461 visitors.

Macao has many other smaller libraries, including the well known octagonal Chinese Library. In addition, various Government departments and tertiary educational institutions have their own libraries. Each contributes to the ever-expanding supply of books and knowledge available to the people of Macao.

Macao Historical Archives

The Macao Historical Archives is the master archive in Macao. The Archive is mainly responsible for collecting, organising, safekeeping, protecting and providing Macao documents of historical value.

Tap Seac Gallery

The Tap Seac Gallery is the base of visual arts exhibition and arts education in Macao. Built in the 1920s and divided into two blocks, this two-storey building was originally a typical residence of one of Macao's elite families. The two blocks join into one after reconstruction. The ground foor has been converted into a 400-square-metre exhibition venue. The front part forms the main exhibition area, while the rear is ideal for holding exhibitions, seminars and lectures.

The gallery and its peripheral buildings were all constructed during the same period. Together, they form a unique cluster of historic monuments in the Tap Seac area, one of Macao's designated heritage sites. The Cultural Affairs Bureau uses the gallery as a venue for visual arts exhibitions and other cultural activities. During the year, the gallery received 33,110 visitors.

Handover Gifts Museum of Macau

The Handover Gifts Museum of Macau is situated next to the Macao Museum of Art, which is an integral part of the Macao Cultural Centre on Xian Xing Hai Avenue in the Outer Harbour Reclamation Area (NAPE). This was the site of the temporary venue where the Macao Handover Ceremony was conducted by the Chinese and Portuguese governments on 20 December 1999. The structure was dismantled afterwards, and its location became the construction site of the Handover Gifts Museum of Macau, in commemoration of the momentous occasion of Macao's return to the motherland.

The Handover gifts exhibition gallery mainly showcases gifts presented by the State Council, as well as those by provinces, municipalities directly under the central government, autonomous regions and the Hong Kong SAR. The thematic exhibition gallery is the venue for displays about Macao's social and cultural history, which showcases a myriad of Macao's cultural features.

MUSEUMS

Centuries of East-West cultural interaction have endowed Macao with many unique museums. They range from the Museum of Macau, Museum of Sacred Art and Maritime Museum, to the Grand Prix Museum, Wine Museum and Fire Service Museum.

Museum of Macau

The Museum of Macau is situated on the heritage site of Mount Fortress, which is a part of the Historic Centre of Macao, while to its immediate west is the Ruins of St Paul's.

The Museum of Macau houses a rich display of Macao's history and diverse culture. With a collection of deep historical and cultural value, the museum highlights the changes to Macao over several hundred years, and tells the story of people from different countries and cultural backgrounds settling in Macao and living in harmony. The Museum of Macau was opened on 18 April 1998.

In 2012, the Museum of Macau received 206,179 visitors, and provided over 1,761 guided tours to 19,118 people. It also held 45 activities, which attracted 2,312 participants.

Monte Fort Corridor

Located at the foot of Mount Fortress's east, Monte Fort Corridor is a passageway linking the S. Lazaro Area pedestrian zone to Mount Fortress. Thus, it facilitates the robust development of the city's entire historical centre. A public space not to be ignored, the corridor has often been chosen as the venue for various arts exhibitions.

Maritime Museum

One of the oldest museums in Macao, the Maritime Museum was founded in 1987. The museum refects the vital role of the sea in Macao's history, as well as vividly portraying the remarkable achievements of China and Portugal in maritime history. Visitors to the Maritime Museum can gain a deeper appreciation of the relationship between cultural exchange and the sea.

Wine Museum

The Wine Museum was opened in 1995. It introduces the history of wine production from its origin in the Caucasus around 10,000 BC up to the present day, with a special focus on Portuguese winemaking.

Grand Prix Museum

The Grand Prix Museum was inaugurated on 18 November 1993. Various Government departments and private institutions have donated exhibits, such as racing cars driven on the Guia Circuit over the years, including by the late celebrated Ayrton Senna and motor racing champion Michael Schumacher. Valuable pictures and trophies are also exhibited.

Macao Museum of Art

The Macao Museum of Art is the only museum in Macao dedicated to art and cultural heritage. It is also the largest visual arts museum in Macao.

In 2012, the Macao Museum of Art held more than 30 exhibitions and conducted more than 100 activities.

Library of the Macao Museum of Art and the Art Square

The Library of the Macao Museum of Art is a reference library specialising in arts materials. It has a collection of over 20,000 books, primarily about visual arts.

Pawnshop Museum

In partnership with a non-governmental organisation, the Government has established the frst museum dedicated to the pawnshop industry. The opening of the Pawnshop Museum in March 2003 marked the success of a new mode of heritage protection.

Built in 1917 as the Tak Seng On Pawnshop, the museum building consists of a pawnshop and a storage tower. The three-storey pawnshop and its relics offer visitors a clear picture of the pawnshop's layout and operation in its heyday.

In September 2004, the Tak Seng On restoration project was awarded an Honourable Mention in the UNESCO Asia-Pacifc Heritage Awards for Culture Heritage Conservation. The project was awarded the title of Urban Best Practices Area (UBPA) of World Expo Shanghai 2010, demonstrating to the world Macao's fruitful efforts in conserving and recycling historic buildings. The museum received 14,572 visitors during 2012.

Treasure of Sacred Art of St Joseph's Seminary

St Joseph's Seminary was established by the Jesuits in 1728. For more than two centuries, it has made a signifcant contribution to training Catholic clergymen engaged in missionary careers in Macao, the mainland and Southeast Asia. For this reason, it was bestowed the title of "Royal Seminary".

Crypt and Museum of Sacred Art

Between 1990 and 1995, the former Portuguese administration conducted archaeological excavation and repaired the Ruins of St Paul's (the Church of Mother of God or Mater Dei), and built the Museum of Sacred Art and Crypt on the site of the grave of Father Alexandre Valignano, the founder of St Paul's College, according to the research fndings.

Dr Sun Yat Sen Memorial House

Originally built by Dr Sun Yat Sen as a home for his family in the years after 1918, this Islamic style residence was opened as Dr Sun Yat Sen Memorial House in 1958.

Lin Zexu Museum

The Lin Zexu Museum in Lin Fong Temple was completed in November 1997, in memory of Imperial Commissioner Lin Zexu, who defed the powerful and the mighty to institute a ban on opium and the opium trade. On 3 September 1839, Lin Zexu, who was then in charge in Guangdong, and Deng Tingzheng, the Governor of Guangdong and Guangxi, met the Consul of the former Portuguese administration to proclaim the prohibition of opium and China's sovereignty over Macao.

Fire Service Museum

Founded in December 1999, the Fire Service Museum is located inside the central operational fre station on Repouso Road. It is open to the public, and received 31,573 visitors in 2012.

Museum of Nature and Agriculture

The frst museum to be built on Coloane island, the Museum of Nature and Agriculture, under the Civic and Municipal Affairs Bureau, is within the Seac Pai Van Country Park. Built by the then Municipal Council of the Islands, the museum was opened on 21 March 1997. It is a cultural amenity with an educational purpose. The museum's fve thematic exhibitions are devoted to the Geography of Macao, Farming Tools of the Islands in Olden Days, the Specimens of Animals, the Specimens of Plants, and the Simulated Mangrove Swamp.

Taipa Houses-Museum

The Taipa Houses-Museum is a collection of residential buildings that form one of Macao's eight most famous landmarks. Constructed in 1921, these fve European-style buildings were the offcial residences of the island's offcers and the homes of Macanese families. The former Portuguese administration's Tourist Department bought and redecorated them in the 1980s. In 1992, they were collectively classifed as an architecturally important monument. The government thoroughly refurbished them and converted three of them into a museum. From east to west, they are known as the Macanese House, the House of the Islands and the House of Portuguese Regions. The other two buildings are the exhibition gallery and reception hall. The museum opened in December 1999, and it offcially adopted the name Taipa Houses-Museum in 2002.

In 2012, the Taipa Houses-Museum received 104,073 visitors. They included 1,995 visitors on 101 guided tours for overseas visitors, local students and community groups. The museum also participated in various major celebratory events organised by the Civic and Municipal Affairs Bureau and other Government departments. Since March, it has also staged eight performances of the play New Tenant in an Old Mansion, which attracted 319 people to watch and learn about the history of Taipa and Coloane in a relaxed atmosphere.

Communications Museum of Macao

Inaugurated on 1 March 2006, the Communications Museum of Macao aims to promote stamp collecting and the stamps of Macao to citizens and tourists. In 2012, it received a total of 32,811 visitors, most of which were arranged visits by local schools and groups.

MACAO SCIENCE CENTER

After seven years of preparation and construction, the Macao Science Center was inaugurated on 19 December 2009, and opened to the public on 25 January 2010. Designed by Ieoh Ming Pei, the Macao Science Center is a public cultural facility with an educational mission that comprises an exhibition centre and a planetarium. Its exhibits focus on public participation and fun.

MACAO TEA CULTURE HOUSE

The Macao Tea Culture House, which is managed by the Civic and Municipal Affairs Bureau, is the frst exhibition gallery in Macao devoted to displaying tea-related artefacts. It was opened to the public on 1 June 2005. Through short-term and long-term exhibitions of various formats, as well as various tea culture activities, it is dedicated to demonstrating Macao's tea culture and everything about tea in China and the West. It also hopes to promote worldwide tea culture, knowledge and studies.

During 2012, the Tea Culture House attracted a total of 42,064 visitors. It also provided 10 free guided tour services, joined by 225 people. The House organised 12 'Taste the Tasty Culture - Tea Culture Promotion Programme' events, in which 640 visitors participated.

MUSEUM OF TAIPA AND COLOANE HISTORY

Opened on 7 May 2006, the Museum of Taipa and Coloane History consists of nine exhibition rooms and a souvenir shop. Built in 1920, the 638-square-metre, two-storey museum building was formerly the building of the former Island Municipal Council of Taipa. On the frst foor are relics unearthed in Coloane, stone architectural remains of the basement, religious and cultural documents and relics from the transformations of the villages on the two islands. These items provide visitors with an overview of the early history and culture of Coloane and Taipa. The exhibition rooms on the second foor have various themes, including the history of the former Municipal Council of the Islands, a look back at agriculture and handicrafts in the old days, the architectural features of buildings on Coloane and Taipa and the recent development of the two islands.

The Museum of Taipa and Coloane History attracted a total of 43,332 visitors in 2012. It provided 13 free guided tours, joined by a total of 553 people.

IONG SAM TONG PAVILION

Managed by the Division of Cultural Facilities of the Civic and Municipal Affairs Bureau, Iong Sam Tong Pavilion was built in the early 20th century as part of Yu Yuen (the former name of Lou Lim Ieoc Garden). The renovation of Iong Sam Tong Pavilion was completed in 2011 and it was reopened on 18 May 2011. It showcases 50 historical items of the Lou family including photographs, letters, biographical materials, handwritten drafts and recordings. It received a total of 14,377 visitors in 2012.

Lou Kau Mansion

Completed in 1889, Lou Kau Mansion was formerly the residence of the prominent merchant Lou Kau and his family. It retains a large number of exquisite carvings in wood, stone and brick; plaster mouldings; pottery decoration; murals; and garden designs, which are typical of the architectural style of traditional Lingnan dwellings.

With a mission to promote Chinese traditional culture by introducing outstanding Chinese folk crafts and conducting arts activities, Lou Kau Mansion conducts regular live demonstrations by famous Chinese folk craft masters. A different theme is introduced each week, attracting many citizens and visitors to exchange ideas and learn from the master craftsmen. In 2012, Lou Kau Mansion attracted 234,989 visitors.

Mandarin's House

The Mandarin's House is the ancestral family residence of the modern Chinese master Zheng Guanying. Zheng's world-famous book Shengshi Weiyan (Words of Warning in Times of Prosperity) was completed here. The building of the Mandarin's House was initiated by Zheng Wenrui, the father of Zheng Guanying, and the Zheng brothers expanded it. The house was probably built before 1869.

In February 2010, the Mandarin's House was opened to the public. During 2012, it attracted 97,842 visitors.

Kun Iam Statue

The Kun Iam Statue is a 32-metre-tall structure on an artifcial island in NAPE, which is connected to the land by a 60-metre bridge. Comprising the statue and lotus fower base, the Kun Iam Statue was completed in March 1999. It received 68,583 visits in 2012.

Macao Cultural Centre

The Macao Cultural Centre is situated on Xian Xing Hai Avenue in NAPE. Completed and opened in March 1999, the complex comprises the Auditoria Building, the Macao Museum of Art Building, Macao Cultural Centre Square and the Handover Gifts Museum of Macao.

The Auditoria Building contains two performance venues. One is a 1,076-seat multipurpose complex theatre, while the other is a 389-seat mini-theatre.

During 2012, the Macao Cultural Centre organised spectacular performances that included dance, music, drama and multimedia. There were 53 programmes with a total of 566 performances or activities. The centre also continued to offer cultural facilities and professional services to various local groups and organisations. During the year, 223 programmes and 884 performances or activities were organised by the centre and its tenants, receiving 180,520 visits.

CULTURAL AND RECREATIONAL ACTIVITIES

The Government is committed to promoting sport for all, encouraging citizens to participate in all kinds of sports and recreational activities as a way to promote good health. Upholding the values of sport-for-all and life-long ftness spelled out in public slogans, the Government has led citizens towards building healthy lives by enjoying everyday sports. At the same time, the Government emphasises enhancing the standards of sports at the local level, and fully supports and encourages local sports institutions with organising and participating in tournaments in Macao and overseas.

The coordinated development of popular sports and athletics can only be realised through the provision of comprehensive modern sports facilities and sports medicine, thereby allowing citizens to exercise conveniently and scientifcally, ultimately enhancing their quality of life.

Macao Sports Development Board

Macao Sports Development Board is responsible for instructing, encouraging, assisting and promoting sports events, establishing the requisite conditions for the development of sports, and coordinating between sports organisations and related staff.

Sport for All

In 2012, a total of 364,165 people took part in the 19 activities organised by the Macao Sports Development Board, of whom 49,290 participated in the 1,978 Sport for All Fitness and Recreational Classes. In 2012, the annual summer activities accommodated a total of 47,726 people, among which 21,539 places were for sport activities. In all, 102 activities and 692 classes were arranged.

Competitive Sport

In 2012, the Macao Sports Development Board supported the Macao Sports Association to organise and participate in 433 competitions, 134 training sessions and 51 international conferences through special funding.

During 2012, a total of 88 athletes and coaches in nine sports were awarded cash prizes in 12 events for their outstanding performances, while 238 athletes and coaches from 22 sports associations were awarded certifcates of merit.

Sports Medicine

In 2012, the board and the China Institute of Sport Science of the General Administration of Sport of China co-organised the Conference for the Third China's National Physical Fitness Surveillance (CNPFS) and International Seminar of Physical Fitness Research. Over 300 professionals from Finland, Austria, Japan, the United States, Macao and mainland China participated in the conference, with more than 100 papers submitted.

In 2012, the Sports Medical Centre served more than 8,451 people.

Major Multi-sport Events

The 4th East Asian Games, held from 29 October to 6 November 2005, was the frst major multi-sports event hosted by Macao. Later, Macao held the First Lusofonia Games in 2006. The 2nd Asian Indoor Games was the third multi-sports event organised by Macao, which was also the frst Asian multi-sports event held by Macao.

Sports and Recreation Venues

Most sports and cultural activity venues in Macao are managed by the Macao Sports Development Board or the Civic and Municipal Affairs Bureau.

In response to the ever-changing demands of users and to meet the needs of different sports, the board constantly improves and diversifes the venues under its jurisdiction. These facilities are conveniently located for Macao residents, and the Sports Development Board intends to eventually establish a sports complex in every district.

At present, major sports facilities in Macao include Tap Seac Multisport Pavilion, Victory Sports Centre, Artur Tamagnini Barbosa Sports Centre, Bosco Sports Complex, Lin Fong Sports Centre and Nam Van Lake Nautical Centre, while those in Taipa include the Olympic Complex, Carmo Swimming Pool, football pitch / athletics ground of the Macao University of Science and Technology (MUST), and Sports Training Centre. Sports facilities in Cotai comprise the Macao East Asian Games Dome, International Shooting Range, Bowling Centre, Tennis Academy, Cheoc Van Nautical Club, Hac-Sa Nautical Centre, and in Coloane, the Go-Kart Racing Course. All of the above are managed by the Macao Sports Development Board.

The Civic and Municipal Affairs Bureau is also responsible for the sports and recreation venues at Dr Sun Yat Sen Municipal Park, Mong Ha Municipal Park, Guia Hill Municipal Park, Ho Yin Garden, the Municipal Swimming Pool, Cheoc Van Swimming Pool, Hac Sa Park and Swimming Pool, Water Activities Centre at Hac Sa Reservoir, Hac Sa Summer Camp Area, Ponte Negra Municipal Recreation Centre (ftness centre), Carmo Sports and Recreation Ground, Ilha Verde Sports Ground, Avenida do Comendador Ho Yin Sports Ground, Avenida do Conselheiro Borja Sports Ground, Weng Neng Sports Ground, Rua Central da Areia Preta Sports Ground, Almirante Magalhaes Correia Sports Ground , Doca Lam Mau Sports Ground, Coloane Sports Ground, Hac Sa Beach Sports Ground, Canal dos Patos Sports Ground and Barra Sports Ground.

There are also many other sports venues owned by associations, institutions and individuals, such as the Workers' Soccer Pitch and a golf course.

Macao Forum

The Macao Forum is one of the most popular venues in Macao for entertainment and sporting events. Opened on 27 May 1985, Macao Forum is divided into two sections. Forum I has a seating capacity of 4,062 and an area of 7,280 square metres. It houses a lobby and an exhibition gallery, which can accommodate displays and exhibitions.

Public Swimming Pools and Beaches

Swimming is one of the most popular recreational activities among Macao residents. The swimming pools managed by the Civic and Municipal Affairs Bureau include the Municipal Swimming Pool, and the swimming pools at Dr Sun Yat Sen Municipal Park, Cheoc Van and Hac Sa Park. The Macao Sport Development Board also manages a number of swimming pools, including those at the Lin Fong Sports Centre, Bosco Sports Complex, Artur Tamagnini Barbosa Sports Centre, Olympic Sports Centre and Carmo.

In Macao, only two beaches -Hac Sa Beach and Cheoc Van Beach, both managed by the Maritime Administration - are available for public use.

Trails

Topographically, Macao has a lower elevation in the north and a higher elevation in the south. Thirteen trails covering a total length of 33 kilometres are located on Taipa and Coloane islands. These provide access to replanted forest areas where saplings still require care, and serve as frebreaks and access routes for fre fghters. For the vast majority of Macao's residents and visitors, however, the primary function of the trails is to facilitate exploration and enjoyment of the natural attractions of the islands.

The 13 trails are Ka Ho Reservoir Trail (1,550 metres), Coloane Fitness Trail (1,225 metres), Taipa Grande Trail (4,000 metres), Taipa Pequena Trail 2000 (2,300 metres), Coloane Trail (8,100 metres), Coloane Northeast Trail (4,290 metres), Hac Sa Reservoir Circuit (2,650 metres), Hac Sa Reservoir Fitness Circuit (1,505 metres), Hac Sa Long Chao Kok Circuit (2,150 metres), Ka Ho Height Circuit (1,490 metres), Seac Pai Van Park Trail (1,680 metres), Coloane Stone Washbasin Ancient Route (about 1,500 metres), and Long Chao Kok Coastal Trail in Hac Sa (about 1,120 metres).

Gardens and Parks

Though small in area, Macao is renowned for its many gardens in a variety of scenery and styles, offering a host of attractions. These form one of Macao's unique features as a tourist destination. The gardens are not only tourist attractions, but are also popular spots where local residents relax and exercise.

Guia Hill Municipal Park

Guia Hill Municipal Park is one of Macao's major venues to enjoy fresh air. This tourist attraction boasts extensive natural resources. Of all the parks in Macao, it ranks frst as a site for Chinese red pines, both in terms of their quantity and age.

Luis de Camoes Garden

Luis de Camoes Garden is one of the oldest gardens in Macao. It was the residence of a rich Portuguese merchant named Lourenco Marques. He loved to feed the pigeons and hundreds of birds nested around his home, creating a spectacular view. From a distance, the garden looked like one giant bird's nest, and the name has been used ever since.

Ho Yin Garden

Ho Yin Garden is situated to the north of Amizade Avenue. It was built to commemorate the late Chinese community leader, Ho Yin, and was opened to the public in 1993.

Carlos d'Assumpcao Park

Carlos d'Assumpcao Park is situated to the south of Amizade Avenue. It commemorates the Macanese community leader and former president of the Legislative Assembly, Carlos d'Assumpcao, and it was opened to the public in 1996.

Flora Garden

Flora Garden is located at the foot of Guia hill. At the end of the 19th century, it was bought by the former Portuguese administration to serve as the Governor's summer residence. Sir Robert Ho Tung, a philanthropist, later bought it, but afterwards returned it as a gift to the former

Portuguese administration. For this reason, the garden is still called "Ho Tung Garden" in Chinese. It is also known as "I Long Hau Fa Yun", as it is at close proximity to a spring.

A cable car was completed and went into service in 1997. It runs from the garden entrance to the top of Guia Hill Reservoir, conveniently linking the two locations.

Lou Lim Ieoc Garden

Lou Lim Ieoc Garden is the only garden in Macao with the classic ambiance of those found in Suzhou. It features pavilions, terraces, lakes, zigzag bridges, rocks and cascades, all of which refect the beautiful scenery of the Jiangnan area on the southern, lower reaches of the Changjiang River.

Dr Sun Yat Sen Municipal Park

Dr Sun Yat Sen Municipal Park is located at Ilha Verde in northern Macao near the Border Gate.

At the centre of the park is a 500-metre-long cloister, the longest of any in Macao's parks, linking most of the scenic spots of the park. Other facilities include an open-air theatre, a sport court, other sports facilities, a swimming pool, and a public library.

There are many other gardens and parks in Macao, including Mong Ha Hill Municipal Park, Russa Hill Park, St Francis Garden, Victory Garden, Vasco da Gama Garden and Areia Preta Seaside Park, Iao Hon Market Garden, Art Garden, and Areia Preta Urban Park on the Macao peninsula; Lakeside Garden, Flower City Garden, Monument Garden, Laurinda Marques Esparteiro Garden and Pier Garden on Taipa island; and Hac Sa Sports and Recreation Park, Hac Sa Arboretum and Coloane Height Park on Coloane island.

Macao Arts Festival

The 23rd Macao Arts Festival was held from 1 May to 2 June 2012. Enriched with fascinating performances, the festival featured performances by leading groups and artists from the United Kingdom, Argentina, Spain, Portugal, Italy, France, the United States, mainland China, Hong Kong and Macao.

MEDIA, COMMUNICATIONS AND INFORMATION TECHNOLOGY

Macao enjoys freedom of the press, freedom of speech and freedom of publishing. Despite its relatively small size, it has a sophisticated and well-developed media industry.

The Government strives to enhance the transparency of its administration and facilitate communication and dialogue with the media. This enables Government messages to be delivered to the public promptly and accurately, and provides a wide range of information via the media. Furthermore, the Government expects the media to act as a watchdog, continually prompting every Government department to improve its work and provide better-quality services to the community.

Macao's laws protect the rights of journalists to gather and receive news and information, and to report it, assuring their journalistic independence.

Mass Media Electronic Media

Macao has one free-to-air TV station, two radio stations and one cable TV station, as well as four locally based satellite TV stations.

Teledifusao de Macau (Macau Broadcasting Company, TDM) began provision of a public broadcasting service in February 1988. Digital broadcasting commenced in 2008. Currently, both analogue broadcasting and digital broadcasting are available. On top of the two round-the-clock channels (Chinese and Portuguese), there are digital channels including sports, information, high defnition (HD), CCTV-13, CCTV news, CCTV documentaries, Fujian TV Station Haixia Satellite Channel and Hunan TV World.

Radio Macau, a subsidiary of TDM, and the privately owned Radio Vila-Verde (Green Village) are Macao's two radio stations. Both broadcast 24 hours a day.

Macau Cable TV has been broadcasting since July 2000, and offers 101 channels (including 20 test channels, and one dedicated hotel channel), all 24 hours.

MSTV Satellite TV Company Limited - originally known as the Cosmos Satellite Television Company, which was the frst operator to be granted a licence to provide satellite television services in Macao - now offers four channels: MSTV's News Channel (launched in January 2009) and Newsky Satellite TV (launched in August 2010) - both on air 24 hours a day; and Kung-fu TV Channel (launched in February 2009) and Zhongbo Satellite TV, which offcially began broadcasting in November 2011. The latter two channels broadcast 16 hours a day.

China Satellite TV (Group) Company was licensed in 2000 to provide satellite television broadcasting services. China Satellite TV offcially began its broadcasting services on 28 March 2008, via the CSTV-1 24-hour channel on health and lifestyle.

The Chinese channel of the MASTV Company began operations in June 2001. It broadcasts 24 hours a day.

On 2 December 2008, Macau Lotus Satellite TV Media Limited was granted a 15-year licence to provide satellite television services in Macao. It started its broadcasting service on 1 January 2009, on its Macao Lotus TV 24-hour channel.

Print Media

The history of Macao's newspaper industry can be traced back over 100 years. From 1839 to 1840, while enforcing the opium ban in Guangdong, Lin Zexu commissioned a selective translation of *the English Macao Monthly* and, for administrative purposes, published *Journal News of Macao* in Guangzhou. On 18 July 1893, Dr Sun Yat Sen and a Macanese named Francisco H. Fernandes worked together and founded *Echo Macanese*, which was published in Chinese and Portuguese. On 22 February 1897, Kang Youwei and Liang Qichao founded *The Reformer China*. After the 1911 Revolution in China, Macao's Chinese newspapers began to fourish. Several newspapers, such as *Ao Men Shi Bao* (Macao Times), *Hao Jing Wan Bao* (Oyster Mirror Evening Post), *Ao Men Tong Bao* (Macao Bulletin), and *Hao Jing Ri Bao* (Oyster Mirror Daily), were founded at this time.

Macao has 10 Chinese daily newspapers, which currently print a total of 100,000 copies each day. They are *Ou Mun Iat Pou* (Macao Daily News), *Jornal Va Kio* (Overseas Chinese Journal), *Tai Chung Pou* (The Public), *Si Man Pou* (The Citizen), *Jornal Seng Pou* (Star Journal), *Cheng Pou* (Righteousness), *Today Macau Jornal*, *Jornal San Wa Ou* (New Chinese Macau Journal), *Hou Kong Daily* and the free newspaper *Exmoo News*.

The main Chinese weeklies published in Macao include: *Jornal Informação* (Information Journal), *Pulso de Macau* (Macau Pulse), *Semanário Recreativo de Macau* (Macau Entertainment Weekly), *Jornal Si Si* (Current Affairs Journal), *Semanário de Desportivo de Macau* (Macau Sports Weekly), *Observatório de Macau* (Macau Observer), *Agora Macau* (Now Macau), *Macao Commercial Post* and *the Macau Convention and Exhibition Economy Journal*.

Portuguese daily newspapers have an even longer history than the Chinese dailies. In 1822, *Abelha da China*, the frst-ever daily in China, was founded and published in Portuguese. Other early-founded Portuguese papers founded in Macao include *Gazeta de Macau* (Macau Gazette), *Imparcial* (The Impartial), and *Correio de Macau* (Macau Post). Macao currently has three Portuguese dailies primarily intended for a local Portuguese readership. These are *Ponto Final* (Full Stop), *Jornal Tribuna de Macau* (Macau Tribune Journal) and *Hoje Macau* (Today Macau). *O Clarim* (The Bugle) is a Portuguese weekly.

The English daily newspapers in Macao are *the Macau Post Daily*, *the Macao Daily Times* and *the Macau Business Daily*.

Every day, dozens of Hong Kong newspaper and magazine titles are transported to Macao. Some daily newspapers published on the mainland are also available on local newsstands. In addition, Macao residents enjoy access to radio and TV programmes made in Hong Kong and mainland China.

Media Stationed in Macao

Macao does not have its own news agency. However, both Xinhua News Agency and Lusa-Portuguese News Agency have branches or representative offices in Macao. Other media organisations with accredited correspondents in the territory include China News Service (CNS); China Central Television (CCTV); China National Radio (CNR); China Radio International (CRI); the State Administration of Radio, Film and Television; People's Daily; Wen Hui Bao (Shanghai); South China Morning Post (SCMP); Hong Kong Economic Journal (HKEJ); Asia Television (ATV); Hong Kong Cable Television (HKCTV); Radio Television Hong Kong (RTHK); Ta Kung

Pao; Wen Wei Po; Hong Kong Daily News; China Economic Weekly; Hong Kong Commercial Daily; Oriental Press Group; EyePress News; and China Trade News.

Press Associations

The press associations in Macao include the Macao Chinese Media Workers Association, the Macao Journalists Club, the Macao Journalists Association, the Macao Media Club, the Macau Sports Press Association, the Macau Press Photographers Association, and the Portuguese and English Speaking Media Association and the Macao Media Workers Welfare Association.

The Press Law

The Press Law (Law No. 7/90/M), promulgated in August 1990, guarantees the freedom of the press and its right of access to information; and governs activities regarding newspapers and magazines, publishers and news agencies.

Macao's Press Law consists of six chapters and 61 articles. This law protects the rights of journalists, including those to gather, receive and report information. By law, journalists have the right to access information from Government authorities, public administrations, public corporations and joint ventures formed by the Government; private organisations of which the Government or its subsidiaries are major shareholders; corporations that operate public assets; and contractors that provide public works or services. This freedom of access is not applicable to information regarding judicial confdentiality and state secrets, or facts and documentation protected by law as private and confdential information.

Journalists have the right to protect their sources of information and they will not be penalised directly or indirectly while exercising that right. Likewise, there is no obligation for media owners and publishers, individual publications or news agencies to reveal their sources of information. In this way, the law protects journalistic independence. However, in the event of suffcient evidence of criminal involvement, the media's right to protect its sources of information can be terminated by a court order.

The Press Law allows freedom of discussion and criticism of politics, society, religious views and laws, as well as the acts of the Government itself and its departments and personnel.

Publishers or other entities publishing periodicals, and correspondents of non-local media organisations based in Macao, are legally required to register with the Government Information Bureau (GCS).

In 2010, the Government proposed to review and revise the 20-year old Press Law, thereby providing local media with a legal environment that is both supportive and conducive to its healthy development. In March 2010, the Government Information Bureau announced that the process would be in three phases: research, consultation, and drafting. In June, the bureau invited local academic institutions to conduct a study on the direction for amendments to the Press Law and the Broadcasting Law of Macao. The tender for gathering public opinions on the revision was launched in the frst quarter of 2011. Deliberative opinion polling was frst introduced in Macao to conduct extensive, objective and scientifc opinion gathering and analyses. In addition, the GCS actively liaised with the newspaper industry and professional organisations to listen to all opinions.

After gathering and analysing the views of the press industry and the results of the deliberative opinion polling, the Government decided to defer any amendment of the Broadcasting Law while proceeding to amend the Press Law under the principle of "limited to deletion only" any clause to the law. The controversial provisions to be deleted included the one regulating the Press Council, and the other on the Code of Practice for Journalists. Some wording was also amended to align with relevant laws. Another round of public consultation will be launched upon completion of the draft.

Government Information Bureau

The Government Information Bureau (GCS) is a bureau-level administrative entity under the supervision of the Chief Executive. It assists Government departments and the media by coordinating and conducting research regarding public communication, disseminating Government information and arranging media interviews. The GCS regularly publishes *Macao* magazine, the *Macao Information* booklet and the *Macao Yearbook* in Chinese, Portuguese and English.

In line with the development of civil society and information technology in mass media, in March the Government promulgated the by-law, Organisation and Operation of the Government Information Bureau (GCS), to enhance the transparency of administration, facilitate communication with citizens and further safeguard the public interests and the right to information.

Under the new framework, the GCS is restructured from one department with three divisions and one team to two departments with fve divisions: the Information Department - under which is the Media Relations Division; the Research and Publicity Department - under which are the Publicity and Promotion Division and the Publication Division; the IT and Archive Division; and the Administration and Finance Division.

Disseminating Government Information

The GCS has also established the Information Broadcast System (IBS) for local media and accredited correspondents. The IBS facilitates media access to offcial information and photographs by distributing them via the Internet. This enables the media to remotely access offcial information at any time.

During 2012, the Information Department wrote and distributed more than 9,996 press releases, interview notices, important notices, and speeches in Chinese, Portuguese and English; and distributed 1,426 photographs on behalf of the MSAR Government and its departments.

Registration of Periodical Publications

The Administration and Accounting Section of the GCS is responsible for registering newspapers, publishers and periodicals. Under the Media Registration Regulations, if a daily publication is registered but has not been published for 180 days, or if other registered periodicals have not been published for a period of one year or have been suspended for a period of one year, their registration will be cancelled. Registration of publications is free of charge.

Forty-fve new publications were registered with the GCS in 2012, including daily, weekly, biweekly, monthly, bimonthly and quarterly publications. Six new publishers were also registered.

The Government Portal

The Government portal (www.gov.mo) was offcially launched in December 2004. It offers a comprehensive platform for information and e-services provided by all Government departments. The portal gives the public access to information from various public administrative departments, the Legislative Assembly, courts, the Public Prosecutions Offce and tertiary education institutions.

Available in both traditional and simplifed Chinese, Portuguese and English versions, the Government portal provides general information and updates about Macao to local residents, tourists and the business community. The portal covers Government information and announcements, fact sheets about Macao, city information, cultural and recreational activities, e-services, legal advice, and comments and complaints from the public.

The portal's objectives are to announce Government policies in a timely manner, enhance communication between the Government and the public, maintain administrative transparency, and collect public opinion.

Government Printing Bureau

The Government Printing Bureau implements the Government's publishing policy. It is responsible for the publication of the *Macao Special Administrative Region Gazette* (the Macao SAR Gazette) and its supplements; the laws and regulations of Macao (in both separate and omnibus formats); the general budget of Macao and related budgets of Government departments and public bodies; Macao's accounting records; Government policy addresses; legally defned offcial forms; and any offcial printed matter that uses the emblem of Macao. It also undertakes the layout, proofreading and printing of printed matter that requires special security measures or close supervision.

The Macao SAR Gazette

Sections One and Two of the *Macao SAR Gazette* are published at 9.00am every Monday and Wednesday, respectively; unless either of these days is a public holiday, in which case the pertinent section is published on the next working day. Announcements of urgent or ad-hoc matters that occur outside this schedule may be issued in a supplement or special section.

Publication of all the following items in Section One of the *Macao SAR Gazette* is mandated by law, and they only come into legal effect thereby: laws, by-laws, Legislative Assembly resolutions, administrative orders and orders approved by the Chief Executive, orders approved by principal offcials of the Government, international treaties signed in the name of "Macao, China", Legislative Assembly election results, the appointment of members of the Legislative Assembly, the appointment and termination of members of the Executive Council, the appointment and termination of presidents and judges at all levels of the courts and of public prosecutors, as well as other announcements of appointments and terminations under the law and documents whose announcement is required by law.

The following announcements must also be made in Section One of the Macao SAR Gazette:

Amendments to the Basic Law of the MSAR, proposals to amend the Basic Law, and interpretations of the Basic Law by the authorised entity;

National laws that apply to the MSAR, and interpretations of those laws by the Standing Committee of the National People's Congress (NPC);

Documents adopted by the NPC and its Standing Committee regarding the MSAR;

Regulatory documents adopted by the NPC's Preparatory Committee for the Macao Special Administrative Region, regarding the establishment and operation of the MSAR;

Documents authorised by the NPC and its Standing Committee and the central government; and orders, instructions and documents issued by the Central People's Government in accordance with the Basic Law of the MSAR;

Documents regarding the appointment and termination of the Chief Executive, principal Government offcials and the Public Prosecutor-General by the Central People's Government; and

The Chief Executive's annual policy address. The following announcements must be made in Section Two of the Macao SAR Gazette:

International treaties applicable to the MSAR;

Agreements on judicial mutual assistance, and mutual exemption of visa requirements by the MSAR and other countries or regions with the assistance and authorisation of the central government;

Judicial mutual assistance agreements signed with judicial authorities in other areas or regions on the mainland;

Statements and announcements made by the Legislative Assembly;

Statements and announcements made by the Government; and

Other documents that are to be announced in this section by law.

Since 2000, the Government Printing Bureau has posted the complete contents of Sections One and Two of the *Macao SAR Gazette* on its website (www.io.gov.mo) for public access and information. By the end of 2011, the Government Printing Bureau had established an online database containing the full text of 19,800 laws and regulations. This includes all the laws and regulations published since the establishment of the MSAR, as well as laws, decree-laws and other regulations gazetted between 1976 and 19 December 1999 that remain in effect. In 2012, the bureau's offcial website recorded an average of more than 268,000 hits per month.

Laws of the Macao Special Administrative Region

Prior to the establishment of the MSAR, the Government Printing Bureau published Macau Laws. Since the establishment of the MSAR, it has published The Macao Special Administrative Region Laws, a semi-annual reference document that provides easy access to major laws, by-laws, resolutions of the Legislative Assembly and administrative orders published in the Macao SAR Gazette. The bureau also published a CD ROM, The Macao Special Administrative Region Laws, in Chinese and Portuguese, which consolidates all the laws announced between 20 December 1999 and 31 December 2012.

Information Technology Science and Technology Committee

The Science and Technology Committee is a consultative body that advises the Government on the formulation of policies to promote technological development and modernisation.

Chaired by the Chief Executive, the Science and Technology Committee was formed with committee members including the Secretary for Transport and Public Works, the Secretary for Economy and Finance, the Secretary for Social Affairs and Culture, the Rector of the University of Macau, the Rector of the Macao Polytechnic Institute, the Rector of the Macau University of Science and Technology, the President of the Macao Foundation, the President of the Board of Directors of the Macau Productivity and Technology Transfer Center (CPTTM), the Director of the United Nations University International Institute for Software Technology, and the President of INESC Macau (Macau Institute of System and Computer Engineering), plus 20 other members who have excelled in the felds of science, technology and innovation, and who are appointed by the Chief Executive.

The Chief Executive has also appointed nine overseas scholars who are renowned in their areas of expertise as advisors to the council. They include Tsung Dao Lee, Lu Yongxiang, Zhu Lilan, Lu Zhonghe, Hui Yongzheng, Zhu Gaofeng, Charles K. Kao, Li Lianhe and Song Yonghua.

Science and Technology Development Fund

The Science and Technology Development Fund was established under By-law No. 14/2004 of the Macao SAR and is supervised by the Chief Executive. In line with Macao's policies on science and technology, the fund subsidises the development of educational programmes, research and other related projects. It especially focuses on the following:

Projects that help to promote and enhance knowledge about science and technology;

Projects that improve productivity and competitiveness;

- Innovative projects that facilitate the development of the science and technology industry;

- Cultural and environmental projects that beneft scientifc and technological innovation and development;

-High-priority technology-transfer projects that enhance socio-economic development; and

-Patent applications.

Groups eligible to receive subsidies include local universities and academies and their affliated research and development centres; local non-proft private organisations, laboratories and entities; registered entrepreneurs and enterprises; and individuals involved in research and development projects in Macao.

In 2012, the Science and Technology Development Fund spent more than 70.87 million patacas to subsidise 84 science research projects, of which 30 were concluded, yielding a total of 137 theses. The projects also trained 28 master's degree candidates and 18 doctoral candidates. In terms of science popularisation projects, in 2012 the Science and Technology Development Fund received 159 applications for total funding of over 14.12 million patacas. The projects involved 6,808 students.

Macau New Technologies Incubator Centre

Co-founded by the Government and the private sector, the Macau New Technologies Incubator Centre (Manetic) was established in 2001, marking Macao's frst step towards the development of innovative hi-tech industries.

Manetic is an incubator centre for new technology. Its major objective is to help turn business or product ideas into commercial ventures as quickly as possible. Manetic's targets include: to strengthen technological development in Macao and improve career opportunities for the next generation; to effectively utilise Macao's professional resources through cooperation with multinational companies; and to tap international resources through developing Macao as the technological development centre in the Greater China region.

Telecommunications Services

The objective of Macao's telecommunications policy is to liberalise the regulation of the public telecommunications infrastructure and service provision gradually, in order to maximise public benefits, create investment opportunities and enhance the competitiveness and long-term development of the economy and the community. This policy strives to ensure that quality and effcient telecommunications services are always available to the entire community and businesses at reasonable cost and in a non-discriminatory manner. A further goal is network interconnection and number portability.

The Telecommunications Law

The Telecommunications Law (Law No. 14/2001) was gazetted on 20 August 2001. The construction, management and operation of a telecommunications network, and its service provision, are legally deemed to be matters of public interest, and they can only be undertaken by a public entity or by a private organisation that complies with applicable regulations and demonstrates its business capability. In 2012, the Government conducted preliminary consultations with the industry regarding amendment of the Telecommunications Law to accommodate the opening up of Macao's telecommunication market to enable better development of the industry.

Bureau of Telecommunications Regulation

Under the supervision of the Secretary for Transport and Public Works, the Bureau of Telecommunications Regulation (DSRT) oversees telecommunications and information technology in Macao.

Fixed-network and External Telecommunications Services

Macao's fxed-network and external telecommunications services are currently operated by Companhia de Telecomunicacoes de Macau (CTM) under a franchise contract. In November 2009, the Government and CTM signed a revised franchise contract on public telecommunications services, regarding the early opening-up of local and international network rental services, and transit services. Other franchise services will be completely liberalised in 2012. In December 2011, the Government formulated the Regulations on the Provision and Operation of Fixed Public Telecommunication Networks (By-law No. 41/2011). In 2012, an open tender for the provision and operation of fxed public telecommunication networks was launched, and the new licences were slated to be issued by the frst quarter of 2013.

At the end of 2012, there were 161,752 fxed-network lines in Macao, along with 781 public pay phones offering local call services and IDD access from public locations throughout the Macao peninsula and the two islands. Callers in Macao can currently make IDD calls to 246 countries and regions.

Public Mobile and Wireless Communications Services

The wireless telecommunications market was offcially opened up in 2000, advancing the Macao telecommunications and information industry into a new era. In the early 2000s, Companhia de Telecomunicacoes de Macau (CTM), Hutchison Telephone (Macau) Company and SmarTone Mobile Communications (Macau) were awarded eight-year licences to offer public mobile phone services. Kong Seng Paging Ltd. was also granted a virtual mobile operator licence to provide public mobile telecommunication services, despite not having its own public telecommunication network and frequency.

The Regulation on the Interconnection of Public Telecommunication Networks (By-law No. 41/2004), stipulates the establishment of a level playing feld for the interconnection of public telecommunications networks, in order to ensure the implementation of interconnection at an opportune time and at a reasonable cost.

In accordance with regulations, in 2005 the Government issued a licence to China Unicom (Macau)1, allowing them to establish a CDMA2000 1X network and provide roaming mobile telecommunications services. After one year of operation, the company successfully applied to the Government for a licence to provide local services.

At the beginning of 2006, China Unicom (Macau), Hutchison Telephone (Macau), Comphania de Telecomunicacoes de Macau (CTM) and SmarTone Mobile Communications (Macau) were granted licences to provide public networks for terrestrial third-generation (3G) mobile telecommunications and roaming 3G mobile telecommunications services. Citizens could enjoy 3G communication services since the second quarter of 2007. The 2G licence of China Unicom (Macau)[1] was revoked at its own request in April 2010; the other three telecom carriers had their 2G licences renewed to 8 July 2012. In 2012, the Government decided to extend the use of 2G service to June 2015 and made corresponding amendments to the 3G licences of Comphania de Telecomunicacoes de Macau (CTM), Hutchison Telephone (Macau) and SmarTone Mobile Communications (Macau) so as to extend their provision of 2G service to that date.

As at year-end 2012, the fve mobile telecommunication providers had 1,613,457 registered users, and per capita cell phone ownership was 279.8 percent.

Internet and Broadband Services

Macao's internet-enabled population continued to increase at a stable pace. At the end of 2012, there were 145,120[2] internet subscribers. In accordance with the regulations of By-law No. 24/2002, in November 2002 internet service providers (ISPs) were formally included in the licensing mechanism. Currently, 21 companies have been granted ISP licences.

CTM began offering internet broadband services in July 2000. By the end of 2012, there were 144,297 registered broadband subscribers, an increase of 7,038 or 5.1 percent over the fgure of 137,259 a year earlier. The Macao peninsula, Taipa and Coloane islands have 100 percent broadband coverage.

Moreover, the urban wireless broadband network project financed by the Government, commenced in 2009, and began providing services to residents and tourists in September 2010.

At the end of 2012, there were 132 WiFi Go service spots, and approximately fve million successful connection instances were recorded.

Registration and Management of Internet Domain Names

The University of Macau's appointment to manage and register the top-level domain ".mo" for the Macao SAR ended in 2010. Consequently, in March 2011, the Government launched the Macao Network Information Centre and awarded a service contract to HNET Asia Ltd to administer and operate Macao domain names. In 2012, the DSRT liaised with relevant service operators regarding necessary preparation and publicity work to introduce registration services for Chinese and Portuguese domain names.

Development of Terrestrial Digital Broadcasting

Following the global trend of terrestrial digital broadcasting, the number of terrestrial digital broadcasting channels provided by Teledifusao de Macau (Macau Broadcasting Company, TDM) increased to 11. To ensure the availability of quality products that meet residents' needs, and to enable residents to enjoy the programmes aired on Macao's terrestrial digital broadcasting channels, the Bureau of Telecommunications Regulation built the Digital Terrestrial Television Research and Testing Centre, which commenced operation on 20 September 2010, in partnership with Macao Polytechnic Institute.

Radio Frequency Allocation and Coordination with Neighbouring Regions

After signing the Mainland China and Macao Frequency Coordination Agreement for Terrestrial, Mobile/Fixed Broadcasting (Audio and Television) in 2002, the two regions have been maintaining strong linkages in the development of wireless communication services.

In November 2012, the State Radio Regulation Bureau of the Ministry of Industry and Information Technology and related authorities met to consider coordination of radio communication frequencies in mainland China and Macao. The parties discussed the cross-border public land mobile network signal coverage and related measures, mobile network coverage at the new University of Macau campus in Hengqin and nearby areas, coordination of 3G networks and frequencies, and new developments in telecommunication services and technology.

Authentication of Electronic Documents and Digital Signatures

Law No. 5/2005, which was passed by the Legislative Assembly in August 2005, forms the key legal basis for regulating and authenticating electronic documents and digital signatures. This law is essential for the long-term development of e-government and e-commerce. Executive Order No. 376/2005 designated the Bureau of Telecommunications Regulation (DSRT) as the authority responsible for authenticating electronic documents and signatures.

Postal Services The Development of Macao's Postal Services over Three Centuries

Since it foundation on 1 March 1884, the Macao Post Offce has operated as a provider of postal services, complying with international conventions. On the same day, the frst Macao stamp, titled "Crown", entered into circulation. In fact, Macao Post's history dates back a century earlier, in 1798, when sea mail services began.

Many new services have been introduced since the establishment of Macao Post. Alongside traditional postal services and the Macao Postal Savings, established in 1917, Macao Post took over the operation of telephone services in 1927. Then, as society developed, these services were conceded to other entities or public sector bodies. In 1981, the Companhia de Telecomunicacoes de Macau (CTM) took over the operation of telecommunications. In 2000, the Post Offce's role as the supervisory body for telecommunications services was transferred to the DSRT.

The Post Offce

To respond to rapid technological developments, the Post Offce is committed to providing modern, diversifed services. In 2006, the Post Offce introduced Electronic Certifcation Services (eSignTrust), becoming the only certifcation service provider accredited by the Government. In the same year, the Communications Museum of Macao was inaugurated, focused on postal services and telecommunications. The museum seeks primarily to serve young people, to satisfy their thirst for knowledge. In 2008, Secure Electronic Postal Services were introduced. The Electronic Postal Certifcation Mark is a trusted time stamp service issued on electronic documents to certify the integrity of document content and its creation time.

In 2012, the volume of local mail was three percent lower than that in 2011, mainly because the Government delivered mail relating to the Wealth Partaking Scheme only once in 2012 instead of twice in 2011.

As the global economic recovery remains sluggish, the volume of outbound surface mail dropped by four percent while the volume of air mail remained the same as the previous year. As for the volumes of inbound surface mail and air mail, there was a decrease of three percent and an increase of four percent, respectively. The main sources and destinations of mail were mainland China, Hong Kong, Taiwan, Singapore, Malaysia, Australia, Canada, Portugal, Belgium, the United Kingdom and the United States.

Regarding registered mail, in 2012 the volume of local mail was three percent higher than in 2011. The volumes of outbound international surface mail and air mail increased by 25 percent and two percent, respectively, while the volume of inbound international surface mail remained the same. There was a rise of four percent in inbound international air mail.

Regarding Express Mail Service (EMS), in comparison with 2011, Macao Post recorded a 10 percent increase in the number of outbound EMS items and a 10 percent increase in inbound EMS items. The chief sources and destinations of EMS items were mainland China, Hong Kong, the United States, Taiwan, Japan and Portugal.

Secure Electronic Postal Services

During 2011, Macao Post employed electronic registered mail technology to build up a secure electronic mailbox system. In addition, it completed its study and examination of integrating electronic postal certifcation, image scanning technology and fax server technology.

The electronic postal certifcation mark has many applications for services such as e-payroll advice, e-bidding and e-report fling.

In the legal sphere, Macao Post is drafting the Electronic Registered Mail Postal Services bylaw and provisions to regulate public electronic registered mail services. Regarding international cooperation, the Council of Administration (CA) of the Universal Postal Union passed Macao Post's proposal to add new provisions on defnitions of electronic registered mail postal services and electronic mailboxes to the Universal Postal Convention, which became effective on 1 January 2012.

To promote electronic postal services, Macao Post participated in IT Week 2012 exhibitions, which showcased the electronic document fling system and electronic bidding system developed from electronic postal certifcation technology.

Philately

Thematic philatelic products issued in 2012 included two thematic packs of I ching, Pa Kua, an album of Literature and its Characters - A Journey to the West, and a philatelic collection of Collect Stamps, Learning with Idioms jointly compiled by Macao Post, Guangdong Philatelic Corporation and Hongkong Post. Showcasing valuable Chinese culture, these three philatelic products are ideal for stamp collectors and Chinese culture lovers.

Macao Post provides different channels for overseas collectors to purchase philatelic products. Collectors around the world can enter Macao Post's website (www.macaupost.gov.mo) to obtain the most recent philatelic information and enrol in the Collector's Plan Subscription. They can also purchase philatelic products directly from local postal organisations or through authorised dealers in Macao philatelic products.

Caixa Economica Postal

Caixa Economica Postal (Postal Savings Offce or CEP) is a credit institution operated by the Macao Post Offce that serves as the post offce's cashier. It also provides a wide range of bank related services, such as credit facilities, remittance services for the public and electronic payments.

In terms of credit facilities, CEP chiefy provides civil servants and employees of public services and private companies who sign an employee credit service agreement with guaranteed short-term credit. In 2012, CEP approved loans worth nearly 194 million patacas.

CEP and Western Union also jointly provide an express money transfer service. Using its advanced IT, global computerised money transfer system and counter network, customers can transfer money safely to over 200 countries and regions within a few minutes. There were over 30,000 transactions in 2012. There are currently nine outlets for this service, at CEP, Central Post Offce, Airport Post Branch, Ferry Terminal Post Branch, eSignTrust Registration Authority, the Communications Museum Shop, the Almirante Lacerda Post Branch, the Ocean Garden Post Branch, and the Coloane Post Offce.

Furthermore, CEP also established an electronic payment platform in 2006. The public can also apply for or settle payments of various Government services online in real time. By the end of 2012, more than 73,000 people had settled payments via the platform.

eSignTrust

As the only authentication entity approved by the Government, eSignTrust has been providing citizens, corporations and Government departments with online identity authentication services since it commenced operation in 2006. An electronic document signed by the user, and with qualifed electronic certifcation provided by eSignTrust services, will have legal effect.

In 2012, to achieve the objectives of the Eighth Supplementary Protocol to the Mainland and Macao Closer Economic Partnership Arrangement on the development of pilot applications of mutual recognition of electronic signature certifcates in Macao and Guangdong, Macao Post, the Department of Information Security Coordination of the Ministry of Industry and Information Technology, the Economic and Information Commission of Guangdong Province and the Bureau of Telecommunications Regulation established a working group to provide suggestions on the framework for the mutual recognition of certifcates issued by Guangdong and Macao to facilitate future planning and implementation.

[1] In line with the reconstruction of mainland China's telecommunications industry, China Telecom has officially acquired the CDMA mobile telephone network and business of China Unicom. China Unicom (Macao) Limited was offcially renamed China Telecom (Macau) Co Ltd on 27 November 2008, when the legal procedures involved in the changes were completed.

[2] According to the results of the 2011 population census, the number of households at year-end was 172,600 (excluding collective households in hotel and hostel services).

Communications Museum of Macao

Opened on 1 March 2006, the Communications Museum of Macao promotes philately and Macao stamps to local residents and visitors.

LAND, INFRASTRUCTURE, HOUSING AND PUBLIC UTILITIES URBAN PLANNING

To satisfy the needs arising from Macao's rapid urban development, the Government has drawn up a long-term plan for major infrastructure, traffc and transportation and other urban development projects, under the policymaking principles of "putting people frst" and "sustainable development". This aims to upgrade infrastructure, transportation and related facilities and improve the quality of life of the community.

Lands, Public Works and Transport Bureau

The Lands, Public Works and Transport Bureau (DSSOPT) is a public administrative authority that provides support to other branches of government in matters of land utilisation and management, urban planning, infrastructure, and basic services. It strives to develop Macao into a sustainable modern city with a favourable environment for both living and working.

In 2012, the DSSOPT actively promoted projects under the Guangdong-Macao Cooperation Framework Agreement, which included compiling the Action Plan for the Bay Area of the Pearl River Estuary, the Plan for the Coordinated Development of Macao and Zhuhai, and the Western Pearl River Delta Development Plan. The DSSOPT also published a digest of the second-phase public consultation on the Master Plan for Macao's New Districts, following completion of the consultation, and held exchange sessions and expert forums in the second half of the year. The third-phase of the public consultation would be launched by the end of 2013, to enrich the plan.

In 2012, the DSSOPT continued to launch and follow up on various plans for smaller areas and studies on key projects. These included detailed planning of the shipyard at Lai Chi Vun, Coloane; planning of Hac Sa Village in Coloane; the overall conceptual urban design of the Border Gate checkpoint and its surrounding environment; the plan for urbanisation of Seac Pai Van in Coloane; the overall urban design of A-Ma district; the Inner Harbour redevelopment plan; the overall plan for the heart of the Historic Centre (Ruins of St Paul's); a planning study for northwest Macao; a study on the Urban Climatic Map of Macao; a study on the adaptive re-use of the area around Lilau Square and the Mandarin's House; a land categorisation study; and an in-depth study on land utilisation.

Regarding the management of urbanisation: the DSSOPT created 290 street alignment charts, of which 218 are for streets on the Macao Peninsula, 37 for streets on Taipa, and 35 for streets on Coloane. In addition, it sent out 492 proposals regarding construction plans.

Construction Companies and Contractors

According to statistics from the Lands, Public Works and Transport Bureau, the numbers of construction contractors and construction companies that have either registered or renewed their registrations by the end of 2012 were as follows:

Engineers and Architects

According to statistics from the Lands, Public Works and Transport Bureau, the numbers of architects and engineers that had registered or renewed their registrations by the end of 2012 were as follows:

Architect Engineer (urban construction) Engineer (gas) Engineering Technician Total

Infrastructure Development Offce

The Infrastructure Development Offce is responsible for facilitating and coordinating the execution, maintenance, modernisation and development of major construction projects in Macao. It also researches, follows up and develops cooperative construction projects with the Greater Pearl River Delta region.

The Infrastructure Development Offce is responsible for planning and launching a number of public projects. Examples of traffc and transportation projects during 2012 included the Taipa Ferry Terminal, the Cotai underground roundabout on the Taipa-Coloane Causeway, Coloane-Ka Ho Tunnel, a study on the construction of Taipa Grande Tunnel, and the Hong Kong-Zhuhai-Macao Bridge.

Regarding public housing, a number of projects were expedited to meet the housing demands of the residents, while public facilities and car parks were also included in these projects in order to cater to the needs of the community.

Projects	No. of residential units	Other facilities
Seac Pai Van Public Housing Estate	8,649	Car park, social facilities
Edifcio do Lago, Taipa	2,703	Car parking spaces, motorcycle parking spaces, public transport interchange, dry markets and social facilities
Fai Chi Kei Public HousingEstate	737	Public car park with car and motorcycle parking spaces
Rua Central De Toi San Public Housing Estate	578	Public car park with a total of about 200 car and motorcycle parking spaces
Bairro da Ilha Verde Public Housing Estate, Lot 1, 2	2,356	Public car park with 1,190 car and 1,600motorcycle parking spaces, bus interchange,commercial and social facilities
Bairro da Ilha Verde Public Housing Estate, Lot 3	770	Public car park with about 400 parking spaces, commercial and social facilities

Hengqin Campus of the University of Macau

The construction of the new campus of the University of Macau (UM) on Hengqin island started in November 2010, and completed by the end of 2012. Final inspections and preparation for the relocation of UM were made in early 2013.

Transportation Infrastructure Offce

On 1 November 2007, the Government established the Transportation Infrastructure Offce, aiming to foster the modernisation and improvement of transportation infrastructure as well as the construction of the Macao Light Rail Transit (LRT) System, to provide comfortable and highly effcient modern transportation for citizens and tourists.

After the public bidding and evaluation of bids, the offce awarded the contract for the supply of Rolling Stock and Systems of Macao LRT Phase I to Mitsubishi Heavy Industries, Ltd. on 3 March 2011 at a contract value of 4.688 billion patacas.

The foundation works of the Light Rapid Transit System (LRT) depot commenced on 23 November 2011, followed by the project on the central Taipa section, which commenced on 21 February 2012, and later, construction of the Cotai and Taipa terminal sections commenced on 13 June 2012. By then the construction of LRT in Taipa was in full swing. Moreover, on 7 August 2012 a ceremony was held for the commencement of the construction of the public transport interchange at Estrada Governador Albano de Oliveira in Taipa.

Infrastructure Projects Private Construction Projects

According to statistics from the Lands, Public Works and Transport Bureau, 30 building projects providing 2,443 private fats with a total foor area of 325,050 square metres, 98 commercial units with a total foor area of 10,536 square metres, and 2,218 parking spaces in car parks with a total area of 73,026 square metres were completed in 2012. Also during the year, construction commenced on 26 private projects providing 2,279 units with a total foor area of 267,093 square metres.

Furthermore, by the end of 2012, 30,698 units were pending approval, of which 29,527 were residential units with a total foor area of 3,949,147 square metres, 1,163 were commercial units with a total foor area of 30,334 square metres, eight were offce units with a total foor area of 8,340 square metres, and the remainder were industrial units with a total foor area of 57,195 square metres, and 32,644 parking spaces in car parks with a total area of 1,000,697 square metres. By 2012, a total of 7,636 units were still under construction, of which 7,254 were residential units with a total foor area of 991,112 square metres, 246 were commercial units with a total foor area of 566,441 square metres, 136 were offce units with a total foor area of 26,255 square metres, and the remainder were industrial units with a total foor area of 38,250 square metres, and 8,786 parking spaces in car parks with a total area of 294,236 square metres.

Public Construction and Infrastructure Projects

To meet the needs arising from social development, the DSSOPT put forward a number of projects in 2012, including the frst-phase expansion of the Emergency Service Building and ancillary facilities of Conde S. Januario Hospital, the Rua de Francisco Xavier Pereira public housing project, the frst-phase construction of the new Coloane Prison, construction of the Cheang Kun Ying Memorial Hall, maintenance of the Kun Iam Statue, construction of the Pou Tai Social Service Building, installation of barrier-free facilities in the car park at Alameda Dutor Carlos d'Assumpcao, and the frst-phase construction of a vehicle examination centre in Cotai.

With regard to infrastructure, to support implementation of the Government's public housing policy and the plan for urbanisation of Seac Pai Van in Coloane, public drainage systems, and tap water and recycled water pipelines were built in the area, slope upgrading and greening works were carried out, and pedestrian footbridges and road-crossing facilities were built in tandem with the development of public housing estates. Furthermore, basic ancillary facilities including two temporary carriageways and a walkway were constructed near Edifcio do Lago (TN27) in Taipa. To facilitate public transportation, road networks were developed. In 2012, Rua Lei Pou Chon and Avenida do Ouvidor Arriaga were opened to traffc, and Avenida Marginal do Patane was extended to connect Travessa dos Estaleiros and Avenida Marginal do Lam Mao, providing linkage between districts.

Macao Civil Engineering Laboratory

The Macao Civil Engineering Laboratory was established in 1988, and is a non-proft public legal body engaged in science and technology, which is autonomous in terms of technology, budget and assets. The chairpersons of the Board of the General Assembly and Board of Directors are both appointed by the Government.

The responsibilities of the Macao Civil Engineering Laboratory are to provide civil engineering and related technical support to the Government, public and private civil engineering frms, and any net value companies in related felds.

Housing Housing Bureau

The main functions of the Housing Bureau are to ensure the execution of public housing policies, projects and work, as well as to assist with and support the management of the common areas of buildings.

Home-Ownership Scheme Housing

Under Decree-Law No. 13/93/M of 12 April 1993, the Housing Bureau invited contractor companies in Macao to build homes on land granted by the Government under Home-Ownership Scheme Housing Development Contracts, the land-grant contracts between the companies and the Government. When a development was completed, some units were reserved for the Government, to repay the costs of concessions and subsidies of land grants. The rest were sold to families on the Housing Bureau's waiting list, in accordance with terms and prices stipulated in the land grant contracts by the bureau.

Under Law No. 10/2011 of 1 October 2011, the construction of Home-Ownership Scheme Housing is led by the government and executed by the Housing Bureau or other public authorities appointed by the Chief Executive.

Rationale for Home-Ownership Scheme Housing

Home-Ownership Scheme Housing is intended to assist Macao residents of a particular income level and fnancial situation to meet their housing needs, and to promote a housing supply that suits the practical needs and purchasing power of Macao residents.

Eligibility for Home-Ownership Scheme Housing

Residents wishing to purchase Home-Ownership Scheme Housing need to fle applications with the Housing Bureau. Applicants must be at least 18 years old or be released from parental authority, and have lived in Macao for at least fve years. In addition to a maximum permissible total income, there are strict regulations regarding family fnancial status. Applicants cannot own any private residential property or land including Home-Ownership Scheme Housing, and may not give up a fat received under the Home-Ownership Scheme Housing or sell their purchased Home-Ownership Scheme Housing fat or mortgage subsidy of private property in any form within fve years prior to signing the housing purchase certifcate. Multiple applications from one or more family members are not permitted. Moreover, applicants involved in cases in which the pre-sale contract of the Home-Ownership Scheme housing unit of a family member has been annulled or declared void over the past two years, or in which an application has been rejected due to false declarations or deception, were ineligible for re-application.

Housing Allocation

In 2012, 8,585 applications were processed, of which 5,431 were allocated Home-Ownership Scheme housing units. At present, there are 3,615 families on the waiting list.

Public Housing

Public housing refers to units built by the Government or by private developers on land granted to them by the Government. Upon completion, a stipulated number of units are handed over to the Government for leasing to low-income families and those in adverse circumstances. Methods for the allocation and management of public housing are governed by By-law No. 25/2009.

Public housing is distributed to families of weak fnancial standing in the form of leasing. Families of weak fnancial standing are defned as those whose household incomes fall beneath the legally stipulated levels.

Requirements for Applications for Public Housing

Applications for public housing will open at a time deemed appropriate by the Housing Bureau. Households applying to lease public housing should fulfl the following requirements: the applicant should be aged at least 18, have resided in Macao for at least seven years, and be a holder of a Macao permanent resident identity card. The applicant and the members of the household should not be the owner or the appointed buyer of any buildings or independent units during the three years before the application, the owner or lessee of any private land, the member of another household which have purchased Home-Ownership Scheme housing, the member of another family that was granted housing through the regulations of the Home Acquisition or Renting Loan Subsidy Scheme and the Home Purchase Loan Subsidy Scheme, or the member of a family that has been punished for violating public housing regulations. In addition, the total monthly income and the total net assets of the household should not exceed the limit stipulated by law.

The Upper Limit of Monthly Household Income and Total Net Assets

Under Executive Order No. 297/2009, the monthly household income and the total net assets of households applying for renting public housing should not exceed the amounts in the following table:

Granting of Public Housing

Since 1996, public housing leases have been awarded through fve rounds of open bidding. In 2012, 1,943 applications were processed, 666 of which were successful. There are currently 6,207 families on the waiting list.

In addition to open applications, people seeking public housing may also apply in writing. In accordance with By-law No. 25/2009, families facing mental or physical danger in their present residences are exempted from the application process and granted public housing directly.

In 2012, the bureau received 729 applications under this category. Of these, 4.9 percent were determined to fall within its legal defnition and were granted public housing.

Temporary Subsidies for Families on the Waiting List for Public Housing

In the wake of economic infation, in September 2012, the Government renewed the Subsidy Scheme for Families Awaiting Public Housing to relieve the housing burden of families on the waiting list for public housing. A family awaiting public housing with a total monthly income not more than the statutory cap is eligible for one of the following: a monthly subsidy of 1,350 patacas for a family of one or two people; or a monthly subsidy of 2,050 patacas for a family of three or more people. In 2012, 224 applications were approved. Together with the 4,536 applications approved from 2008 to 2011 that remained eligible for the subsidies, housing subsidies disbursed amounted to 89 million patacas.

Building Management

According to the laws and regulations of the Home-Ownership Scheme, the Housing Bureau is empowered to monitor and supervise the operation of Home-Ownership Scheme Housing, including building maintenance and property management. In accordance with relevant laws, the bureau can also impose penalties on tenants or management entities that violate its regulations.

The Housing Bureau also assists owners of Home-Ownership Scheme Housing units with setting up management committees, for better housing management through direct participation by homeowners. At the end of 2012, there were 54 such management committees. The Housing Bureau also assists owners of Home-Ownership Scheme Housing units with resolving disputes about building management - providing analyses and advice as a third party, in order to achieve settlement of disputes through reasoning and negotiations. In 2012, it assisted management committees with handling 1,258 disputes.

The Housing Bureau also keeps abreast of all necessary renovation and improvement works for public housing. In addition to public facilities of housing estates, it strives to improve indoor facilities, so as to improve the quality of life of its tenants, particularly for elderly single people.

During 2006, the Housing Bureau started to further strengthen the public-area management function of private buildings. By the end of 2012, the bureau had followed up on 1,304 cases.

Building Maintenance Fund Schemes

To encourage and help homeowners to perform their duties regarding maintenance of common building areas, to improve the living environments and enhance the property value of old buildings, in March 2007 the Housing Bureau established the Building Maintenance Fund to provide for private building maintenance and repair work that ensure safety and adequate levels of environmental hygiene. Schemes under the funding programme include: the Interest-free Loan Scheme for Building Maintenance; Subsidy Scheme for Building Maintenance; Subsidy Scheme for Building Management; Provisional Subsidy Scheme for Common Parts Maintenance of Low-rise Buildings; and Building Maintenance Projects Support Scheme.

There were 274 enquiries concerning the various schemes of the Building Maintenance Fund by the end of 2012.

Joint Centre for Building Leakage Issues

Building leakage caused by blocked drains is a long-standing problem in residential environments and is a concern for many residents. Through cross-departmental cooperation among the Lands, Public Works and Transport Bureau, Civic and Municipal Affairs Bureau, Health Bureau, Legal Affairs Bureau and Housing Bureau, along with technical evaluations carried out by the Civil Engineering Laboratory, the Government established the Joint Centre for Building Leakage Issues on 1 February 2009. Led by the Housing Bureau, the centre provides a one-stop platform for fling and handling residents' complaints, to address and solve building leakage issues simply and effciently. By the end of 2012, 1,961 cases had been fled for investigation. With the cooperation of the Housing Bureau staff, property management companies, homeowners' councils, and the owners of the affected units, 1,048 cases were successfully resolved.

Squatter Area Clearance

To comply with Macao's urban planning policies and the reallocation of land use, the Housing Bureau is committed to clearing squatter camps and relocating affected residents. In 2012, 23 squatters'dwellings were demolished. By the year-end, 509 squatters dwellings remained, of which 229 were on the Macao peninsula and 280 on the two islands.

Land Management Lands Committee

The Lands Committee is a consultative body whose work is supervised by the Secretary for Transport and Public Works. The committee is responsible for advising on land use by recipients of land grants, in terms of legal and contractual obligations. It also advises on:

i) Fines or other penalties on land grant recipients who fail to comply with the laws and terms of their contracts;

ii) Cases concerning the public use of granted land; and

iii) Granting, renewing, renouncing or cancelling temporary land-occupation licences.

The Consultative Committee on the Renewal of Macao’s Old Districts

The Consultative Committee on the Renewal of Macao's Old Districts was established under Executive Order No. 354/2005. The committee is in charge of gauging public opinion at all levels on various issues on redevelopment, as well as producing analyses and making recommendations to the Government or relevant institutions.

Land Concessions

According to the DSSOPT's statistics, a total of 223,272 square metres of land out of 6117,998 square metres of developed foor area was granted in 2012; the total premiums amounted to 3,435,807,279 patacas. In all, 48 land grant contracts were signed in 2012. They involved eight aspects of land grants: leases and grants, amendments to leases, amendments to long-term leases, grants of public housing, transferrals, return of land, land designation for public/private use, and unifcation of the legal system.

Most of this land was granted for residential, commercial and industrial uses, offces, hotels, car parks and facilities; land was also granted for other uses. Income from land premiums in 2012 totalled 2,900,334,991 patacas. There were no overdue payments in 2012.

Water Disposal System

Macao's water disposal system includes the independent networks of the Macao peninsula and Taipa and Coloane islands. Specifc data are as follows:

The Drainage Division of the Civic and Municipal Affairs Bureau is responsible for cleaning and dredging the drainage systems of Macao, inspecting and monitoring their operations, making improvements, and registering relevant information.

During 2012, the Drainage Division received 15 complaints regarding street fooding caused by rainstorms. There were 151 complaints about silting of main drains. In 2012, there were 23 prosecutions concerning violation of the General Regulations Governing Public Places, and 226 subpoenas were issued to illegal polluters.

Slopes

According to the Lands, Public Works and Transport Bureau, at the end of 2012, Macao had 193 dangerous slopes.

The Lands, Public Works and Transport Bureau and the Civic and Municipal Affairs Bureau are responsible for maintaining roadside slopes and slopes in public parks, respectively. In 2012, the Lands, Public Works and Transport Bureau carried out nine slope upgrading projects.

Surveying and Mapping Cartography and Cadastre Bureau

The Cartography and Cadastre Bureau is supervised by the Secretary for Transport and Public Works. It specialises in setting up and maintaining the Government's Geodetic Control Network and Geometric Levelling Network. In addition, the bureau supports land-management activities, drafts maps of various types and scales, and maintains the cadastre management.

Cadastre Management

The Cadastre Division of the Cartography and Cadastre Bureau has operated a cadastral database since 1983. The bureau also produces cadastral maps in accordance with the provisions of the Cadastre Law (Decree-Law No. 3/94/M issued on 17 January 1994). The division continuously updates and organises related information and strives to improve its management. The Cartography and Cadastre Bureau launched the Cadastral Information Net in 2008 and an online shop for cadastral maps in 2011.

The Cadastre Division also provides survey information from its database to land owners who need to re-measure land boundaries for valuation, transaction or development purposes.

Land Surveying and Cartography

The Cartography and Cadastre Bureau provides a wide range of land survey and cartography services. It also provides topographical maps at various scales with Chinese and Portuguese footnotes, digital cartography of Macao, printed aerial survey photos taken in 1941, 1980, 1988, 1993 and 1998, posters, the map of the Macao SAR and its peripheral regions, and thematic maps.

In 2012, the Cartography and Cadastre Bureau introduced the new version of Macao Special Administrative Region and Adjacent Regions Map, which includes the entrance of The

Guangzhou-Macau Expressway at Jinding Town to the north, Changlanwan at Hengqin to the south, the Zhuhai Bridge to the west, and waters of the Pearl River estuary to the east, covering the Macao Special Administrative Region, Zhongshan, Hengqin, Qiao and the Jiuzhou Islands.

GPS Reference Station

The Cartography and Cadastre Bureau opened three Global Positioning System (GPS) reference stations, in Mount Fortress, Alto de Coloane and Taipa Grande on Taipa island in 2002, 2005 and 2008, respectively. The reference stations use a dual-satellite system that can receive GPS signals as well as data from the Russian GLONASS system (Global Navigation Satellite System). By integrating signals from these three stations, it is possible to effectively cover the whole of Macao, further enhancing land, cadastral and engineering surveys of Macao, as well as data collection for the Geographic Information System (GIS).

In 2009, the Macao Satellite Positioning Reference Station Service (www.dscc.gov.mo/mosref) was launched, making satellite reference data offcially available to the public, through registration. In addition, an NTRIP (Networked Transport of RTCM via Internet Protocol) service was launched in 2012. Real Time Kinematic (RTK) corrections were provided to professional users through 3G mobile communication and internet technologies, enabling them to use real-time GPS applications accurate to within a centimetre.

Geographic Information System

In response to society's needs, the Cartography and Cadastre Bureau has introduced various kinds of geographic information systems, including the Cadastre Information Web (adastre.gis.gov.mo), a comprehensive land information platform that combines information from various departments on land and buildings. Users can inquire about buildings, locations, drawing easement, street alignment, district planning, property registration and other relevant regulations and orders. In addition, the website contains statistical data, executive procedures and laws related to land. By the end of 2012, the website had received over 280,000 visitors since its launch in 2008.

The Macao Online Map (webmap.gis.gov.mo) provides geographical information to meet citizens' everyday needs in traditional Chinese, simplifed Chinese, Portuguese and English. Users can search for all buildings, streets, and various categories of location including government departments, tourist spots and banks in Macao. Since its launch in 2001, it has received more than one million visitors.

Apart from viewing a map and searching for locations, users of the Macao Map - Personal Computer Version can also search for the shortest route and driving directions with the electronic road maps. The geographical information in the Macao Map is updated every half-year, and is free for citizens and tourists to download.

In line with the development of information technology and in response to the demand of the public, in 2012 the Cartography and Cadastre Bureau introduced the Macao Map iOS / Android (Apps) and the mobile version of the Macao Online Map. Its major functions include map browsing, searching for landscapes, searching for nearby tourist spots, measuring distances and areas, GPS positioning, favourite tourist spots and offine caching.

The Cartography and Cadastre Bureau also introduced another mobile version of the Macao Online Map for common mobile phone web browsers (webmap.gis.gov.mo). Its design is simple and straight-to-the-point, to help residents and tourists with browsing and viewing Macao maps.

The Traffc and Geographic Information Web (traffc.gis.gov.mo) is a cooperative project between the Cartography and Cadastre Bureau and the Transport Bureau, providing locations of roadworks and related traffc diversions in Macao. In addition, thanks to cooperation between the two bureaus, the public can browse the point-to-point map for information about bus stops on the Public Bus Information Station of the Transport Bureau (www.dsat.gov.mo/bus).

The website for the Environmental Geographic Information System (http://www.dspa.gov.mo/gis/Default.aspx) was created jointly by the Cartography and Cadastre Bureau and the Environmental Protection Bureau. The other two participating organisations are the Meteorological and Geophysical Bureau and the Macao Water Supply Company. The system uploads environmental data and related processed information through the Internet.

The Cadastral Information Net - Intranet provides real-time land information for public works, housing, land planning and management, environment supervision and municipal administration. As well as information available on the Cadastral Information Net, the intranet provides Government departments with information such as forms of land use, aerial photos (1980, 1988, 1993, 1998 and 2009), land area and housing record codes.

Offce for the Development of the Energy Sector

The Offce for the Development of the Energy Sector (GDSE) was established on 1 January 2005 under Executive Order No. 11/2005, and it comes under the supervision of the Secretary for Transport and Public Works. Its purpose is to promote and coordinate all activities related to the energy sector, and thus help to implement the Government's energy policy. The offce's major functions are to assist the Government in formulating policies for the energy sector; formulate development plans and relating laws and regulations, and follow up on and monitor their implementation; coordinate, promote the study on and monitor the effciency, impacts on the environment, price and services, and technical regulations of energy products.

Electric Power

According to the working plan of the Framework Agreement on Cooperation between Guangdong and Macao, the frst two 220 kV power cables between Avenida Marginal Flor de Lotus, Cotai and Qinyun, Hengqin, went into operation in the middle of 2012, increasing the capacity of electricity transmissions between Guangdong and Macao by 50 percent. This was the second 220 kV electric transmission system installed since the power cable system between Canal Dos Patos, Macao and Gongbei, Zhuhai, came into operation in 2008, greatly improving the capacity and stability of power supplies in Macao.

In 2012, the GDSE summarised and analysed the opinions collected during the frst-phase public consultation on the Electricity Tariff System and the Setting of Electricity Prices. Revisions were made to the consultation paper to include the proposal for further reducing the electricity tariffs charged to residential users and small and medium sized enterprises, before the second-phase public consultation was launched. It was hoped that the new electricity tariff system would be implemented in 2013, to alleviate the burden of electricity costs on residential users and small and medium sized enterprises.

Furthermore, to ease infationary pressure and lower residents' burdens, the Government continued to offer the electricity fee subsidy, the amount of which was increased from 180 patacas to 200 patacas per month per household.

Natural Gas

On 27 July 2012, the Government signed a 25-year natural gas supply contract with Nam Kwong Petroleum and Chemical Company Limited, confrming the gradual introduction of natural gas to residential, industrial and commercial units, we well as its application in the transport system. It was expected that natural gas could be supplied to residents of Seac Pai Van Public Housing Estate and the Hengqin campus of the University of Macau by early 2013; and to Taipa within two years at the earliest. It would take fve years to complete major natural gas networks covering all Macao.

To address the need to allocate and sell natural gas according to different types of users, the Government began studying the natural gas price structure and system during the year, in order to set a retail price in 2013 that could facilitate development of the natural gas market and promote market competition.

Energy Conservation

The Energy Management System under the Public Departments and Organisations Energy Effciency and Conservation Programme was implemented by 54 departments, to continuously promote energy conservation. Following preparatory work in 2013, the replacement of streetlights by LED lights would start in early 2013. It was expected that a total of 17,000 LED lights would be installed within fve years. Moreover, the Safety Regulations on Solar Photovoltaic Grid-connected Systems were drafted, to regulate the installation and safety of solar photovoltaic grid-connected system.

The Offce for the Development of the Energy Sector (GDSE) continued to organise large-scale publicity programmes, such as the ffth Macao Energy Saving Week, the Energy Effciency Educational Programme, and the Campus Energy Conservation Programme, in order to promote energy saving.

Drinking Water Macao Water Supply Company (Macao Water)

The Macao Water Supply Company (Macao Water) was established in 1932, and is privately owned. Sino-French Holdings (Hong Kong) acquired 85 percent of the company's shares in 1985 and signed a 25-year water-supply concession contract with the former Portuguese administration. In 2009, the contract was extended for 20 years. Today, Sino-French Holdings (Hong Kong) is a joint venture between the French-based Suez Lyonnaise des Eaux Group (a new company formed after the merger of the French Lyonnaise des Eaux Group and Suez Group in 1997) and NWS Holdings (a subsidiary of New World Development).

Raw Water Supply

Macao's raw water supply from Zhuhai has two main components: the southern pumping station opened in 1988 and part of the Zhuyin Pumping Station opened in 2007. The two stations are connected by the Guangchang Pumping Station. The layout of the whole system is shown in the map below.

Zhu Zhou Tou pumping station

Feng Huang Shan reservoir Zhu Yin reservoir

Ping Gang pumping station

Yue Keng reservoir

Da Jing Shan reservoir

<table>
<tr><td colspan="3">Yu Zhou</td></tr>
<tr><td colspan="3">Pumpingstation</td></tr>
<tr><td colspan="3">Nan Ping reservoir</td></tr>
<tr><td colspan="3">Zhu Xian Dong reservoir</td></tr>
<tr><td colspan="3">She Di Keng reservoir</td></tr>
<tr><td>Gua Ding Jiaosluice gate</td><td>Hong Wansluice gate and pumpingstation</td><td>Yin Keng reservoir</td></tr>
</table>

On the map, the red labels mark Macao's raw water intake. Some 95 percent of Macao's raw water comes from the Modaomen estuary of the Xijiang (West River) in adjacent Zhuhai. In the recent decades, to mitigate salinity effects, the raw water intake for Zhuhai and Macao has been moved upstream. At the moment, there are fve major water intake locations of Macao's raw water.

The blue labels identify reservoirs. Recently, to mitigate salinity effects, the Zhuyin Reservoir was built in Pinggang and trial operation began in autumn 2011.

Zhuhai currently supplies about 234,000 cubic metres of water to Macao each day. In 2012, it supplied a total of 85.66 million cubic metres of raw water. Other than during occasional salt tides in winter and spring resulting in a higher degree of water chloride and a slightly higher degree of faecal coliforms in some seasons, the water quality was certifed as Grade II, according to mainland China's Environmental Quality Standards for Surface Water (GB3838-2002).

Water Treatment, Storage and Transportation

Macao's water treatment capacity increased from 85,000 cubic metres per day in 1985 to 330,000 cubic metres at present. The combined storage capacity of Macao's reservoirs (including the clean water pond and high pool in the water treatment works) rose from 17,000 cubic metres in 1985 to 120,000 cubic metres at present. A total of 97 percent of all the water pipes laid prior to 1982 have been replaced. The total length of pipeline increased from 127 kilometres in 1985 to 513 kilometres in 2012.

At the end of 2012, the total volume of water stored in Macao's reservoirs (including the Main Storage Reservoir (the Outer Harbour Reservoir), the Seac Pai Van Reservoir, the Ka-Ho Reservoir and the Hac Sa Reservoir) was 2.98 million cubic metres, including 1.9 million cubic metres in the reservoir near the Outer Harbour.

Macao has maintained a continuous 24-hour water supply since 1982. A total of 84.58 million cubic metres of water were supplied in 2012, nine percent more than in 2011. The daily average volume supplied in 2012 was around 231,000 cubic metres, with a maximum of 258,000 cubic metres recorded on 21 August. The increase was primarily due to the opening of the casino hotel Sands Cotai Central and the high temperature in summer. In 2012, the total capacity of water sales was 75.28 million cubic metres, with a daily average of 206,000 cubic metres.

Testing Water Potability

The Laboratory and Research Centre of Macao Water is responsible for water quality testing and analysis, and ensuring the quality of water supply. Staff from the Civic and Municipal Affairs Bureau Laboratory and Macao Water take samples from randomly chosen water supply outlets, in order to analyse and monitor water quality. Laboratory staff from Macao Water are responsible for sampling water to monitor quality during weekends and public holidays.

Since 1985, the quality of Macao's tap water has reached the drinking water standards of European countries.

In 1997, the Laboratory and Research Centre of Macao Water participated in a quality-control test administered by laboratories of Lyonnaise des Eaux Group. The Laboratory and Research Centre achieved outstanding results and was again awarded reference laboratory status. In 2000, the centre was awarded a Certifcate of Laboratory Accreditation by the China National Accreditation Committee for Laboratories (CNAL), which is equivalent to ISO 17025. It was only the fourth laboratory in China's water supply industry to be so accredited.

Customer Services

Macao Water established a consolidated customer information system in 1999, to handle customer enquiries promptly and properly and support customer services. The company continues to enhance its services. As well as convenient payment and enquiry services, it also launched the building water supply pipe maintenance service, water-tank-cleaning and water-quality-testing services for buildings, and offers a waiver of fees for the frst fve cubic metres of water used by senior citizens and individuals who receive the Social Welfare Bureau's single-parent or medical subsidies or subsidies for the disabled. On 1 January 2011, a sliding scale of water charges was introduced.

In 2012, Macao Water established a customer service unit, which gather customers' opinions on the water supply services through personal conversations. By the end of 2012, Macao Water had 214,830 customers, including 187,380 households, 25,632 companies and 1,818 government institutions.

Macao Water was awarded an ISO 9001:2000 Quality Management System Accreditation Certifcate in 2003, and OHSAS 18001:1999 Occupational Health and Safety Management System certifcation in 2005. In 2008, it was awarded the ISO 14000 certifcate.

Power Supply Companhia de Electricidade de Macau

Companhia de Electricidade de Macau (CEM) is a public utility company with the sole concession to generate, transmit, distribute, sell, import and export electricity in Macao.

From 1906 to 1972, the electricity supply service was managed by the Macau Electric Lighting Company, headquartered in Hong Kong. In 1972, the company was replaced by CEM.

CEM was restructured with the former Portuguese administration's support in 1982. In 1984, CEM was linked to the primary networks of Macao and Guangdong Province through two 110 kV overhead lines. In 2006, a second network that also comprises two 110 kV overhead lines commenced operation, increasing Macao's standby electricity supply and directly improving the reliability and fexibility of electricity supply services.

Comprising two 110 kV power cables, the third Macao-Zhuhai electricity power grid came into operation in July 2007, and was further upgraded with in June 2008, with 220 kV power capacities and 1050 MVA transmitting capacity. In June 2012, the second 220 kV power grid came into service. By that time, there were a total of fve 220 kV power cables with a transmitting capacity of 1,750 MVA.

In November 2010, the Government and the CEM signed a contract stipulating a 15-year extension to power supply services. The new contract terms came into effect on 1 December 2010.

Since 1987, the Government, which was previously the largest shareholder in CEM, has reduced its holding to just eight percent. Currently, 84 percent of CEM's shares are owned by two major shareholders: the Sino-French Group which holds 42 percent, followed by EDP Asia which holds 21 percent. Moreover, Polytec Industrial Limited and Asiainvest (IP Holding) hold 11 percent and 10 percent respectively. China Power International Holding holds six percent of the shares, and local shareholders own the remaining two percent.

Electricity consumption in Macao increased rapidly during the 1990s. In 1998, CEM decided to invest in developing Coloane B Power Station, which uses multi-cycle gas turbine technology.

In 2012, CEM's capacity peaked at 757 MW on 28 August, 4.4 percent more than the peak capacity in 2011.

The Macao electricity transmission network comprises 24 primary substations and 281 kilometres of 66 kV high-voltage cables, 110 kV cables and 220 kV cables. The Guangdong-Macao electricity network included two 110 kV cables and two 220 kV cables connecting Zhuhai and Nanping, and Gongbei and Zhuhai, respectively.

The 11 kV medium-voltage electricity transmission network comprises 35 user substations and 1,245 user transformer rooms (11 kV / 400 V) connected by cables with a total length of 617 kilometres. The low-voltage transmission network is made up of 780 kilometres of cable, while the street lighting network comprises 524 kilometres of cable and 16,168 streetlights. Almost all of CEM's power network comprises underground cables.

Electricity Output and Consumption

CEM generated 376 GWh of electricity during 2012, a decrease of 49.5 percent over 2011. The amount of electricity imported from mainland China was 3,855 GWh, an increase of 21.8 percent over 2011, accounting for 88 percent of total electricity consumption; and electricity purchased from the Macao Central Incineration Centre totalled 113 GWh. CEM's sales for 2011 totalled 4,142 GWh.

Customer Services

CEM established the CEM Customer Liaison Committee in 2000. With its 19 members coming from 17 different community organisations, the committee serves to refect public views of CEM's services, and to receive and make suggestions for improvement. At the end of 2012, CEM was providing services to 229,449 households. The Macao peninsula accounted for 86.31 percent of the total customer base, Taipa island 12.99 percent, Coloane island 0.69 percent, and COTAI 0.01 percent.

Public housing

The Government expedited public housing construction projects in 2012. A total of 19,260 public housing units were planned to be built; of these, 4,189 were completed and 15,071 units were under construction by year-end. All public housing projects have public facilities and car parks to satisfy the needs of the community.

Transport Roads and Bridges

Macao has 314.5 kilometres of roads and highways, including 183.1 kilometres on the Macao peninsula, 80.9 kilometres on Taipa island and its reclaimed areas, and 40.6 kilometres on Coloane island.

Three bridges and a strip of reclaimed land link the Macao peninsula with Taipa and Coloane. Opened to traffc in October 1974, the Nobre de Carvalho Bridge (also known as the Macao-Taipa Bridge) is 2.5 kilometres long. The 4.4-kilometre Friendship Bridge was completed in April 1994. The 2.1-kilometre Sai Van (West Bay) Bridge was completed in December 2004 and opened to traffc in January 2005. In addition, the 900-metre Lotus Flower Bridge was completed in December 1999 and opened to traffc in March 2000. Linking the reclaimed area between Taipa and Coloane with Zhuhai City's Hengqin island and connected to the Guangzhou-Zhuhai Expressway, this bridge is the second land route between Macao and its neighbouring cities.

Macao has 417.4 kilometres of roads for motor vehicles. This fgure includes 199.5 kilometres on the Macao peninsula, 135.4 kilometres on Taipa island and its reclaimed areas, 61.3 kilometres on Coloane island, fve kilometres on Nobre de Carvalho Bridge, 10.2 kilometres on the Friendship Bridge, 4.2 kilometres on the Sai Van Bridge and 1.8 kilometres on the Lotus Flower Bridge.

Public Transport

Macao has a well-established public transport network connecting the Macao peninsula and the two islands. A variety of vehicles, including buses and taxis, are available for local residents and tourists.

Public Bus Service

The new bus service in Macao was launched on 1 August 2011. The total number of bus operators increased from two to three. At the end of 2012, there were 677 buses in service, including 230 minibuses, 165 medium-sized buses and 282 large buses, on 62 routes. In 2012, a total of 156,749,045 passengers were served, an increase of 14.51 percent over the 2011 fgure, covering a total distance of 39,281,688 kilometres, an increase of 23.42 percent over the fgure in 2011.

The Government signed a seven-year contract with Transportes Urbanos de Macau, Transportes Companhia de Macau and Reolian Public Transport for the provision of mass road passenger transport in Macao. Under the contract provisions, the three companies provide services, vehicles, equipment, staff and supporting facilities, and receive service charges specifed in the contract with the Government. All fares paid by passengers were collected by the MSAR government.

Sociedade de Transportes Colectivos de Macau

Sociedade de Transportes Colectivos de Macau (TCM) (previously known as Companhia de Transporte de Passageiros entre Macau e as Ilhas) originally provided maritime passenger transportation services between Macao and the two islands. During the 1950s, it acquired several bus companies that served residents of Taipa and Coloane, and began to operate public buses. In 1986, Companhia de Transporte de Passageiros entre Macau e as Ilhas was restructured as TCM and became fully responsible for all public buses serving Macao and its islands.

In August 2011, public bus services in Macao began operating under the new government-led model and TCM purchased 63 buses that met Euro IV standards. TCM now has a feet of 145 buses and operates 13 bus routes on Macao peninsula connecting the Macao peninsula and the outlying islands. In 2012, it carried over 32.26 million passengers and covered 6.37 million kilometres.

Transportes Urbanos de Macau (Transmac)

Transportes Urbanos de Macau (Transmac) was previously known as Companhia de Autocarros Fok Lei. Founded in 1952, it was restructured and changed its name to Transportes Urbanos de Macau in July 1988. It is the largest bus company in Macao. The company introduced the ISO Quality Management System in 2004 for overall management, making it the frst franchised bus company in Macao to pass the ISO 9001:2008 Quality Management System.

Transmac has more than 600 employees and a feet of 287 air-conditioned buses that serve 21 bus routes covering Macao, Taipa and Coloane islands. During 2012, over 66.31 million passengers were carried and about 16.57 million kilometres covered.

Reolian Public Transport

Reolian Public Transport is a joint venture between Veolia Transport RATP and HN Group. It has a strong management team and technicians with varied expertise from Macao, France, Australia, the US, mainland China and Hong Kong.

Reolian Public Transport commenced operation in August 2011, running 26 bus routes with a feet of 245 buses. In 2012, it covered about 16.50 million kilometres and carried more than 57 million passengers.

Reolian Public Transport received accreditation for its Occupational Health and Safety System. On 8 December 2012, it became the frst bus company in Macao to secure OHSAS 18001 certifcation.

Taxis

At the end of 2012, Macao had 954 licensed black taxis with cream roofs, plus 100 radio-dispatched yellow taxis. There were 10,911 licensed taxi drivers.

Traffc Management Transport Bureau

The Transport Bureau was established in May 2008. It is responsible for: studying, planning, promoting and implementing road transport policies of the Government; pursuing road improvements; regulation of vehicles; as well as installing, maintaining and improving transportation and pedestrian infrastructure.

Vehicle Statistics

At the end of 2012, there were 217,335 vehicles on Macao's roads, including 115,623 motorcycles, and 95,063 light vehicles. During the year, 17,621 new vehicles were registered, a slight decline of

0.45 percent over the 2011 fgure. Of these, 6,833 were motorcycles and 9,068 were cars.

Traffc Monitoring

Traffc management and monitoring are essential for ensuring the safe and orderly operation of the transport system. The Government has installed closed circuit TV (CCTV) and radar speed monitoring systems to monitor traffc conditions on the Macao-Taipa Bridge and main roads. They include 30 video cameras and six two-way speed monitoring spots on the Friendship Bridge, 65 video cameras, two one-way and one two-way speed monitoring spots on the Sai Van Bridge, and 10 video cameras and two two-way speed monitoring spots on the Ponte Governador Nobre de Carvalho. Also, 157 video cameras, 15 speed monitoring radar units, and 25 sets of electronic systems with a total of 82 cameras for monitoring vehicles jumping red lights have been installed in various downtown locations. During 2012, the monitoring systems identifed 9,752 cases of speeding and 1,114 cases of jumping red lights. A further 9,583 cases were identifed under the illegal parking monitoring system.

Parking

As at 31 December 2012, Macao had 34 public car parks, which together provide 12,515 parking spaces for light vehicles, 730 spaces for heavy vehicles, and 8,498 spaces for motorcycles.

Public Car Parks in Macao	
Name of car park	Available parking spaces
Pak Lane Car Park	519 light vehicles
Pak Tou Car Park	211 light vehicles
Pak Lai Car Park	355 light vehicles
Pak Lik Car Park	417 light vehicles
Pak Lok Car Park	471 light vehicles, 300 motorcycles

Public Car Parks in Macao	
Name of car park	Available parking spaces
Pak Vai Car Park	502 light vehicles
Pak Kai Car Park	208 light vehicles
Pak Wai Car Park	1,019 light vehicles
Pak Keng Car Park	171 light vehicles
Pak Ying Car Park	722 light vehicles
Pak Wu Car Park	682 light vehicles, 196 motorcycles
Pak Kong Car Park	287 light vehicles, 31 heavy vehicles
Sewage Treatment Plant Car Park	276 light vehicles, 459 heavy vehicles
Vasco da Gama Garden Car Park	171 light vehicles, 113 motorcycles
Iao Hon Park Multi-Storey Car Park	406 light vehicles, 404 motorcycles
Art Garden Car Park	351 light vehicles, 446 motorcycles
Ferreira do Amaral Roundabout Car Park	247 light vehicles, 632 motorcycles
Ho Yin Garden Car Park	415 light vehicles, 542 motorcycles
Malaca Street Car Park	215 light vehicles, 563 motorcycles
Taipa Temporary Heavy Vehicle Parking Area	224 heavy vehicles
Flor de Lotus Road Heavy Vehicle Car Park	240 heavy vehicles
S. Lourenco Market Car Park	60 light vehicles, 74 motorcycles
Macao Science Center Car Park	415 light vehicles, 413 motorcycles
Lido Car Park	62 light vehicles, 24 motorcycles

Transport Bureau Car Park	148 light vehicles, 178 motorcycles

Public Car Parks in Macao	
Name of car park	Available parking spaces
Cheng Choi Building Car Park	304 light vehicles, 518 motorcycles
Mong Sin Block Car Park	133 light vehicles, 236 motorcycles
Almirante Sergio Road Car Park	155 light vehicles, 106 motorcycles
Fai Fu Building Car Park	215 light vehicles, 194 motorcycles
Flor de Lotus Road Car Park	416 light vehicles, 512 motorcycles
Tranquilidade Road Car Park	58 light vehicles, 93 motorcycles
Parque Central da Taipa Car Park	1,343 light vehicles (including 10 fordisabled), 1,384 motorcycles
The Taipa Temporary Ferry Terminal Car Park	740 light vehicles, 196 motorcycles
Edificio Mong In Car Park	143 light vehicles, 242 motorcycles
Taipa TN27 Edificio do Lago Public Car Park	678 light vehicles, 1,132 motorcycles

As at 31 December 2012, there were 9,309 parking meters for light vehicles, of which 4,630 were two-hour parking meters, 4,679 were fve-hour parking meters. There were 3,051 non-metered parking spaces. There were also 40,071 motorcycle parking spaces, of which 222 were two-hour parking meters and 382 were fve-hour parking meters.

Road Safety

The Road Traffc Law promotional campaign was held in 2012, jointly organised by the Public Security Police, the Legal Affairs Bureau, the Civic and Municipal Affairs Bureau, the Lands, Public Works and Transport Bureau, and several non-governmental organisations. It publicises the importance of obeying traffc regulations, to strengthen the understanding of laws and sense of road safety among local residents, and thus reduce the number of traffc accidents. The Traffc Department of the Public Security Police also teamed up with schools, transportation companies and non-governmental organisations to stage games and lectures related to road safety. Their objective was to reinforce residents' understanding of road safety by means of long-term educational efforts. During 2012, a total of 5,951 people from 64 schools and 31 other organisations participated in the Traffc Department's road safety promotional activities.

Cross-border Traffc Cross-border Land Routes

Two land routes link Macao and mainland China: the Border Gate and Lotus Flower Bridge Checkpoint (Cotai checkpoint). The volume of cross-border traffc has grown rapidly, in line with increasing exchanges between Macao and the mainland.

The Border Gate Checkpoint is open to passengers from 7.00am to midnight daily, and for cargo from 7.00am to 9.00pm (except for authorised vehicles). The Lotus Flower Bridge Checkpoint is open to passengers from 9.00am to 8.00pm, and for cargo from 8.00am to 8.00pm. The Zhuhai-Macao Crossborder Industrial Zone Border Checkpoint is open 24 hours per day.

A total of 4,465,854 vehicles entered or left Macao by land during 2012. The gross weight of containers imported or exported by land was 30,681 tonnes, a decrease of 13 percent; re-exported containers totalled 10,986 tonnes.

During 2012, there were 14,829,681 visitor arrivals by land, an increase of 3.1 percent over the previous year's fgure. Of these, 13,590,514 entered via the Border Gate; tourists from mainland China and Hong Kong represented 83.1 percent and 11.5 percent of the total, respectively. The number of visitors who arrived via the Cotai checkpoint was 1,217,618. During the year, there were 21,664,342 arrivals of Macao residents via the Border Gate, with 376,552 via the Cotai checkpoint.

Cross-border Marine Transportation Services

The Outer Harbour Ferry Terminal, Taipa Ferry Terminal, and Inner Harbour Ferry Terminal provide cross-border transportation services for passengers travelling between Macao and Hong Kong and the mainland. Scheduled passenger ferries to Hong Kong and the mainland are operated by the Shun Tak-China Travel Ship Management Limited; Far East Hydrofoil Company; Hong Kong-Macau Hydrofoil Company; Shun Tak - China Travel Macau Ferries Limited; Yuet Tung Shipping Company; and Cotai Waterjets (Macau) Limited.

Outer Harbour Ferry Terminal

The Outer Harbour Ferry Terminal commenced operations in 1993. Its two vertical piers provide 14 berths for a total of 14 passenger vessels at one time. The main building has a foor area of over 6,000 square metres, with a helicopter pad on its rooftop.

The Government commenced the Outer Harbour Ferry Terminal expansion project in late 2006, with an aim of increasing the usable area inside the terminal, easing pressure arising from the sharp increase in visitor numbers. The Government installed a self-service clearance system in 2009, and from 2009 to 2011 undertook improvement work at public facilities to provide a more comfortable environment.

The operation management contract of the Outer Harbour Ferry Terminal ended in December of 2011, and from 21 December the management of the harbour was taken up by the Government. The Government plans to commence enhancement work of the Outer Harbour Ferry Terminal in 2013, through improving the overall layout to streamline passenger fow and luggage transfer, to provide quality and convenient services to residents and visitors.

Taipa Ferry Terminal

The permanent Taipa Ferry Terminal was under construction. It will occupy 144,000 square metres with 16 berths for ferries, three multi-functional berths and a helicopter pad on its rooftop.

Inner Harbour Ferry Terminal

The Inner Harbour Ferry Terminal offcially came into service in February 2008, and moved from Terminal 14 to Terminal 11A which has a gross area of over 1,450 square metres. The ferry terminal operates routes to and from Wanzai District from 8.00am to 6.00pm.

According to the Statistics and Census Service, during 2012, there were 112,691 scheduled ferry sailings between Macao and Hong Kong, and 27,264 scheduled ferry sailings between Macao and mainland China.

According to statistics provided by the Public Security Police, during 2012, some 11,484,840 passengers arrived in Macao by sea, an increase of 4.2 percent over the 2011 fgure. Of these,

7,042,005 entered Macao via the Outer Harbour Ferry Terminal, 541,090 visitors via the Inner Harbour, and 3,901,745 via the Taipa Temporary Ferry Terminal.

In 2012, 87,707 containers or 119,927 TEUs (twenty-foot equivalent units) were shipped in and out of Macao by sea, representing increases of 17.10 percent and 17.59 percent, respectively, on the 2011 fgures.

Cross-border Helicopter Services

Helicopters are the most convenient way to travel between Macao and Hong Kong. A helicopter passenger transportation service was inaugurated in November 1990. Jointly operated by Helicopters Hong Kong (Heli HongKong) and East Asia Airlines, the service has reduced the travelling time between Hong Kong and Macao to only 16 minutes. It operates from 9.00am to 11.00pm, with scheduled fights in each direction every 30 minutes. In addition, East Asia Airlines began operating daily passenger helicopter fights between Macao and Shenzhen in April 2002. In 2012, there were 14,920 helicopter fights to and from Hong Kong via the Outer Harbour Ferry Terminal, and 3,412 fights between mainland China and Macao.

Ports Outer Harbour

Located on the east coast of the Macao peninsula, the Outer Harbour is designated for scheduled ferries between Macao and Hong Kong and Shenzhen. Its watercourse is 120 metres wide and 4.4 metres deep.

To streamline the sea passageway to the east of Friendship Bridge, the Maritime Administration restructured a fairway off eastern Friendship Bridge leading to the Inner Harbour, making the fairway straight and setting up a more advanced system of synchronised fashing beacons.

Inner Harbour

Located on the west coast of the Macao peninsula, the Inner Harbour has many piers for loading and discharging cargo, plus Pier 11A, the ferry terminal, used by passenger ferries licensed by the Maritime Administration. The South Sampan Pier between Piers 8 and 9 is used by crewmembers of ships berthed in the Inner Harbour who hold Macao ID Cards, or who are authorised to land and depart by the relevant Government authority, with prior notice to the Macao Customs Service. The Inner Harbour's approach channel is 45 metres wide, and its fairway is 55 metres wide and

3.5 metres deep.

Taipa

The Taipa Temporary Ferry Terminal is situated on the north-eastern tip of Taipa island, and is exclusive for scheduled high-speed ferries shuttling between Macao and Hong Kong, and between Macao and the Pearl River Delta area. Its fairway is 120 metres wide and 4.4 metres deep.

Ka Ho Harbour

Located on the northeast shore of Coloane island, Ka Ho Harbour consists of the Fuel Oil Terminal, Cement Terminal, Ka Ho Container Port, and Power Plant Terminal. Its approach channel is 75 metres wide and 4.4 metres deep.

Ka Ho Container Wharf and Fuel Oil Terminal

Phase One of Ka Ho Container Wharf commenced operations in December 1991. With a total construction area of 42,000 square metres (now 49,524 square metres), it includes a container wharf, container yard and warehouses. At present, it has two berths, of 135 metres and 171.4 metres in length; a 10,428-square-metre cargo working area; a 23,828-square-metre container yard; and 2,850 square metres of cargo warehousing space. The terminal's annual handling capacity is 100,000 TEUs.

In 2012, Ka Ho Harbour handled 12,905 inbound TEUs (twenty-foot equivalent units) and 11,807 outbound TEUs; both fgures include re-exports.

The Fuel Oil Terminal commenced operation in June 1995. It can store a wide variety of fuel oil imported into Macao, and can simultaneously load and unload two fuel-carrying vessels. It has 14 storage tanks with a combined capacity of 86,000 cubic metres.

Marine and Water Bureau

The Marine and Water Bureau is a department with authorities and duties relating to maritime affairs, and is responsible for exercising its power to promote and coordinate the development of maritime activities.

To promote and assist economic development of the fshery sector, in 2007 the Government promulgated By-law No. 3/2007 to establish the Fisheries Development and Support Fund.

The Marine and Water Bureau also provides port management and services including vessel inspections, pilot services, vessel traffc control, search and rescue operations, hydrographic survey, dredging and port cleaning.

Ships Maritime Registration

By law, all vessels engaged in economic activities - including freighters, passenger vessels, fshing boats and auxiliary boats -must be registered with the Marine and Water Bureau and the Commercial and Movable Goods Registry. The registration procedures are designed to verify its conformity with offcial requirements concerning technology, safety and environmental protection. Maritime registration is a prerequisite for vessels seeking commercial registration. There were 300 registered vessels at the end of 2012, including six that were newly registered during the year.

In addition, maritime and commercial registration is required for vessels over 2.5 metres in length that are used for non-proft-making purposes, such as water sports, fshing or recreational activities. These include ocean-going, coastal, inshore, channel and river pleasure boats. There were 107 registered vessels in this category at the end of 2012, including 14 new registrations.

Seafarer Registration

According to the law, Macao residents aged 18 or above may apply for seafarer registration with the Marine and Water Bureau. All Macao residents who wish to conduct professional maritime activities on commercial vessels, auxiliary boats or fshing boats are required to register with the bureau beforehand. At the end of 2012, a total of 251 people held seafarer's books issued by the bureau.

Maritime Training School

The Maritime Training School is Macao's only nautical education institution. Its principal objectives are to provide theoretical and practical training in maritime subjects and harbour management, as well as related scientifc knowledge.

Most of the training school's students are Marine and Water Bureau and Macao Customs Service staff members, as well as sailors, fshermen and nautical athletes in Macao. The training school also provides after-school and summer vacation activities for youngsters.

The Shipyard

The Shipyard is a department under the Marine and Water Bureau. As well as shipbuilding and ship repairs, it is responsible for maintaining and repairing Government vehicles, verifying their status and inspecting them, handling newly purchased vehicles, as well as making and installing vehicle identifcation plates. At present, most of the vessels built and repaired at the Shipyard belong to the bureau and Macao Customs Service. In 2012, the Shipyard monitored the construction and delivery of an 11-metre hydrographic surveying ship and coordinated the building of a rescue ship for the bureau. The Shipyard also monitored the construction and delivery of a 30-metre patrol ship as well as provided technical support to Macao Customs Service. It has carried out 302 vessel maintenance projects, of which 229 projects were completed. In the examination, maintenance and repair of vehicles, the Shipyard carried out 2,151 projects involving 2,694 vehicles.

Civil Aviation Civil Aviation Authority

The Civil Aviation Authority was founded on 4 February 1991, in accordance with Decree-Law No. 10/91/M dated 4 February 1991. It is constituted as a public institution under the Secretariat for Transport and Public Works, and it enjoys autonomy over administration, fnances and property. It is responsible for directing, controlling and monitoring all civil aviation activities in Macao, and the operations of all aircraft registered in Macao.

Aviation Service

To implement its "Open Skies" policy, the Government has adopted a series of measures to enhance Macao's civil aviation infrastructure network. Every effort has been made to attract additional investment from domestic and foreign airlines, to promote the use of Macau International Airport, and to enhance the development of passenger and cargo transportation.

To increase cooperation with the international aviation community, the Government will continue to forge new air services agreements with countries around the world. By 31 December 2012, Macao had initialled air services agreements with 47 nations and regions, among which 40 had been offcially signed.

Luxembourg New Zealand Portugal Switzerland Singapore Malaysia Thailand United States Vietnam Germany DPR Korea Denmark Sweden Norway South Korea The Philippines India Nepal South Africa Brunei United Arab Emirates Russia Myanmar

(Cont.)

Australia Poland Pakistan Czech Republic Cambodia United Kingdom Iceland Maldives France Sri Lanka Mongolia Japan Laos Oman Indonesia Israel Greece Slovakia Cape Verde

As at 31 December 2012, four airlines were registered in Macao and providing fight services: Air Macau, East Asia Airlines, JetAsia and Macau Jet International.

Below are details of the feets and routes that they operated:

The numbers of pilots licensed by the Civil Aviation Authority, as at 31 December 2012, were:

Airline	Number of licensed pilots
Civil Aviation Authority	2
Air Macau	157
East Asia Airlines	28
JetAsia	6
Macau Jet International (Commercial Charter Services)	7
Total	200

Macau International Airport is located at the eastern end of Taipa island and neighbouring waters. The terminal building was constructed on a rock-cut platform at Ponta da Cabrita, while the apron was built on reclaimed land. East of the apron, the air-traffc control building, control tower and ancillary fre station are on Kia Kiong Islet. The runway is on an artifcial island linked to the apron by two taxiway bridges.

The main fre station is on the runway island, next to the oblique taxiway. The airport is within easy reach of the Macao peninsula, the Outer Harbour and Zhuhai via motorway, the Friendship Bridge and the Lotus Flower Bridge. Commuting time from each of these points is less than 20 minutes.

The Macau International Airport handled 4,491,065 passengers during 2012, a rise of 11 percent on the 2011 fgure. Its cargo volume was 27,794 tonnes, a decrease of 29.7 percent. A total of 41,997 fights took off or landed, an increase of 7.8 percent.

Private and commercial air charters saw a steady rise in the number of fights, from 1,010 in 2011 to 1,209 fights in 2012, an increase of 19.7 percent.

Air Traffc Control

Since it opened in 1995, the airport's air traffc control system has maintained excellent standards of service effciency and fight safety. Air traffc control facilities include secondary surveillance radar and the Automatic Terminal System. Telecommunications facilities include AMHS and satellite ground stations, while air-ground communications facilities include a UHF radio station.

Macao's air traffc zone is classifed as Category-C under International Civil Aviation Organization (ICAO) standards. The keyhole-shaped air traffc zone is centred on Macau International Airport. It extends up to an altitude of 3,000 feet and a radius of fve nautical miles. The western boundary is a straight line parallel to and three nautical miles from the runway. To the south, the zone forms a rectangle fve nautical miles wide and extending southwards for 10 nautical miles.

Macao's air traffc zone lies between the Hong Kong and Guangzhou fight information zones. All aircraft, including helicopters entering Macao airspace, are supervised by the airport control tower. Arriving and departing aircraft can land or take off from both the southern and northern approaches. The mainland authorities control air traffc to the north of Macao's air zone, while traffc to the south is controlled by the Civil Aviation Department of Hong Kong. Since traffc in the

Pearl River Delta airspace is busy and complex, the air-traffc control authorities of Macao, the mainland and Hong Kong must work closely together to ensure the safety and effciency of air traffc in Macao and the neighbouring air zone.

Aircraft Noise

Macau International Airport was constructed offshore and far from residential communities, avoiding the need to install soundproofng. However, to protect Zhuhai from noise pollution caused by northbound fights taking off from the runway, aircraft are not allowed to pass the 230-degree radial line of Zhuhai's Jiuzhou omni-directional beacon station.

Security at Macau International Airport

Under Decree-Law No. 36/94/M issued on 18 July 1994 and ICAO regulations, the security systems at Macau International Airport are intended to ensure the safety, normal operations and effciency of international civil aviation activities at the airport. Security measures and procedures are essential to protect passengers, crew, airport staff and the public, as well as ensuring the normal, uninterrupted operations of aircraft, facilities and equipment.

Responsibility for airport security is distributed among the Civil Aviation Authority, the Unitary Police Service, the Macao Customs Service, the Public Security Police, the Judiciary Police, the Fire Service, the Marine and Water Bureau, the airport itself, Companhia de Seguranca de Macau Lda (SEMAC), the private airport security company, aviation companies and other airport departments.

The private airport security company is responsible for implementing the security measures and procedures formulated by the airport operator, and ensuring that the security measures and procedures comply with the International Civil Aviation Organization (ICAO) standards and recommendations. Besides, the company provides professional training, certifed technicians and advanced security equipment to perform security checks on passengers, baggage and cargo.

Macau International Airport Company

Macau International Airport Company (CAM) has been appointed by the Government to operate Macau International Airport. It was responsible for the airport's construction, and it is now responsible for its operation. The Government has approved the company's application in 2001 to extend the period of its franchise by a further 25 years to 2039.

Public bus services

Public bus services in Macao have been operating since last century. A new bus service model was launched on 1 August 2011. The number of bus operators increased from two to three.

OFFSHORE SECTOR IN MACAO

Macau SAR's Offshore Law has been in effect since 18th October 1999.The offshore finance business is regulated and supervised by the Macau Monetary Authority, while the offshore non-finance business is regulated and supervised by the Macau Trade and Investment Promotion Institute (IPIM).

BASIC REQUIREMENTS FOR OPERATING OFFSHORE SERVICE BUSINESS

Firstly, an investor has to obtain a Permit from IPIM, in order to operate an offshore service business in Macau SAR.To operate an offshore service business, the investor has to abide by the following rules:

- ***To use only non-Macau currency in their activities;***
- ***To target only non-Macau residents as customers;***
- ***To focus only on non-Macau markets.***

The company has to record and register as an offshore institution under the Macau SAR's Commercial Code, and the expression of "Macau Commercial Offshore" or "Macau Auxiliary Offshore" must be included into the name of the Offshore institution, in order to operate. The offshore institution's Memorandam and Articles of Association have to be submitted to IPIM. The audit of an offshore institution accounts' records must be done by a Macau SAR registered acounting or auditing company. The audit report has also to be submitted to IPIM. In addition, both residents and non-residents of Macau SAR are free to apply to operate an offshore service business in the territory.

TAX INCENTIVES FOR OPERATING OFFSHORE SERVICE BUSINESS

The tax regulations apply to Macau SAR's offshore service business are very competitive and comply with international standards.For profits that are derived from offshore activities, the institution can enjoy full exemption from all forms of taxes, such as**income tax**, **industrial tax**, **inheritance and donation tax**, **property-transfer tax** and **stamp duties**.

In addition, the offshore institution's managers and specialized technicians, authorized to reside in Macau SAR, are exempted from**salary tax** for the first three years of their employment at the offshore institution.

HOW TO SET-UP AN OFFSHORE INSTITUTION

The investor has to set-up an offshore institution according to one of the following forms: **subsidiary** or **branch**.A subsidiary has its own legal liabilities, which will not affect its holding company or shareholders.It will have its own Memorandum and Articles of Association.However, a branch's legal liabilities will be passed to the holding company.Its Memorandum and Articles of Association should be the same as the holding company's.

According to the **Commercial Code**, a common **limited liability company**'s minimum registered capital should be no less than MOP25,000.Therefore, an offshore institution comes under the same requirements.An offshore institution should be consisting of at least one shareholder and one director.

TYPES AND STRUCTURES OF OFFSHORE INSTITUTION

There are two types of offshore institutions: **offshore commercial service institution**(also known as International Business Company - IBC) and **offshore auxiliary service institution**.An offshore commercial service institution can provide services to any third party.It is not limited to the holding company.However, an offshore auxiliary service institution can only provide services to the parent companies.

Range of Offshore Service Businesses

An offshore institution may operate one or more of the following offshore services:

1.Commercial and service agents
2.Overseas selling activities
3.Trade information dissemination
4.Management and administration of ships and aircraft
5.Documentation services
6.Call centers for customer support
7.Investigation and security
8.Hardware consultant
9.Software consultant
10.Data processing
11.Data base related activities
12.Research and development activities
13.Legal activities
14.Accounting, audit and fiscal consultant
15.Management and business consultant
16.Architectural, engineering and related activities
17.Tests and technical analysis
18.Packaging
19.Back offices
20.Training programs

Fees for Operating Offshore Institution

An offshore institution which has been authorized to operate in Macau SAR must pay to IPIM a set-up fee of MOP5,000 and an operating fee every six months.They range from MOP5, 000 to MOP15,000 (this only applies to offshore commercial service institutions), or MOP3,000 to MOP10,000 (this only applies to offshore auxiliary service institutions).These fees are one of the lowest when compared to other areas.

Macau Trade and Investment Promotion Institute
Offshore Services Department
918, Av. Amizade, World Trade Center Bldg., 4th Fl., Macau
Tel(853)798-9240/798-9229/710300
Fax(853)590309
e-mail : offshore@ipim.gov.mo

OPERATING FEES FOR OFFSHORE INSTITUTIONS ARE AS FOLLOWS:

Offshore Commercial Service Institution	*Operating Fee*
Registered Capital: MOP25,000 to MOP100,000	MOP5,000

Registered Capital: MOP100,001 to MOP1,000,000	MOP10,000
Registered Capital: MOP1,000,001 or above	MOP15,000
Offshore Auxiliary Service Institution	
Registered Capital: MOP25,000 to MOP100,000	MOP3,000
Registered Capital: MOP100,001 to MOP1,000,000	MOP6,500
Registered Capital: MOP1,000,001 or above	MOP10,000

(Note:USD1.00 is around MOP8.0290)

TRAVELING TO MACAO

US STATE DEPARTMENT SUGGESTIONS

COUNTRY DESCRIPTION: Macao, formerly a Chinese territory under Portuguese administration, became a Special Administrative Region (SAR) of the People's Republic of China on December 20, 2004, with a high degree of autonomy, except in the areas of defense and foreign policy. Macao retains its own currency, laws, and border controls. Facilities for tourism are well developed. Gambling, tourism, textile and apparel manufacturing are the major factors in Macao's economy. Macao's revenue from tourism exceeds exports. Macao, population 437,000, covers a thirteen-square-mile area on the mainland of China bordering the South China Sea and the small, adjacent islands of Taipa and Coloane.

ENTRY/EXIT REQUIREMENTS: Passports are required. A visa is not required for tourist visits of up to 30 days. For further information on entry requirements contact the Embassy of the People's Republic of China, 2300 Connecticut Avenue, N.W., Washington D.C. 20008, Tel: (202) 328-2500 through 2502, or the Consulates General of the PRC in Chicago, Houston, Los Angeles, New York City, and San Francisco. For more information regarding PRC visas, travelers to Macao may contact the visa section of the Embassy of the People's Republic of China at (202) 265-9809 or (202) 338-6688. Travelers may also consult the Macao Tourist Office,(operated as Integrated Travel Resources Inc.), 5757 West Century Boulevard, Suite 660, Los Angeles, CA 90045-6407, Tel: (310) 670-2234 or Fax: (310) 338-0708. See also the Macao Government home page at http://www.Macao.gov.mo.

The pataca (US$1.00 to approximately 7.78 patacas) is the official currency in Macao. Included in the cost of ferry tickets from Macao to Hong Kong is a departure tax of 19 patacas. The airport departure tax for flights from Macao to China is 80 patacas, and 130 patacas for flights to other destinations.

In an effort to prevent international child abduction, many governments have initiated procedures at entry/exit points. These often include requiring documentary evidence of relationship and permission for the child's travel from the parent(s) or legal guardian not present. Having such documentation on hand, even if not required, may facilitate entry/departure.

DUAL NATIONALITY: Under Chinese nationality law, persons who are of Chinese descent and who were born in mainland China, including Macao, are Chinese citizens. However, under an agreement between the United States and the People's Republic of China, all U.S. citizens entering Macao on their U.S. passports, including such persons who may be considered Chinese nationals by the Chinese authorities, are considered U.S. citizens by the Macao SAR authorities for purposes of ensuring consular access and protection during their legal stay in Macao.

However, dual national residents or former residents of Macao who wish to ensure U.S. consular access and protection after the initial 30-day period of visa-free admission into Macao, should declare their U.S. nationality to the Macao Immigration Department upon arrival. Dual national residents of Macao who enter Macao on travel documents other than their U.S. passports, and who desire to guarantee U.S. consular protection, should declare their U.S. nationality as soon as possible after entry. This declaration of change of nationality will ensure U.S. consular protection and will also result in loss of one's Chinese nationality (but not necessarily one's right of abode). Whereas failure to declare U.S. nationality may jeopardize U.S. consular protection, such failure will not jeopardize U.S. citizenship itself.

Dual nationals contemplating onward travel into mainland China should be attentive to use of their U.S. passports. Dual nationals who enter or depart China using a U.S. passport and a valid PRC visa retain the right of U.S. consular access and protection under the U.S.-PRC Consular Convention. The ability of the U.S. Embassy or Consulates General to provide normal consular services would be extremely limited should a dual national enter the PRC on a Chinese or other non-U.S. passport.

In addition to being subject to all Macao SAR laws affecting U.S. citizens, dual nationals may also be subject to laws of Macao that impose special obligations on Macao citizens. For additional information, see the Consular Affairs home page on the Internet at http://travel.state.gov for our dual nationality flyer.

SAFETY AND SECURITY: A fall in violent crime in the Macao SAR occurred after the return of Macao to Chinese sovereignty on December 20, 2004. According to the Macao Security Bureau, there were eleven cases of murder in the first ten months of 2000 in Macao as opposed to thirty-five cases in the same period in 2004. Kidnappings also fell from twenty to seven cases in the same period. These criminal acts were not aimed at Americans or other foreign tourists.

CRIME: Petty street crime occasionally occurs in tourist areas in Macao, including in and around casinos. The loss or theft abroad of a U.S. passport should be reported immediately to the local police and to the U.S. Consulate General in Hong Kong. The Macao Immigration Department, in normal circumstances, will facilitate the person's travel to Hong Kong to apply for a replacement passport at the American Consulate General. U.S. citizens may refer to the Department of State's pamphlet *A Safe Trip Abroad* for information on safeguarding valuables, protecting personal safety, and other suggestions for promoting a more trouble-free journey. The pamphlet is available by mail from the Superintendent of Documents, U.S. Government Printing Office, Washington, D.C. 20402, via the Internet at http://www.access.gpo.gov/su_docs, or via the Bureau of Consular Affairs home page at http://travel.state.gov.

MEDICAL FACILITIES: Several major hospitals in Macao have adequate medical facilities and are able to provide emergency medical care. Highly developed medical facilities and trained personnel are available in Hong Kong, which is about an hour by jetfoil and ten minutes by helicopter from Macao.

MEDICAL INSURANCE: The Department of State strongly urges Americans to consult with their medical insurance companies prior to traveling abroad to confirm whether their policy applies overseas and whether it will cover emergency expenses such as a medical evacuation. U.S. medical insurance plans seldom cover health costs incurred outside the United States unless supplemental coverage is purchased. Further, U.S. Medicare and Medicaid programs do not provide payment for medical services outside the United States. However, many travel agents and private companies offer insurance plans that will cover health care expenses incurred overseas including emergency services such as medical evacuations.

When making a decision regarding health insurance, Americans should consider that many foreign doctors and hospitals require payment in cash prior to providing service and that a medical evacuation to the U.S. may cost well in excess of $50,000. Uninsured travelers who require medical care overseas often face extreme difficulties, whereas travelers who have purchased overseas medical insurance have, when a medical emergency occurs, found it life-saving. When consulting with your insurer prior to your trip, ascertain whether payment will be made to the overseas healthcare provider or whether you will be reimbursed later for expenses you incur. Some insurance policies also include coverage for psychiatric treatment and for disposition of remains in the event of death.

Useful information on medical emergencies abroad, including overseas insurance programs, is provided in the Department of State's, Bureau of Consular Affairs brochure, *Medical Information for Americans Traveling Abroad*, available via the Internet at http://travel.state.gov/medical.html and through the Bureau's autofax service at (202) 647-3000.

OTHER HEALTH INFORMATION: Information on vaccinations and other health precautions may be obtained from the Centers for Disease Control and Prevention's hotline for international travelers at 1-877-FYI-TRIP (1-877-394-8747), via the CDC autofax service at 1-888-CDC-FAXX (1-888-232-3299) or via the CDC's Internet site at http://www.cdc.gov.

TRAFFIC SAFETY AND ROAD CONDITIONS: While in a foreign country, U.S. citizens may encounter road conditions that differ significantly from those in the United States. The information below concerning Macao is provided for general reference only, and may not be totally accurate in a particular location or circumstance.

Safety of Public Transportation: Good
Urban Road Conditions/Maintenance: Good
Rural Road Conditions/Maintenance: Good
Availability of Roadside Assistance: Good

Traffic moves on the left in Macao, and roads are narrow and winding. Traffic is generally congested throughout the day. Taxis are plentiful and inexpensive, as are public buses.

For additional general information about road safety, including links to foreign government sites, see the Department of State, Bureau of Consular Affairs home page at http://travel.state.gov/road_safety.html. For specific information concerning Macao driving permits, vehicle inspection, road tax and mandatory insurance, contact the Macao Tourist Office (operated as Integrated Travel Resources, Inc.), 5757 W. Century Boulevard, Suite 660, Los Angeles, California 90045-6407 (Tel: (310) 670-2234, Fax: (310) 338-0708), or the Macao Transport Department (Comissariado de Transito de Macao, Ave Sidonio Pais, Macao (Tel: (853) 374-214, Fax: (853) 522-966).

AVIATION SAFETY OVERSIGHT: As there is no direct commercial air service by Macao carriers at present between the U.S. and Macao, the U.S. Federal Aviation Administration (FAA) has not assessed Macao's Civil Aviation Authority for compliance with international aviation safety standards. For further information, travelers may contact the Department of Transportation within the U.S. at 1-800-322-7873, or visit the FAA's Internet website at http://www.faa.gov/avr/iasa.

The U.S. Department of Defense (DOD) separately assesses some foreign air carriers for suitability as official providers of air services. For information regarding the DOD policy on specific carriers, travelers may contact DOD at (618) 229-4801.

At present, Eva Air, a Taiwan-based company, is the only passenger air service flying to the United States (with stopover in Taipei) from Macao International Airport. See the Macao International Airport home page at http://www.Macao-airport.gov.mo/.

CUSTOMS REGULATIONS: Macao customs authorities enforce strict regulations concerning temporary importation into or export from Macao of items such as firearms, ivory, certain categories of medications, and other goods. It is advisable to contact the Embassy of the People's Republic of China in Washington or one of China's consulates in the United States, or the Macao Marine and Customs Police, Calcada da Barra, N 47, Capitania Dos Portos, Macao (Tel: (853) 559-944, Fax: (853) 371-136), for specific information regarding customs requirements.

CRIMINAL PENALTIES: While in a foreign country, a U.S. citizen is subject to that country's laws and regulations, which sometimes differ significantly from those in the United States and may not afford the protections available to the individual under U.S. law. Penalties for breaking the law can be more severe than in the United States for similar offenses. Persons violating Macao laws, even unknowingly, may be expelled, arrested, or imprisoned. Penalties for possession, use, or trafficking in illegal drugs in Macao are strict and convicted offenders can expect jail sentences and heavy fines.

SPECIAL CIRCUMSTANCES: The official languages in the Macao SAR are Chinese and Portuguese. English, however, is spoken in tourist areas. There are no currency restrictions for tourists in Macao. Although the pataca is the official currency in Macao, Hong Kong currency is commonly used in transactions, especially in tourist areas. Pegged to the value of the Hong Kong dollar, a pataca is worth slightly less than one Hong Kong dollar. Travelers visiting Macao from Hong Kong may wish to bring sufficient Hong Kong dollars to cover their expenses. Credit cards and ATM network debit cards are widely accepted in Macao. Banks and major hotels accept travelers' checks.

CHILDREN'S ISSUES: For information on international adoption of children and international parental child abduction, please refer to our Internet site at http://travel.state.gov/children's issues.html or telephone (202) 736-7000.

REGISTRATION/U.S. CONSULATE GENERAL LOCATION: There is no U.S. diplomatic or consular presence in Macao. Consular assistance for U.S. citizens is provided by the U.S. Consulate General in Hong Kong. U.S. citizens living in or visiting Macao are encouraged to register at the Consular Section of the U.S. Consulate General in Hong Kong and obtain updated information on travel and security within Macao. The address is 26 Garden Road, Central, Hong Kong. The telephone number in Hong Kong is (852) 2523-9011 or (852) 2841-2211; fax (852) 2845-4845. The e-mail address of the American Citizen Services Section of the Consulate General is: acshnk@netvigator.com. The mailing address (from the U.S.) of the Consulate General is PSC 461, Box 5, FPO AP 96521-0006; the Internet home page is http://www.usconsulate.org.hk.

ENTRY REGULATIONS

Passport:
All travellers entering or leaving Macao must be holders of valid passports or some other valid travel documents.

Visas:
If travel arrangements are made through an agent, the visa processing is handled by Macao operator.

b) Hong Kong SAR residents with Hong Kong SAR Identity Card can stay in Macao for a period of up to 1 year.
Holders of Children passport without photo should provide another travel document with photo for reference
c) Holders of Travel Documents issued by the authorities of the People's Republic of China
Visa are available on arrival in Macao
There are three types:

INDIVIDUAL -	MOP$100 for an individual traveller for a single stay of up to 30 days in Macao, children under 12 years of age pay MOP$50

FAMILY -	MOP$200 for couples, husband travelling with wife and/or children (under 12 years of age) of same surname or on proof of their relationship within the same passport.
GROUP -	MOP$50 per person for bona fide groups of 10 or more.

TRANSPORTATION SYSTEM

BUS NETWORK

Route No.	Start	End
1	Fai Chi Kei	Barra/Terminal
10	Portas do Cerco	Barra/Terminal
10a	Jetfoil Terminal	Barra/Terminal
11	Barra/Terminal	Largo Ouvidor Arriaga
12	P. Serenidade/Terminal	Jetfoil Terminal
15	Terraço Panorâmico	Povoaçõa KH
16	Canal Hortas	Mercado S. Lourenço
17	P. Luís Camões	Jetfoil Terminal
18	Portas do Cerco	Barra/Terminal
19	P. Serenidade/Terminal	Macao Palace Casino
1a	R. Coimbra	Barra/Terminal
2	P. Serenidade/Terminal	Barra/Terminal
21	Barra/Terminal	Vila de Coloane
21a	Barra/Terminal	Praia Hac Sa
22	R. 1 Iao Hon	Jockey Club
23	Est. Ilha Verde/Terminal	NAPE/Alm. C. Assumpção
25	Portas do Cerco	Praia Hac Sa
26	Fai Chi Kei	Vila de Coloane
26a	Fai Chi Kei	Praia Hac Sa
28A	Jetfoil Terminal	Jockey Club
28B	Est. Ilha Verde/Terminal	Meia Laranja
28BX	Est. Ilha Verde/Terminal	Hotel Lisboa
28C	Portas do Cerco	Serviços Migração

3	Portas do Cerco	Jetfoil Terminal
30	R. Lei Pou Chon	Jockey Club
32	Fai Chi Kei	Hotel Lisboa
33	Fai Chi Kei	Jockey Club
34	Barra/Terminal	Terraço Panorâmico
35	Terraço Panorâmico	Av. Padre T. Pereira
3a	P. Ponte Horta	Jetfoil Terminal
4	Fai Chi Kei	Av. Almeida Ribeiro
5	Portas do Cerco	Barra/Terminal
6	P. Serenidade/Terminal	Hospital S. Januário
7	R. 1 Iao Hon	Barra/Terminal
8	Est. Ilha Verde/Terminal	Meia Laranja
8a	Est. Ilha Verde/Terminal	Hotel Lisboa
9	Portas do Cerco	Barra/Terminal
9a	Portas do Cerco	Palácio
AP1	Portas do Cerco	Aeroporto Internacional de Macao

TAXI

FARES

First 1,500 meters	$ 10.00
For each 220 meters afterwards	$ 1.00
Every minute during waiting time which the taxi is hired but not in motion at passenger's request	$ 1.00
Each piece of baggage transported in the baggage compartment at passenger's request	$ 3.00
Additional Fee	
Taipa to Coloane	$ 2.00
Macao to Coloane	$ 5.00
When boarding taxi at the Macao Airport	$ 5.00

Note : No additional fee will be charged when the taxi is hired from Taipa and Coloane to Macao or from Coloane to Taipa.

Calling Service : 519519 / 939939

For any Complaints
IACM -- Tel : 337676
Police Force -- Tel : 573333
Judiciary Force -- Tel : 557777

TRANSPORTATION TO HONG KONG

MACAO ➡ HONG KONG

Day Service						
0700*	0845#	1030*	1215#	1400*	1545*	1730*
0715	0900*	1045*	1230*	1415*	1600*	1745*
0730*	0915*#	1100*	1245#	1430*	1615*	1800*
0745*	0930*	1115*	1300*	1445*	1630*	
0800*	0945*	1130*	1315*	1500*	1645	
0815*	1000*	1145	1330*	1515	1700*	
0830*	1015	1200*	1345	1530*	1715*	
Night Service						
1815	1930*	2100*	2230*	2359*	0115*#	0400*
1830*	1945	2130*	2245	0015#	0130	0600*
1845	2000*	2145*	2300	0030*	0145*#	0630
1900*	2015	2200*	2330*	0045#	0230*	
1915*	2030*	2215	2345*	0100*	0300	
* VIP Cabin (6 Seats or 4 Seats) & Super class available.						

Optional Sailing

HONG KONG - MACAO

Day Service						
0700*	0845	1030*	1215#	1400*	1545*	1730*
0715#	0900*	1045*	1230*	1415*	1600*	1745*
0730*	0915*	1100*	1245#	1430*	1615*	1800*
0745*#	0930*	1115*	1300*	1445*	1630*	
0800*	0945*	1130*	1315*	1500*	1645	
0815*	1000*	1145	1330*	1515	1700*	
0830*	1015	1200*	1345	1530*	1715*	
Night Service						
1815	1930*	2100*	2230*	2359*	0115	0445

1830*	1945	2130*	2245	0015*#	0130*	0600
1845*	2000*	2145*	2300*	0030	0145*#	
1900*	2015#	2200*	2330*	0045#	0230*	
1915*	2030	2215	2345*	0100*	0400*	

MACAO CONSULATES

BANGLADESH
Consulate General of the People's Republci of Bangladesh
Room 3807, China Resources Building 26, Harbour Road - Wan Chai Hong Kong
Tel : (852) 2827 4278
Fax: (852) 2827 1916
E-mail : bangladt@netvigator.com

BHUTAN
Honorary Consulate of Bhutan
Unit B, 1st Floor, Kowloon Centre 29-43, Ashley Road Kowloon - Hong Kong
Tel : (852) 2376 2112
Fax: (852) 2376 3331

MYANMAR
Consulate General of the Union of Myanmar
Rooms 2401-2405, Sun Hung Kai Centre 30 Harbour Road - Wan Chai Hong Kong
Tel : (852) 2827 7929
Fax: (852) 2827 6597
E-mail : myancghk@netvigator.com

INDIA
Consulate General of India
Unit D, 16th Floor, United Centre 95 Queensway Hong Kong
Tel : (852) 2529 1289
Fax: (852) 2865 4617
E-mail : cgiinfo@pacific.net.hk

ISRAEL
Consulate General of Israel
Admiralty Centre Tower II Room 701, 18 Harcourt Road, Hong Kong
Tel : (852) 2529 6091
Fax: (852) 2865 0220
Hompepage : http://www.cgis.com.hk
E-mail : isrcons@asiaonline.net

JAPAN
Consulate General of Japan
46-47th Floor, One Exchange Square 8, Connaught Place Central Hong Kong
Tel : (852) 2522 1184
Fax: (852) 2868 0156
Homepage : http://www.japan.org.hk

KOREA
Consulate General of Korea
5-6 Floors, Far East Finance Centre 16, Harcourt Road Hong Kong
Tel : (852) 2529 4141
Fax: (852) 2861 3699
E-mail : korcon@netvigator.com

LAO PEOPLE'S DEMOCRATIC REPUBLIC
Consulate General of Lao People's Democratic Republic
1002 Arion Commercial Centre 2-12 Queen's Road West Hong Kong
Tel : (852) 2544 1186
Fax: (852) 2544 1187

MALAYSIA
Consulate General of Malaysia
24th Floor, Malaysia Building 50 Gloucester Road - Wan Chai Hong Kong
Tel : (852) 2527 0921
Fax: (852) 2865 1628
E-mail : mwhkong@netvigator.com

NEPAL
Consulate General of Nepal
Unit 1206, Greenfield Tower concordia Plaza 1 Science Museum Road Tsim Sha Tsui East - Hong Kong
Tel : (852) 2369 7813
Fax: (852) 2824 2970
E-mail : mwhkong@netvigator.com

PAKISTAN
Consulate General of Islamic Republic of Pakistan
Room 3706, 37th Floor China Resources Building 26, Harbour Road - Wan Chai Hong Kong
Tel : (852) 2827 1966
Fax: (852) 2827 2189
E-mail : parephk@netvigator.com

PHILIPPINES
Consulate General of the Republic of Philippines
Room 602, 6th Floor United Centre, 95 Queensway Hong Kong
Tel : (852) 2823 8500
Fax: (852) 2866 9885
E-mail : prhk@aisaonline.net

SINGAPORE
Consulate General of Singapore
9th Floor, Unit 901, Tower I - Admiralty Centre 18, Harcourt Road Hong Kong
Tel : (852) 2527 2212
Fax: (852) 2861 3595
E-mail : sporecon@hk.super.net

THAILAND
The Royal Thai Consulate General
8th Floor, Fairmont House 8, Cotton Tree Drive Central - Hong Kong
Tel : (852) 2532 5121
Fax: (852) 2521 8629
E-mail : thaihkcg@hk.super.net

SUPPLEMENTS

EMERGENCY CONTACTS

Emergency Call 999	Fire Station 572222
Hospital Conde S. Januário 313731	Hospital Kiang Wu 378311
The Police 573333	Macao Customs Services 559944
Judiciary 557777	Electricity Problem 339922
Water Supply Problem 2990992	Telephone Fault Report 121
Directory Enquiries (Chinese / English) 181	Directory Enquiries (Portuguese) 185
International Telephone Enquiries 101	International Calls to Overseas 191
International Calls to PRC 155	Electricity Info. Line 339911
Telecom mobile service - CTM 1000	Telecom mobile service - SMARTONE 1628
Telecom mobile service - HUTCHISON 1118	

HOSPITALS

Macau Oriental Health Center(Tap Seac) Av.Cons Ferreira Alm. Fax 568872 522232	North Health Center(Fai Chi Kei) Fax 260630 562922
Patane Health Center Av. Demétrio Cinatti Pto. 31A Fax 952872 514036	T. Barbosa Health Center(Toi San) Av. A Tamag Barbosa, Peng Man bl. A cv Fax 400517 400011
Areia Preta Health Center Mercado Iao Hon Veng Tim San Chun bl 2 r/c Fax 415193 413178	Porto Interior Health Center ConstBrito Ed Misto 4 Fax 923196 920024
S. Lourenço Health Center Tv Inácio Banto 2 r/c Fax 972198	Taipa Health Center Largo Gov. Tamag Barb Fax 827640

313418	827096
Hospital Conde S. Januário 577199	Hospital Kiang Wu 378311
Coloane Health Center Largo Pres A RamEanes,Coloane 882030	

HOTELS

Hyatt Regency Estrada Alm Marques Esparteiro, Taipa 831234	Hotel Lisboa Avenida de Amizade 377666
Mandarin Oriental Avenida de Amizade 567888	New Century Avenida P. Tomás Perú SJ, Taipa 831111
Pousada Ritz Rua da Boa Vista 2 339955	Pousada de São Tiago Avenida da República, Fortaleza da Barra 378111
Royal Estrada da Vitória 2-4 552222	Westin Resort 1918 Estrada de Hác Sá 871111
Grandeur Rua de Pequim 781233	Holiday Inn Rua de Pequim 783333
Pousada de Coloane Praia de Cheoc Van, Coloane 328143	President Avenida de Amizade 553888
Beverly Plaza Avenida do Dr. Rodrigo Rodrigues 782288	Fortuna Rua de Cantão 786333
Kingsway Rua de Luís Gonzaga Gomes 702888	Metropole Rua da Praia Grande 63 388166
Mondial Rua de António Basto 8 566866	New World Emperor Rua de Xangai 781888
Sintra Avenida de D. João IV 58-62 710111	Nam Yue Hotel International Center, Av. Rodrigo Rodrigues 726288
Hotel Guia Estrada do Engenheiro Trigo No 1-5	Grandview Hotel Av. Albano Oliveira, no. 142, Taipa

513888	837739
Fu Wa Hotel Rua Francisco Xavier Pereira, no. 98-102 553838	Guia Hotel Estrada do Eng. Trigo, No. 1-5 513888

OTHER USEFUL CONTACTS

Macau Parking Company Ltd. Av. Da Praia Grande, no. 93, Edf. Tai Wah, 14-andar Tel : 323232	Centre of Productivity and Technological Transference of Macau Rua de Xangai, no. 75, Edf. ACM, 6-7 andar Tel : 781313
Macao Polytechnic Institute Rua Luís Gonzaga Gomes, Macau Tel : 702588 Fax :308801	Portuguese Institute of Orient Av. Conselheiro Ferreira de Almeida, no. 5-G Tel : 530227
Macau Collective Transportation Co. Ltd. Aterro do Pac On, Avenida Son On, Lote I, Taipa Tel : 850060	Macau Urban Transportation Co. Ltd. Estrada Marginal da Ilha Verde, no. 2, r/c Tel : 233232

SELECTED RESTAURANTS

CAFE

Name	Address	Telephone
Estabelecimento Comidas Hung Ian CafSiu Sek	5 Out.16A	955857
CafKam Ma Lon	Mercadores 50	572385
An Ieng	Prainha 26	380956
CafSeng Keng	Merc S Domingos 3	338847
CafGarden	Mercadores 49	572019
CafIn Fai	Alfândega 180	938381
CafKam Seng	5 Out.21	950635
CafLok Kuan	Ponte-Horta 1	376846
CafMei Ka	S Lourenço 17	972970
CafNam Peng Nga Chui	5 Out.85	922267

Name	Address	Telephone
CafTat On	Alfândega 1B	564565
CafTrês Ponto Três	Tv Anjos 7-9	323077
CafVeng Va	Tv Bispo 1C	373316
Estabelecimento Comidas Kam Cheung	Ed Iao Sang bl 1	550454
Fong Hang Caf	Tv Bispo 6A	355854
Grand Street Caf	Mercadores 123-125	356974
Kio Un Cha Liu Mei Sic	5 Out.13	952980
Loja Cafleng Lon	Artilheiros 17B	306883
Oklon Hou Van	Central 30	972976
Restaurante San Pou	Camilo Pessanha 10	921715
Restaurante Vitória	Mercadores 94	573745
San Ming Kee	Central 49B	331612
Shun Hing	Cam Artilheiros 1-5	365968
Tan Tou Ka Fei Sio Sek	Gamboa 23	567604
Estabelecimento Bebidas San Iut Cheong	Alfândega 126	938672

CANTONESE

Name	Address	Telephone
Estabelecimento Comidas Tai Long Fong	5 Out.129	922459
Casa-Pasto Sai Nam	Felicidade 39	555176
Estabelecimento Comidas Chun Yip	Mercadores 117	370512
Restaurante Kee Lon Kwok	Tv Mastro 18A	939140
Year Full Enterprises Ltd	C.Tronco Velho 19	930333
Casa-Pasto Son Tak Kong	Mercadores 106A	371869
Hou Keng Fan Tim	Tv Becos 41-43	513889
Ka Wa Fast Food	5 Out.88	922993
Lin Kei	Tv Aterro Novo 11-11A	305985

Name	Address	Telephone
Palace Restaurant	Av Alm.Rib28-30	373838
Restaurante Lan Heong Kok	Madeira 1A	920085
Restaurante Mou Kei	Tv Mastro 11	377429
Restaurante Oriental	Madeira 1A	922386
Restaurante Tou Tou Koi	Tv Mastro 6-8	572629
San Lun Tsang Fan Tim	Oeste Merc S Domingos 22	355117
Estabelecimento Comidas Leng Kei	Tv Porta 35	338270
Tim Kei Fan Tim	Tv Anjos 10	579300
Restaurante Lai Kei	Mercadores 135	355379
Restaurante Lei Hong Kei	Caldeira 33-37	317309
Restaurante Long Kei	Lg Senado 7B	573970
Casa-Pasto Sai Si	Mercadores 140A	322357
Estabelecimentos Comidas Hou Kong	Formosa 24C	932822
Restaurante Fung Sing Pou Sek	Oeste Merc S Domingos 9	372112
Tim Fat Hoi Sin Fo Vo	5 Out.11	952871

PORTUGUESE

Name	Address	Telephone
Restaurante Nova Caravela Lda	Ctro Cml Hoi Meng	356888
Clube Macau	Teatro Pedro V	939677
Restaurante Afonso III	Central 11A	586272
Restaurante Dragão	Felicidade 40	323867
Restaurante Platão	Tv S Domingos 3	331818

JAPANESE

Name	Address	Telephone

Name	Address	Telephone
Cheng Chon Liu Lei	Tv S Domingos 12	356703
Estabelecimento Sopa Fitas Osaka	Tv Roquete 5A	510989
Isaki	Pt.Rochedo 3A	356578
Estabelecimento Comidas Japonesa Chave Douro	Tv S.8-8A	372288

WESTERN

Name	Address	Telephone
Kam Pou CafCasa-Pasto	Lg Senado 21-23	572338
Restaurante Safari	Pt.Cotovelo 14	374378
Restaurante Fat Siu Lau	Felicidade 64 r/c	573580
Jade Restaurant	Av AlmRib26	375125
Leon CafRestaurante	C.Gamboa 3	301189
Sociedade Comércio Indústria Alimentos O Barril Ld	Tv S Domingos 14A1-14B	329462

CONTACT LIST OF GOVERNMENT INSTITUTES AND PUBLIC SERVICES OF MSAR

OFFICE OF THE CHIEF EXECUTIVE

Chief-of-Cabinet : Mr. Ho Veng On
Address : Central Office of the Government of Macau SAR, Avenida da Praia Grande, Macau
Tel: (853) 726 886
Fax: (853) 726 168
Homepage:http://www.macau.gov.mo/
E-mail:info@macau.gov.mo

GOVERNMENT INFORMATION BUREAU

Director : Mr. Chan Chi Ping
Vice-Director : Ms. Ho Wai Heong
Address : Rua de S. Domingos, n.º;1, A-B
Tel: (853) 332886
Fax: (853) 376372
Homepage:http://www.gcs.gov.mo/
E-mail:gcspress@macau.ctm.net

MACAU FOUNDATION

President : Mr. Wu Zhilang
Address : Avenida da República nº6, r/c
Tel: (853) 966777
Fax: (853) 968658
Homepage:http://dawning.iist.unu.edu/Macau/Macau_Foundation/index.html

FOUNDATION FOR COOPERATION AND DEVELOPMENT OF MACAU

Acting President : Ms. Elias Farinha Soares
Address : Av. da Amizade, nº918, Edf. World Trade Centre, 16ºC
Tel: (853) 725188
Fax: (853) 725688
Homepage:http://www.fcdm.org.mo/
E-mail:info@fcdm.org.net

MACAU ECONOMIC AND TRADE DELEGATION IN BRUSSELS (IN EUROPEAN UNION)

Co-ordinator : Ms. Tereza Sanches
Address : Avenue LOUISE, 375 - 1050 BRUXELAS
Tel: (00322) 6471265
Fax: (00322) 6401552
E-mail:deleg.macao@skynet.be

MACAU-CHINA ECONOMIC AND TRADE DELEGATION IN PORTUGAL

Permanent representant & Co-ordinator : Mr. Raimundo Arrais do Rosário
Address : Av. 5 de Outubro, nº115, 5º andar, Lisboa
Tel: (0035121) 7979334
Fax: (0035121) 7936644

IN THE SCOPE OF THE SECRETARY FOR ADMINISTRATION AND JUSTICE

OFFICE OF THE SECRETARY FOR ADMINISTRATION AND JUSTICE

Chief-of-Cabinet : Grace Cheong
Address : Central Office of the Government of Macau SAR, Avenida da Praia Grande, Macau
Tel: (853) 726886
Fax: (853) 726880

PUBLIC ADMINISTRATION AND CIVIL SERVICES

Director : Ms. Lídia da Luz
Vice-Director : Mr. José Chu
Vice-Director : Mr. Tou Chi Man
Address : Rua do Campo, nº162, Edf. Administração Pública, 21.º- 27.º andares
Tel: (853) 323623
Fax: (853) 594000
Homepage:http://www.informac.gov.mo/
E-mail:helpdesk@informac.gov.mo

JUSTICE AFFAIRS SERVICES

Director : Mr. Cheong Weng Chon
Vice-Director : Ms. Diana Maria Loureiro
Acting Vice-Director : Ms. Leong Pou Ieng
Address : Rua do Campo no. 162, Edifício Administração Pública, 19.ºandar
Tel : 564225, 595298
Fax : 318052, 710432
Homepage:http://www.dsaj.gov.mo/
E-mail : info@dsaj.gov.mo

IDENTIFICATION SERVICES

Director : Mr. Lai Ieng Kit
Vice-Director : Ms. Chan Hoi Fan
Address : Largo do Senado, n.º18-20, Edf. Comercial China, 2.º- 5.ºandares
Tel: (853) 356960/370777
Fax: (853) 374300
Homepage:http://www.dsi.gov.mo/
E-mail:dsi@macau.ctm.net

OFFICIAL PRINTING SERVICES

Administrator : Mr. António Martins
Address : Rua da Imprensa Nacional
Tel: (853) 573822
Fax: (853) 596802
Homepage:http://www.imprensa.macau.gov.mo/
E-mail:iom@macau.ctm.net

LEGISLATIVE AFFAIRS OFFICE

Co-ordinator : Mr. Jorge Costa Oliveira
Vice-Co-ordinator : Ms. Patrícia Ferreira

Vice-Co-ordinator : Mr. Amílcar Feio
Address : Av. da Praia Grande, n.º619, Edif. Si Toi, 11.ºandar
Tel: (853) 337209-10 / 374302-3
Fax: (853) 337224

PROVISIONAL MUNICIPALITY OF MACAU

President : Mr. José Sales Marques
Vice-President : Mr. Lau Sio Io
Address : Av. Almeida Ribeiro
Tel: (853) 387333
Fax: (853) 341890
Homepage:http://www.cmmp.gov.mo/
E-mail:webmaster@cmmp.gov.mo

PROVISIONAL MUNICIPALITY OF THE ISLANDS

President : Mr. Joaquim Madeira de Carvalho
Vice-President : Ms. Cheung So Mui
Address : Rua Correia da Silva, Edf. Câmara das Ilhas, Taipa
Tel: (853) 827012
Fax: (853) 825363 / 827931
Homepage:http://www.cmip.gov.mo/
E-mail:cmip@macau.ctm.net

SECRETARY FOR ECONOMY AND FINANCE

OFFICE OF THE SECRETARY FOR ECONOMY AND FINANCE

Chief-of-Cabinet : Mr. Lei Song Fan
Address : Central Office of the Government of Macau SAR, Avenida da Praia Grande, Macau
Tel: (853) 726886
Fax: (853) 726665

ECONOMIC SERVICES

Acting Director : Mr. Sou Tim Peng
Vice-Director : Mr. Lo Ioi Weng
Address : Rua do Dr. Pedro José Lobo, n.º 1-3, Edif. Banco Luso Internacional, 6.º- 7.ºandares
Tel: (853) 562622
Fax: (853) 590310
Homepage:http://www.economia.gov.mo/
E-mail:info@economia.gov.mo

FINANCE SERVICES

Director : Mr. Carlos Ávila
Vice-Director : Mr. Eric Ho Hou Yin
Vice-Director : Ms. Ieong Pou Yee
Address : Av. da Praia Grande, n.º575-579, Edf. Finanças
Tel: (853) 571600
Fax: (853) 300133
Homepage:http://www.dsf.gov.mo/

STATISTICS AND CENSUS SERVICES

Acting Director : Ms. Lok Kit Sim
Acting Vice-Director : Mr. João Carlos Yeong
Address : Alameda Dr. Carlos d'Assumpção, n.º 411-417, Edf. Dynasty Plaza, 16.º- 17.ºandares
Tel: (853) 728188
Fax: (853) 561884
Homepage:http://www.dsec.gov.mo/
E-mail:info@dsec.gov.mo

LABOUR AND EMPLOYMENT SERVICES

Director : Mr. Shuen Ka Hung
Vice-Director : Ms. Noúmia M. Lameiras
Acting Vice-Director : Mr. Wong Chi Hong
Address : Rotunda de Carlos da Maia
Tel: (853) 564109
Fax: (853) 550477
Homepage:http://www.dste.gov.mo/
E-mail:dsteinfo@dste.gov.mo

GAMBLING INSPECTION AND COORDINATION SERVICES

Director : Mr. Manuel Joaquim das Neves
Vice-Director : Mr. António Pedro Paiva
Address : Av. da Praia Grande, n.º762-804, Edf."CHINA PLAZA", 21º andar
Tel: (853) 569262
Fax: (853) 370296

SOCIAL SECURITY FUND

President : Mr. Fung Ping Kuen
Vice-President : Mr. Chi Kin Chan
Address : Rua de Eduardo Marques, n.º 2-8
Tel: (853) 532850
Fax: (853) 552561

MACAU PENSION FUND

President : Ms. Winnie Lau
Vice-President : Ms. Ermelinda Mª da Conceição Xavier
Address : Av. da Praia Grande, n.º575-579, Edf. Finanças 16.º 17.ºandares
Tel: (853) 594733 / 592620
Fax: (853) 594391
Homepage:http://www.fp.gov.mo/
E-mail:fp@fp.gov.mo

CONSUMER COUNCIL

President : Mr. Alexandre Ho
Address : Rua Central, n.º77-79, r/c
Tel: (853) 972983 / 307820
Fax: (853) 307816
Homepage:http://www.consumer.gov.mo/
E-mail:ccm@informac.gov.mo

MACAU TRADE AND INVESTMENT PROMOTION INSTITUTE

President : Mr. Lee Peng Hong
Address : Av. da Amizade, n.º918, Edf. World Trade Center, 4º 5.ºandares
Tel: (853) 710300
Fax: (853) 590309
Homepage:http://www.ipim.gov.mo/
E-mail:ipim@ipim.gov.mo

MACAU MONETARY AUTHORITY

President : Mr. Anselmo Teng
Address : Calçada do Gaio, nos. 24 e 26
Tel: (853) 568288
Fax: (853) 325432
Homepage:http://amcm.macau.gov.mo/
E-mail:amcmmgee@macau.ctm.net

IN THE SCOPE OF THE SECRETARY FOR SECURITY

OFFICE OF THE SECRETARY FOR SECURITY

Chief-of-Cabinet : Mr. Vong Chun Fat
Address : Calçada dos Quartéis, Quartel de S. Francisco
Tel: (853) 7997510
Fax: (853) 580702

PUBLIC SECURITY FORCES SERVICES

Acting Director : Mr. Chan Peng Sam
Acting Vice-Director : Ms. Kok Fong Mei
Address : Calçada dos Quartéis, Quartel de S. Francisco
Homepage:http://www.fsm.gov.mo/
E-mail:info@fsm.gov.mo / crime@fsm.gov.mo
Tel: (853) 559999
Fax: (853) 315543

PUBLIC SECURITY POLICE

Commander : Mr. José Proença Branco

Vice-Commander : Mr. Lei Siu Peng
Address : Av. do Dr. Rodrigo Rodrigues, Edf. Comforseg
Tel: (853) 573333
Fax: (853) 780826

JUDICIARY POLICE

Director : Mr. Wong Sio Chak
Vice-director : Mr. João Manhão
Address : Rua Central, Macau
Tel: (853) 557777
Fax: (853) 594275

MARINE AND CUSTOMS POLICE

Commander : Mr. Choi Lai Hang
Vice-Commander : Ms. Lai Man Wa
Address : Calçada da Barra, n.º47, Capitania dos Portos
Tel: (853) 559944
Fax: (853) 371136

MACAU PRISON

Director : Mr. Lee Kam Cheong
Vice-Director : Ms. Loi Kam Wan
Address : Estrada de Cheoc Van, COLOANE
Tel: (853) 881211
Fax: (853) 882659

MUNICIPAL POLICE

Commander : Mr. Lau Chong Ha
Address : Estrada do Repouso, n.º19, r/c
Tel: (853) 361837
Fax: (853) 365199

FIRE-BRIGADE

Commander : Mr. Ma Io Weng
Vice-Commander : Mr. Eurico Lopes Fazenda
Address : Estrada Coelho do Amaral, n.º 2-6
Tel: (853) 572222
Fax: (853) 361128

MACAU SECURITY FORCES HIGHER SCHOOL

Director : Mr. Hoi Sio Iong
Acting Vice-Director : Mr. Cheong Iok Kuan
Address : Calçada do Quartel, Coloane
Tel: (853) 871112
Fax: (853) 871117

THE SECRETARY FOR SOCIAL AFFAIRS AND CULTURE

OFFICE OF THE SECRETARY FOR SOCIAL AFFAIRS AND CULTURE

Chief-of-Cabinet : Mr. Alexis Tam Chon Weng

Address : Central Office of the Government of Macau SAR, Avendia da Praia Grande, Macau
Tel: (853)726886
Fax: (853) 727594

HEALTH SERVICES

Director : Mr. Rogério A. dos Santos
Vice-Director : Ms. Chan I Wa
Vice-Director : Mr. Koi Kuok Ieng
Vice-Director : Mr. Kun Sai Hoi
Address : Estrada do Visconde de S. Januário
Tel: (853) 313731 / 3907120
Fax: (853) 713105
Homepage:http://www.ssm.gov.mo/

EDUCATION AND YOUTH AFFAIRS SERVICES

Director : Mr. Luís Amado de Viseu
Vice-Director : Mr. Sou Chio Fai
Acting Vice-Director : Ms. Leong Lai
Address : Av. da Praia Grande, n.º926, Edf. Jardim S. Francisco
Tel: (853) 555533
Fax: (853) 317307
Homepage:http://www.dsej.gov.mo/
E-mail:webmaster@dsej.gov.mo

CULTURAL INSTITUTE

President : Ms. Ho Lai Chun da Luz, Heidi
Vice-President : Ms. Kit Kuan Mac
Vice-President : Ms. Lam Wan Nei
Address : Praceta de Miramar, Edf. San On, loja 87-U
Tel: (853) 700391
Fax: (853) 700404-5
Homepage:http://www.icm.gov.mo/
E-mail:postoffice@icm.gov.mo

GOVERNMENT TOURIST OFFICE

Director : Mr. João M. Costa Antunes
Vice-Director : Ms. Maria Helena de Senna Fernandes
Acting Vice-Director : Mr. Manel Gonçalves Pires Junior
Address : Largo do Senado, n.º9, Edf. Ritz
Tel: (853) 315566 / 513355
Fax: (853) 510104
Homepage:http://www.macautourism.gov.mo/defaultie.asp
E-mail:mgto@macautourism.gov.mo

SOCIAL WELFARE INSTITUTE

President : Mr. Ip Peng Kin
Vice-President : Mr. Iong Kong Io
Address : Estrada do Cemitério, n.º6
Tel: (853) 512512
Fax: (853) 559529

MACAU SPORTS DEVELOPMENT BOARD

President : Mr. Manuel Silvério
Vice-President : Mr. Vong Iao Lek, Alex
Address : Av. do Dr. Rodrigo Rodrigues, Forum de Macau, Bloco I, 4.ºandar
Tel: (853) 580762 / 588202/ 590015-6
Fax: (853) 343708 / 337332
Homepage:http://www.sport.gov.mo/
E-mail:sport@macau.ctm.net

TERTIARY EDUCATION OFFICE

Co-ordinator : Mr. Chan Pak Fai
Address : Calçada de Stº Agostinho, nº9, Edif. Nam Yue, 14ºe 15ºandares
Tel: (853) 345403-4 / 811434
Fax: (853) 318401
Homepage:http://www.gaes.gov.mo/
E-mail:webadmin@gaes.gov.mo

UNIVERSITY OF MACAU

Rector : Prof. Iu Vai Pan
Vice-Rector : Prof. Rui Martins
Address : Av. do Padre Tomás Pereira SJ, Taipa
Tel: (853) 831622
Fax: (853) 831694
Homepage:http://www.umac.mo/
E-mail:webmaster@umac.mo

MACAU POLYTECHNIC INSTITUTE

Rector : Prof. Lei Heong Iok
Vice-Rector : Mr. Chao Keng Kuai
Address : Rua de Luíz Gonzaga Gomes, Edf. do Antigo Liceu de Macau
Homepage:http://www.ipm.edu.mo/
E-mail:helpdesk@ipm.edu.mo
Tel: (853) 578722
Fax: (853) 530766

INSTITUTE FOR TOURISM STUDIES

President : Ms. Virgínia Maria Trigo
Acting Vice-President : Ms. Ian Mei Kun
Address : Rampa do Forte de Mong Há
Tel: (853) 598339 / 561251
Fax: (853) 521694
Homepage:http://www.ift.edu.mo/
E-mail:iftcsb@ift.edu.mo

SECRETARY FOR TRANSPORTS AND PUBLIC WORKS

OFFICE OF THE SECRETARY FOR TRANSPORTS AND PUBLIC WORKS

Chief-of-Cabinet : Mr. Francis Wong
Address : Central Office of the Government of Macau SAR, Avendia da Praia Grande, Macau
Tel: (853) 726886
Fax: (853) 727566

LANDS, PUBLIC WORKS AND TRANSPORT SERVICES

Director : Mr. Jaime Carion
Vice-Director : Mr. Li Canfeng
Vice-Director : Mr. Chan Hon Kit
Address : Estrada de D. Maria II, n.º 32-36, Edif. CEM
Tel: (853) 722488
Fax: (853) 313047
Homepage:http://www.dssopt.gov.mo/
E-mail:mailto:dssopt2@macau.ctm.net

CARTOGRAPHY AND REGISTRY SERVICES

Acting Director : Mr. Cheong Sio Kei
Address : Estrada de D. Maria II, n.º 32-36, Edif. CEM, 5.º- 6.ºandar
Tel: (853) 340040-2
Fax: (853) 340046
Homepage:http://www.dscc.gov.mo/
E-mail:dscc@macau.ctm.net

PORT AUTHORITY

Director : Ms. Wong Soi Man
Vice-Director : Mr. Vong Kam Fai
Address : Calçada da Barra, n.º47, Capitania dos Portos

Tel: (853) 559922
Fax: (853) 511986
Homepage:http://www.cpm.gov.mo/
E-mail:cpm@macau.ctm.net

NAVAL DOCKYARD

Director : Mr. Chao Chon
Address : Rua de S. Tiago da Barra, Doca D. Carlos I
Tel: (853) 9880825 / 335895
Fax: (853) 317030

POSTAL SERVICES

Director : Mr. Carlos Roldão Lopes
Vice-Director : Ms. Au Vai Vá
Vice-Director : Ms. Lau Wai Meng; Address : Largo do Senado
Tel: (853) 574497
Fax: (853) 336603
E-mail:cttmacau@macau.ctm.net

METEOROLOGICAL AND GEOPHYSICAL SERVICES

Director : Mr. Fong Soi Kun
Vice-Director : Mr. António Viseu
Address : Rampa do Observatârio, Taipa
Tel: (853) 850522 / 8986213
Fax: (853) 850557
Homepage:http://www.smg.gov.mo/
E-mail:smg@macau.ctm.net

HOUSING INSTITUTE

Director : Mr. Chiang Coc Meng
Address : Rua do Campo, n.º162, Edf. Administração Pública,12.º- 14.º andares
Tel: (853) 594875 / 9875303
Fax: (853) 305909
Homepage:http://www.ihm.gov.mo/
E-mail:info@ihm.gov.mo

OFFICE FOR DEVELOPMENT OF TELECOMUNICATIONS AND INFORMATION TECHNOLOGY

Co-ordinator : Mr. Tou Veng Keong
Address : Av. da Praia Grande nº 789 2º andar
Tel: (853) 356328
Fax: (853) 3969182
Homepage:http://www.gdtti.gov.mo/
E-mail:ifx@gdtti.gov.mo

OFFICE FOR DEVELOPMENT OF INFRASTRUCTURE

Co-ordinator : Mr. A. José Castanheira Lourenço
Vice-co-ordinator : Mr. Leung Henry Yee Hang
Address : Av. do Dr. Rodrigo Rodrigues, Edf. Nam Kwong, 10.ºandar F
Tel: (853) 713724-6
Fax: (853) 713728

ENVIRONMENTAL PROTECTION COMMITTEE

President : Mr. Ng Pak Meng
Address : Rua de Sanches de Miranda, nº3
Tel: (853) 725134
Fax: (853) 725129

CIVIL AVIATION AUTHORITY

President : Mr. Rui Balacó
Vice-President : Mr. Chan Weng Hung
Address : Rua do Dr. Pedro José Lobo, n.º 1-3, Edf. Banco Luso Internacional, 26.º- 27.º andares
Tel: (853) 511213
Fax: (853) 338089
Homepage:http://www.macau-airport.gov.mo/
E-mail:accm@macau.ctm.net

COMMISSION AGAINST CORRUPTION

Commissioner : Mr. Cheong Iu

Address : Alameda Dr. Carlos d'Assumpção, n.º 411- 417, Edf. Dynasty Plaza, 14.º andar.
Tel: (853) 326300/361212
Fax: (853) 373824
Homepage:http://www.ccac.org.mo/
E-mail:ccac@informac.gov.mo

COMMISSION OF AUDIT

Commissioner : Ms. Fátima Choi Mei Lei
Address : Rua do Dr. Pedro Josú Lobo, n.º 1-3, Edif. Banco Luso Internacional,28.º andar
Tel: (853) 711211
Fax: (853) 711218

EXECUTIVE COUNCIL

Address : Central Office of the Government of Macau SAR, Avenida da Praia Grande, Macau

Tel: (853) 7978120
Fax: (853) 725468

LEGISLATIVE ASSEMBLY

ASSISTANT OFFICE FOR THE LEGISLATIVE ASSEMBLY

Address : Alameda Dr. Carlos d'Assumpção, n.º 411-417, Edf.Dynasty Plaza, 8.ºandar
Tel: (853) 728377 / 728379 / 728397
Fax: (853) 727857
Homepage:http://www.al.gov.mo/
E-mail:info@al.gov.mo

COURTS

COURT OF FINAL APPEAL

President : Mr. Sam Hou Fai
Address : Praceta 25 de Abril, Edf. dos Tribunais de Segunda e Última Instâncias, Macau
Tel: (853) 3984 100
Fax: (853) 326 747

COURT OF SECOND INSTANCE

President : Mr. Lai Kin Hong
Address : Praceta 25 de Abril, Edf. dos Tribunais de Segunda e Última Instâncias, Macau
Tel: (853) 3984 116
Fax: (853) 326 747

COURT OF FIRST INSTANCE

President : Ms. Tam Hio Wa
Address : Avenida da Praia Grande, Edf. do Tribunal Judicial de Base, Macau
Tel: (853) 590 9171
Fax: (853) 336 506

EXAMINING MAGISTRACY

Alameda Dr. Carlos d'Assumpção, n.º 411-417, Edf.Dynasty Plaza, 4º andar
Tel: (853) 7966 513
Fax: (853) 728 275

ADMINISTRATIVE COURT

Av. da Praia Grande, Edf. BCM, 10ºandar, Macau
Fax: (853) 355 593

PROCURATORATE

Procurator-General of Procuratorate : Mr. Ho Chio Meng
Alameda Dr. Carlos D' Assumpção, NAPE, Edf. Comercial Tai Fung Macau
Tel: (853) 7978271
Fax: (853) 727621

STRATEGIC BUSINESS CONTACTS IN MACAO

OFFICIAL DEPARTMENTS

ECONOMIC AFFAIRS
Direcção dos Serviços de Economia
Rua Dr. Pedro José Lobo, 1-3
Edif. Luso-Internacional, 25th Floor,
Macau
Tel : (853) 562622
Fax : (853) 590310

FINANCE
Direcção dos Serviços de Finanças
Av. Praia Grande, 575,
Macau
Tel : (853) 571600
Fax : (853) 300133

MONETARY AUTHORITY
Autoridade Monetária e Cambial de Macau
Rua Pedro Nolasco da Silva, Nº 45,
Macau
Tel : (853) 325416
Fax : (853) 325433
Telex : 88480 AMCM OM

PUBLIC WORKS AND TRANSPORT
Direcção dos Serviços de Solos,
Obras Públicas e Transportes
Estrada de D. Maria
Edif. CEM 1-5 Ground Floor
Macau
Tel : (853) 722488
Fax : (853) 340019

STATISTICS
Direcção dos Serviços de Estatística
Alameda Dr. Carlos
Assumpção, 411-417,
Edf. Dynasty, 17° andar
Macau

Tel : (853) 728188
Fax : (853) 972705

TOURISM
Direcção dos Serviços de Turismo
Largo do Senado, Nº 9 Edif. Ritz,
Macau
Tel : (853) 315566
Fax : (853) 510104

OFFICE OF THE FUTURE MACAU SPECIAL ADMINISTRATION REGION OF P.R. CHINA
Office of the Chief Executive of Macau S.A.R. of P.R.China
Edif. Tai Fung,
418, Alameda Dr. Carlos d' Assumpção,
Macau
Tel : (853) 377935
Fax : (853) 345851

TRADE / INVESTMENT PROMOTION ORGANISATIONS

EURO-INFO CENTRE, MACAU
Av. da Amizade 918, Edf. World Trade Centre,
17° andar, Macau
Tel : (853) 713338
Fax : (853) 713339

I.C.E.P.
Av. da Amizade, No. 918,
Edif. World Trade Centre, 16° " D",
Macau
Tel : (853) 728300
Fax : (853) 728303

MACAU TRADE AND INVESTMENT PROMOTION INSTITUTE
Av. da Amizade 918,
Edf. World Trade Centre, 4° & 5° andares,
Macau
Tel: (853) 710528
Fax: (853) 590309

WORLD TRADE CENTER MACAU
Av. da Amizade, N° 918
Edif. World Trade Centre, 17° Andar,
Macau
Tel : (853) 727666
Fax : (853) 727633

INDUSTRIAL PARK & PRODUCTIVITY CENTER

SPIC - CONCORDIA INDUSTRIAL PARK LTD.
Av. da Amizade, 918 14/F Apartment

A & B Edf. World Trade Center,
Macau
Tel : (853) 786636
Fax : (853) 785374

MACAU PRODUCTIVITY AND TECHNOLOGY TRANSFER CENTER
Rua de Xangai, 175,
Edf. ACM, 6 andar,
Macau
Tel: (853) 781313
Fax: (853) 788233

BUSINESS ASSOCIATIONS

ASSOCIAÇÃO DE BANCOS DE MACAU
Av. da Praia Grande, N° 575
Edif. Financas, 15th Floor, Macau
Tel: (853) 511921, 511922
Fax: (853) 346049

BUILDING CONTRACTORS & REAL ESTATES
Associação dos Construtores Civis e Empresas de Fomento Predial de Macau
Rua do Campo, 103, 6th Floor A, Macau
Tel : (853) 573226
Fax : (853) 345710

MACAU REAL ESTATE AGENTS ASSOCIATION
Rua Luis Gonzaga Gomes,
Ed. Lei Kai 3B,
Macau
Tel: (853) 316600/706204
Fax: (853) 701686

ASSOCIAÇÃO DOS MEDIADORES DO FOMENTO PREDIAL DE MACAU
Avenida do Dr. Rodrigo Rodrigues,
First International Commercial Center,
1st Floor, Rm P109-110,
Macau
Tel : (853) 707171
Fax : (853) 705527

CHAMBER OF COMMERCE
Associação Comercial de Macau
Rua de Xangai, N° 175,
Edif. ACM, 5/F,
Macau
Tel : (853) 576833
Fax : (853) 594513
Telex : 88229 TWHMA OM

CHINESE ENTERPRISES ASSOCIATION
Associação das Empresas Chinesas de Macau
Av. do Dr. Rodrigues, 223-225,

Edf. Nam Kwong, 8 andar, Macau
Tel : (853) 576833
Fax : (853) 594513
Telex : 88229 TWHMA OM

EXPORTERS AND IMPORTERS
Associação dos Exportadores e Importadores de Macau
Av. Infante D. Henrique N° 60-62,
3rd Floor Centro Comercial " Central",
Macau
Tel: (853) 375859, 553187
Fax: (853) 512174

INDUSTRY
Associação Industrial de Macau
Rua Dr. Pedro José Lobo, 34-36
Edif. AIM, 17th Floor,
Macau
Tel : (853) 574125
Fax : (853) 578305

Associação dos Industriais de Tecelagem e Fiação de Lã de Macau
Av. da Amizade 57-67B,
Edif. Kam Wa Kok, 6th Floor A,
Macau
Tel : (853) 553378
Fax : (853) 511105

LAWYER'S ASSOCIATION
Associação de Advogados de Macau
Av. de Amizade, No. 918,
Edif. World Trade Centre, 12° A-B,
Macau
Tel: (853) 728121, 728122
Fax: (853) 728127

SHIPPING
Macau Shipper's Association
Rua do Comandante Mata e Oliveira, No.32,
Edf. A.I.M., 17° Andar,
Macau
Tel : (853) 574125
Fax : (853) 578305

Macau Air Freight Forwarding Association
Av. Cons. Ferreira de Almeida, No. 36A-B,
Multigroup Comm. Bldg.,
Macau
Tel: (853) 312312
Fax: (853) 335563

Macau Shipping Agencies Association
Av. Horta e Costa, N° 7, D-E, Macau

Tel : (853) 528207
Fax : (853) 302667

SME ASSOCIATION
Associação de Pequenas e Médias Empresas de Macau
Avenida Doutor Mario Soares,
Yang Cheng Commercial Centre,
9° andar F, Macau
Tel : (853) 750507
Fax : (853) 750508

TRAVEL AGENTS

Associação de Agências de Turismo de Macau
Rua de Nagasaki ZAPE,
Edif. Xin Hua, 10° Andar,
Macau
Tel : (853) 7998811
Fax : (853) 706611

PUBLIC UTILITY COMPANIES

ELECTRICITY
CEM-Companhia de Electricidade de Macau, S.A.R.L.
Est. D. Maria II, Ed. CEM, r/c,
Macau
Tel : (853) 339933
Fax : (853) 308361

TELECOMMUNICATION
CTM-Companhia de Telecomunicações
Rua de Lagos, Telecentro, Taipa
Tel : (853) 8913822
Fax : (853) 8913813

WATER
SAAM - Sociedade de Abastecimento de Águas de Macau, S.A.R.L.
Avenida do Conselheiro Borja N° 718, Macau
Tel : (853) 233332
Fax : (853) 234657

MACAU REPRESENTATIVE OFFICES ABROAD

MISSÃO DE MACAU EM LISBOA
Av. 5 de Outubro, 115, 5° 1050, Lisboa
Portugal
Tel : (351-1) 7979334
Fax : (351-1) 7979328

DELEGAÇÃO DE MACAU EM BRUXELAS
Av. Louise, 375-BTE 9, B-1050, Brussels
Belgium
Tel : (32-2) 6471265
Fax : (32-2) 6401552

AIRLINES

AIR KORYO
Rua da Praia Grande, No. 55,
Edif. Cen. Com. Hoi Wong, 20° Andar, "C",
MACAU
Tel : 356635
Fax : 356631

AIR MACAU
Av. da Praia Grande,
Edif. Tai Wah, 9/F,
MACAU
Tel : 3966888
Fax : 3966866

CNAC-CHINA NATIONAL AVIATION CORP.
Av. Dr. Mário Soares,
Edif. Bank of China, 28/F, Bloco C,
MACAU
Tel : 788034
Fax : 788036

EAST ASIA AIRLINES (HELICOPTER)
Ground Floor, Macau Maritime Terminal,
Av. de Amizade,
MACAU
Tel : 725939
Fax : 725942

EVA AIRWAYS
Novos Aterros do Porto Exterior,
Edif. Dynasty Plaza, Lote 8, 21/F,
MACAU
Tel : 726866
Fax : 726840

SINGAPORE AIRLINES
Rua Dr. Pedro Jose Lobo, No. 1-3,
Edif. Banco Luso Internacional, 10° Andar,
MACAU
Tel : 711728/9
Fax : 711732

TRANS ASIA AIRWAYS
Rua de Pequim, 244-246,
Edif. Macau Finance, 11° Andar, B-C,
MACAU
Tel : 701777/556
Fax : 701565

BANKS

BANK OF AMERICA (MACAU LTD.)
Av. de Alm. Ribeiro, 70-76, Macau
Tel : (853) 568821
Fax : (853) 570386

BANK OF CHINA
Av. Dr. Mário Soares, Edif. Banco China, Macau
Tel : (853) 781828
Fax : (853) 781833

CITIBANK NA
Av. da Praia Grande, 251-253, Macau
Tel : (853) 378188
Fax : (853) 578451

BANCO COMERCIAL DE MACAU
Av. da Praia Grande, 572, Macau
Tel : (853) 7910000
Fax : (853) 580967

BANCO COMERCIAL PORTUGUÊS
Av. Dr. Mário Soares, Edif. Banco China,
21° Andar "F", Macau
Tel : (853)786769
Fax : (853) 786772

BANCO DELTA ASIA S.A.R.L.
Avenida do Conselheiro Ferreira de Almeida No. 79, Macau
Tel : (853) 559898
Fax : (853) 570068

DEUTSCHE BANK
90, Ave. Alm. Ribeiro, 7° Andar,
Nam Wah Comm. Edif. Macau
Tel : (853) 378440
Fax : (853) 304939

BANCO ESPÍRITO SANTO DO ORIENTE
Av. Dr. Mário Soares BOC Bldg., 28, E&F,
Macau
Tel : (853) 785222
Fax : (853) 785228

FINIBANCO (MACAU)
Av. da Praia Grande No. 811, r/c, P.O. Box 3110,

Macau
Tel : (853) 322678
Fax : (853) 322680

GUANGDONG DEVELOPMENT BANK, MACAU
Av. da Praia Grande, No. 269, Macau
Tel : (853) 323628
Fax : (853) 323668

HONG KONG & SHANGHAI BANKING CORP.
Av. da Praia Grande, 639, Macau
Tel : (853) 553669
Fax : (853) 322831

LIU CHONG HING BANK LIMITED
Avenida da Praia Grande, No. 693,
Edif. Tai Wah, r/c, Macau
Tel : (853) 339982
Fax : (853) 339990

BANCO LUSO INTERNACIONAL LTD
Av. Dr. Mário Soares, 47, Macau
Tel : (853) 378977
Fax : (853) 578517

BANCO NACIONAL ULTRAMARINO
Av. de Alm. Ribeiro, No. 22-38, Macau
Tel : (853) 355111
Fax : (853) 355653

BANQUE NATIONALE PARIS
Av. Alm. Ribeiro No.61, Central Plaza,
10° Andar C & D, Macau
Tel : (853) 562777
Fax : (853) 560626

OVERSEAS TRUST BANK
Rua da Santa Clara, No. 5-7,
Edif. Ribeiro R/C C-D, Macau
Tel : (853) 329338
Fax : (853) 323711

SENG HENG BANK LTD.
18/F, Seng Heng Bank Tower, Macau Landmark
Avenida da Amizade
Tel : (853) 555222
Fax : (853) 338064

STANDARD CHARTERED BANK
Av. de Amizade, Z. A. P. E., 8/F,
Office Tower Macau Landmark, Macau
Tel : (853) 786111
Fax : (853) 786222

TAI FUNG BANK LTD.
418, Alameda Dr. Carlos Assumpção, Macau
Tel : (853) 322323
Fax : (853) 570737

TAIPEI BUSINESS BANK
Nos. 52-58, Av. Infante D. Henrique, Macau
Tel : (853) 715175
Fax : (853) 715035

BANCO TOTTA & AÇORES
Av. da Praia Grande, 429, 21° andar, Macau
Tel : (853) 573299
Fax : (853) 563852

BANCO WENG HANG
Av. Almeida Ribeiro, 241, Macau
Tel : (853) 335678
Fax : (853) 576527

HOTELS

HOTEL BEVERLY PLAZA
Av. do Dr. Rodrigo Rodrigues, Macau
Tel: 782288
Fax: 780684

HOTEL FORTUNA
63, Rua de Cantão, Macau
Tel: 786333
Fax:786363

HOTEL FU HUA LDA.
98, 102, R. Francisco Xavier Pereira, Macau
Tel: 553838
Fax:527575

GRAND VIEW HOTEL
142, Est. Governador Albano de Oliveira, Taipa, Macau
Tel: 837788
Fax:837777

HOTEL GRANDEUR
Rua de Pequim, Outer Harbour, Macau
Tel: 781233
Fax: 781211

HOTEL GUIA
1-5, Estrada do Engenheiro Trigo, Macau
Tel: 513888
Fax: 559822

HOLIDAY INN MACAU
Rua de Pequim, Macau
Tel: 781707
Fax: 782321

HYATT REGENCY MACAU
Estrada Almirante Marques Esparteiro No.2, Taipa Island, Macau
Tel: 831234
Fax: 830195

HOTEL KINGSWAY
Rua de Luis Gonzaga Gomes No. 230, Macau
Tel: 702888
Fax: 702828

HOTEL LISBOA
Avenida de Amizade, Macau
Tel: 577666
Fax: 710574

MANDARIN ORIENTAL
Avenida de Amizade, Outer Harbour, Macau
Tel: 567888
Fax: 594589

HOTEL METRÓPOLE
No. 493-501, Rua da Praia Grande, Macau
Tel: 388166
Fax: 388553

HOTEL MONDIAL
No. 8-10, Rua de António Basto, Macau
Tel: 566866
Fax: 514083

HOTEL NAM YUE
International Center Avenida do Dr. Rodrigo Rodrigues , Macau
Tel: 726288
Fax: 726726

HOTEL NEW CENTURY
Av. Padre Tomás Pereira No. 889, Taipa Island, Macau
Tel: 831111
Fax: 832222

HOTEL NEW WORLD EMPEROR
Rua de Xangai, Macau
Tel: 781888
Fax: 782287

HOTEL PRESIDENTE
355, Av. de Amizade, Macau
Tel: 553888
Fax: 552735

HOTEL RITZ MACAU, LTD.
Rua Comendador Kou Ho Weng, Macau
Tel: 339955
Fax: 317826

HOTEL ROYAL
Estrada da Vitoria No. 2-4, Macau
Tel: 552222
Fax: 563008

HOTEL SINTRA
Avenida D. João IV, Macau
Tel: 710111
Fax: 715057

POUSADA DE S. TIAGO
Fortaleza de S. Tiago da Barra, Av. da República, Macau
Tel: 378111
Fax:552170

POUSADA DE COLOANE
Praia de Cheoc Van, Coloane Island, Macau
Tel: 882144
Fax: 882251

THE WESTIN RESORT
Estrada de Hac Sa Coloane Island, Macau
Tel: 871111
Fax: 871122

MACAU OVERSEAS REPRESENTATIVE OFFICES

The Macau Overseas Representative Offices of the Macau Government Tourist Office carry out various activities for tourist promotion, including providing travel information, distribution of news, organization of seminars, incentives or special interest programmes, and handling arrangements for special educational trips to Macau for trade and media people.

MGTO Marketing Representative
Suite 1303, Shun Tak Centre
200 Connaught Road, Central
Hong Kong
Tel: (852) 2549-8884
Fax: (852) 2559-6513
e-mail: dnetwork@netvigator.com

Contact: Ms. Winnie Pau

JAPAN

Mile Post Consultants, Inc.
Sanden Building, 3rd Floor
5-5, Kojimachi 3-chome
Chiyoda-ku, Tokyo 102-0083,
Japan
Tel: (81) 3-5275-2537
Fax: (81) 3-5275-2535
e-mail: macau@milepost.co.jp
Contact: Ms. Fumihiro Sakakibara

TAIWAN

Compass Public Relations Ltd.
3rd Floor, 150 Tun Hwa North Road
Taipei, Taiwan
Tel: (886) 2-2546-6086
Fax: (886) 2-2546-6087

email: mgtottwn@ms27.hinet.net
Contact: Ms. Pauline Leung

SOUTH KOREA

Glocom Korea Co. LTD.
Suite 1105, Paiknam Building (President Hotel)
188-3, Eulchiro 1-Ka, Chung-Ku,
Seoul, Korea
Tel: (82) 2-778-4402
Fax: (82) 2-778-4404
e-mail: glocomco@chollian.net
Contact: Mr. Lew Hwa-Kyu
Cti Network Pte Ltd.
321, Orchard Road
#09-01 Orchard Shopping Center
Singapore 238866
Tel: (65) 7323239
Fax: (65) 7323205

e-mail: cti-network@pacific.net.sg
Contact: Ms. Grace Tong

MALAYSIA

Pacific World Travel Sdn Bhd
2.5 & 2.6, Bangunan Angkasa Raya Jalan Ampang,
50450 Kuala Lumpur
Malaysia
Tel: (60-3) 241-2899
Fax: (60-3) 248-1357
e-mail: pwt@melewar.com

Contact: Ms. Cherry Lee

PHILIPPINES

Asia Pacific Projects, Inc
9th Floor PDCP Bank Centre
Herrera corner Leviste Streets
Salcedo Village, Makati City, Philippines
Tel: (63-2) 817-2644
Fax: (63-2) 813-4781
e-mail: mgtophil@info.com.ph
Contact: Ms. Narzalina Z. Lim

THAILAND

Pacific Leisure (Thailand) Ltd.
8th Floor, Maneeya Center Building
518/5 Ploenchit Road, Patumwan Bangkok 10330
Thailand
Tel: (66) 2-2555989
Fax: (66) 2-6520509
e-mail: destinations@plt.co.th
Contact: Ms. Jarunee Tantinukul

AUSTRALIA

ICON Services Pty.Ltd.
Level 5, 17 Bridge Street
Sydney, NSW 2000,
Australia
Tel: (61) 2-8272-7878 (or 1300 300 236 in Australia only)
Fax: (61) 2-9241-6510
e-mail: macau@icongsa.com.au

Contact: Ms. Nicki Keegan

NEW ZEALAND

Aviation & Tourism International / ICON Aviation
P.O.Box 99230 Newmarket
Auckland
New Zealand
Tel: (64) 9 522 5948
Fax: (64) 9 522 2429
e-mail: chrisj@iconaviation.co.nz
Contact: Mr. Chris Jones

MEMBERS OF THE CONSULAR CORPS ACCREDITED TO MACAU SAR

HONORARY CONSULS ACCREDITED TO MACAU SAR

BHUTAN
Unit B, 1st Floor, Kowloon Centre
29-43, Ashley Road
Kowloon - Hong Kong
Tel : 23762112
Fax: 23763331

ESTONIA
13/F A-B, World Trade Centre
918, Avenida da Amizade
Macau
Tel : (853) 332266
Fax: (853) 727768

GUINEA-BISSAU
Avenida da Amizade, R/C
Edf. Chong Yu, Loja N
Macau
Tel : (853) 703333
Fax: (853) 702663

GUINEA-CONACRY
Macau Finance Centre, 9K
Rua de Pequim
Macau
Tel : (853) 703233
Fax: (853) 703214

MALI
Rua de Foshan, 51
Centro Comercial San Kin Yip, 19A
Macau
Tel : (853) 786638
Fax: (853) 780383

MOZAMBIQUE
Suite G, 6th Floor, Shun Kit Bld.

OFFICIALLY RECOGNISED REPRESENTATIVES OF INTERNATIONAL ORGANIZATIONS

EUROPEAN UNION OFFICE OF THE EUROPEAN COMMISSION
19th Floor, St. John's Bld.
33, Garden Road
Central - Hong Kong

Rua Inacio Baptista, 1
Macau
Tel : (853) 970003
Fax:(853) 970481

NAMIBIA
Room 509, Manning House
38-48, Queen's Road
Central
Hong Kong
Tel : 25861339
Fax: 28771264
E-mail : henry@spider.net.hk

PERU
Av. Almeida Ribeiro, 54-60 R/C
Macau
Tel : (853) 574344
Fax:(853) 593199

UNITED KINGDOM
Hong Kong & Shanghai Banking Corp. Ltd.
Macau Managemnet Office
73-75, Av. da Praia Grande
Macau SAR
Tel : (853) 553670
Fax: (853) 315421

SURINAME
Shun Tak Holdings Ltd.
Penthouse 39/F West Tower
Shun Tak Centre
200, Connaught Road
Central - Hong Kong
Tel : 28594855
Fax: 28574377

Tel : 25376083
Fax: 25221302

UNITED NATIONS HIGH COMMISSIONER FOR REFUGEES SUB-OFFICE
9th Floor, Yau Ma Tei Carpark Bld.
250, Shanghai Street
Kowloon
Hong Kong

Tel : 27809271
Fax: 27705504
E-mail : chiho@unhcr.ch

COUNTRY REPRESENTATIONSARGENTINA
Suite 1210-1212, Jardine House
1, Connaught Place
Hong Kong
Tel : 2523 3208
Fax: 2877 0906
E-mail : consarhk@netvigator.com

AUSTRALIA
Harbour Centre, 21st-24th Floors
25 Harbour Road
Hong Kong
Tel : 2827 8881
Fax: 2585 4457
E-mail : Webmaster@australia.org.hk

AUSTRIA
Room 2201, Chinachem Tower
34-37 Connaught Road
Central - Hong Kong
Tel : 25228086
Fax: 25218773
E-mail : autconhk@pacific.net.hk

BANGLADESH
Room 3807, China Resources Building
26, Harbour Road - Wan Chai
Hong Kong
Tel : 28274278/9
Fax: 28271916
E-mail : bangladt@netvigator.com

BELGIUM
9th Floor, St. John's Building
33, Garden Road
Hong Kong
Tel : 25243111
Fax: 28685997
E-mail : consulhk@netvigator.com

BRASIL
Room 2014-21, Sun Hung Kai Centre
30 Harbour Road
Hong Kong
Tel : 25257002
Fax: 28772813
E-mail : cgbrahkg@netvigator.com

CANADA
One Exchange Square, 14th Floor
8, Connaught Place
Hong Kong
Tel : 28104321
Fax: 28106736
Homepage : http://www.canada.org.hk

CHILE
Suite 1408, Great Eagle Centre
23, Harbour Road - Wan Chai
Hong Kong
Tel : 28271826
Fax: 28272060
E-mail : cghonghk@netvigator.com

COLOMBIA
Unit A, 6th Floor - C.M.A. Building
64-66 Connaught Road - Central
Hong Kong
Tel : 25458547
Fax: 25448347
E-mail : concolhk@hutchcity.com

CZECH REPUBLIC
Room 1204-05, Great Eagle Centre
23 Harbour Road - Wan Chai
Hong Kong
Tel : 28022212
Fax: 28022911
E-mail : gkcrhk@netvigator.com

DENMARK
Room 2402 B, Great Eagle Centre
23 Harbour Road - Wan Chai
Hong Kong
Tel : 28278101
Fax: 28274555
E-mail : danconhk@netvigator.com

EGYPT
Suite No. 1, 22 Floor, Sino Plaza
255-257 Gloucester Road,
Causeway Bay Hong Kong
Tel : 2827 0668
Fax: 2827 2100
E-mail : egyptcg@netvigator.com

FINLAND
1818, Hutchison House
10, Harcourt Road
Hong Kong
Tel : 25255385

Fax: 28101232
E-mail : sanomat.hng@formin.fi

FRANCE
26th Floor, Admiralty Centre, Tower II
18 Harcourt Road
Hong Kong
Tel : 25294351
Fax: 28669693
E-mail : consinfo@france.com.hk

GERMANY
21st Floor, United Centre
95 Queensway
Hong Kong
Tel : 25298855
Fax: 28652033
E-mail : germancg@netvigator.com

GREECE
Suites 2503/2504, Two Pacific Place
88, Queensway
Hong Kong
Tel : 27741682
Fax: 27059796

HUNGARY
Suite 3202, Citibank Tower
3, Garden Road
Central
Hong Kong
Tel : 28787555
Fax: 28787010
E-mail : consulhu@netvigator.com

INDIA
Unit D, 16th Floor, United Centre
95 Queensway
Hong Kong
Tel : 25291289
Fax: 28654617
E-mail : cgiinfo@pacific.net.hk

ISRAEL
Room 701 - Admiralty Centre, Tower II
18, Harcourt Road
Hong Kong
Tel : 25296091
Fax: 28650220
Hompepage : http://www.cgis.com.hk
E-mail : isrcons@asiaonline.net

ITALY
Room 805, Hutchison House
10, Harcourt Road
Hong Kong
Tel : 25220033/6
Fax: 28459678
Homepage :
http://home.netvigator.com/~itconshk
E-mail : itconshk@netvigator.com

JAPAN
47th Floor, One Exchange Square
8, Connaught Place
Central - Hong Kong
Tel : 25221184
Fax: 28680156
Homepage : http://www.japan.org.hk

KOREA
5-6 Floors, Far East Finance Centre
16, Harcourt Road
Hong Kong
Tel : 25294141
Fax: 28613699
E-mail : korcon@netvigator.com

MALAYSIA
24th Floor, Malaysia Building
50, Gloucester Road - Wan Chai
Hong Kong
Tel : 25270921
Fax: 28651628
E-mail : mwhkong@netvigator.com

MEXICO
Room 1304, Great Eagle Centre
23, Harbour Road - Wan Chai
Hong Kong
Tel : 25113305
Fax: 28453404
E-mail : mexicohk@netvigator.com

MYANMAR
Rooms 2401-24/F Sun Hung Kai Centre
30 Harbour Road - Wan Chai
Hong Kong
Tel : 28277929
Fax: 28276597
E-mail : myancghk@netvigator.com

NETHERLANDS
Suite 5702, 57/F, Cheung Kong Center
2, Queens Road - Central
Hong Kong

Tel : 25225127
Fax: 28685388
Homepage : http://www.neth-consulate-hk.org
E-mail : nlgovhon@netvigator.com

NEW ZEALAND
Room 6501, Central Plaza
18, Harbour Road - Wan Chai
Hong Kong
Tel : 25255044
Fax: 28452915
E-mail : nzcghk@netvigator.com

NIGERIA
Rooms 3309-10, 33rd Floor
China Resources Building
26, Harbour Road - Wan Chai
Hong Kong
Tel : 28278813
Fax: 28278892
E-mail : ngrconhk@netvigator.com

NORWAY
Room 1502, Great Eagle Centre
23, Harbour Road - Wan Chai
Hong Kong
Tel : 25879953
Fax: 25871786
E-mail : generalkonsulat-hong-kong@ud.dep.telemax.no

PAKISTAN
Room 3706, 37th Floor China Resources Building
26, Harbour Road - Wan Chai
Hong Kong
Tel : 28271966
Fax: 28272189
E-mail : parephk@netvigator.com

PERU
10th Floor, Wong Chung Ming Commercial House
16, Wyndham Street
Central - Hong Kong
Tel : 28682622
Fax: 28400733
E-mail : Conperhk@netvigator.com

PHILIPPINES
Room 602, 6th Floor
United Centre, 95 Queensway
Hong Kong
Tel : 28238503
Fax: 28669885
E-mail : prhk@asiaonline.net

POLAND
Suite 1006, One Pacific Place
88, Queensway
Hong Kong
Tel : 28400779
Fax: 25960062

PORTUGAL
Consulate General of Portugal
Rua Pedro Nolasco da Silva, 45
Macau SAR
Tel : (853) 356660
Fax :(853) 356658

RUSSIA
Rooms 2932-2940
29th Floor, Sun Hung Kai Centre
30, Harbour Road
Hong Kong
Tel : 28777188
Fax: 28777166
E-mail :cgrushk@hknet.com

SAMOA
Unit A, 30th Floor, Morrison Plaza
5-9A Morrison Hill Road Wan Chai
Hong Kong
Tel : 25722777
Fax: 25752666

SINGAPORE
9th Floor, Unit 901, Tower I
Admiralty Centre
18, Harcourt Road
Hong Kong
Tel : 25272212
Fax: 28613595
E-mail :sporecon@hk.super.net

SOUTH AFRICA
27/F, Great Eagle Centre
Rooms 2706-2710
23 Harbour Road - Wan Chai
Hong Kong
Tel : 25773279
Fax: 28901975
E-mail :sacghgk@netvigator.com

SPAIN
8th Floor, Printing House
18, Ice House Street
Hong Kong
Tel : 25253041
Fax: 28772407

Sweden
8th Floor, The Hong Kong Club Bld.
3A, Chater Road
Hong Kong
Tel : 25211212
Fax: 25960308
E-mail :generalkonsulat.hongkong@foreign.ministry.se

SWITZERLAND
3703, Gloucester Tower
The Landmark - 11, Pedder Street
Hong Kong
Tel : 25227147/8
Fax: 28452619
E-mail :Swisscg@hon.rep.admin.ch

THAILAND
8th Floor, Fairmont House
8, Cotton Tree Drive
Central - Hong Kong
Tel : 25216481/5
Fax: 25218629
E-mail :thaihkcg@hk.super.net

TURKEY
3rd Floor, Sino Plaza, Room 301
255-257, Gloucester Road
Causeway Bay - Hong Kong
Tel : 25721331
Fax: 28931771
E-mail :turkcons@netvigator.com

UNITED KINGDOM
1, Supreme Court Road
Hong Kong
Tel : 29013020/1
Fax: 29013066
E-mail :information@britishconsulate.org.hk

USA
26, Garden Road
Hong Kong
Tel : 25239011
Fax: 28451598
Homepage : http://www.usconsulate.org.hk

URUGUAY
Room 1701, Dina House
11, Duddell Street
Central - Hong Kong
Tel : 28680330
Fax: 25301287
E-mail :urukong@hk.super.net

VENEZUELA
Suite 3902, Central Plaza
18 Harbour Road - Wan Chai
Hong Kong
Tel : 27308099
Fax: 27366519
E-mail :consulve@hk.net

BASIC TITLES ON MACAO

IMPORTANT!
All publications are updated annually!
Please contact IBP, Inc. at ibpusa3@gmail.com for the latest ISBNs and additional information

Title
Macao A "Spy" Guide - Strategic Information and Developments
Macao Business and Investment Opportunities Yearbook
Macao Business and Investment Opportunities Yearbook Volume 1 Strategic Information and Opportunities
Macao Business Intelligence Report - Practical Information, Opportunities, Contacts
Macao Business Law Handbook - Strategic Information and Basic Laws
Macao Business Law Handbook - Strategic Information and Basic Laws
Macao Company Laws and Regulations Handbook
Macao Country Study Guide - Strategic Information and Developments
Macao Customs, Trade Regulations and Procedures Handbook
Macao Diplomatic Handbook - Strategic Information and Developments
Macao Ecology & Nature Protection Handbook
Macao Economic & Development Strategy Handbook
Macao Export-Import Trade and Business Directory
Macao Foreign Policy and Government Guide
Macao Government and Business Contacts Handbook
Macao Government and Policy Guide
Macao Industrial and Business Directory
Macao Internet and E-Commerce Investment and Business Guide - Strategic and Practical Information: Regulations and Opportunities
Macao Investment and Business Guide - Strategic and Practical Information
Macao Investment and Business Guide - Strategic and Practical Information
Macao Investment and Trade Laws and Regulations Handbook
Macao Recent Economic and Political Developments Yearbook
Macao Recent Economic and Political Developments Yearbook
Macao Recent Economic and Political Developments Yearbook
Macao Starting Business (Incorporating) in....Guide
Macao Taxation Laws and Regulations Handbook
Macao Telecom Laws and Regulations Handbook
Macao Telecommunication Industry Business Opportunities Handbook
Macao Transportation Policy and Regulations Handbook
Macao Starting Business (Incorporating) in Macao Guide
Macao Ecology & Nature Protection Laws and Regulation Handbook
Macao Energy Policy, Laws and Regulation Handbook

GLOBAL ARMY, DEFENSE, INTELLIGENCE, COUNTERINTELLIGENCE, NATIONAL SECURITY HANDBOOK LIBRARY

(PRICE $149.95 each)

Ultimate handbooks on army, defense policy, intelligence, counterintelligence, national security and related operation, conducted by specific countries. National security and intelligence agencies operations and structure

TITLE
1. Albania Army, National Security and Defense Policy Handbook
2. Argentina Intelligence & Security Activities & Operations Handbook
3. Australia Army, National Security and Defense Policy Handbook
4. Australia Intelligence & Security Activities & Operations Handbook
5. Bangladesh Army, National Security and Defense Policy Handbook
6. Bulgaria and NATO Handbook
7. Bulgaria Department of Defense Handbook
8. Canada Intelligence & Security Activities & Operations Handbook
9. Canadian Security Intelligence Service (CSIS) Handbook
10. China Army, National Security and Defense Policy Handbook
11. Cuba Army, National Security and Defense Policy Handbook
12. Czech Republic Army, National Security and Defense Policy Handbook
13. Estonia Army, National Security and Defense Policy Handbook
14. Estonia Intelligence & Security Activities & Operations Handbook
15. EUROPOL – EUROPEAN POLICE OFFICE Handbook
16. Finland Army, National Security and Defense Policy Handbook
17. Finland Intelligence & Security Activities & Operations Handbook
18. France Army, National Security and Defense Policy Handbook
19. German Intelligence & Security Activities & Operations Handbook
20. Germany Army, National Security and Defense Policy Handbook
21. Global Counter-Terrorism Handbook
22. Global National Intelligence and Security Agencies Handbook
23. Global Terrorism Attacks Encyclopedic Handbook
24. Greece Army, National Security and Defense Policy Handbook

---

To order and for additional analytical and marketing information, please contacrt
International Business Publications, USA at:
P.O. Box 15343, Washington, DC 20003, USA. Phone: (202) 546-2103. Fax: (202) 546-3275.
E-mail: rusric@erols.com
http://www.ibpus.com

TITLE
25. Greece Intelligence & Security Activities & Operations Handbook
26. Hungary Army, National Security and Defense Policy Handbook
27. Hungary Intelligence & Security Activities & Operations Handbook
28. India Army, National Security and Defense Policy Handbook
29. India Intelligence & Security Activities & Operations Handbook
30. Iraq Economic Sanctions, Customs, Trade Regulations and Procedures Handbook
31. Ireland Army, National Security and Defense Policy Handbook
32. Ireland Intelligence & Security Activities & Operations Handbook
33. Israel Army, National Security and Defense Policy Handbook
34. Israel Intelligence & Security Activities & Operations Handbook
35. Italy Intelligence & Security Activities & Operations Handbook
36. Japan Army, National Security and Defense Policy Handbook
37. Japan Intelligence & Security Activities & Operations Handbook
38. Jordan Intelligence & Security Activities & Operations Handbook
39. Korea North Army, National Security and Defense Policy Handbook
40. Korea South Army, National Security and Defense Policy Handbook
41. Korea South Intelligence & Security Activities & Operations Handbook
42. Latvia Army, National Security and Defense Policy Handbook
43. Lebanon Army, National Security and Defense Policy Handbook
44. Lithuania Army, National Security and Defense Policy Handbook
45. Macedonia National Security, Army and Defense Policy Handbook
46. Malaysia Army, National Security and Defense Policy Handbook
47. Myanmar Army, National Security and Defense Policy Handbook
48. New Zealand Army, National Security and Defense Policy Handbook
49. New Zealand Intelligence & Security Activities & Operations Handbook
50. Norway Army, National Security and Defense Policy Handbook
51. Pakistan Army, National Security and Defense Policy Handbook
52. Pakistan Intelligence & Security Activities & Operations Handbook
53. Philippines Army, National Security and Defense Policy Handbook
54. Poland Army, National Security and Defense Policy Handbook
55. Portugal Intelligence & Security Activities & Operations Handbook
56. Romania Army, National Security and Defense Policy Handbook
57. Romania Intelligence & Security Activities & Operations Handbook
58. Russia Army, National Security and Defense Policy Handbook
59. Russia Intelligence & Security Activities & Operations Handbook
60. Russian KGB Handbook: Past and Present
61. Russian Navy Handbook: History and Modern Situation

TITLE
62. Russia-NATO Cooperation Handbook
63. Singapore Army, National Security and Defense Policy Handbook
64. Slovak Republic Army, National Security and Defense Policy Handbook
65. South Africa Army, National Security and Defense Policy Handbook
66. South Africa Intelligence & Security Activities & Operations Handbook
67. Sri Lanka Army, National Security and Defense Policy Handbook
68. Starting Business (Incorporating) in India Encyclopedic Guide
69. Sweden Intelligence & Security Activities & Operations Handbook
70. Switzerland Army, National Security and Defense Policy Handbook
71. Switzerland Intelligence & Security Activities & Operations Handbook
72. Taiwan Army, National Security and Defense Policy Handbook
73. Taiwan Intelligence & Security Activities & Operations Handbook
74. Thailand Royal Army, National Security and Defense Policy Handbook
75. The French Foreign Legion Handbook
76. The INTERPOL Handbook
77. The United Stated Ambassadors Yearbook
78. Turkey Army, National Security and Defense Policy Handbook
79. Turkey Intelligence & Security Activities & Operations Handbook
80. UK Department of Trade and Industry (DTI) Handbook
81. UK Intelligence & Counterintelligence Handbook
82. UK Intelligence & Security Activities & Operations Handbook
83. UK Intelligence and Security Policy Handbook
84. UK MI5 Security Service Handbook
85. UK Military Intelligence Handbook
86. UK National Intelligence Service Handbook
87. UK National Police Handbook
88. UK Royal Air force Handbook
89. UK Royal Army Handbook
90. UK Royal Navy Handbook
91. Ukraine Army, National Security and Defense Policy Handbook
92. Ukraine Intelligence & Security Activities & Operations Handbook
93. United Kingdom Army, National Security and Defense Policy Handbook
94. US Arms Sales to Foreign Countries Handbook
95. US Business Intelligence Handbook
96. US Counterintelligence Operations against Cuba Handbook
97. US Defense Policy Handbook
98. US Federal Depository Libraries Directory

TITLE
99. US Federal Government Directory
100. US Federal Grant Management Handbook
101. US Military Intelligence Handbook
102. US Ocean Transportation Companies Directory
103. US Political Intelligence Handbook
104. US War Against International Terrorism Handbook
105. US War Against Iraq Handbook: Political Strategy and Operations
106. US-Russia Cooperation Against Terrorism Handbook
107. US-Russia Economic & Financial Cooperation Handbook
108. US-Russia Military Cooperation Handbook
109. US-Russia Political Cooperation Handbook
110. US-Russia Scientific & Technological Cooperation Handbook
111. US-Russia Space Cooperation Handbook

www.ingramcontent.com/pod-product-compliance
Lightning Source LLC
LaVergne TN
LVHW080028210926
848481LV00011B/3133